THE FUTURE OF GOSPELS AND ACTS RESEARCH

Edited by Peter G. Bolt

SCD Press
2021

CGAR SERIES, NO 3

The Future of Gospels and Acts Research
CGAR Series, No 3
Edited by Peter G. Bolt

© SCD Press and contributors 2021

SCD Press
PO Box 1882
Macquarie Centre NSW 2113
scdpress@scd.edu.au

ISBN-13: 978-1-925730-43-2 (Paperback)
ISBN-13: 978-1-925730-44-9 (E-book)

Cover design and typesetting by Lankshear Design.

THE FUTURE OF GOSPELS AND ACTS RESEARCH

Edited by Peter G. Bolt

SCD Press
2021

CGAR SERIES, NO 3

CGAR Series:

1. Peter G. Bolt & James R. Harrison (eds.), *The Impact of Jesus of Nazareth: Historical, Theological, and Pastoral Perspectives*. Vol. 1: *Historical and Theological Studies* (Macquarie Park, NSW: SCD Press, 2020).

2. Peter G. Bolt & James R. Harrison (eds.), *The Impact of Jesus of Nazareth: Historical, Theological, and Pastoral Perspectives*. Vol. 2: *Social and Pastoral Studies* (Macquarie Park, NSW: SCD Press, 2021).

3. Peter G. Bolt (ed), *The Future of Gospels and Acts Research* (Macquarie Park, NSW: SCD Press, 2021).

CONTRIBUTORS

Peter G. Bolt is the Academic Director of Sydney College of Divinity, the Director of the Centre for Gospels and Acts Research, and the executive editor of the *Journal of Gospels and Acts Research*. He has published *Jesus' Defeat of Death. Persuading Mark's Early Readers* (CUP, 2003), and *The Narrative Integrity of Mark 13:24–27* (Wipf & Stock, 2021).

Timothy P. Bradford is the Senior Pastor of Petersham Baptist Church and a PhD student at Sydney College of Divinity researching the Gospel of Matthew and theological anthropology.

John A. Davies is an Honorary Research Associate of the Sydney College of Divinity and Principal Emeritus of Christ College, Sydney, where he has taught biblical studies. He holds the degrees of MA (Hons) and PhD from the University of Sydney and MDiv from Westminster Theological Seminary, Philadelphia. He is the author of *A Royal Priesthood* (2004), *A Study Commentary on 1 Kings* (2012), *Unless Someone Shows Me* (2015), *Lift Up Your Heads* (2018), and *Heaven—Ain't Goin' There: A Down-to-Earth Look at Eternal Life* (2019).

Emily Fero-Kovassy is a PhD candidate in Biblical and Early Christian studies at the Australian Catholic University in Melbourne. In 2020 she completed a Master of Arts (Research) at Monash University. Her Masters thesis explored the motif of "the will of the Father in heaven" in the Gospel of Matthew. Her current research areas include the Gospel of Matthew, James and the Jerusalem Church, and the Jewish context of the New Testament.

James R. Harrison studied Ancient History at Macquarie University and graduated from the doctoral program in 1997. Professor Harrison, FAHA, is the Research Director at the Sydney College of Divinity. His recent monographs include *Paul and the Imperial Authorities at Thessalonica and Rome* (Mohr

Siebeck, 2011), *Paul and the Ancient Celebrity Circuit* (Mohr Siebeck, 2019), and *Reading Romans with Roman Eyes* (Lexington/Fortress, 2020). He is also the chief editor of *New Documents Illustrating the History of Early Christianity Vols. 11–16* (forthcoming), co-editor with L. L. Welborn of *The First Urban Churches Vols. 1–6* (SBL, 2015–2020; *Vols. 7-9* forthcoming 2022–2024), and is editor of the collection of E. A. Judge, *The Conflict of Cultures: The Legacy of Paul's Thought Today* (Cascade, 2019).

Michael J. Kok received his PhD in Biblical Studies at the University of Sheffield and is the New Testament Lecturer at the Perth Campus of Morling College, Australian College of Theology. His research focuses on the origins of the Gospels and their reception in the Patristic period, the development of Christology, and early Christian identity formation.

Mary J. Marshall PhD is a Honorary Research Fellow of Murdoch University, Western Australia. Since completing her doctorate in 2002, Mary has widened her field of research, and current interests include: Historical Jesus; Gospels and Acts; Last Supper; James, the brother of Jesus; Essenic influence; Christian origins; Parting of the Ways; and Jewish–Christian relations. She is passionately committed to fostering interfaith relations, working especially through her membership of the Council of Christians and Jews, at local, national, and international levels.

Stephen Rockwell has been lecturing Greek and New Testament at George Whitefield College, Cape Town, South Africa since 2015.

Christopher Seglenieks PhD lectures in New Testament and Greek at the Bible College of South Australia and Tabor Adelaide. He is author of *Johannine Belief and Graeco-Roman Devotion* (Mohr Siebeck, 2020), as well as several articles and book chapters. His research interests include John's Gospel, faith, and christology. Most recently, he has applied his interest in faith to the Synoptic Gospels, as well as 1 John, in several forthcoming publications.

Chris Spark studied theology at Moore Theological College and has an ongoing interest in the Gospel of Luke and its connections to Graeco-Roman culture. He is the minister of St Peter's of the Rock Anglican Church, Rangiora in New Zealand.

Andrew Stewart grew up in Northern Ireland, where he studied Law at The Queen's University of Belfast, and Theology at the Reformed Theological College, Belfast, and the Reformed Presbyterian Theological Seminary in Pittsburgh. Following ordination in 1990 he has served pastorates in Northern Ireland, Cyprus and Australia. Since 1998 he has been Minister of the Reformed Presbyterian Church in Geelong. He has written commentaries on First and Second Chronicles and Deuteronomy for the Welwyn Commentary Series published by Evangelical Press. Since 2019 Andrew has served as Adjunct Lecturer in New Testament and Theology at the Reformed Theological College, Melbourne. In August 2020 he was awarded a Doctor of Theology degree by the Australian College of Theology for a thesis entitled, 'The Three Accounts of Paul's Conversion in Acts 9, 22 and 26: A Study of Consistency and Creativity in Narrative Retelling'.

CONTENTS

1. Peter G. Bolt, *Introduction: The Future is Now* 1

2. James R. Harrison, *Social Stratification and Poverty Studies in First-Century Roman Palestine: An Evaluation of Recent Research on the Economic Context of the First Disciples* 7

3. Mary J. Marshall, *Essenic Influence on Jesus, His Brothers, and the Early Church* 51

4. Emily Fero-Kovassy, *'Doing the Will of the Father in Heaven' in Matthew 7:21: Polemics and Law Observance* 77

5. Timothy P. Bradford, *Born Eunuch: Recovering an Ancient Metaphor* 101

6. Michael J. Kok, *Jesus' Imperial Authority over the Sea in Mark 6:45–52* 123

7. Chris Spark, *'With a Noble and Good Heart'. ἐν καρδίᾳ καλῇ καὶ ἀγαθῇ (Luke 8:15) in Graeco-Roman Cultural-Communicative Context* 139

8. Peter G. Bolt, *Breathing in Enoch to Breathe out Jesus. Two Examples of Luke's Apocalypticism* 153

9. Stephen Rockwell, *Nathanael as a Remnant Figure in the Gospel of John: A Fresh Look at an Enigmatic Character* 189

10. John A. Davies, *Many Abidings (John 14:2)* 209

11. Christopher Seglenieks, *The Meaning of πιστεύω in the Gospel of John* 233

12. Andrew Stewart, *What Did Paul's Companions Hear? How the Syntax of ἀκούω Aids the Interpretation of Acts 9:7 and 22:9*.. 255

CHAPTER 1

Introduction: The Future is Now

Peter G. Bolt

Who can predict the future of anything, let alone an academic field such as Gospels and Acts research? In 2019, the first biennial conference for the Centre for Gospels and Acts Research set itself the task of 'Discerning the Trends'. Rather than bringing out the crystal balls, or donning the garb of a prophet, presenters interacted around papers arising from their own current research. Since the current generation of researchers is the bridge between the past and the future, a snapshot of the research being conducted in the present is one way of 'Discerning the Trends'. The future is now.

This volume of essays represents a selection of eleven of the papers from the conference, duly revised after that interaction. With two discussing issues of method and historical background (Harrison; Marshall), two on Matthew (Fero-Kovassy; Bradford), one on Mark (Kok), two on Luke (Spark; Bolt), three on John (Rockwell; Davies; Seglenieks), and one on Acts (Stewart), the collection provides a sample of research from across the full range of the texts in the field. Each builds on current research and opens up new questions which chart a direction for research in the future. The now is the future.

James R. Harrison opens the volume with a review of the influential model of social stratigraphy in Gospel studies dating to Lenski and Alföldy, in the light of the demands of recent scholarship for a more sophisticated approach to New Testament social and economic studies. Despite significant challenges to the model, it nevertheless retains some advantages. On this base, the essay charts the way forward for future research into social stratification and poverty in the Gospels, focusing methodologically upon the iconographic, epigraphic, and papyrological evidence, as well as the rhetoric of the evangelists themselves. The essay concludes by exploring a case study of the 'impoverished widow-benefactor' (Luke 20:45—21:4) with a view to understanding this paradoxical vignette better in its first-century A.D. context.

Evaluating and expanding on Simon Joseph's publication *Jesus, the Essenes, and Christian Origins* (2018), **Mary J. Marshall** continues her previous research on James, the brother of Jesus, the Last Supper, and Jesus' links with the Essenes — including the converted priests mentioned in Acts 6:7. Assessing three legends about James in the light of other early church traditions, she explores the brothers' mixed ancestry linking them through Mary with both Judah and Aaron, giving them a priestly connection. As *mebaqqer* (guardian) of his household, James may have hosted the Last Supper in the Essene quarter of Jerusalem, at which Jesus was recognised as the anticipated royal anointed one, and later deemed the Davidic and priestly Messiah.

With a similar regard for the Jewish context of earliest Christianity, **Emily Fero-Kovassy** examines the Gospel of Matthew's emphasis on 'doing the will of the Father in heaven' (Matt 7:21), tracing the semantics of the 'will of God' in Jewish thought, and exploring continuities and developments of these semantics in the New Testament. Drawing upon the commitment in Jewish thought to law-observance being inherent to 'doing God's will', Matthew 7:21 takes its part in Matthew's purposeful use of this motif within the strategically polemical context of his narrative.

Seeking some biblical resources to engage with the contemporary interest in thinking theologically and pastorally about important questions raised by Intersex/Disorders of Sexual Development (DSD), **Timothy P. Bradford** also turns to Matthew's Gospel. Given that the ambiguity of intersexed bodies jars with the biblical 'male and female, he created them' (Genesis 1:27), attempts to address these issues have seen a renewed engagement with Jesus' eunuch logion (Matthew 19:12). The essay reconsiders εὐνοῦχοι οἵτινες ἐκ κοιλίας μητρὸς ἐγεννήθησαν οὕτως as a metaphor, arguing that the (male) child is not born castrated, rather the image of the eunuch is being applied to the image of the newborn in order to create a new meaning. Further associations of these images in Matthew's literary and social world strengthen the correspondence between εὐνοῦχοι ... ἐγεννήθησαν and Intersex conditions, in order to provide new avenues for resourcing the church's theological and pastoral understanding of Intersex/DSD.

In seeking to understand the Christology of the Marcan version of Jesus walking on the water (Mark 6:45–52), **Michael J. Kok** draws upon some recent scholarship that reads Mark's language of divine sonship in light of the Davidic messianic expectations within Second Temple Judaism on the one hand, and the Roman imperial cult on the other. With Mark influenced by an older imperial ideology, the essay proposes Davidic Christology as the hermeneutical key to interpreting the incident. Jesus was empowered to conquer and rule over the forces of chaos symbolised by the sea as the representative of the God of Israel and the royal heir of King David.

Discussing the usage of καλὴ καὶ ἀγαθή in Luke's rendition of the Parable of the Sower, **Chris Spark** demonstrates that Luke's use of ἀγαθός regularly carries ethical weight in characterisation, consistent with the use of this term in the Graeco-Roman benefaction system. Literary and inscriptional evidence shows that the fuller expression, καλὴ καὶ ἀγαθή, carried significant cultural weight in describing the ideal person. Although this cultural weight is also reflected in Jewish sources, the fact that these are limited points to the predominantly Graeco-Roman currency of the expression. The essay concludes that Luke intentionally uses this addition to interpret Jesus' meaning for Graeco-Roman ears.

Apocalyptic Judaism was simply the air breathed by Jesus and by the early Jesus movement. **Peter G. Bolt** draws attention to the wide influence on these apocalyptic perspectives of the literature associated with the name of Enoch. Whereas previous scholarship has discussed potential Enochic influences within the Gospel of Luke, this chapter draws particular attention to the Enoch-influenced genealogy, and the Lucan additions to the Parable of the Figtree. Although lying on the 'surface' of the narrative, these two examples indicate a deeper connection with the 'Enochic' world-view, especially in relation to time. These soundings add further weight to the suggestion that Luke's Gospel is, in fact, an apocalyptic narrative about Israel's Messiah/Son of Man at the End of Days, which necessitates a continuing re-evaluation of previous scholarly views of its character.

Dissatisfied with prevailing explanations of Nathanael as 'truly an Israelite in whom there is no deceit' (1:47), **Stephen Rockwell** examines the three key terms (ἀληθῶς, Ἰσραηλίτης, δόλος) related to the description. While by broad consensus the expression should be read against the backdrop of the Jacob narrative in Genesis and also Psalm 32, drawing upon prophetic writings the essay proposes that both Jesus and the Gospel of John present Nathanael as a remnant figure of faithful Israel.

John A. Davies argues that Jesus' words of comfort to his disciples on the eve of his 'glorification' about the 'many abidings' in his 'Father's house' (John 14:1–4), say nothing about what is to happen after their deaths. At this Passover time, Jesus employs the language of Jewish eschatological temple-building, the culmination of the exodus, to speak of the fulfilment of the divine dwelling with his people on earth. The case is strengthened by John's account utilising a bilingual play on words and a chiastic arrangement of Chapter 14, revealing a sustained theme of the coming of Jesus through the Spirit to empower the church for its continuing mission.

Christopher Seglenieks continues his interest in belief (πίστις) and believing (πιστεύω) in the Gospel of John. Interacting with Nadine Ueberschaer, it is evident that Johannine belief has a propositional dimension focused on the identity of Jesus. Yet the contextual study by Teresa Morgan demonstrates that the use of πίστις and *fides* in the Graeco-Roman world had a primarily relational focus. Considering a third alternative from Matthew Bates, the translation 'allegiance' rather than 'faith' does not fit in the Johannine context, but the term 'allegiance' is nevertheless useful for discussing the broader concept of belief in John, which involves words and deeds, as well as trust and propositional belief.

Luke's three accounts of Paul's conversion have long been at the centre of discussions about the historicity of Acts, including the question of what Paul's companions saw or did not see in Acts 9:7 and 22:9. Since various formulations of the syntax of ἀκούω have shaped this discussion, **Andrew Stewart** examines the linguistic data in Luke-Acts and Paul in light of the basic functions of the accusative and genitive cases. He suggests an alternative formulation which may aid the reader's understanding of the use of ἀκούω both in the wider context of Acts, and in the conversion narratives.

In one sense, the lines of inquiry represented by these essays are thoroughly familiar: the use of interpretive models and the need for their evaluation; attempts to better understand the variegated Jewish environment in which Jesus lived and from which the Gospels and Acts emerged; attempts to better understand the Graeco-Roman hearers to whom these documents directed their persuasive attempts; careful attention to their original language and their narrative art; questions about the historical Jesus; questions about the Gospels portrayal of him; apocalyptic perspectives from the first century, and their abiding relevance (or not?) for the centuries after Christ; the Christian hunch that these marvelous records at the foundation of the Christian movement still have something to say, even to complex and confused discussions in our contemporary world; the conviction that they continue to move Christ's people to engage in his mission in the present times of distress.

But it would miss the significance of contemporary research being done on the Gospels and Acts to domesticate it to the known 'business as usual', declaring 'the old is better' (Luke 5:39). Lasting change comes by degrees. Trajectories are only seen in retrospect. Like the man with the rich and interesting attic (Matt 13:52), or the Lord's mercies every morning (Lam 3:23), Gospels and Acts research will be ever-new, as it continues to explore and discover, evaluate and re-evaluate, refute and propound, invite and proclaim. By seeking to better understand Jesus of Nazareth in the past, through these documents, such research will engage with issues of the present. By returning to these foundational accounts of events of fundamental significance, the good news of Jesus Christ will be re-visited, re-formulated, and re-proclaimed in order to shape the future by means of Christ's continuing mission.

The future is now. Now is the future.

Peter G. Bolt
Director, Centre for Gospels and Acts Research

CHAPTER 2

Social Stratification and Poverty Studies in First-Century Roman Palestine: An Evaluation of Recent Research on the Economic Context of the First Disciples

James R. Harrison

Abstract

This essay explores the extended use of the Lenski and Alföldy model of social stratigraphy in Gospel studies. Recent scholarship (Scheidel, Friesen, Longenecker, Keddie) has demanded a more sophisticated approach to New Testament social and economic studies. It is argued in this essay that despite these significant and telling challenges, the model of Lenski still retains the advantage of bringing the evidence of the Jewish historian Josephus into sympathetic dialogue with the Gospel narratives in a helpful and enlightening manner. From here the essay charts the way forward for future research into social stratification and poverty in the Gospels, focusing methodologically upon the iconographic, epigraphic, and papyrological evidence. Finally, in coming to grips with social stratification and poverty in Gospel studies, the rhetoric of the evangelists themselves has to be reckoned with. In this regard, Luke's portrait of the 'impoverished widow-benefactor' in 20:45—21:4 is explored as a case study in its epigraphic, numismatic, and Graeco-Roman literary context, with a view to understanding this paradoxical vignette better in its first-century A.D. context.

Social Stratification and Poverty in Roman Palestine: The Contribution of the Lenski and Alföldy Model to Gospel Studies

Studies in the social stratification of Roman Palestine have led to extensive investigations of the social consequences of poverty in its Herodian, imperial and rabbinic contexts.[1] The conceptual starting point for stratification research has been Josephus' statement that Palestine was an agricultural economy, as opposed to a maritime economy (Josephus, C. Ap. 1.60, 195; cf. Let. Aris. 112). Josephus' estimate probably betrays the strong Roman bias against traders that is found in the agricultural treatises of Cato (Agr. 1.2–4), Varro (Rust. 2.10.1–3), and Columella (Rust. 1.1–17).[2] We would, therefore, be unwise to infer that trade had little or no part in the economy of Roman Palestine.[3] But the assessment of Roman Palestine as an agricultural economy meant that scholars were inevitably drawn to social-scientific studies of peasant societies for explanatory models.[4]

The sociological and historical models of Gerhard E. Lenski and Geza Alföldy have been pivotal in enabling Gospel scholars to conceptualise at a macro level the social stratification of early first-century Jewish agricultural society.[5] A sociologist, Lenski proposed an evolutionary theory of human development in which the dominant forms

---

1   Schottroff and Stegemann, *Jesus and the Hope of the Poor*; Hamel, *Poverty and Charity*; Rosenfeld and Perlmutter, 'The Poor as a Stratum'; Wilfand, *Poverty, Charity and the Image of the Poor*; Sandford, *Poverty, Wealth, and Empire*; Häkkanin, 'Poverty in the First-Century Galilee'.
2   See Harland, 'The Economy of First-Century Palestine', 518.
3   On Palestinian trade, see Mattila, 'Revisiting Jesus' Capernaum', 105–9; Harland, 'The Economy of First-Century Palestine', 518–20; Pastor, 'Trade, Commerce, and Consumption', 297–307. On agricultural societies generally, see Herzog, *Parables as Subversive Speech*, 56–66. On agriculture and the economy in Roman Palestine, see Broshi, 'Agriculture and Economy'; Safrai, *The Economy of Roman Palestine*; Pastor, *Land and Economy*; Gill, 'The Decline of Agrarian Economy'.
4   For discussion of the key representatives in the social-scientific literature, see Harland, 'The Economy of First-Century Palestine', 511–13.
5   See the diagram of Lenski, *Power and Privilege*, 284 Fig. 1, on the relationships between the classes in agrarian societies. Additionally, see Oakman, 'The Countryside in Luke-Acts'.

of production (hunting and gathering, horticulture, agriculture, and industry) revealed particular systems of stratification.[6] Two propositions of Lenski have been central for studies of the economic background to the Gospels:[7] that (a) the Graeco-Roman world was an advanced agrarian society, characterised by superior technology (e.g. iron ploughs, a professional army), and (b) it was riven by social inequality. Consequently, the landowning élites rented out their large estates (*latifundia*) throughout the Empire, including Roman Palestine, and, in the process, dispossessed many of the peasantry, reducing them to indebtedness and subsistence.[8] The two-strata model (upper and lower strata) of the historian Geza Alföldy for Roman society,[9] coupled with Lenski's suggestion of a 'vassal' class in the upper stratum (i.e. a 'retainer class'),[10] provided the paradigm for the Stegemanns' highly influential social history of the first Christians.[11] David A. Fiensy, in his impressive social history of the Herodian period in Palestine, has also profitably utilised the model of Lenski.[12] Most recently, Ben Rosenfeld and Haim Perlmutter have produced the first definitive historical study of the social stratification of Roman Palestine from 70 C.E. to the Mishnaic period, though the model of Lenski and Alföldy has not been the conceptual driving force of this study.[13] The pre-70 C.E. period of social stratification still awaits a comprehensive study for Roman Palestine.

Other useful sociological models have added to our understanding of the internal frictions, violence, and factionalism characteristic of social stratification in Roman Palestine. Richard Horsley, rejecting Gerd Theissen's abstract use of a structural-functionalist sociology, in his *Sociology of Early Palestinian Christianity*[14] posited instead the

---

6 For the most recent discussion of Lenski as a sociologist, see Barnett, *Gerhard Lenski's Sociological Theories*.
7 The pioneering work in the discipline was Grant, *The Economic Background of the Gospels*.
8 Lenski, *Power and Privilege*, 189–296.
9 Alföldy, *The Social History of Rome*, 94.
10 Lenski, *Power and Privilege*, 325–26.
11 On stratification and its social consequences, see Stegemann and Stegemann, *The Jesus Movement*. On social stratification at Jerusalem, see Jeremias, *Jerusalem in the Time of Jesus*.
12 Fiensy, *Social History of Palestine*, 155–76.
13 Rosenfeld and Perlmutter, *Social Stratification*. On stratification, see Scheidel, 'Stratification', 40–59.
14 Horsley, *Sociology*, 15–64, 147–55.

sociological model of 'Conflict Theory'[15] as a more concrete way of explaining the economic and political tensions affecting Palestinian village communities. R. C. Hanson and Douglas E. Oakman, noting the dysfunctional nature of Jesus' society, also affirm that a 'conflict' approach 'attends to the tensions between social factions, institutions and subcultures that are the product of power relations in which one group seeks to dominate, control, manipulate or subdue the others for its advantage'.[16]

Despite the advances in scholarship generated by the Lenski and Alföldy model of social stratigraphy, the Roman historian Walter Scheidel has decisively challenged Alföldy's dichotomisation of Roman society. Scheidel has argued that models derived from the Roman *ordo* system—in which the *honestiores*, belonging to the three élite orders (senators, knights, municipal *decurions*), are polarised against the *humiliores* (everyone else)—are sociologically deficient because they overlook the possibility of a middle class in the Roman world.[17] The Stegemanns adhere closely to Alföldy's upper and lower-stratum groups, but they nuance economic differences between urban and rural contexts and highlight groups (e.g. richer merchants and tradesmen) who attain a measure of prosperity and acquire honorific status via their involvement in the local associations.[18] Recently, Steven J. Friesen and Bruce Longenecker have proposed more sophisticated stratification scales. They have not only jettisoned Alföldy's binary model but also have critiqued Justin Meggitt's vast overestimation of the ratio of the destitute non-elite poor (99%) to the elite rich (1%) in another binary construal of the social pyramid in the Roman Empire.[19] Both Friesen and Longenecker allow for a 'middling' group (ES4 Scale), comprising 7% of the Empire's population in the case of Friesen, and 15% in the case

---

15 Horsley, *Sociology*, 67–145, 156–65. Horsley, *Jesus and the Spiral of Violence*, 22–26, in conceptualising structural violence against oppressive governments, employs neo-colonial theories of a three stage 'spiral of violence,' suggested by Dom Helder Camara, Archbishop of Recife in northeast Brazil.
16 Hanson and Oakman, *Palestine in the Time of Jesus*, 9.
17 Scheidel, 'Stratification', esp. 41–46. See also Harris, 'Poverty and Destitution', 31–32.
18 Stegemann and Stegemann, *The Jesus Movement*, 85–86.
19 Meggitt, *Paul, Poverty and Survival*, 33, 99. For an appreciative but incisive critique of Meggitt's seminal monograph, see Martin, 'Review Essay: Justin J. Meggitt'.

of the Longenecker.[20] In sum, subsequent scholarship has challenged Alföldy's dichotomisation of Roman society and New Testament scholars have adjusted their conception of the social pyramid accordingly, with Longenecker in particular discussing the upwardly mobile *apparitiones* and the *Augustales* as instances of the middling group.[21]

Nevertheless, the Lenski and Alföldy model of social stratigraphy, as pursued in New Testament Gospel studies, has had the distinct advantage of bringing the evidence of Josephus into close dialogue with the Gospels in a valuable manner. The social hierarchy devolved from the upper stratum (Roman provincial administrators, the Herodian house, aristocratic élites, the Sanhedrin), resourced and aided by its retainers (Sadducean priests, scribes, military administration, merchant classes), to the lower stratum.[22] The lower stratum ranged from prosperous craftsmen/traders[23] to peasant farmers,[24] tenants,[25] fishermen,[26] shepherds,[27] day-labourers,[28] and the destitute.[29] Crucially, Lenski highlighted the plight of the 'unclean and degraded' at the base of the social pyramid (lepers, 'sinners').[30] Tradesmen were also despised by the élites because they worked with their hands (Sir.

---

20 Friesen, 'Poverty in Pauline Studies', 323–62; Longenecker, *Remember the Poor*, 53. Scheidel and Friesen, 'The Size of the Economy', 62, argue that within the Roman Empire 'economically "middling" non-élite groups accounted for a population (around 10 per cent) but perhaps another fifth of annual income'.
21 Longenecker, *Remember the Poor*, 329–32.
22 On the scribes, see Arnal, *Jesus and the Village Scribes*.
23 Acts 16:14.
24 See Oakman, *Jesus and the Peasants*.
25 Mark 12:1–12.
26 Matt 4:17–22; Mark 1:16–17; Luke 5:11.
27 Luke 2:8–20.
28 Matt 20:1–16; Mark 1:20b; John 10:11–13.
29 Beggars: Matt 21:14; Mark 10:46; Luke 14:21; 16:20; John 5:3; 9:1; Acts 3:2; widows: Luke 7:11–12; 20:47–21:4. For discussion, see Stegmann and Stegemann, *The Jesus Movement*, 129–36.
30 Lepers: Mark 1:40; 14:3; Luke 17:12. 'Sinners', Mark 2:14–17; Luke 15:1–2 (cf. *Sir* 12.13–14). Ritually impure: Mark 1:40–44; 5:25–29; Luke 8:43–48; 14:1–4; 11:11–19. On sinners, see Horsley, *Jesus and the Spiral of Violence*, 217–23; Dunn, 'Pharisees, Sinners, and Jesus'; Chilton, 'Jesus and Sinners and Outcasts'. On the ritually impure, see Evans, '"Who Touched Me?"'; Kim, 'Jesus and the Purity Paradigm'; Jensen, 'Purity and Politics', 3–34. On the exclusion of people with disabilities from Judaism, see *m. Kelim* 1:6–9, *t. Meg.* 2.7, 4QMMT 39–40, 1QSa II 5–11. For discussion, see Shemesh, '"The Holy Angels are in Their Council"'; Olyan, 'The Exegetical Dimensions of Restrictions'; Marx, *Disability in Jewish Law*; Dorma, *The Blemished Body*. For Jesus' interaction with people with disabilities, see Gosbell, *'The Poor, the Crippled, the Blind, and the Lame'*.

38.25–34, esp. vv.32b–33; cf. Xenophon, Oec. 4:14; Dio Chrysostom, Or. 7.110; Lucian, Fug. 1213; Cicero, Off. 1.42; Brut. 73).[31] To the lowest echelon of Lenski's social stratigraphy belonged the 'expendables', including beggars[32] and bandits.[33] Notably, the social location of the first Palestinian Christians—with the exceptions of Herodian court contacts[34] and members of the retainer class[35]—are, at first glance, all lower stratum, a conclusion in line with Justin Meggitt.

The literature and documents of Second Temple Judaism and the Graeco-Roman world, as well as the Gospels, confirm the Lenski and Alföldy model, notwithstanding its deficiencies, when it is applied to Palestine at a macro level. First, the presence of *latifundia* in Seleucid Palestine was a prominent feature of agricultural life, as elsewhere in the Roman Empire. During the rule of the Seleucid King over Syria, Antiochus III (241–187 B.C.E.), Ptolemaios, the military governor and chief priest of Koile Syria, sent several letters to the King in 219 B.C.E. In a Greek inscription near the village of Hefzibah, Ptolemaios suggests that his own villagers should be allowed to transfer products to other nearby villages, as opposed to those outside of his territory (Document III. IIIa ll. 10–14).[36] In another letter (V. II ll. 27–33), King Antiochus prohibits travelling military commanders from lodging 'by violence' in the villages of Ptolemaios, fining the officials tenfold for damages done. Thus, by the time of Seleucid Palestine, there were large *latifundia* owned by absentee powerbrokers, with the

---

31   Herzog, *Parables as Subversive Speech*, 65, 69. On Graeco-Roman and Jewish attitudes to artisans, see Fiensy, 'Jesus' Socioeconomic Background', 239–41.
32   Luke 16:19–31; cf. Acts 3:2.
33   Lenski, *Power and Privilege*, 280–84. On bandits, see Horsley, 'Josephus and the Bandits'; Horsley, *Jesus and the Spiral of Violence*, 37–39; Horsley and Hanson, *Bandits*, 48–87.
34   Luke 8:3; cf. Acts 13:1.
35   'Chief tax collector' Zachaeus: Luke 19:1–8; Levi: Luke 5:27. Jewish priests, Acts 6:7. A scholarly dispute exists over the status of tax-collectors. Some scholars regard the *telônai* to be lower echelon subordinate officials who collect indirect taxes for the Herods and Romans *specifically* at the tollbooths at commercial and transport centres: Donahue, 'Tax Collectors and Sinners', who prefers the term 'toll-collector' for the term *telônês*. Alternatively, other scholars consider them to be small tax farmers, that is, local contactors charged with the responsibility for collecting revenue for Rome: see Herrenbrück, *Jesus und die Zöllner*; cf. Herrenbrück, 'Wer waren die "Zölner"'. In other words, Donahue sees *telônai* as the equivalent of the Roman *portitores* (i.e. servants of the *publicani*), whereas Herrenbrück understands *telônai* to be the familiar tax officials of the Hellenistic world.
36   See Landau, 'A Greek Inscription Found Near Hefzibah'.

potential for the abuse and exploitation of villagers.

Secondly, regarding the upper stratum in Roman Palestine,[37] Herod Antipas' councillor, Ptolemy, owned Arus, a local village (Josephus, A.J. 17.11). Herod also had his own estates in Perea, the Great Plain, and Galilee (Josephus, Vita 33, 119; A.J. 18.92), producing 200 talents annually (A.J. 17.318). Loyal officers were rewarded with estates, as was Herod Agrippa I's prefect, Crispus, described as 'absent on his estates beyond the Jordan' (Vita 33; cf. the prefect Philip, Vita 47; A.J. 17.29–30). Imperial (Vita 71–73) and Herodian granaries (Berenice, sister of Agrippa II: Vita 118–119) were also located in the villages of Upper Galilee, along with five groups of twenty storage chambers for the produce of Herod the Great's estate along the coastline of Caesarea Maritima (Acts 12:20), storage which Herod Agrippa utilised for trade.[38]

Crucially, however, Jesus' contemptuous dismissal of Herod Antipas as a weak and wily 'fox' (Luke 13:32),[39] lampooning the ruler as one who had insulated himself in soft clothing within the security of his palace (Matt 11:8), underscores Jesus' radical up-ending of social stratification (Matt 19:30; 26:16; Mark 10:31; Luke 13:30). Furthermore, Jesus' parables are replete with graphic accounts of the workers on the large Galilean estates (Matt 13:24–30; 20:1–15; Mark 12:1–12; Luke 12:16–21; 15:1–31; 16:1–9), including estate bailiffs who oversaw their master's finances (Luke 12:42–48; 16:1–8).[40] From the sociological and literary evidence above, it has been inferred that large estate owners deprived some peasants of their land, driving them over the precipice into subsistence. However, the scholarly inference of acquisitive estate owners in Galilee has not commanded the support of all, including Richard A. Horsley, who has denied the presence of large Galilean estates during the ministry of Jesus.[41]

---

37 On local village notables and aristocrats (e.g. Josephus, *Vita* 43–45, 123–125), see Fiensy, 'Jesus' Socioeconomic Background', 231–32; Fiensy, *Christian* Origins, 11.
38 On the archaeological evidence, see Keener, *Acts: An Exegetical Commentary. Volume 2: 3:1–14:28*, 1958.
39 Hoehner, *Herod Antipas*, 220–21.
40 The foundational article is Herz, 'Grossgrundbesitz in Palästina im Zeitalter Jesu', not available to me.
41 Horsley, *Galilee: History, Politics, People*, 213–14. Pace, Fiensy, *The Social History of Palestine*, 21–73.

Given the upper stratum dominance of Palestine by Roman officials and Herodian client-kings, the question arises whether the cities of first-century C.E. Palestine became increasingly Romanised. An interesting case study in this regard is entertainment.[42] Theatres were a Hellenistic phenomenon, but they were built by Herod the Great in Jerusalem, Jericho, and Caesarea Maritima, with only the latter two appearing in the archaeological record. Significantly, they did not follow the Greek paradigm, which specified round orchestras, but rather the Roman semi-circular prototype of Vitruvius in *De Architectura*.[43] Herod also introduced spectacles and competitions as a new provincial entertainment, including gladiatorial games and wild beast spectacles, a uniquely Roman activity. These were held at the Herodian hippodromes—along with chariot races and athletic competitions—which Herod had also built at Jerusalem, Jericho, and Caesarea Maritima. From the end of the first century C.E. and increasingly so into the second and third centuries, Roman buildings for entertainment populated Roman Palestine. Notwithstanding, in the third century C.E., Rabbi Shimon ben Pazi could still denounce theatres, circuses, and the contests of wild beasts as the preserve of idolaters (b. 'Abod. Zar 18b).[44] No matter how much Roman culture impacted upon Palestine, the traditions of Israel's ancestral faith still remained at the forefront of Jewish identity, including the early Jewish Christ-followers in Palestine.

Thirdly, regarding the retainers who collaborated with Rome, four high priestly houses are portrayed in rabbinic tradition as acting violently towards the people (b. Pesahim 57a; t. Menahot 13.21; cf. T. Mos. 7.3–10).[45] Other retainers of Rome, such as the tax-collectors, are well known from Josephus (B.J. 2.287) and the Gospels (Luke 5:29; 19:1–10).[46] Significantly, Tacitus highlights the heavy burden of taxation imposed upon Judaea (Tacitus, Ann. 2.42). Although there

---

42 For the literary and archaeological evidence, see Weiss, 'Buildings for Entertainment'.
43 Chancey and Porter, 'The Archaeology of Roman Palestine', 191.
44 See Ratzlaff, 'The Effects of Empire on Daily Life', 449–50.
45 See Herzog, 'Why Peasants Responded', 49. Note the Egyptian scribe (*P. Salier* I. 6.9–7.9) who, in collecting the harvest tax, violently beats impoverished farmers and their families (Simpson, *The Literature of Ancient Egypt*, 343–44). Similarly, note the violence perpetrated against the families of tax-evaders in Egypt at the time of Philo of Alexandria (*Spec.* 3.159–162).
46 Horsley, *Jesus and the Spiral of Violence*, 212–17.

were occasional tax remittances under Herod the Great (A.J. 15.365; 16.64), with less tribute collected in times of drought (A.J. 15.300, 303; cf. Acts 11:28–30), severe taxes were laid upon all produce when Archelaus came to power (A.J. 17.205). The competing demands of two taxation systems, one Judean and the other Roman, resulted in requests for tax relief (A.J. 15.365; 16:64; 18:90; 19:299). This culminated, it is argued, in the Jewish insurgents burning the office where the tax records were kept in Jerusalem at the beginning of the war against Rome (B.J. 2.427: 'eager to destroy the money-lenders' bonds and to prevent the recovery of debts'; cf. Antioch, B.J. 7.61).[47]

The parables and logia of Jesus reveal an awareness of the dynamics of indebtedness in Palestine (Matt 18:23–35; Matt 5:25–26/Luke 12:58–59; Luke 7:41–42; 12:58–59; 16:1–8; 20:47–21:4). Jesus' prayer for the release of our debts (Matt 6:12/Luke 11:4) could conceivably be a 'petition for release from the earthly shackles of indebtedness' as opposed to 'release from infractions against God', though the divine focus of the petition remains much more likely.[48] Significantly, whether Jesus discusses the payment of the tribute or the temple tax (Mark 12:13–17; Matt 17:22–27), he endorses its payment, but pointedly calls into question the ultimacy of the Caesars and their priestly collaborators (Mark 12:17b; Matt 17:25–26 [cf. Matt 12:6]).

Fourthly, those who belonged to the lower stratum have been mentioned above, including the economically destitute. The sudden unemployment of 18,000 workers upon the completion of the Temple demonstrates how easily many could slide into poverty (A.J. 20.219). Significantly in this regard, Jesus, son of Sapphias, an aristocrat from a high priestly family (B.J. 2.566), turned his back upon his privileged class origins and led a revolt of the mariners and the destitute at Tiberias in the late 60s (Vita 66–67; cf. 134–135; J.W. 3.450–52, 467–68).

Jesus of Nazareth, by contrast, highlighted the precariousness of wealth (Matt 6:24; Mark 10:25; Luke 6:24–26 [cf. 1 En. 94:8; 96:8];

---

47 See Oakman, *Jesus and the Economic Questions,* 72–77, 153–55; Oakman, *Jesus, Debt, and the Lord's Prayer,* 23–29. On taxation in Roman Palestine, see Udoh, *To Caesar What is Caesar's.*

48 Oakman, *Jesus and the Economic Questions,* 155; contra, Carson, 'Matthew', 172–73.

8:14; 11:39, 42–44; 12:13–21; 16:19–31; 18:22–30; 20:47; 21:34),[49] announcing good news for the poor, and proclaiming the Jubilee release of the oppressed and the seventh-year debt release (Luke 4:18–19; 6:20–23; cf. Lev 25:8–10; Deut 15:1).[50] In sum, Jesus demonstrated a deep awareness of the wide economic divide in Galilee and his message must have resonated deeply with the destitute.

Fifthly, we are faced with the question of Jesus' social location. This critical question revolves around what is meant by τέκτων in Mark 6:3 and Matthew 13:55. The word referred to a builder of any kind, not necessarily the traditional carpenter, but rather a stonemason (possibly even a metalworker) or a builder at a nearby city such as Sepphoris.[51] The meaning, however, seems to be primarily 'carpenter'.[52] The meaning of 'carpenter' as opposed to stonemason, is certainly the referent for τέκτων that predominates in the papyri when the word is given precise contextualisation, as opposed to just appearing in a list. A few examples will suffice to establish the case.

A contract (22nd April 111 B.C.E.) from Pathyrus in Upper Egypt states: 'Petes, son of Pelaios, carpenter, agrees with Horos, Persian of the epigone, son of Nechoutes, grandson of Aratres, to make a satisfactory wagon yoke and a basket before Tybi 3rd of the 7th year'.[53] A contact of association (A.D. 568, 28th April, Antinoopolis) between two carpenters, Aurelius Psois and Aurelius Iosephis, outlines how the profits and losses should be born between both parties.[54] In a private letter (A.D. 250–268: Theadelphia [Arsinoites]) of Geminus to Heroninos, it is said that 'Hermes (the) carpenter has my 160 drachmai for two wheels eight cubits long.'[55] The sale of a vacant lot is 'on the

---

49 See Schmidt, *Hostility to Wealth in the Synoptic Gospels*; Hayes, *Luke's Wealth Ethics*; Giesen, 'Poverty and Wealth'.
50 See Sloan, *The Favourable Year of the Lord*; Ringe, *Jesus and Liberation*; Gunjevic, *Jubilee in the Bible*, 139–83.
51 Batey, 'Is Not This the Carpenter?'; Häkkanin, 'Poverty', 8. Louw and Nida, *Greek English Lexicon*, 520, write: 'There is every reason to believe that in biblical times one who was regarded as a τέκτων would be skilled in the use of wood and stone and possibly even metal'.
52 See BAGD, τέκτων, ονος, ὁ. Moulton and Milligan, *Vocabulary*, 628–29, conclude: 'The ordinary limitation of this word to "a worker in wood", "a carpenter", as in Mat 13:55, Mk 6:3, is supported by P Fay 110 (AD 94)'.
53 P.Corn. 4.
54 P.Cair. Masp. 2. 67158.
55 P.Flor. 2.262.

west of the lots of the sons of Pasion, the carpenter (first century A.D.: Tebtynis)."[56] The subscription to a contract for the sale of a courtyard (first century A.D.: Tebtynis) mentions that the total number of cubits have been 'measured with the carpenter's standard wooden cubit'[57] In an account of expenses (A.D. 184: Ptolemais Hormou), 4 drachmae is paid to the carpenter, along with interestingly, 10 drachmai to the thief-catchers.[58] There is also mention of a carpenter from the city of Arsinoition (574 A.D.)[59] and an apprenticeship for a carpenter (28th August, A.D. 128).[60] In sum, there is little doubt that Jesus was a carpenter as opposed to a stonemason on the basis of the Egyptian papyri, though we must not rule out the possibility of multi-skilling in a village context. What is especially interesting about some of the examples above, spanning first century B.C.—sixth century A.D., is the contractual nature of the work, demonstrating that artisans lived above subsistence levels within city and village contexts, with agreed payments specified and accounted for. At the very least, while certainly falling short of the 'middling' group (ES4 Scale), the Egyptian carpenters in the late Hellenistic and Roman ages would have had modest means.

So where does Jesus as a Palestinian carpenter fit into this wider economic spectrum? Oakman argues that although Jesus was socialised within a village context (Mark 6:1–3; Luke 2:51), he is 'best understood as a peasant child forced to leave the village in search of a livelihood (Mark 6:3)',[61] as opposed to being a resident village artisan. If the Egyptian Satire on the Trades, *The Instruction of Dua-Khety*, reflects social realia, notwithstanding its elements of caricature, it is significant that the family of the carpenter suffered while he was absent labouring at non-local worksites: 'But as for the food which is to be given to his household (while he is away), there is no one who provides for his children' (Section 11).[62] That Jesus himself came from

---

56 P.Mich. 5.291.
57 P.Mich. 5.306.
58 P.Petaus. 34. See also the account of 5 drachmai and double obol for a carpenter from an unknown Egyptian city (O.Camb. 99).
59 P.Muench.3.1.100.
60 BASP 48 (2011) S. 47.
61 Oakman, *Jesus and the Peasants*, 171.
62 Simpson, *The Literature of Ancient Egypt*, 329–36.

a poor family is evidenced by Mary's offering of two doves for her purification (Luke 2:24; cf. Lev. 12:8). His itinerant life of privation (Matt. 8:20; Luke 9:58; Mark 15:24), dependence upon the beneficence of others (Luke 8:1–3; 10:38–42; John 11:1; cf. Matt. 10:10; Luke 9:3; 10:4, 7–8) and inability to produce a coin when required (Matt. 17:24–27; Mark 12:13–17), underscore his personal poverty.[63] There may well have been more prosperous carpenters in the larger cities of Roman Palestine, but the evidence of the Gospels speaks against this in the case of Jesus. One has to ask how Jesus had such an acute eye in delineating the experience of poverty and indebtedness in his parables: his own periodic experiences of privation as a carpenter in a village of little significance, perhaps forcing him intermittently to seek work elsewhere, seems to be the answer.

In conclusion, the sociological and historical models of Lenski and Alföldy might be said to be flawed because they do not reflect accurately enough the 'middling' group present minimally in the Roman Empire. That is certainly true. However, in terms of the Palestinian disciples, there are no obvious candidates for such a 'middling' group (e.g. *apparitiones*, *Augustales*) as there are arguably in the later eastern Mediterranean churches. There is a minority who have 'retainer' status because of their personal connections with the Herodian court or with the Roman government as its tax collectors, but next to them in the social stratification of Palestine, we can only speak of those with very modest wealth in the lower stratum amongst the first disciples. This means that the Lenski and Alföldy model still retains considerable value for assessing the Gospel evidence against the stratification that we find in the narratives of Josephus. Care, nevertheless, has to be exercised lest we read the evidence of Josephus and the Gospels through the lens of our sociological theory, seeing connections that are only very minimally there, if at all. But, as we have seen, we can test our conclusions against the epigraphic and papyrological evidence to test the reality of the implications we are drawing, such as the presence of large estates in first-century Galilee, or the proposed modest

---

63 Stegemann and Stegemann, *The Jesus Movement*, 90, 199. Contra, see Fiensy (*Christian Origins*, 23–33) who argues that Jesus was an artisan of modest means.

wealth of Jesus as an artisan. Finally, we must be discerning regarding the rhetoric of the writings of Josephus and the Gospels themselves, lest we overlook the complexity and subtlety of what individual evangelists are attempting to establish for their contemporary readers in a later generation, a theme to which we will return in the last section of this essay.

We turn now to a methodological assessment of the model of Lenski and Alföldy and its continuing application to the social pyramid of Roman Palestine. In what ways might the debate regarding social stratification and its relation to poverty studies in the Gospels be advanced methodologically? What qualifications to the so-called 'consensus', emanating from the model of Lenski and Alföldy, should be considered?

Social Stratification and Poverty in Gospel Studies: The Way Forward for Future Research

Several methodological observations pertinent for future studies in Gospel Studies on social stratification and its relation to poverty are made below.

There needs to be a closer analysis of the language of 'poverty' in each corpus of Jewish evidence (e.g. LXX, Second Temple literature, Gospels, Josephus, Philo, epigraphy). Although poverty terminology is notoriously slippery,[64] an awareness of contextual nuances can be very helpful (e.g. the distinction between the indigent widow [Mark 12:38–40] and the totally destitute Lazarus [Luke 6:19–31]).[65] In this regard, a poverty scale of five levels, based on the terminology of the Mishnah, has been charted by Rosenfeld and Perlmutter. This is a fine example of the close lexical work that needs to be pursued.[66] The difficulty of the task, however, should not be underestimated. As W. V. Harris writes, 'Greek *ptochos* and *penes*, Latin *egens* and *pauper*—and all the other words that refer to persons short on resources—are not of

---

64 See Hamel, *Poverty*, 167–211; Longenecker, *Remember the Poor*, 37–40; Harris, 'Poverty and Destitution', 30–31.
65 See Rosenfeld and Perlmutter, 'The Poor as a Stratum', 279–80.
66 See Rosenfeld and Perlmutter, 'The Poor as a Stratum', 292–93.

course meaningless terms, but they are highly subjective, flexible, and relative."[67]

Attention should be given to the relevant visual evidence in discussions of tax indebtedness and depictions of the impoverished. First, an interesting sidelight to the burning of the tax records in Josephus (B.J. 2.427) is the official ceremonial burning of the debt records in front of Vespasian at Rome, who, in the Adlocutio relief, is seated atop the Rostra Augusti before the Temple of Saturn, the state treasury. Soldiers carry heavy account books towards the fire consuming the records, while senators (identified by the *toga*) and the poor (identified by the *paenula*) strain forward to view the spectacle, though the poor are pushed to the rear.[68] Here the imperial propaganda of debt remission stands in contrast to the efforts of the Jewish revolutionaries to obliterate the tax records from memory: either way, a consciousness of the burden of tax is envisaged, even if cynically manipulated by Vespasian for political purposes.

Nevertheless, we have to ask whether the debt record burning at Jerusalem (Josephus, B.J. 2.427) represents the policy of the insurgents. Lyn Cohick has argued that in the case of Sepphoris, as opposed to Jerusalem, there was no instance of the burning of debt records (Josephus, Vita 67).[69] So was the action at Jerusalem a deliberate act of debt erasure, undertaken as a policy decision, or simply a measure intended to muster popular support? But Cohick has posed a false dilemma here: the burning of the archives was simultaneously policy-based and an act of follower recruitment. Why the strategy adopted at Sepphoris was different to Jerusalem is difficult to determine: we have to allow for the fluidity of the revolt in its local expressions and not expect rigid consistency in each instance.

Second, the visual evidence of the ancient Near East ought to be pursued for insights into poverty. An Egyptian relief (Figure 1) reveals the harsh social conditions for the destitute, depicting starving

---

67 Harris, 'Poverty and Destitution', 31. On the Latin terminology of poverty, see Esser, *De Pauperum cura apud Romanos*, esp. Appendix 275–81. The thesis is now online and has been recently published by Wentworth Press, 2019.
68 See Favro and Johanson, 'Death in Motion', 14 Fig. 3.
69 Cohick, 'Poverty and Its Causes', 25.

nomads in a time of famine, their emaciated bodies revealing the outline of their rib cages. At the bottom lower left of the relief, a woman picks vermin from her hair with her left hand and conveys the morsels to her mouth with her right hand.⁷⁰

Figure 1: Egyptian Relief

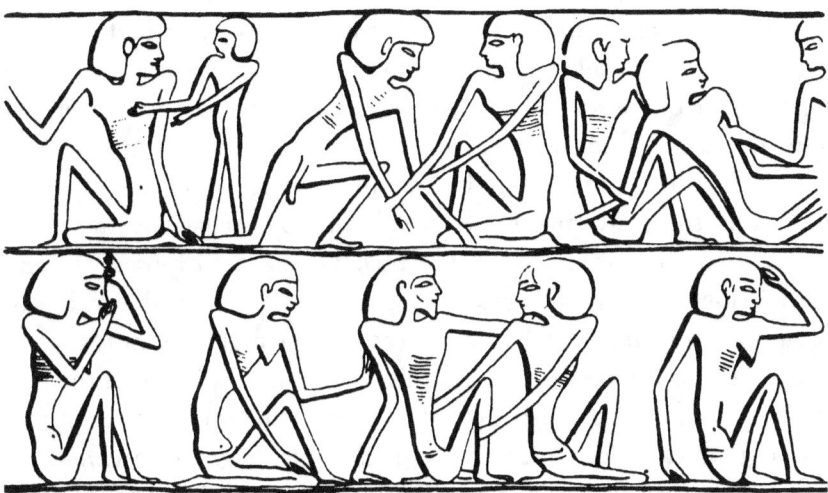

Indeed, food, to pursue a brief aside here, is indicative of levels of poverty. Harris notes, citing Petronius, Sat. 14, that the poor did not eke out an existence solely on wheat and barley but on even cheaper fare such as peas and lupin seeds.⁷¹ Notably, in the Parable of the Prodigal Son (Luke 15:11–32), the errant son, working as an impoverished hired hand during a famine and facing death-foreshadowing hunger pangs (Luke 15:17b), was longing to be fed pods, the staple diet of the pigs (15:15–16: κεράτιον).⁷² The pods of the pigs and the vermin of the hair

---

70 Keel, *The Symbolism of the Biblical World*, 76 Fig. 88. Picture used with author's permission.
71 Harris, 'Poverty and Destitution', 41.
72 Snodgrass, *Stories with Intent*, 126, writes: 'Carob pods were known throughout the Mediterranean region as fodder for animals and the food of desperation for humans'. Galen, the physician, describes *keratia* ('carobs') as follows (*Foodstuffs* 6.615): 'Carobs are a food that is unwholesome and woody, and necessarily difficult to concoct for nothing woody is easy. But the fact that they are also not excreted quickly is a considerable defect with them. So that it would be better for us not even to import them from the eastern regions where they are produced'. Cited by Wau, *The Path to Salvation*, 50.

illustrate graphically the extremes of poverty experienced during famine in agricultural communities in the Mediterranean the Middle East.

Further, at the Smithsonian National Museum of Natural History, Washington, there is a wooden carving of a starving naked man, sitting squat on a support, with both hands placed on his knees, staring at the viewer with gaunt eyes. Dated to the Late New Kingdom Period of Egypt (1298–1064 B.C.E.), the carving of the man is identified as starving by his six exposed ribs on the right and left sides of his torso. The Smithsonian Museum exhibit comments that while the significance of the statue in the tomb is far from certain, it was perhaps intended to ward off hunger, which, it is suggested, was considered a source of cosmic and social imbalance in Egyptian belief.

While there are methodological limitations regarding the interpretation of the visual evidence of poverty (e.g. are exposed ribs and emaciation always an accurate iconographic signal of malnutrition or simply a case of physical disease?),[73] the graphic nature of these ancient Near Eastern vignettes are consonant with Jesus' depiction of the destitute Lazarus (Luke 6:19–31). We have seen the poor are sometimes iconographically identified by their clothing (e.g. the *paenula*, i.e. a hooded cloak, noted above). But ambiguity of interpretation can remain even when clothing indicates poverty.[74]

---

73 See Harrison, 'Beneficence to the Poor in Luke's Gospel in Its Mediterranean Context', 33–34. On the depiction of poverty in Roman art, see Larsen, *The Representation of Poverty in the Roman Empire*, 240–83, with images in 'Appendix: Images'.

74 We should also note here the literary stereotypes of the clothing of the poor, including Juvenal's famous description (*Sat.* 3.170): '... his torn and dirt-caked top-coat, his grubby toga, one shoe agape where the leather's split—those clumsy patches'. On clothing and economic disparity, see Wau, *The Path to Salvation*, 55–58.

Figure 2: Wall Hanging from Pompei

Image credit: Fondo Antiguo de la Biblioteca de la Universidad de Sevilla from Sevilla, España

For example, a wall painting from the villa of Julia Felix at Pompeii (Figure 2) shows a readily identifiable beggar, semi-naked and dressed in rags, holding a staff in his left hand and a tethered dog in his right hand.[75] With his left knee extended, the beggar leans towards a well-dressed woman and her young bowl-holding attendant in an open street,[76] with large civic statues to his left. The woman seems to be offering a coin to the beggar. Longenecker speculates that the beggar may also be a youth, like the attendant, because of their comparatively small size.[77] This may be true, but the stunted size of the beggar may also be the inevitable results of lifelong malnutrition, or, in the case of the original painter of the wall painting, it may simply be a symbolic touch denoting the social inferiority of the beggar.[78] The sharp contrast between the privation of the beggar and the wealthy accoutrements of Roman urban civilisation in the wider frieze is well depicted. The interpretative uncertainty, noted above, is whether the scene shows a professional beggar (e.g. a

---

75 Baudrillart, 'Mendicatio, Mendici', 1713. The wall-painting has long since faded and we are dependent on an eighteenth century sketch of the three panels of the original frieze. For the full frieze, see Longenecker, *Remember the Poor*, 80, Illustration 1.
76 On the public places that beggars inhabited, see Parkin, *Poverty in the Early Roman* Empire, 46–47.
77 Longenecker, *Remember the Poor*, 79.
78 We should remember the social contempt expressed in the telling graffito from Pompeii: 'I hate the poor' (*CIL* 4.9839b).

Cynic philosopher, a priest of Cybele?)[79] or a destitute beggar unable to support himself. Certainty of interpretation is unachievable. However, Longenecker has astutely noted that the woman is only accompanied by a single attendant as opposed to a wider retinue, as would be expected of an elite female. Therefore, she is probably a sub-elite Pompeian, belonging to the 'middling' group (ES4 Scale).[80]

Archaeological evidence needs to be brought more regularly into the debate, with a view to testing assumptions inherited from the literary evidence and our socio-scientific and anthropological models. At the outset, however, the limitations of the archaeological evidence have to be acknowledged. Rosenfeld and Perlmutter correctly observe regarding the social stratification debate: 'it is difficult to create a clear distinction of poverty based on the archaeological evidence'.[81] Furthermore, the importance of not overstating the significance of the evidence is important.

First, Mattila has demonstrated that the socio-economic level of the villagers in Capernaum in Jesus' time was certainly above subsistence level. Fine free-blown Roman glassware (late first century C.E.), amphorae from Rhodes (second century B.C.E.), Hellenistic table wares, and the modest wealth of the houses in Insula 2, including the large triple courtyard house demonstrate this.[82] A subsistence constituency among the Galilean disciples from Capernaum, inferred from the model of Lenski and Alföldy, is questioned by this data. As fishermen with their own business in Capernaum, James, John, Peter, and Andrew probably lived above subsistence level, as certainly did Matthew the tax-collector (Matt. 4:13). But we have to be careful not to overstate the archaeological evidence in this instance. We cannot assume that all Galilean villages were so well placed as Capernaum.[83] We have argued above that though Jesus lived as a peasant artisan at

---

79 See Eidinow, 'In Search of the "Beggar Priest"'.
80 Longenecker, *Remember the Poor*, 79–80.
81 Rosenfeld and Perlmutter, 'The Poor as a Stratum', 300.
82 Mattila, 'Revisiting Jesus' Capernaum', 75–138.
83 Reed, 'Instability in Jesus' Galilee', 343–65, argues that a modest or vibrant urban economy did not necessarily ensure that the residents of Sepphoris and Tiberias were better off than nearby subsistence villagers: '... overall population growth, newly built cities, considerable migration, and extensive malaria caution against an optimistic view of economic life under Antipas' (p.364).

Nazareth, he was forced intermittently to leave home and seek work elsewhere due to family poverty.

Second, Fiensy has argued on the basis of the literary and archaeological evidence that there was a series of medium-sized estates in the Bet Netova valley. These were owned by elites in Lower Galilee, evidenced by the remains of three buildings in Shikhin and by the remains of houses in Sepphoris in the first half of the first century C.E.[84] Horsley is incorrect in denying the existence of estates in first-century Galilee. Fiensy concludes that these were not the large estates implied in Jesus' parables.[85] But we must not overgeneralise from the archaeological evidence: the papyri should also be consulted lest we construct a skewed picture of Palestinian agriculture. Ernest van Eck points to Apollonius, finance minister of Ptolemy II Philadelphos, as an important figure who owned several large estates, including one in Galilee (PSI VI 554; P.Lond. VII 1948). Large estates, therefore, had already established a foothold in Galilee by Hellenistic times.[86]

The Jewish literature has to be supplemented by an investigation of the documentary evidence. We have already seen that the epigraphic (n. 36, supra) and papyrological evidence (n. 86 supra) has confirmed the presence of large estates in Galilee in Seleucid and Hellenistic times, presaging those later in Roman Palestine. The evidence for the poor in Jewish inscriptions is scant but nevertheless significant. Two examples with suffice.[87]

First, a fragmentary letter in Aramaic on an ostracon (first century B.C.E.—first century C.E.), found in the upper city area of Jerusalem, says: '... the miserable poor ... that something bad ... in all (his?) ... Mattatiya has not been destroyed ... peace, in peace' (CIIP I.1. §629). The meaning and context of the inscription is obscure due to the highly damaged state of the ostracon. However, the description of the poor is arresting. Is the phrase, 'miserable poor', contemptuous or sympathetic in its intent? Either option is potent in its interpretative import.

---

84 Fiensy, 'Large Estates', 140–53.
85 Fiensy, 'Large Estates', 153.
86 See van Eck, *The Parables of Jesus the Galilean*, 146 n. 26.
87 See also the two uses of the laudatory epithet πενιχρός ('poor man'), cited by Hamel, *Poverty*, 187 n. 129, from the tombs of Beth She'arim (third century A.D.), originally belonging to a Jewish family from Palmyra.

Second, a paleo-Hebrew inscription from Giv'atha-Mitvar near Jerusalem, datable to the late Second Temple period, sets out the circumstances of Abba's life:

> I, Abba, son of the priest Ele-
> az(ar), son of Aaron the elder,
> Abba, the oppressed (ma'anyeh) and the perse-
> cuted who (was) born in Jerusalem
> and went into exile to Babylon, brought (back to Jerusalem) Matta-
> thi(ah), son of Jud(ah); I buried him in the
> cave which I had acquired by writ.[88]

The word ma'anyeh, as Hamel notes, may also mean 'made poor' or 'humiliated'.[89] If this lexical nuance is present, then the economic implications of Abba's socially humiliating persecution, resulting in his exile to Babylon, is implied by the careful word choice. The world of honour and shame is fused with socio-economic realities of an externally imposed poverty. In both inscriptions more than economic realities are aired: the social implications of poverty, including its dishonour, are canvassed or at least implied. Part of the problem with an exclusively statistical approach to poverty is that such social realities are anaesthetised.

Social-scientific models need to be tested carefully against the ancient evidence, fragmentary though it is, in order to test the assumptions generated, the anachronisms inadvertently imposed unless due caution is exercised, and the danger of models themselves becoming the evidence.[90] Nevertheless, the model of Lenski and Alföldy has stood the test of time in Gospels scholarship as far as still being a useful paradigm for understanding social stratification in agricultural Roman Palestine.

Perhaps one final area that needs to be explored in a Roman context is how Roman officialdom defined poverty. Here taxes are useful evidence for official conceptions of poverty because the poor often fall far short of the fiscal level determined by the state. Parkin has highlighted the importance of a mother's letter (P.Oxy. 251 ll. 7–23: A.D. 44) to

---

88   Hamel, *Poverty*, 186–87.
89   Hamel, *Poverty*, 187.
90   On the latter point, see Fiensy, *Christian Origins*, 84.

two officials of the Oxyrhynchite nome pleading regarding tax exemptions because of the poverty of her son. She requests that his name be removed from the census list because his impoverishment has forced him to leave the area, either in search of work, as Parkin hypothesises, or possibly to alleviate the dire straits that feeding another mouth is imposing upon his family.[91] Did the fact that the mother was writing the letter indicate that she was a widow and thus was financially vulnerable in a time of general privation? And would the officials reading her letter about her impoverished son leaving home have considered her plea to be nothing else than a clever tax dodge?[92] As Parkin correctly observes, the defensiveness of the mother ('I swear ... that the aforesaid are true') shows that she is very much aware that she might be dismissed as a tax evader.[93] The papyrus is set out below:

My son Thoönis, son of Dionysius,
who has no trade,
having been registered in the quar[t]er of Temouenouthis,
with[d]rew to the
[fo]reign country in the intervening
[t]ime. [Wh]erefore I ask that [t]his (person) be e[ntered]
[i]n the (list of people) wi[thdrawn]
[f]rom this present fourth
year of Tiberius Claudius
Caes[ar] Augustus
[Ger]m[anic]us Imperator,
and I [s]wear by Tiberius
[Claudiu]s Caesar Augustus
[Germani]cus Imperator
that the a[f]or[esaid] things [are true]
[and that no] resources belong
to Thoönis [.....]

Additionally, an official certificate of poverty (literally, ἄποροι, 'poor', 'without resources', 'destitute'), datable to 5th August 49 C.E. (P.Lond.

---

91   Parkin, *Poverty*, 23–24.
92   Parkin, *Poverty*, 24.
93   Parkin, *Poverty*, 23–24.

III 911), establishes the grounds—which are not specified because they are known to the parties involved at the time—for the person named to be entitled to poor-relief:

> Copy of a certificate of poverty (ἀντίγραφον γραφῆς ἀπόρων)
> recorded in the 12th year
> of Antoninus Caesar
> the lord. Mesore 12th.
> D[.....]ia [
> There is among the paupers (ἐν ἀπόροις)
> Petesorapis the son of Penaus,
> the son of Petesorapis, his mother being ...[94]

What precisely the poor person was exempted from is also not clear. Harris speculates that the exemption may have been made 'perhaps on the basis of physical disability'.[95] But this is extremely unlikely because it infers that there was a favourable attitude to people with disability in Roman Egypt. A telling papyrus from Egypt reveals the local village discrimination against people with disabilities (P.CollYoutie 1.16.5, 30):

> To Ptolemaios, kinsman [of the king] and *strategos*, from Petermouthis son of Pteesis, a *makhismos* with seven *arounai* among those recruited by Khomenis, being also a crippled tailor, from Tebtynis in the district of Polemon, and living at Oxyrhynchos in the same district ... despising me as being without help and a cripple.[96]

A more positive assessment of how people with disabilities were treated by officialdom in Roman Egypt emerges from the four petitions of visually impaired Gaius Gemellus Horigenes (born c. A.D. 171), a member of the provincial elite.[97] Gaius' petitions recount instances of his personal harassment (including magical spells launched by his enemies),

---

94 Milligan, 'A Certificate of Poverty from the Greek Papyri'. There is no other case of such a certificate revealed in a search of the online papyrological data base www. papyri.info. This document is unique.
95 Harris, 'Poverty and Destitution'. 36 n. 53.
96 Lee and Horsley, 'A Lexicon of the New Testament with Documentary Parallels: Some Interim Entries. 2', 64.
97 Draycott, 'Reconstructing the Lived Experience', 189–205.

physical assault, theft of his crops, and verbal abuse. Remarkably, an Egyptian official, an *epistrategos* called Calpurnius Concessus, stipulates in an additional notation that the petition of Gaius Gemellus Horigenes should be taken seriously: 'Petition his excellency the *epistrategos*, who will not be found wanting in matters within his jurisdiction. Return to the petitioner (P.Mich. V 425.23–24)'.[98] But we must remember that the petitioner is a powerful representative of the provincial élite. Would the Egyptian poor have commanded the same attention from officialdom? That eventuality is highly unlikely.

Thus our two documents above (P.Oxy. 251, P.Lond. III 911) confirm that there was an official definition of 'poverty' in Roman Egypt from the early first century A.D. onwards, or, at least, in specific locations thereof. But nothing is revealed regarding the criterion used at the level of Egyptian officialdom to determine the legitimacy of the poverty certificates or requests for census-based tax exemptions. So, as documentary comparanda to the situation in Roman Palestine, we cannot make any legitimate inferences regarding decisions of officialdom from these documents about the fate of the poor in Roman Palestine. The systems put in place seem to be uniquely Egyptian, though care must be taken with such a sweeping assessment because our papyrological evidence is almost exclusively Egyptian.

Last, in coming to grips with social stratification and poverty in Gospel studies, we must be attuned to the rhetoric of the evangelists themselves. How do they present the vulnerable poor in the Gospel stories in an age characterised by overflowing civic beneficence? How do they transition their narratives about Jesus and the dominical logia, forged in first-century Roman Palestine, to the wider world of the eastern Mediterranean basin, with its imperial officials and local civic elites? Does Jesus' radical counter-cultural critique of the wealthy and powerful become blunted in the process or is it repositioned in its new context with equal force? Does Jesus remain a troubling figure who undermines the oppression and social superiority arising from social stratification, as each evangelist reconfigures the Jesus tradition for a new audience? We will conclude our study with Luke's paradoxical

---

98 Draycott, 'Reconstructing the Lived Experience', 201.

presentation of the paradigm of an 'impoverished benefactor' in Luke 20:25–21:4.

Social Stratification and Poverty in Gospel Studies: Taking into Account the Benefaction Rhetoric of Luke 20:45–21:4

The pericope of Jesus' commendation of an impoverished widow benefactor in Mark 12:41–44 has provoked considerable discussion. It has been viewed as a story inculcating a moral exemplum of whole-hearted fidelity, in which the widow has agency and honour, with the result that she models the ideals of discipleship already espoused by Mark (6:8; 10:21, 25).[99] Indeed, her self-impoverishment becomes the precursor of the self-sacrifice and cruciform poverty of Jesus himself (Mark 12:6; 14:3–9; 15:24). Conversely, the pericope about the widow has been interpreted as a story about a subjugated victim, oppressed by a collaborationist, elitist, and gender-restricted temple system.[100] She symbolically represents 'one of the last nails in the coffin' of national Israel, summing up the 'chronic disregard of God's law and the sham religion of the nation's leaders'.[101] In sharp contrast to the 'moral exemplum' approach, here the widow has no agency or honour at all. In post-colonial studies, she has been depicted as another hapless victim of imperial rule within Palestine.[102] Most recently, in an Australian feminist reading, Michele E. Connolly presents the widow as an isolated and mute figure, like all the other silenced women of Mark's narrative. In giving to the inept, corrupt, and exploitive Temple system, she colludes 'with a religious disorder in a vicious cycle of illogic', where, now penniless, she will have to draw from the Temple's widow fund in order to survive.[103] The divergences in viewpoint are intriguing, reflecting new critical methodologies and disciplines of study within Markan scholarship and the New

---

99 See Nineham, *The Gospel of St. Mark*, 334–35; Malbon, 'The Poor Widow in Mark and Her Poor Rich Readers'; Gundry, *Mark*, 728–30.
100 See Wright, 'The Widow's Mites: Praise or Lament?'; Waetjen, *A Reordering of Power*, 183–96.
101 Smith, 'A Closer look at the Widow's Offering', 36.
102 See Kim, 'Rupturing the Empire'; Moore, 'Mark and Empire'.
103 Connolly, *Disorderly Women and the Order of God*, 153–54.

Testament guild more generally. However, the fate of the pericope in its Lukan context (21:2–4) has been entirely ignored—but it is a fascinating study which will be the focus of the remainder of the chapter.

The two pericopes comprising the larger literary unit of Luke 20:25–21:4 have not been investigated from an 'honour' perspective in Lukan studies. Two types of leaders are mentioned in each pericope: the scribal élites who seek notability (Luke 20:45–47) and the élite benefactors who underwrite the costs of temple worship by virtue of their extravagant gifts (21:1–5). In each case Jesus punctures the notability of the Jewish elites. Jesus, in a stinging prophetic and eschatological denunciation, exposes the greed and hypocritical piety of the scribes (Luke 20:45), whereas the elite temple benefactors are rebuked with the paradoxical and unexpected exemplum of an 'impoverished' widow, the most vulnerable figure of Second Temple Judaism (21:2–4; cf. 20:47).

The widow stands in sharp contrast to the wealthy widow benefactors of Graeco-Roman antiquity, known to us through the epigraphic and numismatic evidence, though, as we will see, with, very surprisingly, much less frequency than we would imagine. What has been overlooked are the strong echoes of Graeco-Roman honorific and benefaction motifs that unify both pericopes within their wider literary unit, themes which form an important locus of interest in Luke's Gospel (e.g. Luke 6:32–36; 14:7–14; 22:24–30). Contemporary auditors, familiar with the public inscriptions and the operations of benefaction culture, would have recognised the honorific resonances in each pericope: the epigraphic honours and stress on primacy in Luke 20:46 and the figure of the 'impoverished benefactor' in 21:2–4.

This unusual and deeply unconventional civic benefactor, known to us from the Graeco-Roman literature and inscriptions, emptied himself of all reserves in caring for his community, abandoning the right of exemption from public levies (*aleitourgetos*) routinely extended by cities to their overly generous benefactors, lest they impoverish themselves. Luke 20:25–21:4, therefore, prepares us for the public dishonouring of another impoverished benefactor, who, divested of his possessions and naked on the cross, emptied himself of everything for his ungrateful beneficiaries (23:32–49). We now turn to the ancient literary, epigraphic, and numismatic evidence to fill out in greater detail the portrait briefly sketched above.

2.1 The Graeco-Roman Public Commemoration of Women Benefactors and the Paradoxical Counter-Narrative of Luke 21:2–4

Since Jesus commends the impoverished woman benefactor of Luke 21:2–4, we will confine our investigation to honorific references to women benefactors in the eulogistic inscriptions and also in numismatic legends. What is remarkable in each instance is the sparsity of honorific reference to widows in such contexts: there are only two honorific inscriptions praising widows (χήρα) for their benefactions. Moreover, a second century A.D. Colossian benefactor Claudia Eugenetoriane, designates herself as widowed—a designation so far unique within the numismatic corpus. The same sense of rarity of self-designation in a benefaction context is again underscored. It may be reasonably inferred that Jesus is also performing publicly something highly unusual in commending a woman benefactor—even if she is a highly unconventional one, though, as we will see, within an established rhetorical trope.

a) The Epigraphic Evidence and Luke 21:2–4

In the case of the epigraphic evidence, from a search of the Packard Humanities Greek Epigraphy programme, only 44 occurrences of χήρα occur in the entire epigraphic corpus.[104] Of these, only two honorific inscriptions appear, each referring to the same woman (Atalante), from the same region (Pisidia in Asia Minor) and city (Termissos), in the second century A.D. The ἐπεί clause sets out the rationale for the conferral of the substantial honours upon Atalante—a copper statue on the most prominent site of the city, a gold crown, and games in her honour—by the council of the people of Termissos (TAM III,1, 4 ll. ll. 2, 29) and its craftsmen (ll. 25–26, 30):

---

104 Of the ten Ionian occurrences of the word for widow (χήρη), none is used in a benefaction context.

Since Atalante, daughter of Piaterabis, granddaughter of Pillakoas, great granddaughter of Kinnounis,[105] widow (χήρα), adorned with nobility of soul (εὐγενεία) and moderation (σωφροσύνη) and displaying all feminine virtue (πᾶσαν γυναικείαν ἀρετήν), working hard in conformity with her ancestors who often had contributed liberally to (πεφιλοτειμημένος) the city, both in (underwriting) the most remarkable expenses and in loans of silver and voluntary contributions and priestly salaries, has promised, when there was a great scarcity of corn, that abundance (of grain) was be furnished to the people and, (in) discharging this duty, she offered this liberality in plenty (τὴν φιλιτειμίαν δ[α]ψιλῆ ταύτην) from the month of Idalianios (onwards) for the (remainder of the) year ... (the honours given to Atalante are then listed).

Immediately we see that Atalante is designated as belonging to an élite household, modeling her behaviour upon her ancestors who have been already honoured by the city Termissos (cf. Luke 6:23). The beneficence offered elicits from the council the award of civic virtue, though this is understood in terms of its upper class origins ('nobility of soul') and also, significantly, her gender ('feminine virtue'): the hierarchy of her élite male family members has been enriched by her virtue as a woman. Significantly, her virtue breaks out of the confines of the domestic sphere, for which activities other widows are praised, into the public sphere of munificence. Significantly, there is no reference to Atalante's deceased husband. Her status stands independently of his house, whatever status the household might have had. In this regard, the reference at the outset of the inscription to the three generations of her prestigious family is reinforced by their previous philanthropy towards the city. The range of beneficence is wide, not only in terms of its various types, but

---

105 See the three prestigious generations of Atalante's family outlined in an inscription honouring Pillakoas (SEG 41 1258: c.180–200 A.D.), her grandfather. This inscription predates the time when Atalante became a widow, given the omission of the crucial word χήρα from the document. The precise role that Atalante had in relation to her father's will and what she actually performed is unspecified (κατὰ διαθήκην Πιατηραβιος τοῦ πατρὸς αὐτῆς). The inscription is translated as follows: 'Atalante, daughter of Piaterabis, granddaughter of Pillakoas, great granddaughter of Kinnounis, (honours) Pillakoas the grandfather (Πιλλακοαν τὸν παππόν) (the son of) Kinnounis according to the will Piaterabis, her father (Πιατηραβιος τοῦ πατρὸς αὐτῆς)'.

also in terms of its occasion (priestly wages, famine) and duration (a substantial part of the year).

Last, another brief honorific inscription (TAM III.1. 62) offers a vignette of her role as a benefactor in alleviating debt:

> The craftsmen honoured Atalante, daughter of Piaterabis, granddaughter of Pillakoas, great granddaughter of Kinnounis, widow (χήρα), who was their benefactor (εὐεργέτιν), by whom abundance of (provisions) was furnished to all the people when there was a scarcity of corn.

b) The Numismatic Evidence and Luke 21:2–4

Alan Cadwallader, in a forthcoming chapter to be published in Volume 12 of *New Documents Illustrating the History of Early Christianity*, discusses the Colossian female benefactor of the second century A.D.[106] Important for our purposes is that as the moneyer, Claudia Eugenetoriane engages in an almost unique type of female benefaction by reviving the city's coin production as a coin minter, resuscitating in the process the civic pride of the city by astutely chosen iconography on the coins. On the third coin-type produced, Claudia designates herself as χήρη, the Ionian version of the more common Greek word for widow, χήρα. The prominent self-designation is accomplished by the striking addition of XHPH to her name on the coin. It is beyond the scope of this paper to discuss in any detail why she takes such an unprecedented step of self-designation, other than to reiterate the suggestions of Cadwallader: namely, that Claudia is emphasising her conventionality as a women entering the public sphere, perhaps employing a term of official civic recognition from Colossae (and I would add that there are epigraphic lists of widows in eastern Mediterranean cities elsewhere from the Hellenistic age, though their significance is lost to us),[107] and engaging the iconography of Demeter on the reverse: since the latter was used prominently in the reigns of Hadrian and Trajan, Claudia is

---

106 See Cadwallader, 'Wealthy, Widowed, Astute and Beneficent'.
107 See SEG 50.589 (Dion: Hellenistic age). There, under the heading χῆραι πολίτιδες, the names of five women are given: Σικελία Ἐπιγόνου, Νικαρίστη Ἀντιπάτρου, Σαβύθη Θεοξένου, Μικυλὶς Σάμου and Εὐφρονίς.

perhaps thereby asserting her own Asian role comparatively with the key imperial women of the Latin West.

Reflecting on Jesus' Commendation of an Impoverished Benefactor in Light of the Numismatic and Epigraphic Evidence

Against this backdrop, why does Jesus commend the vulnerable widow benefactor who impoverishes herself by donating the mite to the temple treasury? First, the example of this widow excelling the Jewish synagogal benefactors in her piety and personal sacrifice coheres with the Lukan theme of the divine overturning of the élites of this world—including Claudia Eugenetoriane and Atalante—in preference for the lowly in Luke 1:51–52, as well as the paradoxical blessedness of the Lukan poor over the rich (1:53; 6:20–21 [cf. 24–25]).

Secondly, in saying that she has given away everything she had (21:24), Jesus implicitly underscores in a Jewish context how vulnerable she, as a widow, is in a Temple holiness system that is corrupt and which exploits one of the weakest figures meriting divine concern in the literature of the Old Testament and Second Temple Judaism (Luke 21:47a). The reign of élite benefactors is being divinely eclipsed by the marginalised poor and socially vulnerable in the new economy of sacrificial giving. Indeed, Jesus' perceptive phrase in Luke 21:4a that the temple gift givers give out of their abundance (ἐκ τοῦ περισσεύοντες) underscores how benefactors, along with their cities, were careful not to exhaust their reserves lest their future beneficence and acquisition of honour status be imperilled.

But does this vignette provide us another rhetorical perspective when viewed against the backdrop of the wider literature and epigraphy of the Graeco-Roman world? We turn to the trope of the 'impoverished benefactor'.

The "Impoverished" Benefactor: The Paradoxical Counter-Narrative of Luke 21:2–4 in Graeco-Roman Context

Normally, benefactors were regularly accorded as an honorific status of *aleitourgetos* ('free from the public burden') for several years so that they had the time to recoup their reserves and give to the city in the future.[108] However, the motif of the 'impoverished benefactor'—absent from the honorific inscriptions—makes its appearance in the philosophical literature.[109] Here we are interested in a highly unusual feature of benefaction culture in the ancient world: namely, the excessive divestiture of wealth by a benefactor which imperils his status and resources. The evidence is sparse, but tantalising. Dio Chrysostom (Or. 1.61–62) provides us with this striking vignette of the mythical hero, Heracles:

> he went unclothed and unarmed except for a lion's skin and a club, and they add that he did not set great store by gold or silver or fine raiment, but considered all such things nothing save to be given away and bestowed upon others. At any rate he made presents to many men, not only of money without limit and lands and herds of horses and cattle, but also of whole kingdoms and cities. For he fully believed that everything belonged to him exclusively and that gifts bestowed would call out the goodwill of the recipients.

Dio Chrysostom himself lets fall a revealing snippet concerning his pet project of embellishing Prusa, his native city. He comments that 'I have grown much thinner than I was when I came in' (Or., 47.20). The thrust of his comment is fully appreciated when one remembers his continuing financial hardship after his return from exile in A.D. 96, and what had been for him the genuine risk of poverty prior to that (Or., 47.21; 40.2). Notwithstanding, Dio Chrysostom gives himself unstintingly to his efforts on behalf of his citizens.

The Roman collector of moral exempla, Valerius Maximus, nominates Fabius Maximus as a case of such liberality. The Senate had

---

108 Harrison, *Paul's Language of Grace*, 254.
109 The next five paragraphs are drawn from Harrison, *Paul's Language of Grace*, 250–56.

refused to honour the contract he had secured with Hannibal for the release of Roman captives. Instead he sent his son to Rome, sold the only farm he possessed, and paid Hannibal. Valerius (Noteworthy Doings and Sayings, 4.8.1.) provides a homily on the actions of Fabius Maximus:

> If we consider the sum, (it is) but small, as being the price but of seven acres of land, and those lying in Pupinia; but considering the soul of the giver, (it is) a most large sum, and far exceeding the money. For he would rather himself to be destitute in patrimony, than that his country should be poor in credit. So (his act is) much more to be commended, as it is a more certain sign of favourable study, to stretch beyond ability, rather than to do the same act out of superfluity. For the one can do what he performs, the other more than he is able.

Another example of the impoverished benefactor motif is found in Lucian's portrait of Timon (Timon 5), the semi-legendary misanthrope of Periclean Athens. Timon rails against the social misfortune that befalls benefactors like himself who sacrifice everything for their beneficiaries. Now reduced to farm labouring and wearing animal skins, Timon sums up his fate in terminology reminiscent of 2 Corinthians 8:9:

> After raising so many Athenians to high station and making them rich when they were wretchedly poor before and helping all who were in want, nay more, pouring out my wealth in floods to benefit my friends, now that I have become poor thereby I am no longer recognised or even looked at by the men who formerly cringed and kowtowed and hung on my nod.

The generosity of the liberator of Syracuse, Dion, exhausted his personal resources as he distributed favours to his friends and rewards to his allies (Plutarch, Life of Dion 52.1).

In light of the above examples, flashes of cultural recognition might have been initially aroused by Luke's presentation of the impoverishment of the widow benefactor who stretched, like some contemporary benefactors, beyond her reserves. However, paradox is potent because the analogy only goes so far: she never had any reserves that she could exhaust—she was at the margins of society because of her poverty, but nevertheless dispensed with everything she had in sacrificial giving to God. As such, the widow becomes a potent and proleptic example of the self-emptying of the dishonoured Christ, stripped even of his clothing on the cross.

Finally, Jesus redefines the contemporary benefaction system of the Caesars and the Herodian élites in Luke 22:24–27 in light of his counter-narrative, taught and exemplified, of the servant benefactor: the greatest one who becomes the least in service of others.[110] This, Jesus says, stands in sharp contrast to the imperial and Herodian elites who enforce their authority brutally and who enhance their notability by benefactions. The scribes, Jesus says, have imbibed the same honorific culture of the powerful being publicly commended with places of honour at banquets and the synagogues (Luke 21:40)—and, as the inscriptions also reveal, benefactors were honoured with special seats at the theatre and accorded first place in the public feasts (e.g. SEG 11 948).[111] This competition for precedence led to the imperial priesthoods being sold to the highest bidder at Ephesus in the reign of Claudius, an inscription informs us, with a view to embezzling the money (IEph 1a 18 ll. 11–21: A.D. 44).

However, to consider this just a Graeco-Roman phenomenon would be unwise. Josephus' effusive boasting in his priestly ancestry and his own achievements as a scholar in Vita 1–9 in the grand rhetorical style of the inscriptions underscores that the excesses of Graeco-Roman honorific culture were as much present among the Jewish élites as among the Graeco-Roman luminaries.[112] By contrast, the self-effacement and self-sacrifice of Jesus' marginalised widow challenged this boastful construct at its very core. Here we see the seamless transition from Jesus' critique of social stratification and its oppressive results in a Roman Palestinian context to the wider eastern Mediterranean basin.

---

110 See Marshall, *Jesus, Patrons, and Benefactors*.
111 Harrison, *Paul's Language of Grace*, 51.
112 See Harrison, 'From Rome to the Colony of Philippi', 312–19.

Conclusion

This chapter set out to investigate the continuing applicability of the sociological and historical model of Lenski and Alföldy to the debate about social stratification of Roman Palestine at the time of the first disciples and its relation to the issue of poverty and, consequently, the social location of the first generation of believers. We have seen that the new model of Friesen and Longenecker better represents the stratification of the Roman Empire because it recognises the existence of a small 'middling' social echelon.

Among the first disciples were members belonging to the retainer class (those with Herodian contacts and wealthy tax collectors such as Zacchaeus). Seemingly, there were no real candidates among the ES4 Scale, at least as profiled by Longenecker. There was, however, a range in economic profile among the lower strata, ranging from those with a modest income above subsistence level to the utterly destitute. Of great value was Lenski's categorisation of the 'unclean and degraded' at the base of the social pyramid. This allowed New Testament researchers to explore the rich evidence of the Gospels in this regard, underscoring that 'poverty' was as much a social categorisation as an economic one.

It was suggested that the model of Lenski and Alföldy, as well as the stratification scales of Friesen and Longenecker, remained valuable only insofar as they included the backdrop of the epigraphic, papyrological, archaeological, iconographic, and numismatic evidence, in addition the foundational evidence of the Gospels, the literature of Second Temple Judaism, Josephus, Philo, and the later rabbinic corpus. But the model of Lenski and Alföldy, we saw, was especially valuable in helping us to bring the literary evidence of Josephus into critical dialogue with the Gospels.

Notwithstanding, the documentary and material evidence has posed its own methodological issues, especially when defining what 'poverty' actually is and how the lineaments of its evidence related to social stratification. The archaeological evidence by itself does not provide a clear distinction of poverty; the visual evidence of poverty is open to different interpretative construal, even when its implications for poverty analysis seem at first blush incontestable.

Finally, we need to listen very carefully to the rhetorical contexts in which the evangelists place the narratives, as well as the logia of Jesus, touching upon poverty and social marginalisation. When these are investigated against the material, documentary, and literary evidence of the Graeco-Roman world, the counter-cultural portrait of Jesus as the Messiah and Saviour who overturned the hierarchy, violence, and economics of social stratification in favour of God's beneficent community of the poor, disabled, and marginalised, becomes very clear.[113] The hope offered to the powerless in these communities of divine grace would soon move beyond agricultural Roman Palestine to the urban world of the eastern Mediterranean basin and beyond.

---

113 See Harrison, 'The Social Context', 105–26.

Bibliography

Alföldy, G. — *The Social History of Rome* (translated by D. Braund and D. Pollock. Totowa: Barnes & Noble, 1985).

Arnal, W. E. — *Jesus and the Village Scribes: Galilean Conflicts and the Setting of Q* (Minneapolis, MN: Fortress, 2003).

Atkins, M. and R. Osborn, (eds.) — *Poverty in the Roman World* (Cambridge: Cambridge University Press, 2006).

Barnett, B. M. — *Gerhard Lenski's Sociological Theories: Assessments, Extensions, New Directions* (London: Paradigm Publishers, 2020).

Batey, R. A. — 'Is Not This the Carpenter?', *New Testament Studies* 30.2 (1984), 249–58.

Baudrillart, A. — 'Mendicatio, Mendici', in C. Daremburg and M. E. Saglio (eds.), *Dictionnaire des antiquités grecques et romaines d'après les textes et les monuments* (5 vols.; Paris: Hachette, 1873–1819, III.2 [1904]), 1712–16.

Broshi, M. — 'Agriculture and Economy in Roman Palestine: Seven Notes on the Babetha Archive', *Israel Exploration Journal* 42.3/4 (1992), 230–40.

Cadwallader, A. H. — 'Wealthy, Widowed, Astute and Beneficent: Claudia Eugenetoriane and the Second Century Revival of the Colossian Mint', in A. H. Cadwallader and J. R. Harrison, *New Documents Illustrating the History of Early Christianity. Volume 12: Colossae, Hierapolis, and Laodicea*, (Grand Rapids, MI: Eerdmans, forthcoming).

Carson, D. A. — 'Matthew', *The Expositor's Bible Commentary Volume 8* (Grand Rapids: Zondervan, 1984), 3–599.

Chancey, M. A. — *The Myth of a Gentile Galilee* (Cambridge: Cambridge University Press, 2002).

Chancey, M. A. and A. Porter. — 'The Archaeology of Roman Palestine', *Near Eastern Archaeology* 64.4 (2002), 164–203.

Charlesworth, J. H. (ed.) — *Jesus and Archaeology* (Grand Rapids, MI: Eerdmans, 2006).

Chilton, B. — 'Jesus and Sinners and Outcasts', in T. Holmén and S. Porter (eds.), *Handbook for the Study of Historical Jesus. 3: Jesus and the Legacy of Israel* (Leden and Boston: Brill, 2011), 2801–2833.

Cohick, L. H.   'Poverty and Its Causes in the Early Church', in S. Walton and H. Swithinbank (eds.), *Poverty in the Early Church and Today: A Conversation*, (London: T&T Clark, 2019), 16–27.

Connolly, M.   *Disorderly Women and the Order of God: An Australian Feminist Reading of the Gospel of Mark* (London and New York: T&T Clark, 2018).

Donahue, 'J.   Tax Collectors and Sinners: An Attempt at Identification', *Catholic Biblical Quarterly* 33 (1971), 39–61.

Dorma, J. H. J.   *The Blemished Body: Deformity and Disability in the Qumran Scrolls* (Groningen: Rijksuniversiteit, 2007).

Draycott, J.   'Reconstructing the Lived Experience of Disability in Antiquity: A Case Study from Roman Egypt', 62.2 *Greece & Rome* (2015), 189–205.

Dunn, J. D. G.   'Pharisees, Sinners, and Jesus', in J. D. G. Dunn, *Jesus, Paul and the Law* (Louisville: Westminster John Knox Press, 1990), 61–88.

Edwards, D. R. (ed.)   *Religion and Society in Roman Palestine: Old Questions, New Approaches.* (New York, NY and London: Routledge, 2004).

Eidinow, E.   'In Search of the "Beggar Priest"', in G. Richard et al., *Religious Entrepreneurs and Innovators in the Roman Empire* (Berlin/Boston, MA: Walter de Gruyter, 2017), 255–75.

Esser, J. J.   *De Pauperum cura apud Romanos* (PhD thesis, Vrije Universiteit Amsterdam, 1902).

Evans, C. A.   '"Who Touched Me?" Jesus and the Ritually Impure', in B. Chilton and C. A. Evans (eds.), *Jesus in Context: Temple, Purity, and Restoration* (Leiden: Brill, 1997), 353–76.

Favro, D., and C. Johanson   'Death in Motion: Funeral Processions in the Roman Forum', *Journal of the Society of Architectural Historians* 69.1 (2010), 12–37.

Fiensy, D. A.   *Christian Origins and the Ancient Economy* (Eugene, OR: Cascade, 2014).

Fiensy, D. A.   'Did Large Estates Exist in Lower Galilee in the First Half of the First Century CE?', *Journal of the Study of the Historical Jesus* 10.2 (2012), 133–53.

Fiensy, D. A.	'Jesus' Socioeconomic Background', in J. H. Charlesworth and L. l. Johns (eds.), *Hillel and Jesus: Comparisons of Two Major Religious Leaders* (Minneapolis, MN: Fortress, 1997), 225–55.
Fiensy, D. A.	*The Social History of Palestine in the Herodian Period: The Lord is Mine* (Lampeter: Edwin Mellen Press, 1991).
Friesen, S. J.	'Poverty in Pauline Studies: Beyond the So-Called Consensus', *Journal for the Study of the New Testament* 26 (2004), 323–62.
Giesen, H.	'Poverty and Wealth in Jesus and the Jesus Tradition', in T. Holmén and S. Porter (eds.), *Handbook for the Study of Historical Jesus*. 4: *Individual Studies* (Leiden and Boston: Brill, 2011), 3269–3303.
Gill, Mosche	'The Decline of Agrarian Economy in Palestine under Roman Rule', *Journal of the Economic and Social History of the Orient* 49.3 (2006), 285–328.
Gosbell, L. A.	*'The Poor, the Crippled, the Blind, and the Lame': Physical and Sensory Disability in the Gospels of the New Testament* (WUNT II 469; Tübingen: Mohr Siebeck, 2018).
Grant, F. C.	*The Economic Background of the Gospels* (Oxford: Oxford, University Press, 1926).
Gundry, R. H.	*Mark: A Commentary on His Apology for the Cross* (Grand Rapids, MI: Eerdmans, 1993).
Gunjevic, L.	*Jubilee in the Bible: Using the Theology of Jürgen Moltmann to Find a New Hermeneutic* (Biblical Interpretation Series 156; Leiden and Boston, MA: Brill, 2018).
Häkkanin, S.	'Poverty in the First-Century Galilee', *HTS Teologiese Studies/Theological Studies* 72.4 (2016), a3398. http://dx.doi.org/10.4102/hts.v72i4.3398.
Hamel, G. H.	*Poverty and Charity in Roman Palestine, First Three Centuries CE* (Berkeley, CA and Los Angeles, CA: University of California Press, 1990).
Hanson, K. C. and D. E. Oakman	*Palestine in the Time of Jesus: Social Structures and Social Conflicts* (Minneapolis, MN: Fortress, 1998).
Harland, P. A.	'The Economy of First-Century Palestine: State of the Scholarly Discussion', in A. J. Blasi et al. (eds.), *Handbook*

	of Early Christianity: Social Science Approaches (Walnut Creek, CA: AltaMira Press, 2002), 511–27.
Harris, W. V.	'Poverty and Destitution in the Roman Empire', in W. Scheidel (ed.), *Rome's Imperial Economy: Twelve Essays* (Oxford University Press: Oxford, 2011), 27–54.
Harrison, James R.	'The Historical Jesus as "Social Critic": An Investigation of Luke 6:27-36', *Journal of the Gospels and Acts Research* 2 (2018), 53–74.
Harrison, James R.	'From Rome to the Colony of Philippi: Roman Boasting in Philippians 3:4-6 in Its Latin West and Philippian Epigraphic Context', in J. R. Harrison and L. L. Welborn (eds.), *The First Urban Churches. Volume 4: Roman Philippi* (Atlanta: SBL Press, 2018), 307–70.
Harrison, James R.	'Beneficence to the Poor in Luke's Gospel in Its Mediterranean Context: A Visual and Documentary Approach', *Australian Biblical Review* 65 (2017), 30–46.
Harrison, James R.	'The Social Context', in M. Harding and A. Nobbs (eds.), *The Content and Setting of the Gospel Tradition* (Grand Rapids, MI: Eerdmans, 2010), 105–26.
Harrison, James R.	*Paul's Language of Grace in Its Graeco-Roman Context* (WUNT II 172; Tübingen: Mohr Siebeck, 2003).
Hayes, C. M.	*Luke's Wealth Ethics: A Study in Their Coherence and Character* (WUNT II 275; Tübingen: Mohr Siebeck, 2010).
Herrenbrück, F.	*Jesus und die Zöllner: Historische und neutestamentlich-exegetische Untersuchungen* (WUNT II 41; Tübingen: Mohr Siebeck, 1990).
Herrenbrück, F.	'Wer waren die "Zölner"', *Zeitschrift für die neutestamentliche Wissenschaft* 72 (1981), 178–94.
Herz, Johannes	'Grossgrundbesitz in Palästina im Zeitalter Jesu', *Palästina Jahrbuch* 24 (1928), 98–113.
Herzog, W. R. II.	'Why Peasants Responded to Jesus', in Richard Horsley (ed.), *Christian Origins: A People's History of Christianity* (Minneapolis, MN: Fortress, 2005), 47–70.
Herzog, W. R. II.	*Parables as Subversive Speech: Jesus as Pedagogue of the Oppressed* (Louisville, KY: Westminster John Knox Press, 1994).

Hetzer, C. (ed.) *The Oxford Handbook of Jewish Daily Life in Roman Palestine* (Oxford: Oxford University Press, 2012).

Hoehner, H. W. *Herod Antipas: A Contemporary of Jesus Christ* (Grand Rapids, MI: Zondervan, 1980 repr. [1972]).

Horsley, R. A. *Galilee: History, Politics, People* (Valley Forge, PA: Trinity Press International, 1995).

Horsley, R. A. *Sociology and the Jesus Movement* (2nd edn; New York, NY: Continuum, 1994).

Horsley, R. A. *Jesus and the Spiral of Violence: Popular Jewish Resistance* (San Francisco, CA: Harper and Row, 1987).

Horsley, R. A. 'Josephus and the Bandits', *Journal for the Study of Judaism* 10 (1979), 37–63.

Horsley, R. A. and J. S. Hanson *Bandits, Prophets, and Messiahs: Popular Movements at the Time of Jesus* (San Francisco, CA: Harper and Row, 1988).

Jensen, M. H. 'Purity and Politics in Herod Antipas' Galilee: The Case for Religious Motivation', *Journal for the Study of the Historical Jesus* 11 (2013), 3–34.

Jeremias, J. *Jerusalem in the Time of Jesus* (Göttingen: Vandenhoeck & Ruprecht, 1962; rev. 1967; ET: London: SCM, 1969).

Keel, Oscar *The Symbolism of the Biblical World: Ancient Eastern Iconography and the Books of Psalms* (London: SPCK, 1972).

Keener, C. S. *Acts: An Exegetical Commentary. Volume 2: 3:1–14:28* (Grand Rapids, MI: Baker Academic, 2013), 1958.

Kim Huat Tan, 'Jesus and the Purity Paradigm', in T. Holmén and S. Porter (eds.), *Handbook for the Study of Historical Jesus. 3: Jesus and the Legacy of Israel* (Leden and Boston: Brill, 2011), 2709–2744.

Kim, S. H. 'Rupturing the Empire: Reading the Poor Widow as a Postcolonial Female Subject (Mark 12:41–44)', *Lectio Difficilior* 1 (2006), 1–21.

Landau, Y. H. 'A Greek Inscription Found Near Hefzibah', *Israel Expedition Journal* 16 (1966), 54–70.

Larsen, M. R. 'The Representation of Poverty in the Roman Empire' (Ph.D. diss. University of California, Los Angeles, 2015).

Lee, J. A. L., and G. H. R. Horsley   'A Lexicon of the New Testament with Documentary Parallels: Some Interim Entries. 2', *Filologia Neotestamentaria* 21–22 (1998), 57–84.

Lenski, G. E.   *Power and Privilege: A Theory of Social Stratification* (2nd edn.; Chapel Hill and London: University of North Carolina Press, 1984).

Longenecker, B. W.   *Remember the Poor: Paul, Poverty, and the Greco-Roman World* (Grand Rapids, MI: Eerdmans, 2010).

Louw, J. P., and E. A. Nida   *Greek English Lexicon of the New Testament Based on Semantic Domains, Volume 1* (New York: United Bible Societies, 1988).

Malbon, E. S.   'The Poor Widow in Mark and Her Poor Rich Readers', *Catholic Biblical Quarterly* 53.4 (1991), 589–604

Marshall, J.   *Jesus, Patrons, and Benefactors: Roman Palestine and the Gospel of Luke* (WUNT II 259; Tübingen: Mohr Siebeck, 2009).

Martin, Dale B.   'Review Essay: Justin J. Meggitt, *Paul, Poverty and Survival*', *Journal for the Study of the New Testament* (2001), 51–64.

Marx, T. C.   *Disability in Jewish Law* (London: Routledge, 2002).

Mattila, S. L.   'Revisiting Jesus' Capernaum: A Village of Only Subsistence-Level Fishers and Farmers?', in D. A. Fiensy and R. K. Hawkins (eds.) *The Galilean Economy in the Time of Jesus* (Atlanta, GA: Scholars, 2013), 75–138.

Meggitt, J.   *Paul, Poverty and Survival* (Edinburgh: T&T Clark, 1998).

Milligan, George   'A Certificate of Poverty from the Greek Papyri', *The Expository Times* 20.2 (1908), 90–91.

Moore, S. D.   'Mark and Empire: "Zealot" and "Postcolonial" Readings', in R. S. Sugirtharajah (ed.), *The Postcolonial Biblical Reader* (Malden: Blackwell, 2006), 193–205.

Moulton, J. H., and G. Milligan   *Vocabulary of the Greek Testament* (Grand Rapids, MI: Baker Academic, 1995).

Nineham, D. E.   *The Gospel of St. Mark* (Pelican New Testament Commentaries; Baltimore, MD: Penguin, 1963).

Oakman, D. E.   *Jesus, Debt, and the Lord's Prayer: First-Century Debt and Jesus' Intentions* (Eugene, OR: Cascade, 2014).

Oakman, D. E. *Jesus and the Peasants* (Eugene, OR: Cascade Books, 2008).

Oakman, D. E. 'The Countryside in Luke-Acts', in J. H. Neyrey (ed.) *The Social World of Luke-Acts: Models for Interpretation*, (Peabody: Hendrickson, 1991), 151–79.

Oakman, D. E. *Jesus and the Economic Questions of His Day* (Lewiston, NY: Edwin Mellen, 1986).

Olyan, S. M. 'The Exegetical Dimensions of Restrictions on the Blind and the Lame in Texts from Qumran' *Dead Sea Discoveries* 2 (2001), 38–50.

Parkin, Anneliese R. 'Poverty in the Early Roman Empire: Ancient and Modern Conceptions and Constructs' (Ph.D. thesis, Girton College, Cambridge, 2001).

Pastor, Jack 'Trade, Commerce, and Consumption', in Catherine Hetzer (ed.), *The Oxford Handbook of Jewish Daily Life in Roman Palestine* (Oxford: Oxford University Press, 2012), 297–307.

Pastor, Jack *Land and Economy in Ancient Palestine* (London: Routledge, 2005).

Ratzlaff, A. L. 'The Effects of Empire on Daily Life in the Provincial East (37 BCE–313 CE)', in A. Yasur-Landau et al. (eds.), *The Social Archaeology of the Levant: From Prehistory to the Present* (Cambridge: Cambridge University Press, 2019), 438–57.

Reed, J. L. 'Instability in Jesus' Galilee', *Journal of Biblical Literature* 129.2 (2010), 343–65.

Reed, J. L. *Archaeology and the Galilean Jesus: A Re-examination of the Evidence* (Harrisburg, PA: Trinity Press International, 2002).

Ringe, S. H. *Jesus and Liberation, and the Biblical Jubilee: Images for Ethics and Christology* (Overtures to Biblical Theology 19; Philadelphia: Fortress, 1985).

Rosenfeld, B. Z. and H. Perlmutter *Social Stratification of the Jewish Population of Jewish Palestine in the Period of the Mishnah, 70–250 CE* (Leiden and Boston, MA: Brill, 2000).

Rosenfeld, B. Z. and H. Perlmutter 'The Poor as a Stratum of Jewish Society in Roman Palestine 70–250 CE: An Analysis', *Historia* 60.3 (2011) 273–300.

Safrai, Ze'ev *The Economy of Roman Palestine* (London and New York: Routledge, 1994).

Sandford, M. J. 'Poverty, Wealth, and Empire: Jesus and Postcolonial Criticism Israel' (*NTM* 35; Sheffield: Sheffield Phoenix Press, 2014).

Scheidel, W. 'Stratification, Deprivation, and Quality of Life', in M. Atkins and R. Osborn (eds.) *Poverty in the Roman World* (Cambridge: Cambridge University Press, 2006), 40–59.

Scheidel, W. and S. J. Friesen 'The Size of the Economy and the Distribution of Income in the Roman Empire', *Journal of Roman Studies* 99 (2009), 61–91.

Schmidt, T. E. *Hostility to Wealth in the Synoptic Gospels* (JSNTSup 15; Sheffield: Sheffield Academic, 1987).

Schottroff, L. and W. Stegemann *Jesus and the Hope of the Poor* (Maryknoll: Orbis, 1986 [German: 1978]).

Shemesh, A. '"The Holy Angels are in Their Council": The Exclusion of Deformed Persons from Holy Places in Qumranic and Rabbinic Literature', *Dead Sea Discoveries* 4 (1997), 179–206.

Simpson, William Kelly (tr.) *The Literature of Ancient Egypt: An Anthology of Stories, Instructions, and Poetry* (New Haven and London: Yale University Press, 1972), 343–44.

Sloan, R. B. *The Favourable Year of the Lord: A Study of the Jubilary Theology in the Gospel of Luke* (Ann Arbor, MI: Scholars, 1977).

Smith, G. 'A Closer look at the Widow's Offering: Mark 12:41–44', *Journal of the Evangelical Theological Society* 40 (1997), 27–36.

Snodgrass, Klyne R. *Stories with Intent: A Comprehensive Guide to the Parables of Jesus* (Grand Rapids: Eerdmans, 2008).

Stegemann, E. W. and W. Stegemann *The Jesus Movement: A Social History of Its First Century* (Edinburgh: T&T Clark, 1999).

Udoh, F. E.	*To Caesar What is Caesar's: Tribute, Taxes, and Imperial Administration in Early Roman Palestine 63 BCE–70 CE* (Brown Judaic Studies 343; Providence, RI: Brown University, 2005).
van Eck, E.	*The Parables of Jesus the Galilean: Story of a Social Prophet* (Eugene, OR: Cascade, 2016).
Waetjen, H. C.	*A Reordering of Power: A Social-Political Reading of Mark's Gospel* (Minneapolis, MN: Fortress Press, 1989).
Wau, M.	*The Path to Salvation in Luke's Gospel: What Must We Do?* (LNTS 607; London: T&T Clark, 2019).
Weiss, Zeiv	'Buildings for Entertainment', in Daniel Sperber (ed.), *The City in Roman Palestine* (New York and Oxford: Oxford University Press, 1998), 77–102.
Wilfand, W.	'Poverty, Charity and the Image of the Poor in Rabbinic Texts from the Land of Israel' (SWBA 9; Sheffield: Sheffield Phoenix Press, 2014).
Wright, A.G.	'The Widow's Mites: Praise or Lament?—A Matter of Context', *Catholic Biblical Quarterly* 44 (1982), 256–65.

CHAPTER 3

Essenic Influence on Jesus, His Brothers, and the Early Church

Mary J. Marshall

Abstract

The essay builds on the contention that Jesus' last meal, on Wednesday 1 April 33 C.E., was held in an Essenic household where his brother James was a resident. Simon Joseph's 2018 publication *Jesus, the Essenes, and Christian Origins*, is evaluated and several sections are expanded. Some Acts accounts of events after the Last Supper are studied, further endorsing Essenic influence; and three legends concerning James the Just are considered. Findings are then assessed over against early church traditions about Jesus and his brothers. The datum that through Mary, the family has both Judahite and Aaronic ancestry is found to be significant. It is posited that James was the *mebaqqer* of his household, and this has implications for the events of the Last Supper, and for the identification of Jesus as Messiah. The scroll 4Q521 is found to be relevant to both Jesus and James.

1. Introduction

This essay builds on my previous exploration of the extraordinary advancement of Jesus' brother James, from almost complete obscurity to a positon of great authority in the early church.[1] That study, drawing primarily on Luke's passion narrative and Acts, is grounded on the contention that at Jesus' last meal, he and his disciples were guests at an Essenic establishment in the southwest quarter of Jerusalem where James was a resident.[2] It is asserted that this commemoration of Passover, without a lamb, was held on Wednesday evening, 1 April 33 C.E. at the beginning of Nisan 15 according to the lunisolar calendar of the Essenes.[3] Following Jesus' death, while James would have remained in that household, the proposal has Jesus' mother, his other siblings, and the various disciples who had come to Jerusalem for Passover, taking up residence nearby, perhaps in a guesthouse,[4] as would be consistent with Acts 1:13–14.

The current study provides a summary and assessment of the relevant findings of Simon Joseph in his 2018 publication *Jesus, the Essenes, and Christian Origins*, before offering further reflections on the hypothesis, taking into account insights gained from Joseph's work. The main aims are to:

> (1) affirm the proposed scenario concerning the Last Supper and subsequent events, assembling further evidence by exploring Acts 6:1–7, and particularly the nature of the 'priests' in v. 7;
>
> (2) examine relevant legends and traditions about James the Just, and ascertain whether they cohere with the hypothesis concerning the Last Supper, and possibly shed light on his position in the Essenic household; and

---

1   In particular, the essay 'The Rise and Rise of James the Just', presented in the Lukan stream at the ANZATS conference held at the Emmanuel College, St Lucia, QLD, 1–4 July 2018, to be published in *JGAR* 6 (2022).
2   Regarding the Essene quarter in Jerusalem, see e.g. B. Pixner, 'Mount Zion, Jesus, and Archaeology', 309–21.
3   The chronology draws on Saulnier, *Calendrical Variations*.
4   See Riesner, 'Jesus, the Primitive Community', 198–234 (201); Pixner, 'Mount Zion, Jesus, and Archaeology', 321.

(3) assess the findings against traditions and beliefs about Jesus and his brothers in the early church.

2. Assessment of Joseph's Findings

While I concur with Joseph's conclusion that Essenic influence on Jesus and early Christianity is certain,[5] it is necessary to treat the several components of his findings separately, as many aspects relevant to research in the field are controversial.

2.1 Identity of the Qumran Group

Joseph identifies the Qumran sect as Essenes, but acknowledges that the hypothesis has limitations.[6] This is the majority view among scholars,[7] although the matter remains fiercely contested, notably between prominent scholars VanderKam and Schiffman.[8]

2.2 Origin of The Name

The background to the name 'Essene' remains a mystery, though the Aramaic word meaning 'pious' or 'holy' is probably the most popular suggestion, according to Joseph.[9] This coheres with the descriptions of the Essenes' holiness, as given by both Philo and Josephus.[10] Philo refers to them in Greek as 'Essenes or holy ones', indicating this title is merited,[11] while Josephus also regards them as especially holy.[12] There are

---

5   See Joseph, *Jesus, the Essenes, and Christian Origins*, 164–66.
6   Joseph, *Jesus, the Essenes, and Christian Origins*, 47.
7   Joseph, *Jesus, the Essenes, and Christian Origins*, 27; Goranson, 'Essenes', 425.
8   For arguments for and against the Essene hypothesis, see respectively, VanderKam, 'People of the Dead Sea Scrolls', 50–62; and Schiffman, 'Sadducean Origins', 35–49. For further support of the Qumran Essene hypothesis see Broshi, 'Essenes at Qumran?', 25–33; VanderKam, *Dead Sea Scrolls Today*, esp. 118–19, 125; Cross, 'Historical Context of the Scrolls', 25. Against the hypothesis, see also Golb, 'Qumran Essene Hypothesis'; and Collins, 'Introduction', *Religion in the Dead Sea Scrolls*, 2 n.4, regarding Golb as 'the most vocal critic' of the consensus view.
9   Joseph, *Jesus, the Essenes, and Christian Origins*, 32–34. According to Collins, the Semitic word חסיא ('pious' or 'holy') is considered to correspond most closely to Essaioi (Joseph, *Jesus, the Essenes, and Christian Origins*, 34 n.28).
10 Joseph, *Jesus, the Essenes, and Christian Origins*, 32.
11 Joseph, *Jesus, the Essenes, and Christian Origins*, 32, citing Philo, Hypoth. 1.
12 I.e. σεμνότητα (Joseph, *Jesus, the Essenes, and Christian Origins*, 32, citing Josephus, J.W. 2.119).

other suggestions, but this seems the most likely as there is an instance of its use in Palestinian Aramaic in a fragment from Qumran.¹³

2.3 The Yaḥad

As indicated in the rules contained in the *Damascus Document* (CD),¹⁴ the Essenes associated with Qumran were part of a much wider group living in what were called 'camps',¹⁵ in multiple locations around Judaea. Collectively, this *union-of-communities* comprised the *Yaḥad*.¹⁶ The disparity between the content of CD and that of the *Rule of the Community* (1QS), and the different versions of each, indicate that CD represents an earlier, more rigorous form of the community's legislation.¹⁷ Thus the CD community can perhaps be termed 'the parent group of the *yaḥad*',¹⁸ with the different rule books probably deriving from disparate groups and stages in the history of the movement.¹⁹

According to the evidence in the texts of CD and 1QS, the *Yaḥad* arose from a 'new covenant' movement grounded on a desire to reaffirm loyalty to Mosaic Law, and linked with the ideology expressed in Jeremiah 31:31–33.²⁰ Adherents saw themselves as the real 'remnant of Israel',²¹ a 'kingdom of priests', as in Exodus 19:6, and a people of 'holiness' and 'perfection'.²²

CD refers to families, with members living in 'towns' and 'camps',²³ marrying, and having children. Each of the camps had a supervisor termed a *mebaqqer* (guardian),²⁴ responsible for maintaining boundaries

---

13 Joseph, *Jesus, the Essenes, and Christian Origins*, 34, 34 nn.27–28.
14 Joseph, *Jesus, the Essenes, and Christian Origins*, 48.
15 Joseph, *Jesus, the Essenes, and Christian Origins*, 47, 54, referring to 1QS 6:1b–8.
16 Joseph, *Jesus, the Essenes, and Christian Origins*, 54.
17 Joseph, *Jesus, the Essenes, and Christian Origins*, 51–52. For a completely different (and unpersuasive) view, namely that the Damascus Document was the latest set of rules to be written, see Stegemann, *The Library of Qumran*, 116–18.
18 See Joseph, *Jesus, the Essenes, and Christian Origins*, 53 n.120, citing Hempel, *Laws of the Damascus Document*, 150.
19 Joseph, *Jesus, the Essenes, and Christian Origins*, 45.
20 Joseph, *Jesus, the Essenes, and Christian Origins*, 48–49.
21 Joseph, *Jesus, the Essenes, and Christian Origins*, 49.
22 Joseph, *Jesus, the Essenes, and Christian Origins*, 55.
23 I.e. ערים and מחנות respectively (Joseph, Jesus, the Essenes, and Christian Origins, 49).
24 The Hebrew term for 'guardian', deriving from the verb בקר and the participle as a noun, has the meaning inspector or overseer. See בקר, mng. 2, in Clines, CDCH, 54.

2.4 Zadokite Origin?

In discussing the origins of the Essenes, Joseph displays some uncertainty in citing the theory that the *Yaḥad's* 'Teacher of Righteousness' led a group of Zadokite priests to form the Qumran group, noting that it is 'not clear [...] that there ever really was an exodus of Zadokite priests from the Jerusalem Temple'.[26] In view of Joseph's caution, it is necessary to explore the supposed Zadokite background of the sect more closely.

The priest Zadok himself is of uncertain genealogy, with most scholars regarding the several contradictory OT references to his lineage as fictional, and intended to construct an appropriate ancestry for a priest who was not actually from any priestly family.[27] According to the genealogies in 1 Chronicles 5:24–6:3, he would be an Aaronide,[28] but the intent of this text is most likely to create a new priestly line in place of the northern priesthood.[29] Zadok served as high priest in Jerusalem during the reigns of David and Solomon, and his descendants possibly held that position until the exile.[30] In postexilic literature, the priesthood is attributed to all Aaronides, and Zadokites are promised perpetual priesthood (Numbers 25:10–13).[31] Although the attempt to incorporate the Zadokites into the traditional priesthood was apparently unsuccessful, some scholars maintain they held the office of high priest until the advent of Antiochus Epiphanes, shortly before the 160s B.C.E.[32]

Information in CD 1:5–11 offers some light as to how this period

---

25 Joseph, *Jesus, the Essenes, and Christian Origins*, 49.
26 *Jesus, the Essenes, and Christian Origins*, 53.
27 See Ramsey, 'Zadok', 1034; Boorer, *Vision of the Priestly Narrative*, 328–329 n.320.
28 Schley/Spence, 'Zadok', 1406. See also Hackett, 'Zadok, Zadokites'.
29 Schley/Spence, 'Zadok', 1406.
30 Ramsey, 'Zadok', 1034. Note that Ramsey indicates here that such sons of Zadok may have been appointed on grounds of ability rather than heredity (1036). Furthermore, Boorer regards it as unlikely that a hereditary Zadokite dynasty functioned in Jerusalem during the divided monarchy (*Vision of the Priestly Narrative*, 330, 330 n.326).
31 Ramsey, 'Zadok', 1036.
32 VanderKam, *Dead Sea Scrolls Today*, 129; Ramsey, 'Zadok', 1036. But see again Boorer, *Vision of the Priestly Narrative*, 330 n.326, disputing the veracity of the genealogy given in 1 Chr. 6:1–15.

is linked to the origin of the Qumran community, describing a group of penitents who had realised their sinfulness during a time of divine punishment, and God's raising up for them a teacher of righteousness to guide them on the right path.[33] The relevant Teacher is named as a priest—not high priest—but it is possible that he served as high priest in 159–152 B.C.E. when according to Josephus, there was no official in that role.[34] In 152, the Seleucid king appointed Jonathan, one of the Maccabean brothers, to the office, and so began the Hasmonean high priesthood, which continued until 37 B.C.E.[35] Jonathan is considered likely to have been the 'Wicked Priest' who features in the Scrolls as being in conflict with the Teacher of Righteousness,[36] and it is probable that the latter was driven into 'the place of his banishment' for his safety.[37] The location of that site is unknown, but on the basis of CD 1:5–11, VanderKam states: 'it is evident that before the Qumran settlement was built a new penitential movement came into being and that eventually the person known only by the epithet "the Teacher of Righteousness" became its leader'.[38] He considers that at some time after the death of the Teacher, some of his followers moved to Qumran.[39] This background does provide more certainty for the identity of the Qumran community. Joseph has noted the Hasidean and Zadokite origins of the Qumranites,[40] and states that the site was 'a kind of "Wisdom community" founded by a Teacher of Righteousness', thus endorsing VanderKam's hypothesis as outlined.[41]

The multiple references to Zadok and Zadokite priests give rise to conflicting genealogies and traditions, but Ezekiel 44:15–16 is generally acknowledged as the primary one with regard to the 'sons of

---

33 VanderKam and Flint, *Meaning of the Dead Sea Scrolls*, 289–90.
34 *VanderKam, Dead Sea Scrolls Today*, 129, 131.
35 *VanderKam, Dead Sea Scrolls Today*, 129.
36 Note, however, that many other Hasmoneans have been suggested as the Wicked Priest (VanderKam, *Dead Sea Scrolls Today*, 131–32).
37 VanderKam, *Dead Sea Scrolls Today*, 131; and for relevant text see *Commentary on Habakkuk* 11:6, in Martínez, *Dead Sea Scrolls Translated*, 201.
38 VanderKam, *Dead Sea Scrolls Today*, 128.
39 It is surmised that the phrase 'the gathering in of the Teacher' (CD 20:13–15) refers to his death (VanderKam, *Dead Sea Scrolls Today*, 132–33).
40 Joseph, *Jesus, the Essenes, and Christian Origins*, 85, 32.
41 Joseph, *Jesus, the Essenes, and Christian Origins*, 67 (emphasis original), and n.203.

Zadok'.[42] Nurmela provides a plausible rationale for the privileged status of Zadokites, mentioning that Azariah, high priest during Hezekiah's reign, belonged to the house of Zadok (2 Chr. 31:10).[43] Moreover, according to the Chronicler, Zadok was officer in charge over the tribe of Aaron (1 Chr. 27:17),[44] so the clan apparently had a high position.[45] Citing lack of evidence, Boorer dismisses Nurmela's finding that during and following the exile, Aaronites and Zadokites were part of the same group.[46] However, 'sons of Zadok' feature in the Scrolls with reference to their priestly role,[47] as do 'sons of Aaron', with no apparent distinction,[48] so it seems that the equivalence of the groups was accepted, though likely fictional.[49] Further, it is relevant that the covenanters aspired to be a 'kingdom of priests',[50] and noteworthy that the anonymous 'faithful priest' predicted in 1 Samuel 2:35 is identifiable as Zadok.[51] In his commentary on CD 3.18–4.4, Bruce asserts that in reinterpreting Ezekiel 44:15, the Zadokite author shows that the divine commendation as 'sons of Zadok' applies to the entire community as a 'worthy and legitimate body of men ready to resume the service of God'.[52] These factors provide grounds for the Essenes to have viewed themselves in that light, and hence as 'sons of Zadok', regardless of their actual ancestry.[53]

---

42 Nurmela, *The Levites*, 97.
43 Nurmela, *The Levites*, 76, 170.
44 Nurmela, *The Levites*, 170.
45 Nurmela, *The Levites*, 171.
46 Boorer, *Vision of the Priestly Narrative*, 334 n.339.
47 E.g. 1QS 5:2, 9. On these see Schofield and VanderKam, 'Hasmoneans', 73–87.
48 Schofield and VanderKam, 'Hasmoneans', 83 n.31, citing Kugler comparing 1QS 5 and 1QS 9:7.
49 Boorer notes that in 1 Chr. 6:1–15, Zadok is listed as a descendant of Aaron, and that in Ezra 7:1–6, Ezra is depicted as being a descendant of both Aaron and Zadok. See *Vision of the Priestly Narrative*, 337 n.344.
50 As in Exodus 19:6. On the standard of holiness required of the Essenes, see Harrington, 'Halakah and Religion', esp. 84–89.
51 Nurmela, *The Levites*, 30.
52 See Bruce, *Biblical Exegesis*, 35. Re the term 'sons of Zadok' sometimes referring to the entire community, as in CD 4:3, see also 'sons of Zadok', 1.14, section A, The Community, Kraft et al., *Index to DSS Subjects*, though note that J. Pettis, in his revision of the section, regards CD 4:3 as the only example of such usage.
53 It is important to note that Zadokites were *not* Sadducees, as Schiffman claims (*Reclaiming the Dead Sea Scrolls*, 115). For arguments against Schiffman's view, see VanderKam, *Dead Sea Scrolls Today*, 121; VanderKam and Flint, *Meaning of the Dead Sea Scrolls*, 250–252; Mason, 1151. Note that Bibliowicz errs in regarding the name 'Sadducees' as derived from the Hebrew 'Zadokim' (*Jewish–Christian Relations*, 33, 336 n.30). For an explanation of the linguistic distinction between the terms, see Mason, 1151.

2.5 Substitutionary Sacrifice

The question as to whether the Essenes participated in Temple sacrifices is extremely difficult, especially because of ambiguities in the writings of Josephus, Philo, and Pliny on the subject,[54] and the variety of references in many of the Scrolls. Joseph reaches the conclusion that although the Essenes withdrew from the Temple on grounds of its corruption, they began over time to develop rituals of prayer, Torah study, sacred meal practices, and worship, which they regarded as a substitute for animal sacrifice.[55] He considers that in 30 C.E. it would have been over a century since the *Yaḥad* had been involved in the Temple system.[56] This is significant as it supports the idea that at Jesus' last meal, the paschal celebration would have taken place without a lamb.

2.6 Messianic Expectation

Joseph discusses the great variety of messianic figures anticipated in the period under review, concluding that the most common was of a Davidic-type king.[57] Though relatively few of the Scrolls refer to messianism, it comprised a significant aspect of the Qumranites' worldview and self-identification.[58] Four of the documents—1QS, 1QSa, 1QSb, and CD—indicate the sect's distinctive expectation of two messiahs, one royal and one priestly.[59] The members of the *Yaḥad* are enjoined to be set apart as 'a holy house for Aaron', and to live according to the directives of the community, 'until the prophet comes, and the Messiahs of Aaron and Israel' (1QS 9:11).[60] The anticipation of two messiahs is confirmed in several passages of CD.[61]

---

54 See Joseph, *Jesus, the Essenes, and Christian Origins*, 131.
55 Joseph, *Jesus, the Essenes, and Christian Origins*, 131–148, esp. 144. See also Kugler, 'Rewriting Rubrics', esp. 90–92, 112.
56 Joseph, *Jesus, the Essenes, and Christian Origins*, 146.
57 Joseph, *Jesus, the Essenes, and Christian Origins*, 72.
58 Joseph, *Jesus, the Essenes, and Christian Origins*, 72.
59 Joseph, *Jesus, the Essenes, and Christian Origins*, 72; VanderKam, *Dead Sea Scrolls Today*, 119; Collins, *The Scepter and the Star*, 75.
60 Joseph, *Jesus, the Essenes, and Christian Origins*, 72; Martínez, *Dead Sea Scrolls Translated*, 13–14.
61 Joseph, *Jesus, the Essenes, and Christian Origins*, 74 n.15. For more detailed discussion, see Collins, *The Scepter and the Star*, 75, citing CD 12:23; 14:19; 19:10; 20:1; and VanderKam, *Dead Sea Scrolls Today*, 145–46. According to Kraft, 'messiahs (or, messiah) of Aaron and Israel', these terms refer only to 'the anointed high priest and the anointed king', but this view is unpersuasive.

The *Rule of the Congregation* is of particular interest, referring to a time when the messiah will be 'begotten' among them (1QSa 2:11–12).[62] It probably draws on Psalm 2:7, so indicating that the anointed one could be viewed as a 'son of God' in the pre-Christian era.[63] The same document describes the appearance of the 'messiah of Israel' at a communal meal with what seem to be eschatological connotations.[64] The priest who presides is not named 'messiah of Aaron' but this identification may probably be assumed, as he has precedence over the congregation.[65] Here, as also in 1QSb, the expected messiah is of Davidic descent, and is not a priest.[66]

Collins observes the parallel between the binary messianism in the Scrolls—with a priest and a royal figure—and the 'two sons of oil' of Zechariah 4:12,[67] representative of Joshua and Zerubbabel respectively.[68] He notes that a dual leadership model of high priest and king is found in pre-exilic times, and with Aaron and Moses, and that at Qumran, there are two authority figures, priest and guardian, over the *Yaḥad*, and also over each camp.[69] However, that is an oversimplification of the community's organisation, which is extremely complex, and must be carefully reconstructed from several key Scrolls.[70]

Scrutiny of the *Damascus Document* (CD) over against *The Rule of the Community* (1QS) and *The Rule of the Congregation* (1QSa) yields different impressions. While CD relates to family groups living in towns or camps, 1QS is relevant to a 'monastic' group, and 1QSa refers at least partially to the future.[71] In the present study the context

---

62 Joseph, *Jesus, the Essenes, and Christian Origins*, 72–73. Collins observes that the opening sentence of the passage is fragmentary and that possible alternative restorations are of the messiah being 'sent' (instead of 'begotten'), or that he 'shall assemble with them' (*The Scepter and the Star*, 75–76).
63 Joseph, *Jesus, the Essenes, and Christian Origins*, 72–73.
64 Joseph, *Jesus, the Essenes, and Christian Origins*, 73; Martínez, *Dead Sea Scrolls Translated*, 127–28.
65 Collins, *The Scepter and the Star*, 76.
66 VanderKam, *Dead Sea Scrolls Today*, 146; Martínez, *Dead Sea Scrolls Translated*, 432–33 citing 1QSb.
67 Collins, *The Scepter and the Star*, 77, 96 n.11, referring to articles by S. Talmon.
68 See https://biblehub.com/zechariah/4-12.htm for identification of the figures, and for commentary, Wolters, 'The Meaning of Ṣantĕrôt (Zech 4:12)'.
69 Collins, *The Scepter and the Star*, 77.
70 See Vermes and Goodman, *The Essenes*, 7.
71 Vermes and Goodman, *The Essenes*, 7.

is a small, celibate Essenic household in southwest Jerusalem in 33 C.E.—the surmised venue for Jesus' last meal, hence 1QS and 1QSa are the more significant sources. The smallest permissible household comprised ten members, and required a priest to preside at meals.[72] The group leader (*Mebaqqer*—translated variously as 'Examiner', 'Inspector', 'overseer', and 'Guardian'),[73] was termed 'head of the Many'.[74] His responsibilities included examining newcomers, monitoring discussions in meetings of the community, and controlling common goods.[75] Another authority figure, probably second in command, was the *Paqid* ('Overseer', 'Instructor', 'Inspector'), featuring in 1QS 6:14.[76] His role was to examine and judge those wishing to join the sect.[77] Although the priestly status of the *Paqid* is not stated in 1QS 6:14, he is considered to have had a high profile, equivalent to the Greek term *episkopos*.[78]

It is noteworthy here that although the Qumranites' eschatological expectations were important, of more concern in their daily lives were the Torah, and the responsibility to abide by the *Yaḥad's* original laws until the arrival of the prophet and the anticipated messiahs.[79]

2.7 Significant Scriptures

Qumran prophets were regarded as anointed ones, and their role was to mediate divine revelations through the agency of the Holy Spirit.[80]

---

72 Vermes and Goodman, *The Essenes*, 7, citing 1QS 6:2–5.
73 Martínez, *Dead Sea Scrolls Translated*, 10; Vermes and Goodman, *The Essenes*, 7; Kraft, 'overseer, inspector'.
74 See '*Paqid* (Overseer)', 'Qumran Community Leaders', in which it is noted that the *Paqid* serves as 'head of the community' and the *Mebaqqer* as 'head of the Many', and may perhaps be a single individual.
75 See 'Qumran Community Leaders', citing 1QS 6:11–13; 6:20; Kraft, 'overseer, inspector', citing 1QS 6:12, 19–20, and many CD references.
76 '*Paqid* (Overseer)', 'Qumran Community Leaders'; Kraft, 'inspector'.
77 '*Paqid* (Overseer)', 'Qumran Community Leaders'. The terms מבקר and פקיד seem to be used interchangeably and possibly refer to the same figure ('Qumran Community Leaders'); similarly Collins, *The Scepter and the Star*, 96 n.12, but note that the role of the משכיל (master) differs from the other two. The *Maskil* was a learned teacher who instructed the members and novices ['*Maskil* (Master)', 'Qumran Community Leaders', citing 1QS 3:13; 9:18].
78 See Kraft, 'inspector', where it is noted that both *paqid* and *mebaqqer* were translated as *episkopos* in the LXX; and 'פָּקִיד', mng. 1: *cultic overseer*; at Qumran, *perh. specif. head of priests* 1QS 6:14, *CDCH*, p.364.
79 Joseph, *Jesus, the Essenes, and Christian Origins*, 75.
80 Joseph, *Jesus, the Essenes, and Christian Origins*, 79.

Isaianic texts, notably 52:7 and 61:1–2 were especially important and were drawn on, for instance in 11QMelchizedek, for the annunciation of the Jubilee. Here, Melchizedek appears to be styled as the אלוהים (*Elohim*) in Psalm 82:1.[81] The expected eschatological figure is like a Moses *redivivus*, who will be a revealer of Torah, and continue the mission of the Teacher of Righteousness.[82]

Joseph examines 4Q521 closely, observing its compatibility with Qumran ideology. The messianic figure described is singular, and is a prophet like Elijah. This text is considered very illuminating for the messianic identification of the historical Jesus.[83] In Matthew 11:4–5 and Luke 7:22, Jesus' response to John's question about his credentials does not conform to traditional Jewish expectations of the messiah, but it matches the anointed one anticipated in 4Q521.[84] Joseph concludes that the evangelists were *reconfiguring* a pre-existing tradition known at Qumran, that linked Isaianic prophecies to a coming anointed one.[85] He also posits that Jesus was involved in halakhic debates with his contemporaries as to how to do God's will.[86]

By drawing on Enochic texts, *Jubilees*, the *Temple Scroll*, 4QMMT, CD, and other writings, Joseph is able to resolve the vexed question as to the Essenes' relationship with the Temple.[87] The Enochic tradition is shown to be particularly significant, not only because the *Yaḥad* inherited and developed it, but also because it is apparent that it was respected and utilised in early Christianity.[88] Bauckham has written in detail of the dependence of Jude 14–15 on 1 Enoch 1:9,[89] possibly from the original text in Aramaic.[90] He also argues persuasively that

---

81 Joseph, *Jesus, the Essenes, and Christian Origins*, 80–81.
82 Joseph, *Jesus, the Essenes, and Christian Origins*, 81–82.
83 Joseph, *Jesus, the Essenes, and Christian Origins*, 89.
84 Joseph, *Jesus, the Essenes, and Christian Origins*, 91.
85 Joseph, *Jesus, the Essenes, and Christian Origins*, 95.
86 Joseph, *Jesus, the Essenes, and Christian Origins*, 98.
87 Joseph, *Jesus, the Essenes, and Christian Origins*, 138–147, esp. 138–39.
88 Joseph, *Jesus, the Essenes, and Christian Origins*, 29–31.
89 Bauckham, *Jude and the Relatives of Jesus*, 137–39.
90 Bauckham, *Jude and the Relatives of Jesus*, 139. For translation of the fragmentary Aramaic version (4QEnoch^c 1:1:15–17), see Martínez, *Dead Sea Scrolls Translated*, 250.

Jude 6 draws on Enoch,[91] and for many other allusions to that tradition in the Letter of Jude.[92] Luke's significant use of Enoch is discussed in section 5.

3. Insight on Early Christianity

The summary of Joseph's findings, and further commentary, have provided valuable information about the Essenes, their ideology, and eschatological expectations, and also shown clearly that many, though not all, of their beliefs were similar to those of the historical Jesus. Taking these results into account, we will now consider some passages in Acts, especially 6:1–7, to ascertain whether they reflect Essenic influence on the early Jesus movement.

Following the ascension, Luke depicts the eleven remaining apostles as meeting in the upstairs room where they were staying, and constantly devoting themselves to prayer, together with certain women, including Jesus' mother, and also his brothers (Acts 1:13–14). All of these were presumably at the Last Supper, and are regarded by Luke as being among the earliest believers.[93] Intriguingly, James is not named at this point, raising the question as to his relationship with Jesus, and at what stage he became a believer. This will be considered in section 4.

There is evidence in Acts 6:1–7 of similarities between Christians and Essenes in their care of the poor,[94] and elsewhere regarding common goods (2:44–45; 4:34–35).[95] Interestingly, both the Essenes and

---

91 Bauckham, *Jude and the Relatives of Jesus*, 182–183, referring to (among other phrases) 'for the judgment of the great Day' (NRSV) in Jude 6. For the translation of the relevant text see 4QEn^b 1:4:11, Martínez, *Dead Sea Scrolls Translated*, 250.
92 Bauckham, *Jude and the Relatives of Jesus*, 138–41, 181–201.
93 Bernheim, *James, Brother of Jesus*, 95. As noted in section 1, the other family members and apostles probably stayed in a different household from where the Last Supper was held.
94 Barrett, *Acts of the Apostles*, 310. That no one went in need has been mentioned in Acts 4:34 (305). On Acts 6:1–2, see also Conzelmann, *Acts of the Apostles*, 45.
95 Bruce, *Acts of the Apostles*, 182; Cullman, 'Significance of the Qumran Texts, 215. The matter of community of goods is complex, requiring careful explication, and is best considered together with the account of the believers' care of the needy. Brian Capper concludes that Acts 2–6 provides a historically verifiable account of the practices of the earliest Christians, as being close in form to those of the Essenes. See his 'Palestinian Cultural Context', 356, and 'Essene Community Houses', esp. 486, 490.

Christians called themselves 'the poor'.[96]

The pericope in Acts 6:1–7 is the first in Luke's series of progress reports, here focusing on the church's growth,[97] with vv.1 and 7 forming an *inclusio*. The distinction between 'Hellenists' and 'Hebrews' in the passage is generally regarded as linguistic,[98] the former being Greek-speaking Jews, the latter speaking Aramaic.[99] However, in an essay published in 1955, Oscar Cullman suggested tentatively that the 'Hellenists', and the 'priests' reported in Acts 6:7 as having converted to Christianity, were associated with the Qumran sect.[100] Commentators writing in the 1990s have tended to reject the idea,[101] but from what we now know of the Essenes, it seems highly likely that these were indeed Essenes. As such they would be deemed 'sons of Zadok' and/or 'sons of Aaron'. Luke has already mentioned the Sadducees as fierce opponents of Christians (Acts 4:1,6; 5:17),[102] so if they were to convert, it would be nonsensical for the evangelist not to refer to such a surprising turnaround.[103] Some commentaries mention that in the Essenic community, the Council comprised twelve men and three priests (1QS 8:1),[104] surmising a parallel with the twelve apostles and seven Hellenists of Acts 6, but as Conzelmann rightly notes, the priests added to the Christians in v.7 would have no part in the structure of the group.[105]

That the Last Supper venue and the meeting place of the early Christians were both located in the Essene quarter of Jerusalem is considered reliably established, and the exploration of Acts 6:1–7 adds support for the hypothesis concerning Jesus' final meal.

---

96 Bruce, *Acts of the Apostles*, 182; Cullman, 'Significance of Qumran Texts', 215. Furthermore, Cullman notes that the Qumran sect's name for itself—'the New Covenant'—is equivalent to 'New Testament' (215).
97 Bruce, *Acts of the Apostles*, 185.
98 Bruce, *Acts of the Apostles*, 181; Conzelmann, *Acts of the Apostles*, 45; Cullman, 'Significance of Qumran Texts', 220.
99 Cullman, 'Significance of Qumran Texts', 220.
100 Cullman, 'Significance of Qumran Texts', 223–24.
101 See e.g. Barrett, *Acts of the Apostles*, 307, 311, 317; Bruce, *Acts of the Apostles*, 185. Fitzmyer is supportive (Barrett, *Acts of the Apostles*, 317).
102 Barrett, *Acts of the Apostles*, 317.
103 Barrett, *Acts of the Apostles*, 303, seems to imply such a phenomenal expansion.
104 See Martínez, *Dead Sea Scrolls Translated*, 12; Barrett, *Acts of the Apostles*, 311; Cullman, 'Significance of Qumran Texts', 216.
105 Conzelmann, *Acts of the Apostles*, 46. In fact, the council of twelve should be reckoned as *including* three priests. See Bauckham, *Jude and the Relatives of Jesus*, 75 n.89, following Draper.

4. Legends Concerning James

4.1 The Legend of Jesus' Appearance To James

The Gospel of the Hebrews contains a little-known narrative at or near the end of the fragmentary text. Other parts of the seven fragments relate to incidents in the life of Jesus, including the temptation story, but some have no counterpart in the canonical Gospels.[106] There is sufficient detail in No. 7 fragment for scholars to surmise two missing accounts: one relating to a Last Supper narrative at which Jesus' brother James was present, making a vow to abstain from food until he had seen the risen Jesus.[107] From this it can be assumed that according to the narrative, Jesus spoke at the meal of his coming death and rising. The second account would be one describing the resurrection as viewed by guards at the tomb, and so presupposing a burial account.[108] The story differs from canonical accounts, notably 1 Corinthians 15:7, as it has James as the first witness to the risen Jesus.

The likely provenance of the gospel is Egypt; as it was known to Hegesippus, it is dated to the first half of the second century.[109] The English translation of the legend reads:

> And when the Lord had given the linen cloth to the servant of the priest, he went to James and appeared to him. For James had sworn that he would not eat bread from that hour in which he had drunk the cup of the Lord until he should see him risen from among them that sleep. And shortly thereafter the Lord said: Bring a table and bread! And immediately it is added: he took the bread, blessed it and brake it and gave it to James the Just and said to him: My brother, eat thy bread, for the Son of man is risen from among them that sleep.[110]

---

106 Vielhauer and Strecker, 'Gospel of the Hebrews', 172.
107 For background on the text, see Myllykoski, 'James the Just', Part II, 23–27.
108 Vielhauer and Strecker, 'Gospel of the Hebrews', 172.
109 Vielhauer and Strecker, 'Gospel of the Hebrews', 176; Myllykoski suggests a possible date of the second half of the first century ('James the Just', Part II, 27). The fact that the legend involves only bread could indicate the antiquity of the tradition (Myllykoski, 'James the Just', Part II, 30).
110 Vielhauer and Strecker, 'Gospel of the Hebrews', 178. For a slightly different translation see Myllykoski, 'James the Just', Part II, 27.

ESSENIC INFLUENCE ON JESUS 65

Some aspects of the legend may be drawn from the canonical Gospels,[111] e.g. the servant of the priest from Matthew 26:51;[112] the linen cloth from Matthew 27:59;[113] the oath as a modification of Jesus' words in Mark 14:25;[114] and in the concluding line from Jesus' predictions of his passion.[115] The legend may reasonably be interpreted as indicating that James was already a follower of Jesus before the resurrection.[116]

4.2 The Legend According To Hegesippus

Another legend from the beginning of the second century, or earlier, provides relevant insights on James, drawing on the work of Hegesippus.[117] The material includes traditions about the martyrdom and succession of James, but here we will focus only on matters concerning his lifestyle, leadership, and authority.[118] Details given are his leadership of the church, as 'brother of the Lord'; that he was known as 'the Just'; was holy from birth; abstained from intoxicating drink and meat; and did not cut his hair, anoint himself, or bathe.[119] Astonishingly, he is not only described as conducting priestly intercessions in the temple, but is styled as high priest, wearing linen garments,[120] and entering alone into the holy place.[121] While the majority of scholars view this depiction of James as nonsensical, Myllykoski notes that some 'have accepted the idea that [he] came from a priestly, or at least a Levite, family'.[122] Moreover, as has been observed, the Greek translation for either *mebaqqer* or

---

111 See in citation of legend the references given to: 1 Cor. 15:7; Mark 14:25 and parr.; Mark 14:22 and parr.; 1 Cor. 11:23–24; Mark 8:31 and parr. (Vielhauer and Strecker, 'Gospel of the Hebrews', 178); and discussion in Myllykoski, 'James the Just', Part II, 23–31.
112 Chilton suggested that the cloth is given to the servant of the *high* priest who according to Luke 22:49–51 was wounded, and whom Jesus then healed (Myllykoski, 'James the Just', Part II, 28).
113 See Myllykoski, 'James the Just', Part II, 28.
114 For discussion on James' oath, see Myllykoski, 'James the Just', Part II, 29.
115 See Mark 8:31; 9:31; 10:32–34 and parr.
116 See Myllykoski, 'James the Just', Part II, 28; Bernheim, *James, Brother of Jesus*, 94, 97, 100, 287 n.25, 287–88 n.32, citing and endorsing Bauckham, *Jude and the Relatives of Jesus*, 56–57.
117 The legend is as recounted by Eusebius, *Eccl. Hist.* 2.23.4–7 (Myllykoski, 'James the Just', Part II, 33). For discussion see pp.31–43.
118 Myllykoski, 'James the Just', Part II, 32–33.
119 For discussion of the Nazirite and ascetic characteristics, see Myllykoski, 'James the Just', Part II, 34–35.
120 See Lev. 16:4.
121 For discussion see Myllykoski, 'James the Just', Part II, 33–36.
122 Myllykoski, 'James the Just', Part II, 35.

paqid is *episkopos*, so the tradition that James was the inaugural bishop of Jerusalem deserves further investigation.[123] These points are examined further in section 5.

4.3 The legend in the Gospel of Thomas

A further legend concerning James is found in Logion 12 of the Gospel of Thomas. The dating of this overall collection of sayings is debated, but the antiquity of Logion 12 is almost certain,[124] as is also its Jewish-Christian provenance.[125] Like the Gospel of the Hebrews legend, it implies that James was associated with Jesus before the resurrection, and refers to his righteousness:

> The disciples said to Jesus: 'We know that you will depart from us. Who is to be our leader?' Jesus said to them: 'Wherever you are, you are to go to James the righteous, for whose sake heaven and earth came into being'.[126]

The saying endorses the tradition of James' pre-eminence in the Jerusalem church, and this is further confirmed by a saying attributed to Clement that states that after the resurrection: 'Peter, James and John did not claim pre-eminence because the Savior [...] chose James the Just as Bishop of Jerusalem'.[127]

Myllykoski concludes that the tradition from Thomas rested on a logion that circulated in the years after James' death, depicting him as a highly righteous and faithful leader.[128] It provides a little more material for the following discussion.

---

123 See Myllykoski, 'James the Just', Part II, 43, for Chilton's observation that the duties of 'overseer' at Qumran were similar to those of an *episkopos*.
124 The rationale for an early date is that Logion 13 gives greater authority to Thomas. See Bernheim, *James, Brother of Jesus*, 99.
125 Bernheim, *James, Brother of Jesus*, 99; Myllykoski, 'James the Just', Part II, 52.
126 Bernheim, *James, Brother of Jesus*, 99; Myllykoski, 'James the Just', Part II, 50.
127 The tradition is attested by Eusebius (*Eccl. Hist.* 2.1.3-5), cited in Myllykoski, 'James the Just', Part II, 51.
128 Myllykoski, 'James the Just', Part II, 52.

5. James' Priestly Status

The legend discussed in 4.2 features in a tightly-argued essay by William Adler, which sheds light on the depiction of James as a high priest.[129] The essay focuses on three OT prophecies that predicted the end of a line of hereditary rulers,[130] and efforts of fourth-century Christian exegetes to prove that following Herod's abolition of the Hasmoneans' rule, Jesus and James were rightful heirs to the dual office of high priest and king.[131] Key to the discussion is that Exodus 6:23 refers to the marriage of Aaron to a Judahite woman, Elisheba (sister of Nahshon), thus conferring Levitical/Judahite lineage to their offspring.[132]

Epiphanius, in his *Panarion*, referred to the legend about James, stating that he was qualified to enter the inner sanctum once per annum.[133] According to Hegesippus, James' authority was based on his holiness and asceticism, linked to his Nazirite vows.[134] In a second reference to the legend, Epiphanius used Exodus 6:23 as a prooftext for James' additional credentials, showing that the tribes of Judah and Aaron were linked exclusively.[135] Hence Mary, through intertribal marriage, was a descendant of both Levi and David.[136] The view of the early church was that after Herod acceded to the throne, valid authority passed to Jesus, who was seen as both eternal Davidic king and high priest.[137] This authority then passed to the high priests of the catholic church.[138] To quote Adler, based on Epiphanius: 'James, the "brother and apostle of the Lord" as well as the first bishop, could succeed Jesus in the dual role of high priest and king because, like Jesus himself, he

---

129 Adler, 'Exodus 6:23 and the High Priest', 38–39.
130 Gen. 49:10; Dan. 9:25–26; and Jer. 22:28–30 (Adler, 'Exodus 6:23 and the High Priest', 26).
131 Adler, 'Exodus 6:23 and the High Priest', 24–26.
132 Adler, 'Exodus 6:23 and the High Priest', 24. Re Nahshon's position as head of the house of Judah, see 24 n.5.
133 Adler, 'Exodus 6:23 and the High Priest', 39 n.51, citing *Pan.* 29.4.2–4.
134 Adler, 'Exodus 6:23 and the High Priest', 39 n.50, citing Eusebius, *EH* 2.23.6 (quoting Hegesippus).
135 Adler, 'Exodus 6:23 and the High Priest', 39 n.53, citing *Pan.* 78.11.13.5–6, and noting that Epiphanius misrepresented the text.
136 Adler, 'Exodus 6:23 and the High Priest', 39, 39 n.55. Epiphanius apparently rejected the notion that James was the son of Mary, but accepted that he was Jesus' biological brother only on the basis that he 'was raised with him'. See p.40, and nn.56, 57.
137 Adler, 'Exodus 6:23 and the High Priest', 40.
138 Adler, 'Exodus 6:23 and the High Priest', 40 n.58.

possessed the hereditary birthright to do so'.[139]

Adler shows the likelihood of Eusebius ultimately *altering* the exegetical link between Jesus as a Judahite, and the Levitical high priesthood. Drawing on the Epistle to the Hebrews, Eusebius rejected any ancestral relationship between Jesus' priesthood 'after the order of Melchizedek' and the *hereditary* Jewish high priesthood.[140]

The intention of such early Christian scholars was to demonstrate that Jesus' high priesthood was founded on spiritual authority rather than ancestry. A much more recent viewpoint, Bauckham's analysis of Luke's genealogy (Luke 3:23–38), offers an interesting comparison.[141]

In his introduction to the topic, Bauckham notes that two significant points have generally been overlooked: Luke's use of the Apocalypse of Weeks (1 Enoch 93:3–10; 9:11–17);[142] and an appropriate understanding of OT prophecy concerning the anticipated Davidic ruler.[143] On the first point he shows how Luke has changed the original 10 'weeks' (measured by generations) to 11 weeks (representing 77 generations),[144] with the most important individuals typically located at the end of a 'week', i.e. a sabbath.[145] The genealogy is evidently inspired by 1 Enoch 10:12, but has been reconstructed by Luke.[146] Significant modifications which Bauckham assumes the evangelist made to a pre-Lukan form are: in 3:23, the addition of the words ὡς ἐνομίζετο (hence, 'being *as was thought* the son of Joseph'); and in 3:38, τοῦ θεοῦ (thus, 'Adam *the son of God*').[147]

Bauckham argues convincingly for the plausibility of Luke's claim that Zerubbabel was descended from David's son Nathan.[148] He also shows that the genealogical tradition employed by Luke coheres with

---

139   Adler, 'Exodus 6:23 and the High Priest', 40, 40 n.59, citing Epiphanius, *Pan.* 29.3.9.
140   Adler, 'Exodus 6:23 and the High Priest', 47 n.77, citing Eusebius *EH* 1.3.18.
141   See Bauckham, *Jude and the Relatives of Jesus*, 315–73.
142   Bauckham, *Jude and the Relatives of Jesus*, 315, 320.
143   Bauckham, *Jude and the Relatives of Jesus*, 315.
144   Bauckham, *Jude and the Relatives of Jesus*, 318–19.
145   Bauckham, *Jude and the Relatives of Jesus*, 321, 324. See table showing names and weeks, pp.316–17.
146   Bauckham, *Jude and the Relatives of Jesus*, 319–20 (citing 4QEn^b 1:4:10), 325.
147   Bauckham, *Jude and the Relatives of Jesus*, 368–69.
148   Bauckham, *Jude and the Relatives of Jesus*, 340–47. The relevant prophecy in Isa. 11:1 is a prediction of a rightful ruler—Davidic but not from Solomon's line. Micah 5:2 confirmed that this king would be born in Bethlehem. See p.334.

Paul's reference to Jesus' Davidic ancestry (Romans 1:3), and draws on material from Hegesippus about family members.[149] The reliability of the tradition is bolstered by discussion of Africanus' *Letter to Aristides*, the *desposynoi* (relatives of Jesus), and evidence based on the Letter of Jude.[150]

Despite having successfully argued for the veracity of Luke's genealogy, Bauckham, like Eusebius, rejects the concept that Jesus' priesthood relates to his levitical ancestry via Mary. He simply states that to be legitimate, priesthood must be via the male line from Aaron.[151] In his view, Hebrews 7:14 makes it clear that as a Judahite, Jesus was not a levitical priest.[152]

Bauckham's (and Eusebius') reliance on Hebrews for an assessment of Jesus' priesthood is highly problematical. First, the verse cited clearly has no historical value, and worse, is drawn from what is 'often perceived as the New Testament's most anti-Jewish text'.[153] As Bibliowicz has demonstrated, the epistle is extremely supersessionist, with its author engaging in 'battle against those that advocated continuity with the beliefs and traditions of the founding fathers',[154] i.e. Jesus' disciples and first followers.[155] In Hebrews 7, the author's purpose in deploying the figure of Melchizedek is 'to argue the supremacy of his brand of belief in Jesus over that of his Jewish opponents within the Jesus movement'.[156]

Bibliowicz also provides helpful comments on the 'historical' James, noting his considerable power. The inclusion in the canon of the epistle attributed to James indicates that observance of Torah

---

149 Jude's grandsons, and Symeon, Clopas' son (Bauckham, *Jude and the Relatives of Jesus*, 355 [citing Eusebius *HE* 3:20:1-2; 3:32:3], 355 n.125), 94–97.
150 Bauckham, *Jude and the Relatives of Jesus*, 354–64. Note that Africanus' reference to 'both genealogies' (p.359) pertains to those of Matthew and Luke. See pp.356–359.
151 Bauckham, *Jude and the Relatives of Jesus*, 345.
152 Bauckham, *Jude and the Relatives of Jesus*, 345.
153 See Eisenbaum, 'The Letter to the Hebrews', 406. For comment on Hebrews 7:1–17, see pp.414–15; and for background on Melchizedek, p.415.
154 Bibliowicz, *Jewish–Christian Relations*, 144. Bibliowicz's basic argument, with which I concur, is that the antisemitic polemic encountered in Hebrews, and elsewhere in the NT, is a reflection of conflict between Jewish and Gentile Christians, rather than between Jews and Christians. See pp.15–17.
155 Bibliowicz, *Jewish–Christian Relations*, 25.
156 Bibliowicz, *Jewish–Christian Relations*, 149.

remained authoritative in the fourth century.[157] Although there is doubt as to James' authorship of the letter, it is believed to reflect his views.[158] Citing the M material in Matthew, Bibliowicz observes that '[u]ncompromising ethical demands, Torah observance, and radical anti-establishment and anti-wealth' are common to Jesus' teaching and the Epistle of James.[159]

While this is helpful background, it does not inform us about the priestly status of the brothers. Bauckham's research on Jesus' ancestry also appeared pointless. However, if the doctrine of the virgin birth is set aside, Bauckham's findings have merit. Jesus and James may then be viewed as full siblings, and on the basis of Exodus 6:23, it can be claimed that both were of mixed Levitical and Judahite lineage. This will be taken into account in the findings of our study.

6. Conclusion

The assessment of Joseph's work strongly confirmed his finding of Essenic influence on early Christianity, though there remains some doubt about the Zadokite origins of the Qumran sect, and perhaps members of James' household should be regarded as *Hasidim* rather than strict Essenes. The term 'sons of Zadok' was found to be ambiguous, though *Yaḥad* members seem to have self-identified as such. Several Scrolls led to an expectation of two messiahs, one priestly, and one royal. In the *Rule of the Community*, two authority figures were the *mebaqqer* and *paqid*—perhaps a single individual, the overseer, who could be termed an *episkopos*.

Legends about James confirmed his importance in the early church and affirmed that he was regarded as a priest. The study of Jesus' and James' ancestry showed that the family was aware of their Davidic lineage, and it was noted that their mixed Judahite and Levitical ancestry was widely acknowledged in the fourth century.

It is posited that James was the *mebaqqer* of his household and

---

157 Bibliowicz, *Jewish–Christian Relations*, 72.
158 Bibliowicz, *Jewish–Christian Relations*, 76.
159 Bibliowicz, *Jewish–Christian Relations*, 75.

hence the so-called 'owner of the house' in Mark 14:14, who was consulted as to where Jesus and his followers might eat the Passover.¹⁶⁰ In accordance with 1QS 6:4–6, James would also have presided, and been first to bless the bread and wine for the meal. However, when Jesus followed up with his extraordinary actions and words, those assembled would have recalled the words of 1QSa 2:17–21:

> ¹⁷ [...] And [when] they gather at the table of community [or to drink] the new wine, and the table of community is prepared ¹⁸[and] the new wine [is mixed] for drinking, [no-one should stretch out] his hand to the first-fruit of the bread ¹⁹ and of the [new wine] before the priest, for [he is the one who bl]esses the first-fruit of bread ²⁰ and of the new wine [and stretches out] his hand towards the bread before them. Afterwards, the Messiah of Israel shall stretch out his hand ²¹ towards the bread. [And afterwards, shall] bless all the congregation of the community, each [one according to] his dignity.¹⁶¹

While the context is not identical, it is my belief that Jesus was identified as the anticipated royal anointed one by those present, and that after his death and resurrection, and when his ancestry became known, was deemed to be both Davidic and priestly Messiah. Viewing such recognition in relation to the lambless Passover celebration would also explain the early identification of Jesus by Paul as 'our paschal lamb'.¹⁶²

While Jesus' and James' teaching and ethics were observed to be similar, it is interesting to compare Jesus' reputation for open commensality with James' apparent response in the Antioch incident.¹⁶³ We may reasonably suppose that James, in his leadership position, would wish to take a firm stand on this issue and affirm Torah observance.¹⁶⁴ Nevertheless, it is clear that neither of the brothers adhered to strict

---

160 The *mebaqqer* was the 'official gate-keeper of the community'. See Kraft, 'overseer, inspector', citing CD 13:12–13.
161 Martínez, *Dead Sea Scrolls Translated*, 127–128.
162 1 Cor. 5:7.
163 Gal. 2:11–14; Acts 15:1,5.
164 See Bibliowicz, *Jewish–Christian Relations*, 76.

Essenic views such as exclusion of the blind and lame from their communities.¹⁶⁵ In contrast, several verses of the scroll 4QMessianic Apocalypse (4Q521) express well both what we can discern of the outlook of James, and what we know of Jesus from the canonical Gospels.¹⁶⁶

To summarise: Our study of links between the Essenes and the early church, focusing primarily on James the Just and the occasion of the Last Supper, has yielded valuable insights on the historical Jesus—affirming him as an attractive Torah-observant Jewish teacher, healer, prophet, and holy man—incidentally quite unlike the artificial construct depicted in Hebrews chapter 7.

---

165 See 1QSa 2:3–9; 1QM 7:4-5; 11QT^a 45:12–14; and Olyan, 'Exegetical Dimensions', 47.
166 See 4Q521 frag. 2, 2:5–13 in Martínez, *Dead Sea Scrolls Translated*, 394.

Bibliography

Adler, W.	'Exodus 6:23 and the High Priest from the Tribe of Judah', *JTS*, n.s., 48.1 (1997), 24–47.
Barrett, C. K.	*The Acts of the Apostles* (ICC; 2 vols.; Edinburgh: T&T Clark, 1994).
Bauckham, R.	*Jude and the Relatives of Jesus in the Early Church* (Edinburgh: T&T Clark, 1990).
Bernheim, P.-A.	*James, Brother of Jesus* (trans. J. Bowden; London: SCM, 1997).
Bibliowicz, A. M.	*Jewish–Christian Relations: The First Centuries* (rev. edn; Coppell, TX: Mascarat, 2019).
Boorer, S.	*The Vision of the Priestly Narrative: Its Genre and Hermeneutics of Time* (Ancient Israel and Its Literature 27; Atlanta, GA: SBL Press, 2016).
Broshi, M.	'Essenes at Qumran? A Rejoinder to Albert Baumgarten', *DSD* 14.1 (2007), 25–33.
Bruce, F. F.	*Biblical Exegesis in the Qumran Texts* (London: Tyndale Press, 1960).
Bruce, F. F.	*The Acts of the Apostles: Greek Text with Introduction and Commentary* (3rd rev. and enlgd edn; Grand Rapids, MI: Eerdmans, 1990).
Capper, B. J.	'Essene Community Houses and Jesus' Early Community', in J. H. Charlesworth (ed.), *Jesus and Archaeology* (Grand Rapids, MI: Eerdmans, 2006), 472–502.
Capper, B. J.	'The Palestinian Cultural Context of Earliest Christian Community of Goods', in R. Bauckham (ed.), *The Book of Acts in its First Century Setting*. Vol. 4, *Palestinian Setting* (Grand Rapids, MI: Eerdmans, 1995), 323–56.
Clines, D. J. A. (ed.)	*The Concise Dictionary of Classical Hebrew (CDCH)* (Sheffield: Sheffield Phoenix Press, 2009).
Collins, J. J.	'Introduction', in J. J. Collins and R. A. Kugler (eds.), *Religion in the Dead Sea Scrolls* (Studies in the Dead Sea Scrolls and Related Literature; Grand Rapids, MI: Eerdmans, 2000), 1–8.

Collins, J. J.   *The Scepter and the Star: The Messiahs of the Dead Sea Scrolls and Other Ancient Literature* (ABRL; New York, NY: Doubleday, 1995).

Conzelmann, H.   *Acts of the Apostles* (Hermeneia; trans. J. Limburg, A. T. Kraabel, and D. H. Juel; Philadelphia, PA: Fortress Press, 1987).

Cross, F. M.   'The Historical Context of the Scrolls', in H. Shanks (ed.), *Understanding the Dead Sea Scrolls: A Reader from the Biblical Archaeological Review* (New York, NY: Vintage Books, 1993), 20–32.

Cullman, O.   'The Significance of the Qumran Texts for Research into the Beginnings of Christianity', *JBL* 74.4 (1955), 213–26.

Eisenbaum, P.   'The Letter to the Hebrews', in A.-J. Levine and M. Z. Brettler (eds.), *The Jewish Annotated New Testament: New Revised Standard Version* (New York, NY: Oxford University Press, 2011), 406–426.

Freedman, D. N. (ed.)   *Eerdmans Dictionary of the Bible (EDB)* (Grand Rapids, MI: Eerdmans, 2000).

Freedman, D. N. (ed.)   *The Anchor Bible Dictionary (ABD)* (6 vols.; New York, NY: Doubleday, 1992).

García M. F.   *The Dead Sea Scrolls Translated: The Qumran Texts in English* (trans. W. G. E. Watson; 2nd edn; Leiden: Brill, 1996).

Golb, N.   'The Qumran Essene Hypothesis: A Fiction of Scholarship', *Christian Century* 109.36 (9 Dec 1992), 1138–43.

Goranson, S.   'Essenes', *EDB* 425–26.

Hackett, J. A.   'Zadok, Zadokites', http://www.oxfordbiblicalstudies.com/article/opr/t120/e0785 [accessed 12 September 2019].

Harrington, H. K.   'The Halakah and Religion of Qumran', in J. J. Collins and R. A. Kugler (eds.), *Religion in the Dead Sea Scrolls* (Studies in the Dead Sea Scrolls and Related Literature; Grand Rapids, MI: Eerdmans, 2000), 74–89.

Hebrew University Jerusalem   'Qumran Community Leaders', http://virtualqumran.huji.ac.il/moreInfo/CommunityLeaders.htm [accessed 28 December 2020].

Hempel, C.   *The Laws of the Damascus Document: Sources, Traditions and Redaction* (STDJ 29; Leiden: Brill, 1998).

Joseph, S. J.	*Jesus, the Essenes, and Christian Origins: New Light on Ancient Texts and Communities* (Waco, TX: Baylor University Press, 2018).
Kugler, R. A.	'Rewriting Rubrics: Sacrifice and the Religion of Qumran', in J. J. Collins and R. A. Kugler (eds.), *Religion in the Dead Sea Scrolls* (Studies in the Dead Sea Scrolls and Related Literature; Grand Rapids, MI: Eerdmans, 2000), 90–112.
Kraft, R., et al.	*Index to DSS Subjects*, http://ccat.sas.upenn.edu/rak/courses/427/indices/gaster.htm, accessed 27 December 2020.
Mason, S.	'Sadducees', *EDB* 1150–51.
Myllykoski, M.	'James the Just in History and Tradition: Perspectives of Past and Present Scholarship (Part I)', *Currents in Biblical Research* 5.1 (2006), 73–122.
Myllykoski, M.	'James the Just in History and Tradition: Perspectives of Past and Present Scholarship (Part II)', *Currents in Biblical Research* 6.1 (2007), 11–98.
Nurmela, R.	*The Levites: Their Emergence as a Second-Class Priesthood* (South Florida Studies in the History of Judaism 193; Atlanta, GA: Scholars Press, 1998).
Olyan, S. M.	'The Exegetical Dimensions of Restrictions on the Blind and the Lame in Texts from Qumran', *DSD* 8.1 (2001), 38–50.
Pixner, B.	'Mount Zion, Jesus, and Archaeology', in J. H. Charlesworth (ed.), *Jesus and Archaeology* (Grand Rapids, MI: Eerdmans, 2006), 309–22.
Ramsey, G. W.	'Zadok', *ABD* 6:1034–36.
Riesner, R.	'Jesus, the Primitive Community, and the Essene Quarter of Jerusalem', in J. H. Charlesworth (ed.), *Jesus and the Dead Sea Scrolls* (ABRL; New York, NY: Doubleday, 1992), 198–234.
Saulnier, S.	*Calendrical Variations in Second Temple Judaism: New Perspectives on the 'Date of the Last Supper' Debate* (Supplements to the Journal for the Study of Judaism 159; Leiden: Brill, 2012).

Schiffman, L. H. *Reclaiming the Dead Sea Scrolls: The History of Judaism, the Background of Christianity, the Lost Library of Qumran* (Philadelphia, PA: Jewish Publication Society, 1994).

Schiffman, L. H. 'The Sadducean Origins of the Dead Sea Scroll Sect', in H. Shanks (ed.), *Understanding the Dead Sea Scrolls: A Reader from the Biblical Archaeological Review* (New York, NY: Vintage Books, 1993), 35–49.

Schley, D. G., and M. S. Spence 'Zadok', *EDB* 1406–1407.

Schofield, A., and J. C. VanderKam 'Were the Hasmoneans Zadokites?' *JBL* 124.1 (2005), 73–87.

Smith, M. 'What Is Implied by the Variety of Messianic Figures?' *JBL* 78.1 (1959), 66–72.

Stegemann, H. *The Library of Qumran: On the Essenes, Qumran, John the Baptist, and Jesus* (Grand Rapids, MI: Eerdmans, 1998).

VanderKam, J. C. *Dead Sea Scrolls and the Bible* (Grand Rapids, MI: Eerdmans, 2012).

VanderKam, J. C. *The Dead Sea Scrolls Today* (2nd edn; Grand Rapids, MI: Eerdmans, 2010).

VanderKam, J. C., and P. Flint *The Meaning of the Dead Sea Scrolls: Their Significance for Understanding the Bible, Judaism, Jesus, and Christianity* (San Francisco, CA: HarperSanFrancisco, 2002).

VanderKam, J. C. 'The People of the Dead Sea Scrolls: Essenes or Sadducees?', in H. Shanks (ed.), *Understanding the Dead Sea Scrolls: A Reader from the Biblical Archaeological Review* (New York, NY: Vintage Books, 1993), 50–62.

Vermes, G., and M. D. Goodman *The Essenes: According to the Classical Sources* (Oxford Centre Text-Books; Sheffield: JSOT Press, 1989).

Vielhauer, P., and G. Strecker 'Introduction' to 'The Gospel of the Hebrews', *NTApoc* (2nd edn; Louisville, KY: Westminster John Knox Press, 1991), 172–78.

Wolters, A. 'The Meaning of Ṣantĕrôt (Zech 4:12)', *JHebS* 12 article 1, http://www.jhsonline.org/Articles/article_163.pdf [accessed 27 September 2019].

CHAPTER 4

'Doing the Will of the Father in Heaven' In Matthew 7:21: Polemics and Law Observance

Emily Fero-Kovassy

Abstract

This paper examines the Gospel of Matthew's emphasis on 'doing the will of the Father in heaven' in Matthew 7:21 in light of the Gospel's Jewish context. It briefly outlines the semantics of the 'will of God' in Jewish thought in biblical, apocryphal, pseudepigraphal, intertestamental, and Tannaitic literature, and then traces the continuities and developments of these semantics in the New Testament, and in Matthew 7:21. It also analyses the polemical characteristic of the Matthean motif of 'doing the will of the Father in heaven' by means of a redaction-critical analysis of Matthew 7:21-23. This paper argues that law observance is an inherent part of 'doing God's will' in Jewish thought, and that a comparison with other New Testament texts highlights that Matthew 7:21 draws upon this Jewish semantic. It also argues that Matthew purposefully redacts and rearranges this motif into a strategically polemical context within his narrative.

Amongst the vastness of its pages, the Babylonian Talmud provides a forthright explanation of the relationship between obedience to the 'will of God' and the divine sonship of Israel:

> You are called sons and you are called slaves. When you fulfill the will of the Omnipresent (בזמן שאתם עושין רצונו של מקום), you are called sons; when you do not fulfill the will of the Omnipresent (ובזמן שאין אתם עושין רצונו של מקום) you are called slaves. (*b. Bava Batra* 10a)[1]

This image of sonship as co-dependent on obedience to the divine will evokes further imagery of God's fatherhood, Israel's chosenness, and the covenant which binds them. The tendency of the Amoraim to conceive of God's will through a covenantal lens was inherited from their Tannaitic predecessors, who, when commenting on Deuteronomy 20:19–20, not only associate obedience to the will of their Father in heaven with the performance of Torah, but also with the rewards and punishments that result from obedience and disobedience respectively:

> If trees, which do not see, and which do not hear, and which do not speak, because they do not grow fruits, the Omnipresent did not pity them against removing them from the world, then a man who does not do Torah (אדם שאינו עושה את התורה) and does not do the will of his Father in heaven (ואינו עושה רצון אביו שבשמים), how much more so will the Holy One not pity him against removing him from the world. (Sifra *Kedoshim* 4.11.7)

Such associations were not, however, innovations of the rabbis. Prior to the compilation of the Mishnah and the halakhic midrashim, a first-century Jew, who also perceived of God as a Father in heaven, and of God's chosen people as his children, associated obedience to God's will with obedience to Mosaic law, and warned of the salvific consequences for

---

1   The Hebrew text and English translation of the Babylonian Talmud, and the Sifra below, are taken from The Sefaria Library (https://www.sefaria.org/texts), with minor corrections made by Dr Nathan Wolski.

disobedience to this divine will.² This first-century Jew was likewise informed by the centuries of Jewish reflection on the nature and content of God's will which preceded him. The work of this first-century Jew, however, was not circulated, revered, or preserved in the libraries of Jewish literature, but in the scriptural canon of what would become Christianity in the form of a Gospel according to Matthew.

This essay examines the Gospel of Matthew's emphasis on 'doing the will of the Father in heaven' in Matthew 7:21 in light of the recent scholarly focus on the Gospel's Jewishness.³ In order to provide historical and theological context to the Matthean emphasis on doing the Father's will, this essay outlines the semantics of the 'will of God' in Jewish thought in biblical, apocryphal, pseudepigraphal, intertestamental, and Tannaitic literature, and then traces the continuities and developments of these semantics in the New Testament more broadly, and in Matthew 7:21 more specifically.⁴ It also analyses the polemical characteristic of the Matthean motif of 'doing the will of the Father in heaven' by means of a redaction-critical analysis of Matthew 7:21–23.

This essay seeks to demonstrate that law observance is an inherent part of 'doing God's will' in Jewish thought, and that a comparison with the rhetoric of 'doing God's will' found in other New Testament texts highlights that Matthew's call to 'do the will of the Father in heaven' in 7:21 draws upon this Jewish semantic. In addition, this essay demonstrates that Matthew purposefully redacts and rearranges this motif into a strategically polemical context within his narrative (Matt. 7:21–23) that addresses the issue of entry into the eschatological

---

2   By 'a first-century Jew', I refer to the anonymous author of the Gospel of Matthew, whom I refer to throughout this paper as 'Matthew', although I believe it is highly possible that this statement could also apply to the historical Jesus.
3   A number of monographs from the late 1980's and 1990's instigated a critical re-evaluation of the Gospel's Jewishness in recent times. See for example, Levine, *Social and Ethnic Dimensions*; Overman, *Matthew's Gospel and Formative Judaism*; Saldarini, *Matthew's Jewish Christian Community*; Sim, *Matthew and Christian Judaism*.
4   That is, God's 'will' as denoted variously by θέλημα (*thelēma*, 'will'), as in Matt. 7:21; 12:50; 21:31, or θέλησις (*thelēsis*, 'will') and the Hebrew/Aramaic substantive and verbal equivalents רָצוֹן (*ratson*, 'will'), חָפֵץ (*hafets*, 'to desire, delight in'), צְבָא (*tseva*, Aram. 'desire'), as well as other terms such as βουλή (*boulē*, 'will, counsel'), βούλημα (*boulēma*, 'purpose, will'), βούλησις (*boulēsis*, 'willing, wish, desire'), βουλητός (*boulētos*, 'the object of desire, will'), γνώμη (*gnōmē*, 'thought, understanding, reason, will'), and the verbal cognates ἐθέλω/θέλω (*ethelō/thelō*, 'to be willing, wish') and βούλομαι (*boulomai*, 'to will, want').

kingdom. As other New Testament texts depict obedience to God's will in separation from or opposition to law observance, this essay suggests that the rhetoric of '(dis)obedience to God's will' was used polemically in the debates within the nascent church regarding the relevance of Mosaic law for Christ-believers, and that Matthew 7:21 may be evidence of such debate.

1. The Will of God in Jewish Thought

A survey of the occurrences of 'God's will' in biblical, apocryphal, pseudepigraphal, intertestamental, and Tannaitic literature uncovers three recurring categories of meaning prevalent in Jewish thought in antiquity. In category one, God's will is related to the *unfolding of events*, and in this category, it is God who most often plays the active role. That is, in category one, specific events are said to unfold precisely because it is God's will that they do so. Within this category, the type of events attributed to God's will can be further separated into three groups: 'general' events (any general individual event, or the unfolding of the general course of history more broadly, e.g. Ps. 115:3 MT; Dan. (TH) 4:35; Sir. 43:16b-17a; Josephus, *Ant.* 11.55; 1QS 11:17-18; 1QH^a xviii, 2, 5–6, 9), 'biblical' events (those specifically related to Israelite history as narrated in the biblical accounts, e.g. Ps. 135:6–12 MT; Philo, *Abraham* 115; *Alleg. Interp.* 3.197,239; *Moses* 1.95,287; Josephus, *Ant.* 1.223; 2.209,222; 4.40; 8.207), and 'creative' events (those related to God's act of creation, e.g. 1QH^a ix, 13–15; Philo, *Heir* 246; Josephus, *Ag. Ap.* 2.192).[5] Across these three types of events, we see a number of recurring contextual characteristics. The events can involve God's redemption, preservation, judgement, or punishment of Israel (Isa. 62:4 LXX; Ps. 29:8 LXX; Ezek. 18:23; Pss. Sol. 7:3; Philo, *Heir* 272–73; Josephus,

---

5   When referring to texts common to both the Hebrew Bible and Septuagint, either MT or LXX will follow the chapter/verse citation when there is a need to differentiate between the two (e.g. Isa 48:14 MT; Isa 48:14 LXX). If neither MT nor LXX are stated (e.g. Ezek. 18:23), either the MT is assumed, or the reference is to both. In cases where the numbering of chapters or verses differ between the Hebrew Bible and Septuagint, the Hebrew Bible citation is given in parenthesis (e.g. Ps 39(40):9 refers to Ps 40:9 MT and Ps 39:9 LXX).

Ant. 15.144; 18.119; *m. Avot* 5:20; *t. Berakhot* 3:11), or the defeat of Israel's enemies (1 Macc. 3:58-60; 2 Macc. 12:15–16), and God's will sometimes appears in revelatory contexts (Ps. 102:7 LXX; Tob. 12:14-18; Philo, *Heir* 266; *Rewards* 43–44). This category is perhaps the most common of the three, and finds expression across all the various corpora of Jewish literature surveyed.

Categories two and three, on the other hand, both refer to the individual or collective act of *obeying* or *disobeying* God's will. In category two, (dis)obedience to God's will is defined in terms of complicity with the events from category one which God wants to see unfold. Those who willingly comply with the unfolding of these events are said to 'obey' God's will, while those who resist 'disobey' God's will. This category occurs somewhat frequently in Josephus' *Antiquities* (*Ant.* 1.232,255; 2.291,304,309; 4.8,121; 5.133,278; 6.137,147; 7.373; 8.295; 9.132), but is otherwise relatively infrequent (Isa. 44:24–28; 48:14 MT; Philo, *Moses* 1.95; 1QS 9:23–24; Sifre Deut. 306.7). In category three, however, which is far more common than category two, (dis)obedience to God's will is defined in terms of the observance of Mosaic law. That is, one obeys the will of God through obedience to the stipulations of the law, and disobeys God's will through disobedience to the law. This category occurs in every corpora of Jewish literature surveyed, and is a particularly dominant semantic in apocryphal, pseudepigraphal, intertestamental, and Tannaitic literature (Ps. 39(40):7–9; Ezek. 18:21–23; Ezra 10:10–11 MT; 1 Esd. 8:16; 9:7–9; Jub. 21:2–6; 2 Macc. 1:3–4; T. Iss. 4:2–5:2; 1QS 5:1–13; 9:12–16; 1QS^b 1–5 i, 1–3; CD 3:10–16; Josephus, *Ant.* 1.14; *Ag. Ap.* 2.184; *m. Avot* 2:4; 5:20; *t. Demai* 2:7; Sifra *Kedoshim* 4.11.6,7; Sifre Num. 42.1.2; Sifre Deut. 40.7,12–13; 47.6,9; 114.1; 118.1; 305.3; 306.4,6,9,35). Not only is this semantic rooted in biblical literature, its persistence in Jewish thought well into the First Century, when Matthew's Gospel was itself written, is demonstrated by Josephus:

> [7] Sacrifice and offering you did not want, but ears you fashioned for me. Whole burnt offering and one for sin you did not request. [8] Then I said, 'Look, I have come; in a scroll of a book it is written of me. [9] To do your will (τοῦ ποιῆσαι τὸ

θέλημά σου), O my God, I desired—and your law (τὸν νόμον σου), within my belly.' (Ps. 39:7-9 LXX)[6]

For us, with our conviction that the original institution of the Law was in accordance with the will of God (κατὰ θεοῦ βούλησιν), it would be rank impiety not to observe it. (Josephus, Ag. Ap. 2.184 (Thackeray, LCL))

This common Jewish association of obedience to God's will with law observance becomes crucial when assessing the developing semantics of God's will in the New Testament.

2. The Will of God in the New Testament: Continuities and Developments

In light of the ample concern for God's will found in Jewish textual traditions, it is not surprising that such concern was also prevalent among the earliest followers of Jesus. In the New Testament, the 'will of God' appears in all four Gospels, Acts, in five of the seven undisputed Pauline Letters, four of the seven disputed Pauline Letters, two of the seven universal Letters, and in Revelation—a total of seventeen texts.[7] 'God's will' occurs most frequently in the Gospel of John (8x), followed by Acts (7x), Hebrews (7x), Ephesians (6x), and the Gospel of Matthew (6x), though collectively, it occurs most frequently in the Gospels (18x, though only 1x in Mark and 3x in Luke) and the disputed Pauline Letters (17x), followed by the undisputed Pauline Letters (11x), Acts

---

6   All English translations of the LXX in this paper are taken from NETS.
7   By the 'undisputed' Pauline Letters, I refer to Romans, 1 and 2 Corinthians, Galatians, Philippians, 1 Thessalonians, and Philemon. By 'disputed', I refer to Ephesians, Colossians, 2 Thessalonians, 1 and 2 Timothy, and Titus, as well as Hebrews, which was traditionally attributed to Paul, though the text itself and most modern commentators do not make this claim, and of which the genre is closer to a sermon than a letter. Hence, in addition to the Gospels, Acts, and Revelation, references to 'God's will' (denoted by θέλημα, θέλησις, βουλή, βούλημα, and γνώμη) are found in the following eleven New Testament Epistles: Romans, 1 and 2 Corinthians, Galatians, Ephesians, Colossians, 1 Thessalonians, 2 Timothy, Hebrews, 1 Peter, 1 John.

(7x), the universal Letters (6x), and Revelation (2x).[8]

A survey of the occurrences of 'God's will' in the New Testament highlights a number of continuities and developments within the three recurring categories of meaning found in Jewish texts. In category one, God's will continues to be related to the unfolding of events, whether those events involve the unfolding of the general course of history more broadly (Matt. 6:10; Rom. 9:19; Eph. 1:11), God's preservation of his chosen people (Matt. 18:10–14), or God's act of creation (Rev. 4:11). However, we see two developments within this category regarding the kind of events which God wants to see unfold. Firstly, the events that God 'wills' come to refer to historical events in the life of the early church, particularly those involving the church's ministry and expansion (Acts 5:38–39; Rom. 1:10; 15:32; 2 Cor. 8:5), the most frequent being Paul's apostolic appointment (1 Cor. 1:1; 2 Cor. 1:1; Eph. 1:1; Col. 1:1; 2 Tim. 1:1). Secondly, and more significantly, the events that God 'wills' come to refer specifically to God's salvific plan involving the life, death, and resurrection of Jesus. This development appears throughout the New Testament corpus (John 1:12–13; Acts 22:14–15; Gal. 1:4; Eph. 1:3–10; Heb. 2:1–4; 6:17; 10:10), including the synoptic accounts of Jesus' prayer to his Father prior to his arrest (Matt. 26:36–46 // Mark 14:32–42 // Luke 22:39–46). A particularly clear example of this development occurs in the Gospel of John, in which Jesus defines God's will in terms of the final resurrection promised for those who believe in him:

> [39] And this is the will of him who sent me (τοῦτο δέ ἐστιν τὸ θέλημα τοῦ πέμψαντός με), that I should lose nothing of all that he has given me, but raise it up on the last day. [40] This

---

8 θέλημα is used explicitly or implicitly to denotes God's will fifty times in the following passages: Matt. 6:10; 7:21; 12:50; 18:14; 21:31; 26:42; Mark 3:35; Luke 11:2; 22:42; John 1:13; 4:34; 5:30; 6:38,39,40; 7:17; 9:31; Acts 13:22; 22:14; Rom. 1:10; 2:18; 12:2; 15:32; 1 Cor. 1:1; 2 Cor. 1:1; 8:5; Gal. 1:4; Eph. 1:1,5,9,11; 6:6; Col. 1:1,9; 4:12; 1 Thess. 4:3; 5:18; 2 Tim. 1:1; Heb. 10:7,9,10,36; 13:21; 1 Pet. 2:15; 3:17; 4:2,19; 1 John 2:17; 5:14; Rev. 4:11. The New Testament also represents God's will, though less frequently so, by a variety of other terms, including θέλησις (Heb. 2:4), βουλή (Luke 7:30; Acts 2:23; 4:28; 5:38; 13:36; 20:27; Eph. 1:11; Heb. 6:17), βούλημα (Rom. 9:19), and γνώμη (Rev. 17:17). These passages have been taken from their respective entries in Smith, *Greek-English Concordance to the New Testament*, §2307, §2308, §1012, §1013, §1106, but only represent cases in which θέλημα, θέλησις, βουλή, βούλημα, and γνώμη refer specifically to God.

is indeed the will of my Father (τοῦτο γάρ ἐστιν τὸ θέλημα τοῦ πατρός μου), that all who see the Son and believe in him may have eternal life; and I will raise them up on the last day. (John 6:39–40 NRSV)[9]

In category two, (dis)obedience to God's will is still defined in terms of complicity with the events God wishes to unfold—however, the events requiring complicity are predominantly related to God's salvific plan regarding the life, death, and resurrection of Jesus. As such, one development we find is that Jesus himself becomes the individual 'doer' of God's will by actively complying with his assigned role in God's salvific plan. This development is a noticeable feature of the Gospel of John, but also occurs in Hebrews 10:5–10, and is implicit in the Synoptics (Matt. 26:36–46 // Mark 14:32–42 // Luke 22:39–46):[10]

> [36] Jesus said to them, 'I am the bread of life. Whoever comes to me will never be hungry, and whoever believes in me will never be thirsty. [36] But I said to you that you have seen me and yet do not believe. [37] Everything that the Father gives me will come to me, and anyone who comes to me I will never drive away; [38] for I have come down from heaven, not to do my own will, but the will of him who sent me' (οὐχ ἵνα ποιῶ τὸ θέλημα τὸ ἐμὸν ἀλλὰ τὸ θέλημα τοῦ πέμψαντός με). (John 6:36–38, cf. 4:34; 5:30; 9:31)

Carrying out God's will was not, however, solely understood within the Jesus movement as the responsibility of Jesus alone. Obedience to God's will, being his overall salvific plan, was also the responsibility of the followers of Jesus themselves. Hence, a second development is that followers of Jesus demonstrate their complicity with God's salvific plan, and

---

9   All translations of the New Testament in this paper are those of the NRSV, and the Greek text is that of NA.[28]

10 Mathew Palachuvattil argues that Matt. 26:42 demonstrates that 'Jesus himself fulfilled the will of God and acted as God's chosen instrument in realizing His design of salvation in an exemplary manner'. See Palachuvattil, "*The One Who Does the* Will *of the Father*", 64 (see also pp.260–61, 277, 282). This semantic is also alluded to in Mohrlang, *Matthew and Paul*, 76–77; France, *The Gospel According to Matthew*, 373–74; Harrington, *The Gospel of Matthew*, 373, 377; Keener, *The Gospel of Matthew*, 639.

therefore obedience to God's 'will', by either exhibiting faith in God's plan or Jesus as the Messiah (the logical implication of John 6:40, cf. 3:15–16,18,36; 6:28–29,35,47; 11:25–26), or enduring the suffering involved in following Jesus:

> ¹⁷ For it is better to suffer for doing good, if suffering should be God's will (εἰ θέλοι τὸ θέλημα τοῦ θεοῦ), than to suffer for doing evil. ¹⁸ For Christ also suffered for sins once for all, the righteous for the unrighteous, in order to bring you to God. (1 Pet. 3:17–18, cf. 4:1–2,17–19; Heb. 10:32–39)

These developments, however, are relatively limited, and we now, therefore, turn our attention to the more frequent and significant semantic developments that occur within the third category of meaning. In category three, there arises predominantly in the Pauline literature an important development in relation to the carrying out of God's will—namely, the rhetorical opposition or separation of 'God's will' from Mosaic law. In these texts, (dis)obedience to God's will is either defined in opposition to law observance, or in terms of moral behaviour in separation from law observance. In his Letter to the Romans, for example, Paul critiques Jews who claim knowledge of God's will through their knowledge of the law whilst simultaneously breaking the law (Rom. 2:17–24, cf. John 7:14–24), but without conversely stating that *keeping* the law leads to fulfilment of God's will. On other occasions, Paul presents obedience to God's will for Gentiles as achievable through correct moral behaviour in separation from formal observance of the law in its entirety (Rom. 12:2–13:14; 1 Thess. 4:3–6; 5:12–22). Put another way, *in the Pauline rhetoric of (dis)obedience to God's will,* the law only aids obedience to God's will in its capacity to effect moral behaviour, but not 'as a comprehensive body of rules governing the details of daily life and behaviour'.[11] This semantic development is not without attestation in the disputed Pauline Epistles. The Letter to the Ephesians outlines the behaviour expected of slaves within the household: 'Slaves, obey your

---

11 While I am not advocating that Paul has a completely negative stance towards Mosaic law, this is one of three ways Mohrlang argues that the law has ended in Christ in Pauline thought (*Matthew and Paul*, 34). The other two are 'as a means of salvation', and 'as a power that gives sin its authority'.

earthly masters with fear and trembling, in singleness of heart, as you obey Christ; not only while being watched, and in order to please them, but as slaves of Christ, doing the will of God from the heart (ποιοῦντες τὸ θέλημα τοῦ θεοῦ)' (Eph. 6:5–6).[12] That such conduct is independent of law observance is implied from the Letter's earlier assertion that Jesus 'has abolished the law with its commandments and ordinances' (Eph. 2:15).[13]

The semantic development in which (dis)obedience to God's will is defined either in *opposition* to law observance, or in terms of moral behaviour in *separation* from law observance signifies a significant departure from typical Jewish semantics regarding God's will. Not all New Testament texts that address (dis)obedience to God's will, however, depart from standard Jewish semantics. Matthew's Gospel stands out from the texts cited above in that it remains closely aligned with typical Jewish semantics by presenting (dis)obedience to God's will in terms of law observance.

3. Doing the Father's Will in Matthew 7:21: Polemics and Law Observance

That Matthew's emphasis on 'doing the will of the Father in heaven' in Matthew 7:21 aligns with the standard third category of meaning

---

12   Interestingly, the moral behaviour described in the preceding chapter in Eph. 5:3–20 (namely, avoidance of fornication, impurity, vulgar talk, greed, deception, getting drunk with wine, etc.) is demanded on account of it being the 'Lord's will' (τὸ θέλημα τοῦ κυρίου, Eph. 5:17), though here the 'Lord' refers to Jesus rather than God (see Merkle, *Ephesians*, 173).

13   As with the undisputed Pauline Letters, this is not to say that Ephesians has an entirely negative view of the law. Tet-Lim N. Yee, who re-evaluates chapter 2 of Ephesians in light of the 'new perspectives' on Paul instigated by Sanders and Dunn, posits that Ephesians is written by a Jew from a Jewish perspective, and articulates Jewish attitudes towards Gentiles and notions of 'covenantal ethnocentrism' in order to promote ethnic reconciliation made possible through Christ's blood (see Yee, *Jews, Gentiles and Ethnic Reconciliation*). He argues that Eph. 2:15 is not, therefore, a critique of the law *per se*, but of the law being used as a 'boundary marker' which creates ethnic divisions between Jews and Gentiles, and would restrict God's grace to one particular ethnic group. See particularly Yee's discussion of the 'dividing wall' in Eph. 2:14c and the 'law with its commandments and ordinances' in 2:15a (pp.144–48, 154–61). However, as the Letter is addressed to Gentiles Christians (p.33), it is nonetheless still probable that obedience to God's will through proper household conduct is, in light of Eph. 2:15, portrayed in this context as achievable in separation from law observance.

found in Jewish textual traditions is best articulated by first demonstrating how these passages *do not* exhibit the semantic developments found elsewhere in the New Testament. The motif itself appears within the context of the Sermon on the Mount (Matt. 5:1–7:29):

> ²¹ Not everyone who says to me, 'Lord, Lord,' will enter the kingdom of heaven, but only the one who does the will of my Father in heaven (ἀλλ' ὁ ποιῶν τὸ θέλημα τοῦ πατρός μου τοῦ ἐν τοῖς οὐρανοῖς). ²² On that day many will say to me, 'Lord, Lord, did we not prophesy in your name, and cast out demons in your name, and do many deeds of power in your name?' ²³ Then I will declare to them, 'I never knew you; go away from me, you evildoers.' (Matt. 7:21–23)

Beginning with the second category of meaning, we must first consider whether it is possible (or plausible) that obedience to 'the will of the Father in heaven' is understood here in terms of complicity with specific events. Because God's will came to be understood within the Jesus movement in relation to the unfolding of God's salvific plan through the life, death, and resurrection of Jesus, (dis)obedience to God's will through complicity with this salvific plan came to be understood as achievable in two different ways. Either Jesus himself obeys God's will by actively complying with God's salvific plan, or individuals demonstrate their obedience to God's will through their faith or their endurance of suffering as followers of Jesus.

A plain reading of Matthew 7:21–23 indicates that neither of these interpretations is applicable to this Matthean pericope. In the first instance, Jesus is not presented as the individual 'doer' of God's will—rather, Jesus himself describes obedience to the Father's will as a requirement for others who wish to enter the kingdom of heaven. Secondly, obedience to the 'will of the Father in heaven' cannot be equated with faith in God's plan or Jesus as Christ, precisely because Jesus emphatically denies this—*not* everyone who confesses him as 'Lord, Lord' and performs miraculous acts in his name, but *only* those who do the will of his Father in heaven will enter the kingdom. That obedience to the 'will of the Father in heaven' could refer to enduring suffering, however, is possible. The Sermon's Beatitudes give blessings to those who are reviled and persecuted (5:10–12, cf. 5:44). Persecution, however, receives only minor attention within the overall Sermon, making the connection unlikely.

Moving to the third category of meaning, we must next consider whether obedience to 'the will of the Father in heaven' in 7:21 exhibits the semantic development found elsewhere in the New Testament— that is, whether it refers to moral behaviour in opposition to or separation from law observance. That the action required for fulfilling God's will in 7:21 could refer to the practice of general moral behaviour is supported by the Sermon's overall development, in which Jesus outlines the moral conduct expected of the Sermon's addressees (Matt. 5:3–12; 6:1–8; 6:14–7:5).[14] That such concern for moral behaviour should be understood in opposition to or separation from the stipulations of Mosaic law is, however, fiercely negated by the Matthean Jesus' assertion that the law remains valid (5:17–20, cf. 7:12; 19:16–22; 22:34–40), as well as the Sermon's interpretation of six Mosaic commandments (5:21–48), in which Jesus does not dismiss but rather 'builds a fence around the law' (*m. Avot* 1:1).[15] While moral behaviour is emphasised by both, Matthew's adherence to typical Jewish associations of obedience to God's will with the observance of Mosaic law is illuminated when presented side by side with the opposition of obedience to God's will and Mosaic law found in Ephesians:

---

14   Stanton, *A Gospel for a New People*, 299.
15   The six laws interpreted in the so-called 'antitheses' concern murder (Exod. 20:13; 21:12; Lev. 24:17; Num. 35:16; Deut. 5:17), adultery (Exod. 20:13–14; Lev. 20:10; Deut. 5:17–18), divorce (Deut. 24:1-4), oaths and vows (Exod. 20:7; Lev. 19:12; Num. 30:3–16 Deut. 5:11), the distribution of justice (Exod. 21:23–25; Lev. 24:19–20; Deut. 19:21), and loving one's neighbour (Lev. 19:18). For arguments against reading any of the antitheses as abrogations of the law, see Harrington, *The Gospel of Matthew*, 90–92, and more recently Loader, *Jesus' Attitude towards the Law*, 165–82.

Eph. 2:13–16	Matt. 5:17–20
¹³ But now in Christ Jesus you who once were far off have been brought near by the blood of Christ. ¹⁴ For he is our peace; in his flesh he has made both groups into one and has broken down the dividing wall, that is, the hostility between us. ¹⁵ He has abolished the law with its commandments and ordinances, that he might create in himself one new humanity in place of the two, thus making peace, ¹⁶ and might reconcile both groups to God in one body through the cross, thus putting to death that hostility through it.	¹⁷ "Do not think that I have come to abolish the law or the prophets; I have come not to abolish but to fulfill. ¹⁸ For truly I tell you, until heaven and earth pass away, not one letter, not one stroke of a letter, will pass from the law until all is accomplished. ¹⁹ Therefore, whoever breaks one of the least of these commandments, and teaches others to do the same, will be called least in the kingdom of heaven; but whoever does them and teaches them will be called great in the kingdom of heaven. ²⁰ For I tell you, unless your righteousness exceeds that of the scribes and Pharisees, you will never enter the kingdom of heaven.
Eph. 6:5–6	Matt. 7:21
⁵ Slaves, obey your earthly masters with fear and trembling, in singleness of heart, as you obey Christ; ⁶ not only while being watched, and in order to please them, but as slaves of Christ, doing the will of God from the heart.	Not everyone who says to me, 'Lord, Lord,' will enter the kingdom of heaven, but only the one who does the will of my Father in heaven.

Having established the inherent Jewishness of this Matthean motif, we now turn to explore the polemical function of Matthew's emphasis on 'doing the will of the Father in heaven' in 7:21 through a redaction-critical consideration of the pericope unit 7:21–23. A few clarifications, however, are needed first. The following assessment of Matthew's redactional activity assumes Markan priority. The relationship between Matthew and Luke, however, is complex and widely debated. An increasing number of scholars argue for Lukan dependence on Matthew, while many continue to support the existence of a hypothetical 'Q' source common to Matthew and Luke.[16] Neither hypothesis, however, automatically proves Matthean redaction of traditional material in cases of the double tradition, unless, in the case the existence of Q is assumed, it can be demonstrated that Luke retains the more primitive form of the tradition, which is itself a problematic endeavour. Nonetheless, the following analysis assumes that, as a coherent author, Matthew's choice to include or exclude traditional material from his sources, and how Matthew arranges any traditional material within his wider narrative, is itself a form of redaction which reflects his theological position, and reveals his construction of polemic.

As already noted, the first of the three occurrences of the Matthean motif of 'doing the will of the Father in heaven' (Matt. 7:21; 12:50; 21:31), which is the focus of this essay, appears in Matthew 7:21–23, the second last pericope in the Sermon on the Mount (Matt. 5:1–7:29 // Luke 6:17–49). This pericope has two parallels in Luke (but none in Mark), the first of which also appears in Luke's Sermon on the Plain (Matt. 7:21 // Luke 6:46), while the second appears further on in the Lukan narrative (Matt. 7:22–23 // Luke 13:26–27):

---

16 Lukan dependence on Matthew is known as the 'Farrer hypothesis', named after A. M. Farrer's article 'On Dispensing with Q', 55–88. For a recent critique of the Q hypothesis, see Goodacre, *The Case Against Q*.

Matt. 7:21–23	Luke 6:46
²¹ Not everyone who says to me, 'Lord, Lord,' will enter the kingdom of heaven, but only the one who does the will of my Father in heaven (ὁ ποιῶν τὸ θέλημα τοῦ πατρός μου τοῦ ἐν τοῖς οὐρανοῖς).	⁴⁶ Why do you call me 'Lord, Lord,' and do not do what I tell you?
	Luke 13:26–27
²² On that day many will say to me, 'Lord, Lord, did we not prophesy in your name, and cast out demons in your name, and do many deeds of power in your name?'	²⁶ Then you will begin to say, 'We ate and drank with you, and you taught in our streets.'
²³ Then I will declare to them, 'I never knew you; go away from me you evildoers (ἀποχωρεῖτε ἀπ' ἐμοῦ οἱ ἐργαζόμενοι τὴν ἀνομίαν).'	²⁷ But he will say, 'I do not know where you come from; go away from me, all you evildoers (ἀπόστητε ἀπ' ἐμοῦ πάντες ἐργάται ἀδικίας)!'

In the first parallel (Matt. 7:21 // Luke 6:46), the motif of 'doing the will of the Father in heaven', and the qualification that this is the pre-requisite for inclusion in the eschatological 'kingdom of heaven', appears only in the Matthean logion. In the second parallel (Matt. 7:22–23 // Luke 13:26–27), the actions being criticised also differ between the Matthean and Lukan versions. In Matthew, the individual being chastised mistakenly appeals to their acts of prophecy, exorcism, and doing powerful deeds in Jesus' name, while in Luke they appeal to the fact that they had eaten and drunk with Jesus, and that Jesus had taught in their streets. Finally, Jesus' condemnation in Matthew 7:23 and Luke 13:27 are both quotations of Psalm 6:9, though Matthew remains closer to the wording of the Septuagint by retaining 'οἱ ἐργαζόμενοι τὴν ἀνομίαν' (*oi ergazomenoi tēn anomian*, 'workers of lawlessness') which Luke changes to 'ἐργάται ἀδικίας' (*ergatai adikias*, 'workers of injustice'), though Matthew omits 'πάντες' (*pantes*, 'all'), and has 'ἀποχωρεῖτε' (*apochōreite*, 'go away, depart') in place of 'ἀπόστητε' (*apostēte*, 'go away, depart'):

> Keep away from me, all you who practice lawlessness (ἀπόστητε ἀπ' ἐμοῦ, πάντες οἱ ἐργαζόμενοι τὴν ἀνομίαν), because the Lord listened to the voice of my weeping. (Ps. 6:9 LXX)

David Sim suggests that Matthew 7:21–23 is a Matthean redaction, coming from a combination of two Q texts (Q 6:46; 13:26–27) which Matthew has edited, and is secondary to the more original Lukan parallels, arguing that each individual verse has been purposefully redacted in order to create an anti-Pauline polemic.[17] He argues that v.21 is a response to Paul's affirmation that 'no one can say "Jesus is Lord", except by the Holy Spirit' (1 Cor. 12:3) and that 'everyone who calls on the name of the Lord shall be saved' (Rom. 10:9–13). He also argues that Matthew has changed Luke's 'eating, drinking, teaching' triplet (Luke 13:26) to 'prophecy, exorcism, miracle working' (Matt. 7:22) as these were characteristics of the Pauline churches.[18] Finally, he argues that Matthew's refutation of the 'evildoers', or 'workers of lawlessness' (οἱ ἐργαζόμενοι τὴν ἀνομίαν), is a criticism of those who are not Torah observant, as indicated by the use of ἀνομία (*anomia*, 'lawlessness'), which Matthew has intentionally retained from the Psalm for this purpose.[19]

While Sim's arguments have not been widely accepted, they do highlight the role that Matthew's redactional activity plays in the creation of his polemic. The polemical flavour of this pericope is further enhanced when considering the pericopes which immediately precede and follow it. Preceding Matthew 7:21–23 is an eschatologically inspired analogy of good and bad fruit, which although it has a parallel in Luke, includes an introductory warning against 'false prophets' that is a unique Matthean addition:[20]

---

17 Sim, 'Matthew 7.21–23', 325–43. For the reconstructed Q passages, see Robinson et al., eds., *The Sayings Gospel Q*, 90–91, 130–31.
18 Sim points to 1 Cor. 12:4–11 and 12:27–28 as evidence that prophecy and miracle working were characteristic of the Pauline churches, and argues that while exorcism is not mentioned in Paul's Letters, later traditions (e.g. Acts) testify to Paul as exorcising. He further highlights that Matthew also omits Mark's account of the strange exorcist who casts out demons in Jesus' name (Mark 9:38–40) in order to discredit claims to authority outside of the Jerusalem church and to dismiss that Paul was acting in accordance with Jesus, and that Matthew's omission of this pericope influences his redaction of 7:22. See Sim, 'Matthew 7.21–23', 334–41.
19 Sim, 'Matthew 7.21–23', 341.
20 The identification of the 'false prophets' in Matt. 7:15, and whether they are the same people as the 'evildoers' of 7:23 has long been debated. See Hill, 'False Prophets and Charismatics', 327–48.

Matt. 7:15–20	Luke 6:43–45
¹⁵ Beware of false prophets, who come to you in sheep's clothing but inwardly are ravenous wolves. ¹⁶ You will know them by their fruits. Are grapes gathered from thorns, or figs from thistles? ¹⁷ In the same way, every good tree bears good fruit, but the bad tree bears bad fruit. ¹⁸ A good tree cannot bear bad fruit, nor can a bad tree bear good fruit. ¹⁹ Every tree that does not bear good fruit is cut down and thrown into the fire. ²⁰ Thus you will know them by their fruits.	⁴³ No good tree bears bad fruit, nor again does a bad tree bear good fruit; ⁴⁴ for each tree is known by its own fruit. Figs are not gathered from thorns, nor are grapes picked from a bramble bush. ⁴⁵ The good person out of the good treasure of the heart produces good, and the evil person out of evil treasure produces evil; for it is out of the abundance of the heart that the mouth speaks.

In addition to the warning against 'false prophets' attached to the beginning of the pericope, the polemical nature of Matthew's redaction is further indicated by his use of the same analogy of good and bad fruit in a chastisement and eschatological warning against the Pharisees and Sadducees who come to John for baptism (Matt. 3:7–10). In the Lukan parallel (Luke 3:7–9), this chastisement is directed more generally to the crowds. Matthew applies the fruit analogy again in a similar manner against the Pharisees further on in the narrative:

> ³³ Either make the tree good, and its fruit good; or make the tree bad, and its fruit bad; for the tree is known by its fruit. ³⁴ You brood of vipers! How can you speak good things, when you are evil? For out of the abundance of the heart the mouth speaks. ³⁵ The good person brings good things out of a good treasure, and the evil person brings evil things out of an evil treasure. ³⁶ I tell you, on the day of judgment you will have to give an account for every careless word you utter; ³⁷

for by your words you will be justified, and by your words you will be condemned. (Matt. 12:33–37, cf. 21:43)

Moving to the pericope immediately following Matthew 7:21–23, Matthew 7:24–27 provides an analogy of a house built on rock:

> ²⁴ Everyone then who hears these words of mine and acts on them will be like a wise man who built his house on rock (ἐπὶ τὴν πέτραν). ²⁵ The rain fell, the floods came, and the winds blew and beat on that house, but it did not fall, because it had been founded on rock (ἐπὶ τὴν πέτραν). ²⁶ And everyone who hears these words of mine and does not act on them will be like a foolish man who built his house on sand. ²⁷ The rain fell, and the floods came, and the winds blew and beat against that house, and it fell—and great was its fall! (Matt. 7:24–27)

While this analogy is paralleled in Luke 6:47–49, Sim suggests that the 'house built on rock' in the Matthean version is a reference to Peter (Πέτρος, *Petros*), who is referred to as a 'rock' (πέτρα, *petra*) in Matthew 16:18.[21] This identification of Peter as the rock upon which the church is built is absent from the Lukan and Markan accounts of Peter's confession (Mark 8:27–30 // Luke 9:18–21). Sim argues that the Matthean version of this analogy is intended to promote the apostolic authority of Peter in the early church over Paul, who claims that 'the rock was Christ' (1 Cor. 10:4c), and by placing this analogy immediately following the redacted logia of 7:21–23, Matthew is constructing an extended anti-Pauline polemic.

Matthew's redaction of 7:21–23 and the two pericopes surrounding it indicate that the Matthean motif of 'doing the will of the Father in heaven' (7:21) serves a polemical function. Due to the 'hidden' nature of this polemic, however, the identity of the 'evildoers' who fail

---

21 'And I tell you, you are Peter (Πέτρος), and on this rock (ἐπὶ ταύτῃ τῇ πέτρᾳ) I will build my church, and the gates of Hades will not prevail against it' (Matt. 16:18). See Sim, 'Matthew's Anti-Paulinism', 779; 'Matthew and the Pauline Corpus,' 414–15. Palachuvattil notes that it is the foundation which saves the house from falling in Matthew, while in the Lukan parallel, it is the building of the house which saves it (*'The One Who Does the Will of the Father'*, 115).

to 'do the will of the Father in heaven' has long been debated.[22] David Hill argues that the evildoers of 7:23 refer to members within the Matthean congregation whose reliance on charismatic actions alone are insufficient in gaining entry into the kingdom of heaven.[23] They are not, he argues, antinomians outside of the congregation, as had been suggested by earlier scholars.[24] Anthony Saldarini argues that 7:21–23 addresses several groups and issues within the Jesus movement, possibly the 'leaders who differ from Matthew on how Jesus' teaching is to be understood and lived', though he too implies that these are not outsiders entering the group, but charismatic prophets within the community itself.[25] As already noted, Sim argues that the entirety of 7:13–27 is directed towards rival Pauline, law-free churches whose 'numerical supremacy' is threatening their own law-observant church.[26]

Scholars generally agree that Matthew has intentionally redacted 7:21–23 in order to construct a polemical description of the prerequisite for entry into the kingdom of heaven, and that what is being chastised is a reliance on charismatic works without a concern for good deeds, correct praxis, and 'doing the will of the Father in heaven'. What is not agreed upon, however, is precisely who Matthew is addressing in this pericope, and relatedly, what precisely 'doing the will of the Father in heaven' entails. I argue, however, that Matthew's call to 'do the will of the Father in heaven' in 7:21 draws upon typical Jewish semantics in which obedience to God's will is understood in terms of the

---

22 In an appendix to his study of rival Jewish and Christian biblical interpretations in late antiquity, Marc Hirshman discusses how to interpret polemics in Midrash, in which he differentiates between the 'open' and the 'hidden controversy' (see Hirshman, *A Rivalry of Genius*, 125–30). In an 'open controversy', the polemical text 'explicitly mentions its ideological rival, either by name or appellation' (p.126). The 'hidden controversy', or 'hidden polemic', is one in which certain hermeneutical methods are adopted or changed in order to rebuff a rival's views, though the identity of the rival is not explicitly stated.
23 Hill, 'False Prophets and Charismatics', 340–48. By means of a redactional-critical analysis of Matt. 7:15–23 (see pp.333–40), Hill argues that the charismatic evildoers of vv.21–23 are a separate group from the 'false prophets' Matthew warns against in the preceding verses (vv.15–20). He posits that these 'false prophets' may very well refer to the Pharisees, who are infiltrating the Matthean community from the outside in an attempt to convince its members of their errors.
24 For a critique of the earlier antinomian hypothesis prior to Sim's arguments, see Hill, 'False Prophets and Charismatics', 333–40.
25 Saldarini, *Matthew's Jewish Christian Community*, 104–6. Saldarini agrees with Hill that the false prophets of the preceding vv.15–20 refer to rival Jewish teachers in leadership positions.
26 Sim, *Matthew and Christian Judaism*, 209–11.

observance of Mosaic law, and that Matthew is here making a polemical statement about the necessity of law observance for entry into the eschatological kingdom.

4. Conclusion

The New Testament exhibits a number of continuities and discontinuities within the three recurring categories of meaning regarding God's will found throughout Jewish texts in antiquity. It shows continuity in that each of the three categories remains intact. It shows discontinuity in that each category undergoes certain developments. In category one, in which God's will is related to the unfolding of events, two developments occur within the Jesus movement. In the first, God's will becomes related to the unfolding of historical events in the life of the early church. In the second, God's will is linked to the unfolding of his salvific plan involving the life, death, and resurrection of Jesus. In category two, in which (dis)obedience to God's will is defined in terms of complicity with the events God wants to see unfold, two developments also occur. In the first, Jesus becomes the individual 'doer' of God's will by actively complying with his assigned role in God's salvific plan. In the second, individuals demonstrate their complicity to God's salvific plan, and therefore their obedience to God's will, by either having faith in God's plan, and Jesus as the Christ, or by enduring the suffering inherent in following Jesus. In category three, in which (dis)obedience to God's will is defined in terms law observance, there is one significant development. In this development, (dis)obedience to God's will comes to be defined either in opposition to Mosaic law, or in terms of moral behaviour in separation from Mosaic law (Rom. 2:17–24; 12:2–13:14; 1 Thess. 4:3–6; 5:12–22; Eph. 2:13–16; 6:5–6, cf. John 7:14–24). The Gospel of Matthew's emphasis on 'doing the will of the Father in heaven' in 7:21, however, remains more closely aligned with the standard semantic found in the third category of meaning prevalent among Jewish texts in that it demands a commitment to the observance of Mosaic law, as interpreted by Jesus.

This essay has also demonstrated through a redaction-critical analysis of Matthew 7:21–23 that Matthew has intentionally arranged the motif of 'doing the will of the Father in heaven' in 7:21 into a polemical context which addresses the issue of entry into the eschatological kingdom of heaven. It is therefore tempting to conclude that Matthew's emphasis on doing the Father's will in 7:21 (which is unquestionably directed to fellow Christ-believers) is an intentional corrective to the belief held by other Christ-believers, particularly those of the Pauline persuasion, that law observance was no longer necessary for followers of Jesus. At this point, however, we run into problems regarding textual audience and genre. The Pauline Epistles, which downplay the requirement of law observance for obedience to God's will, are predominantly addressed to *Gentiles*, but as Paula Fredriksen has argued, there is no reason to believe that Paul was opposed to law observance by *Jewish* Christ-believers.[27] Matthew's Gospel, on the other hand, while likely received by some Gentiles, has a predominantly *Jewish* concern, and due to the genre of the Gospel, which narrates the ministry of Jesus *to Israel* (10:5–6; 15:24), Matthew nowhere *explicitly* addresses the issue of *Gentile* law observance.[28] His promotion of the law is addressed to Jews. As Davies and Allison note (though recognising that this is a generalisation), there were three varying attitudes regarding the necessity of law observance amongst followers of Jesus in the First Century: the first believed *both* Jews and Gentiles were required to observe the law, the second believed that *neither* Jew nor Gentile was required to observe the law, while the third believed the law was still binding for Jewish followers of Jesus, but not (or less so) for Gentiles.[29] Whether the Matthean and Pauline definition of (dis) obedience to God's will conflict therefore depends on into which group each is classified—which, for Matthew, remains a contested issue. Debate on whether Matthew belongs to the first or third group rests largely on how you interpret the Gospel's silence on circumcision, and the resurrected Jesus' command to the eleven to 'make disciples

---

27   Fredriksen, 'Why Should a "Law-Free" Mission Mean a "Law-Free" Apostle?', 637–50.
28   Levine, Overman, Saldarini, and Sim believe, however, that Gentile law observance was likely promoted by the evangelist. See Levine, *Social and Ethnic Dimensions*, 77–78, 178–85; Overman, *Matthew's Gospel and Formative Judaism*, 157–58; Saldarini, *Matthew's Jewish Christian Community*, 68–83; Sim, *Matthew and Christian Judaism*, 247–55.
29   Davies and Allison, *Matthew I-VII*, 492–93. Davies and Allison believe Matthew to have belonged to the third group.

of all the nations', 'baptising' them and 'teaching them to obey everything that I have commanded you' (28:19–20).[30] It is not my objective to settle such enormously complex debates. What I do argue, however, is that Matthew uses the rhetoric of 'obedience to the Father's will' as a polemical tactic to make a point about the necessity of law observance, while other New Testament texts use the same rhetoric to make a polemical point about the *limitations* of law observance. I leave the implications of this statement for others to debate. My hope, however, is that my conclusions will be somewhat useful for others who do seek to tackle these more difficult problems within Matthean scholarship— if, of course, that be God's will.

---

30 The Gospel's silence on circumcision, especially in the Great Commission (28:16–20), which mentions only baptism, is taken by some as evidence that it was not required for Gentile followers of Jesus, while others believe the silence indicates an assumption on the part of the evangelist that circumcision was taken for granted. Others argue that we cannot infer conclusions either way from silence. Matthean scholars also debate whether 'everything Jesus has commanded' does or does not include his teachings on the law (5:17–20). For a brief discussion of these points, see Levine, *Social and Ethnic Dimensions*, 178–85; Sim, *Matthew and Christian Judaism*, 251–54.

Bibliography

Davies, W. D., and D. C. Allison. *Introduction and Commentary on Matthew I–VII.* (Vol. 1 of *A Critical and Exegetical Commentary on the Gospel According to Saint Matthew* ICC; Edinburgh: T&T Clark, 1988).

Farrer, A. M. 'On Dispensing with Q', in D. E. Nineham (ed.), *Studies in the Gospels: Essays in Memory of R. H. Lightfoot* (Oxford: Blackwell, 1955), 55–88.

France, R. T. *The Gospel According to Matthew: An Introduction and Commentary* (TNTC; Grand Rapids, MI: Eerdmans, 1985).

Fredriksen, P. 'Why Should a "Law-Free" Mission Mean a "Law-Free" Apostle?', *JBL* 134, no. 3 (2015), 637–50.

Goodacre, M. *The Case Against Q: Studies in Markan Priority and the Synoptic Problem* (Harrisburg, PA: Trinity Press International, 2002).

Harrington, D. J. *The Gospel of Matthew* (SP, 1; Collegeville, MN: Liturgical Press, 1991).

Hill, D. 'False Prophets and Charismatics: Structure and Interpretation in Matthew 7, 15–23', *Biblica* 57, no. 3 (1976), 327–48.

Hirshman, M. *A Rivalry of Genius: Jewish and Christian Biblical Interpretation in Late Antiquity* (Albany, NY: State University of New York Press, 1996 [Hebrew, 1995]).

Keener, C. S. *The Gospel of Matthew: A Socio-Rhetorical Commentary* (Grand Rapids, MI: Eerdmans, 2009).

Levine, A.-J. *The Social and Ethnic Dimensions of Matthean Salvation History: "Go Nowhere Among the Gentiles..." (Matt. 10:5b)* (Studies in the Bible and Early Christianity, 14; Lewiston, NY: Edwin Mellen, 1988).

Loader, W. R. G. *Jesus' Attitude towards the Law: A Study of the Gospels* (Grand Rapids, MI: Eerdmans, 2002).

Merkle, B. L. *Ephesians* (Exegetical Guide to the Greek New Testament; Nashville, TN: B&H Academic, 2016).

Mohrlang, R.   *Matthew and Paul: A Comparison of Ethical Perspectives* (Cambridge: Cambridge University Press, 1984).

Overman, J. A.   *Matthew's Gospel and Formative Judaism: The Social World of the Matthean Community* (Minneapolis, MN: Fortress, 1990).

Palachuvattil, M.   *"The One Who Does the Will of the Father." Distinguishing Character of Disciples According to Matthew: An Exegetical Theological Study* (TGST, 154; Rome: Editrice Pontificia Università Gregoriana, 2007).

Robinson, J. M., P. Hoffmann, J. S. Kloppenborg, and M. C. Moreland (eds.) *The Sayings Gospel Q in Greek and English: With Parallels from the Gospels of Mark and Thomas* (CBET, 30; Leuven: Peeters, 2001).

Saldarini, A. J.   *Matthew's Jewish Christian Community* (Chicago, IL: University of Chicago Press, 1994).

Sim, D.   *The Gospel of Matthew and Christian Judaism: The History and Social Setting of the Matthean Community* (Edinburgh: T&T Clark, 1998).

Sim, D.   'Matthew's Anti-Paulinism: A Neglected Feature of Matthean Studies', *HvTSt* 58, no. 2 (2002), 767–83.

Sim, D.   'Matthew 7.21–23: Further Evidence of its Anti-Pauline Perspective', *NTS* 53, no. 3 (2007), 325–43.

Sim, D.   'Matthew and the Pauline Corpus: A Preliminary Intertextual Study', *JSNT* 31 (2009), 401–22.

Smith, J. B.   *Greek-English Concordance to the New Testament: A Tabular and Statistical Greek-English Concordance Based on the King James Version, with an English-to-Greek Index* (Scottdale, PA: Herald, 1955).

Stanton, G. N.   *A Gospel for a New People: Studies in Matthew* (Louisville, KY: Westminster John Knox Press, 1993).

Yee, T-L. N.   *Jews, Gentiles and Ethnic Reconciliation: Paul's Jewish Identity and Ephesians* (SNTSMS, 130; Cambridge: Cambridge University Press, 2005).

CHAPTER 5

Born Eunuch:
Recovering an Ancient Metaphor

Timothy P. Bradford

Abstract

Intersex/Disorders of Sexual Development (DSD) raise important pastoral and theological questions. The Christian theological tradition has, generally, taken as axiomatic that to be made in the image of God is to be embodied as either male or female. After all, *"Male and female, he created them"* (Genesis 1:27). Yet the ambiguity of intersexed bodies raises significant questions about this axiom. Attempts to address these issues have seen a renewed engagement with Jesus' eunuch logion (Matthew 19:12). This essay reconsiders Matthew 19:12a εὐνοῦχοι οἵτινες ἐκ κοιλίας μητρὸς ἐγεννήθησαν οὕτως as a metaphor, arguing that the (male) child is not born castrated, rather the image of the eunuch is being applied to the image of the newborn in order to create a new meaning. The associations of these images in Matthew's literary and social world are then considered, strengthening the correspondence between εὐνοῦχοι ... ἐγεννήθησαν and Intersex conditions and providing new avenues for resourcing the church's theological and pastoral understanding of Intersex/DSD.

Keywords: Intersex/DSD, Eunuch, Matthew 19:12, metaphor

1. Intersex/Disorders of Sex Development

Intersex/Disorders of Sex Development (henceforth DSD) has become an umbrella term for describing variations in the sexual development of the body.[1] Since the chromosomal sex of an embryo is established at fertilization, an embryo typically will develop during the 6th week of conception internal and external genitalia, either male or female gonads and genitals in accord with the chromosomal combination at fertilization (XX or XY).[2] Intersex/DSD, however, describes the atypical developments when the internal or external sex organs do not match that chromosomal sex.[3] Common conditions include Congenital Adrenal Hyperplasia (CAH) and Androgen Insensitivity Syndrome (AIS). CAH can be a life-threatening condition for genetic males and females alike. This condition occurs when steroidogenic enzymes are deficient in the adrenal cortex, subsequently causing an increase in the production of adrenal androgens.[4] The effect of this increase in androgen upon genetic females with CAH can include a masculinization of the external female genitalia, ambiguous genitalia, or abnormalities at puberty, such as amenorrhoea.[5] Androgen Insensitivity Syndrome (AIS) occurs in genetic males (46,XY) when there is a dysfunction of the androgen receptor subsequently causing insensitivity to the hormone androgen.[6] This insensitivity can range from a partial (PAIS) to a complete insensitivity (CAIS), resulting in a range of effects. Often the testes fail to descend and the effects upon the external genitalia can be quite diverse. While some genetic males will develop external male genitals, other genetic males will develop near or complete female external genitalia at birth.[7] In instances of complete androgen insensitivity, the

---

1   These terms are not without controversy. In the absence of generally agreed-upon terms, I will use the nomenclature Intersex/DSD throughout. For an Intersex person's account of these terms, see O'Brien, 'Intersex, Medicine, Diversity, Identity and Spirituality', 49.
2   Freire, Ropelato, and Rey, 'Chapter 37', 625. 2020
3   For summaries of common DSDs using former and contemporary classification see Mazur, et al., 'Disorders', 222–49.
4   Hewitt and Warne, '46,XY DSD', 53–54.
5   Hewitt and Warne, '46,XY DSD', 53. Mazur, et al., 'Disorders', 242.
6   Hewitt and Warne, '46,XY DSD'74.
7   Hutson, 'Abnormal Embryology', 48. Mazur, et al., 'Disorders', 229.

diagnosis of this condition is usually made at puberty when menstruation is delayed. Other DSD's can include conditions caused by the combination of both testicular and ovarian tissue (Ovotesticular Disorder of Sex Development, formerly True Hermaphroditism), when extra X chromosomes are present in genetic males (Klinefelter Syndrome) or when X chromosomes are deleted or missing in genetic females (Turner Syndrome).[8] Despite the addition of "I" (for Intersex) to the acronym LGBTIQ+, the term 'Intersex/DSD' describes a range of conditions that are a variation to the typical development of male and female and does not necessarily indicate a person's sexual orientation or identity.[9]

These conditions raise important questions. On the one hand, the Christian theological tradition has, generally, taken as axiomatic that to be made in the image of God is to be embodied as either male or female. After all, *'Male and female, he created them* (Genesis 1.27). Yet the complexity and, at times, the ambiguity of intersexed bodies raises significant questions about this axiom. Vanhoozer admits that these conditions appear to make 'a certain reading of Genesis 1 less plausible than it used to be, even for those who subscribe to biblical authority'.[10] DeFranza is more critical, believing that the binary description of sex/gender is 'no longer sufficient' but, in fact, 'dishonest to the diversity of persons created in the image of God'.[11] On the other hand, Intersex/DSD exposes a disparity between the chromosomal constitution of a body and its physical actualization. The physical and external body is developing contrary to its inherent chromosomal constitution in ways that bear upon personal identity, gender and sexuality. At the very least, as Sloane cautions, these conditions 'require us to develop nuanced theologies of the body and understandings of how we relate to each other as embodied beings'.[12] What resources, then, might the Scriptures provide to aid the church's understanding of Intersex/DSD?

---

8   Mazur, et al., 'Disorders' 226–28.
9   Mazur, et al., 'Disorders', 244.
10 Vanhoozer, *Pictures*, 246.
11 DeFranza, *Sex Difference*, 67.
12 Sloane, '"Male and Female"', 358.

2. Theological engagement with Matthew 19:12

Within the existing theological literature on Intersex/DSD,[13] a number have engaged with Jesus' eunuch logion (Matt 19:12).[14] Megan DeFranza's 2015 *Sex Difference in Christian Theology: Male, Female, and Intersex in the Image of God* marked one of the first monographs on Intersex/DSD to be published. For DeFranza, Jesus' eunuch logion provides an important resource:

> Jesus' first type of eunuch—who has 'been so from birth'—provides a biblical door through which theologians may pass to explore the contributions provided by intersex to current concepts of human personhood, identity, image of God, sex, gender, and sexuality.[15]

Joseph A. Marchal, however, is more cautious, asking,

> [i]n adopting a strategy of identification, or claiming correspondence between intersex now and eunuchs then, do we really want to import this fraught and frankly dehumanizing complex of meaning upon bodies today that are not, in fact, ambiguous, but have some (often slight) noncorrespondence to cultural expectations around either infant genital size, or gonads, chromosomes, or hormones?[16]

Marchal is particularly concerned that 'an unreflective, ahistoricizing identification of intersex people with eunuchs has the potential to reinforce the assumed naturalness, normalcy, and timelessness of the current and rather particular understanding of gender, sexuality, and embodiment'.[17] These concerns are valid, particularly given the dis-

---

13 Lebacqz, 'Difference or Defect?', 213–29. Looy, 'Male and Female', 10–20. Hester, 'Intersexes and the End of Gender', 215–25. Hester, 'Queers on Account of the Kingdom of Heaven', 809–823. Jung, 'Christianity and Human Sexual Polymorphism', 293–309. Gross, 'Intersexuality and Scripture', 65–74. Mollenkott, *Omnigender*. Cornwall, *Sex and Uncertainty*. DeFranza, 'Virtuous Eunuchs'. Marchal, 'Who are you calling a Eunuch?!' DeFranza, *Sex Difference*. Cox, *Intersex in Christ*.
14 DeFranza. 'Virtuous Eunuchs', 55–78. Hester, 'Queers on Account of the Kingdom of Heaven', 809–823. Marchal, 'Who are you calling a Eunuch?!', 29–54.
15 DeFranza, *Sex Difference*, 70.
16 Marchal, 'Who are you calling a Eunuch?!', 39.
17 Marchal, 'Who Are You Calling a Eunuch?!', 43.

agreement that exists over what precisely constitutes an intersex condition, and stress the importance of examining Jesus' eunuch logion in its original context lest current understandings of embodiment are pressed unnaturally onto the text. Nonetheless, there is, however, an assumption in Marchal's concern: namely, that Jesus' eunuch logion carries a 'dehumanizing complex of meaning'.

It is not surprising that Marchal and DeFranza disagree about whether the eunuch logion is suitable for resourcing Intersex/DSD because they differ in deciding which eunuch better represents Intersex/DSD. Marchal believes the second category—εὐνοῦχοι οἵτινες εὐνουχίσθησαν ὑπὸ τῶν ἀνθρώπων potentially connects better to those Intersex/DSD individuals who have received sex assignment surgery,[18] while DeFranza approaches Intersex/DSD through the first type of eunuch—εὐνοῦχοι … ἐγεννήθησαν. A reexamination of Jesus' eunuch logion seems warranted before assessing its suitability as a resource for understanding Intersex/DSD.

3. Matthew 19:12

Upon hearing Jesus' teaching on divorce and remarriage (vv.8-9), the disciples object οὐ συμφέρει γαμῆσαι "It is better not to marry" (v.10).[19] The eunuch logion provides the substance of Jesus' response to the disciple's shock at the prospect of celibacy. As Table 1 indicates, the eunuch logion exhibits remarkable parallelism.[20]

---

18 Marchal, 'Who Are You Calling a Eunuch?!', 35.
19 It is beyond the scope of this paper to interact with the debate over divorce and remarriage. For representations of the major positions, see Instone-Brewer, *Divorce and Remarriage*; Blomberg, 'Marriage, Divorce, Remarriage, and Celibacy', and Wenham, *Jesus and Divorce*.
20 Gundry, *Matthew*, 382.

Table 1
The eunuch logion (Matthew 19:12)

εἰσὶν γὰρ	εὐνοῦχοι οἵτινες	ἐκ κοιλίας μητρὸς ἐγεννήθησαν οὕτως,
καὶ εἰσὶν	εὐνοῦχοι οἵτινες εὐνουχίσθησαν	ὑπὸ τῶν ἀνθρώπων,
καὶ εἰσὶν	εὐνοῦχοι οἵτινες εὐνούχισαν ἑαυτοὺς	διὰ τὴν βασιλείαν τῶν οὐρανῶν

Three types of eunuchs are identified. Common to each description is the term εὐνοῦχος, which referred to a castrated male.[21] Various methods were employed in castration, as attested by the Hippocratic author of *The Seed*. Some men had their testicles 'cut off in the operation', others had their testicles 'crushed', and others had an 'incision'. (*The Seed* 2).[22] The Hippocratic authors also knew that if these procedures were performed 'while they are still children' the male body would not develop typical masculine features. The male body would 'neither become pubescent nor grow hair on their chins', but remain 'hairless over their whole body' (Hippocrates, *The Nature of the Child* 20).[23] Castration would generally lead to sterility, and, if performed before puberty, sexual immaturity. Such a body could be derided as soft and effeminate.[24]

It appears significant that Matthew used the term εὐνοῦχος three times and the same verbal form εὐνουχίζω twice in the one saying, given that there were an additional seven descriptions of eunuchs and the castrated available. The terms σπάδων (torn), ἀπόκοπος (cut off), ἐκτομίας (cut out), τομίας (gelded), ἴθρις (eunuch), θλᾰδίας (crushed), θλῐβίας (pressed) reveal, as Alexander observes, 'the diverse types of eunuch-making and the tendency to label eunuchs by the manner in which they were castrated'.[25] It seems significant then that Jesus used this generic term (εὐνοῦχος), which did not indicate the

---

21 LSJ, 'Εὐνοῦχος', 724. Bauer and Danker, *Greek–English Lexicon*, 409.
22 Hippocrates, *Hippocratic Writings*, 318.
23 Hippocrates, *Hippocratic Writings*, 333.
24 Hester, 'Eunuchs and the Postgender Jesus', 21.
25 Alexander, 'Self-Made Eunuchs', 95.

specific manner of castration.²⁶ The effect of the repeating the one term εὐνοῦχος in the logion is that it maintains a degree of commonality across the group despite the different ways they had become eunuchs.

Jesus' first two eunuchs, εὐνοῦχοι ... ἐγεννήθησαν and εὐνοῦχοι ... εὐνουχίσθησαν ὑπὸ τῶν ἀνθρώπων, reflect the well-attested categorization of eunuchs in the ancient world. Rabbinic literature regularly identified two types of eunuchs, distinguishing between those who had been castrated (*saris adam*) and those considered *saris chamma*, literally 'eunuch of the sun' but often translated into English as 'eunuch by nature' (*tMegillah 2.7*). Rabbinic texts define the *saris chamma* as any eunuch 'whom the sun has not seen in a state of validity for even a single moment' (*y.Yebamot 8.5, cf. mZabin 2.1*), identifying a range of physical features such as 'born without testicles' (*t.Berakhot 5.14*) or 'one testicle' (*t.Yebamot 10.3*), an absence of pubic and facial hair, whose skin is smooth, whose 'voice croaks, so on cannot tell whether it is male or female', as well as the inability of the penis to function as expected (*t.Yebamot 10.6*).²⁷ Rabbinic texts also display an awareness of other bodily variations, acknowledging people of unknown sex and even those with sexual traits of both sexes; hermaphrodites (*m.Zabim 2.1, t.Berakhot 5.14, t.Rosh ha-Shanah 2.5, t.Megillah 2.7 t.Yebamot 2.5*) and the alyonith, a woman lacking pubic hair, whose genitals are abnormal and voice is deep (*t.Yebamot 10.7*).²⁸

In contrast to the εὐνοῦχοι ... ἐγεννήθησαν, Jesus' second and third eunuch describe someone becoming a eunuch. The verb εὐνουχίζω is employed to describe the process of becoming castrated either by the agency of others (ὑπὸ τῶν ἀνθρώπων) or of those who have *castrated themselves* for *the kingdom of heaven*.

Ascertaining whether the eunuch logion is an appropriate resource for understanding Intersex/DSD is complicated by the history of interpretation. For many, this passage is considered 'the classic text' regarding celibacy and its implications for the priestly office.²⁹ The

---

26 DeFranza asserts that 'like the term "intersex", "eunuch" was an umbrella term—a word to cover a range of phenomena' without providing any reasons or references for such an idea. *Sex Difference*, 68.
27 See, esp., Lev, 'They Treat Him As a Man', 218.
28 Lev, 'How the 'Aylonit Got Her Sex'.
29 See, esp., Trautman, *The Eunuch Logion*, 496–99.

interpretation of the eunuch logion has long been disputed as the church has wrestled between literal and figurative readings.³⁰ The main lines of the debate surround whether all three eunuchs should be taken metaphorically or 'Literally in the first two and metaphorically in the third only'.³¹ Eusebius would have us believe that Origen interpreted the third eunuch 'in too literal and extreme a sense' (Histories 6.8).³² Origen himself, however, interpreted the logion allegorically. Origen described the noble person who

> cuts out the passion of the soul, without, however, laying a hand on the body, and does so because he understands the kingdom of heaven [...] It is to such persons, and not as those people think who interpret the verse literally, that the saying is applicable: There are eunuchs who have eunuchized themselves for the kingdom of heaven's sake.³³

Modern scholarship has largely followed Josef Blinzler's interpretation of the eunuch logion.³⁴ Blinzler categorized the first two eunuch references as literal, following the two rabbinic categories (*saris adam* and *saris hammah*), while the εὐνοῦχοι ... διὰ τὴν βασιλείαν τῶν οὐρανῶν 'eunuch... for the kingdom of heaven' was to be understood as a metaphor, advocating for celibacy. Recently, however, Llewelyn, Wearne, and Sanderson have questioned Blinzler's classification, asking: 'What is it that alerts the hearer to its metaphoricity?'.³⁵ We believe that a reconsideration of metaphor can illuminate the interpretation of the eunuch logion but we propose turning attention to Jesus' first eunuch, εὐνοῦχοι ... ἐγεννήθησαν. Our focus remains on the suitability of the eunuch logion for resourcing the church's understanding of Intersex/DSD. Appreciating εὐνοῦχοι ... ἐγεννήθησαν as a metaphor, we believe, can create new avenues for considering the correspondence between this body and Intersex/DSD bodies.

---

30 Caner, 'Practice and Prohibition'.
31 Kleist, 'Eunuchs in the New Testament', 447.
32 There is a debate here over the intentions of Eusebius.
33 Origen, *Commentary on the Gospel of Matthew*, 15.4
34 Blinzler, 'Eisen Eunouchoi: Zur Auslegung von Mt 19:12', 264–67.
35 Llewelyn, Wearne, and Sanderson, 'Guarding Entry', 230. Similarly, Moxnes asks: 'Why should it not be understood in the same way in the third part, which refers to self-castration among the followers of Jesus?', Moxnes, 'Body, Gender, and Social Space', 173.

4. Identifying metaphor

According to Aristotle, a metaphor is an application of 'a strange term from the genus to species or from the species to the genus or from the species to [another] species according to analogy' (*Poetics 1457b8-9*). Aristotle's description of 'strange term' has been influential and can be seen in modern discussion. According to Paul Ricoeur, words function as metaphors when

> they are opposed to other words taken literally; this shift in meaning results mainly from a clash between literal meanings, which excludes a literal use of the word in question and gives clues for the finding of a new meaning which is able to fit in the context of the sentence and to make sense in this context.[36]

Richard B. Hays offers a similar understanding:

> Metaphors are incongruous conjunctions of two images—or two semantic fields—that turn out, upon reflection, to be like one another in ways not ordinarily recognized. They shock us into thought by positing unexpected analogies.[37]

The application of strange terms and incongruous images enables 'an audience to "see" something in a particular way and in a way that it might not have seen before'.[38]

When considered, the description εὐνοῦχοι ... ἐγεννήθησαν alerts the reader to an incongruous image. We encounter a clash in literal meaning because the phrase cannot mean that the (male) child is born castrated. As A. E. Harvey observes, rather tentatively, the first eunuch is only a eunuch in an 'extended sense'.[39] Piet Farla sounds a similar caution, noting the 'word castration can only be applied to the second group of eunuchs'.[40] Rather, we contend that the term εὐνοῦχοι ... ἐγεννήθησαν is functioning metaphorically. Two known images are

---

36 Ricoeur, 'Metaphor', 99.
37 Hays, *Moral Vision*, 300.
38 Huber, 'Knowing is Seeing', 236.
39 Harvey, 'Eunuchs for the Sake of the Kingdom', 6.
40 Farla, '"The Two Shall Become One Flesh"', 70.

being brought together. The image of the eunuch is being applied to the image of the newborn in order to create a new meaning. The temporal function of the prepositional phrase ἐκ κοιλίας μητρός (*since the mother's womb*)⁴¹ evokes the scene of labour and the delivery of the child. We imagine the excited questions of the child's identity: 'Is it a boy? Is it a girl?'. But what if determining the sex was not straightforward? What conceptual tools would be available to describe this ambiguous or atypical body? We believe that the metaphor εὐνοῦχοι ... ἐγεννήθησαν offers one such conceptual tool. Vanhoozer observes that metaphors often function to describe 'the less familiar in the context of the more familiar in order to understand it in new ways'.⁴² In this case, the known frame of the castrated body is being applied to the less familiar—the ambiguous or atypical body.

Reading this first eunuch metaphorically may explain the presence of the adverb οὕτως (Matt 19:12a). It is not immediately clear why the adverb οὕτως is required to clarify the manner of the verb (ἐγεννήθησαν), particularly given the mention of the mother's womb. However, if the first eunuch is indeed to be read metaphorically, then the adverb clarifies the analogy being drawn: some eunuchs have been 'born' *this way* since their mother's womb.

Reading εὐνοῦχοι ... ἐγεννήθησαν as a metaphor may not be a novel interpretation so much as recovering an ancient interpretation. In his survey of the history of interpretation of Matthew 19:12, Walter Bauer identified Justin Martyr's second century work, *The First Apology*, as the first citation of the eunuch logion outside of the New Testament. Bauer observes that Justin cites the logion without commenting on the content.⁴³ Justin's citation, however, is worth a closer reading. For ease of comparison, Table 2 reorders Matthew's logion to reflect Justin's ordering.

---

41   Quarles, *Matthew*, 110.
42   Vanhoozer, *The Drama of Doctrine*, 280.
43   Bauer, 'Matth. 19.12', 235–244.

Matthew's Eunuch Logion (Reordered)	Justin's citation of the logion
καὶ εἰσὶν εὐνοῦχοι οἵτινες εὐνουχίσθησαν ὑπὸ τῶν ἀνθρώπων,* εἰσὶν γὰρ εὐνοῦχοι οἵτινες ἐκ κοιλίας μητρὸς ἐγεννήθησαν οὕτως, καὶ εἰσὶν εὐνοῦχοι οἵτινες εὐνούχισαν ἑαυτοὺς διὰ τὴν βασιλείαν τῶν οὐρανῶν. (*12b has been reordered with v.12a)	εἰσὶν τινες οἵτινες εὐνουχίσθησαν ὑπὸ τῶν ἀνθρώπων, εἰσὶ δὲ οἳ ἐγεννήθησαν εὐνοῦχοι εἰσὶ δὲ οἳ εὐνούχισαν ἑαυτοὺς διὰ τὴν βασιλείαν τῶν οὐρανῶν.

Justin's quote shows remarkable care to preserve the eunuch saying. This draws attention to the slight changes that Justin has made. Not only has Justin changed the order of the eunuchs—the first and second eunuchs are reversed—Justin shortens the description of the first eunuch to simply οἳ ἐγεννήθησαν εὐνοῦχοι 'born eunuch' (*Apology 1.15*). We might speculate that Justin's reordering of the first two eunuchs could be interpreted as grouping the metaphorical (*born eunuch, eunuch castrated for the kingdom of heaven*) and distinguishing these from the literal eunuch (*eunuch castrated by men*). Whatever the interpretative reasoning behind Justin's ordering, we suggest the shortened *born eunuch* makes the metaphor even starker. A newborn cannot be born castrated. What associations, then, would Matthew's first readers have drawn from these images?

5. Imagining the born eunuch: mapping the metaphor

The image of the εὐνοῦχοι ... ἐγεννήθησαν would have conjured a complex set of human experiences and associations. The *eunuch / saris* was known but decidedly in the background of the Hebrew Scriptures. The doctrine of creation and the covenants maintained that the foreground was focused on family and national life. The creation narrative described humanity as 'male and female' (Genesis 1:27). This sexual differentiation enables the divinely given blessing of procreation

(Gen 1:28).⁴⁴ Similarly, the covenants focused on Yhwh's promise to bless and increase Abraham's descendants and then bless 'all families of the earth' (כֹּל מִשְׁפְּחֹת הָאֲדָמָה Gen 12:3).⁴⁵ Still, the Torah was well aware of bodily variations. The Holiness Code included a range of physical defects (מוּם) that would exclude a priest from sacred space, including 'crushed testicle' (Lev 21:20).⁴⁶ Deuteronomy would expand this proscription, barring any castrated or emasculated male (פְּצוּעַ־דַּכָּא וּכְרוּת שָׁפְכָה) from the sanctuary of Israel's cult.⁴⁷ This command could also serve as prohibiting castration in Israel, complementing the prohibition against castrating animals (Lev 22:40). Seen against the value placed on family and procreation in creation and covenant, these bodies were considered 'blemished' and 'defective' (מוּם). We hear the eunuch despair: 'Look, I am a dried-up tree', only to find that they will be the object of Yhwh's pity and compassion (Isaiah 56:3–8).

Nevertheless, eunuchs could hold significant roles in the ancient world. The eunuchs mentioned in the Hebrew Bible often appear in court settings where they perform significant roles for kings and queens.⁴⁸ Eunuchs served royal courts as chamberlains to kings (Diodorus Siculus, *Library* 11.69) and even as treasurers (Strabo, *Geographica*, 13.4.1). However, eunuchs were often slaves.⁴⁹ Castration was frequently used as a punishment and as a means of subjugation.⁵⁰ Eunuchs were considered 'objects of contempt' (Xenophon, *Cyropaedia* 7.5.51). Josephus advised that eunuchs be avoided and held 'in detestation' since they 'have deprived themselves of their manhood,

---

44 See, esp., Bird, *Missing Persons*, Chapter 7.
45 Genesis 12:3, 15:5, 17:1-8.
46 Skylar offers a compelling reason for the exclusion: 'One possible explanation is that the tabernacle was like the garden of Eden, where the Lord "walked" among his people . . . As such, it was to be a place of perfection, and those working in it were not to have any physical blemishes as a way to symbolize the perfection that used to belong to all of humanity (Gen. 2:25) and will one day belong again to all those who enter into God's presence in the heavenly tabernacle (Rev. 7:9–17; 21:2–4)'. Skyler, *Leviticus*, 267.
47 Olyan, *Disability*, 11. Deuteronomy 23:1 specifies the means of castration. It is possible then that what is prohibited here is a castrated person (*saris adam*) and not a eunuch by nature (*saris hammah*). McConville believes the castration referred to here assumes a particular religious commitment, *Deuteronomy*, 349.
48 Gen. 37:36, 40:2, Jer. 38:7, 1 Kings 22:9, 22:13, 2 Kings 24:12, Dan. 1:3).
49 Spencer, 'The Ethiopian Eunuch and His Bible: A Social-Science Analysis', 156.
50 Xenophon, *Cyropaedia*, Book 5, Chapter 2.

and of that fruit of generation which God has given to men... Let such be driven away, as if they had killed their children; since they beforehand have lost what should procure them' (*Ant.* 4.290-291). Philo counseled the same exclusion of 'those whose generative organs are fractured or mutilated' considering them 'worthless' (*Special Laws*, 1.325). These attitudes can be found in sources dating to late antiquity, as evidenced by the following from the Babylonian Talmud

> 'O eunuch, O eunuch', he retorted, 'you have enumerated three things to me, [and now] you will hear three things: the glory of a face is its beard; the rejoicing of one's heart is a wife; the heritage of the Lord is children; blessed be the Omnipresent, Who has denied you all these!' (*b. Shabbath* 23.5, 151-153).

These attitudes aid the reader's appreciation to the metaphor εὐνοῦχοι ... ἐγεννήθησαν. At best the eunuch was considered unfortunate for their blemished and defective body, an object of pity. At worst the eunuch was an object of scorn and exclusion.

The second set of images and associations involves the newborn and the womb (ἐκ κοιλίας μητρὸς ἐγεννήθησαν οὕτως). In the Hebrew Bible, 'the Israelites believed that God was ultimately in control of the womb'.[51] The patriarch Jacob responds to Rachel's demand for a child with exasperation (Gen 30:2): Am I in the place of God, who has withheld from you the fruit of the womb? (הֲתַחַת אֱלֹהִים אָנֹכִי אֲשֶׁר־מָנַע מִמֵּךְ פְּרִי־בָטֶן).[52] Passages such as Genesis 29:31 and 30:22 describe Yhwh *opening* wombs. The Hebrew Bible even dares to imagine Yhwh's creative work in the womb. Job's protest reveals the idea that God had poured him out like milk, curdled him like cheese (Job 10.10).

Wolff describes this image as 'an analogy, it helps us understand the pouring out of the milky seminal fluid into the female organism and the development of a firm embryonic body that follows insemination'.[53] The image is similar to Psalm 139 where the Psalmist expresses

---

51 Garroway, *Growing up in Ancient Israel*, 27.
52 The description 'fruit of the womb' (פְּרִי־בָטֶן) serves as an idiom for children (Gen. 30:2, Ps. 132:11, Isa. 13:18.
53 Wolff, *Anthropology*, 97.

his conviction that it was Yʜᴡʜ who wove him together in his mother's womb (139:13). These convictions provide further explanation for why children were considered a blessing *from* the Lord (Ps. 127:3, 5).

We should note that the Hebrew Bible acknowledges Yʜᴡʜ's agency for bodily variations as well. When Yʜᴡʜ responds to Moses' complaint: 'Who gave human beings their mouths? Who makes them deaf or mute? Who gives them sight or makes them blind? Is it not I, the LORD?' (Exod. 4:11), we hear Yʜᴡʜ take responsibility for bodily limitations and dysfunction.[54] The contrasts of the words (אִלֵּם אוֹ חֵרֵשׁ אוֹ פִקֵּחַ אוֹ עִוֵּר) are suggestive that this list is representative and not exhaustive. Moreover, the description of the blind here recalls the blind priest, who was classified in the Holiness Code as having a 'physical defect' (מוּם). The Hebrew conviction that Yʜᴡʜ forms the body of individuals includes bodily limitations, dysfunctions, and even 'defects'.

The phrase εὐνοῦχοι οἵτινες ἐκ κοιλίας μητρὸς ἐγεννήθησαν invokes two contrasting associations. The eunuch's body is associated with infertility and frustration. The Hebrew Bible considered the eunuch blemished because of the physical defects. However, the image of the birth and the mother's womb evoked from ἐκ κοιλίας μητρὸς ἐγεννήθησαν recalls Yʜᴡʜ's intimate forming of the body in the womb. This second aspect of the metaphor ensures that the eunuch's body remains a dignified body. The concerns raised by Marchal, that the eunuch was a dehumanizing complex of meaning, was a valid concern but a premature judgement. The description εὐνοῦχοι ... ἐγεννήθησαν acknowledges the frustration, limitation and pain. This body is blemished and bears the marks of physical defects but the description equally recalls a worldview where Yʜᴡʜ takes responsibility for these dysfunctions, the eunuch's body remains a body 'knitted together' by God and divinely given.

Having argued that εὐνοῦχοι ... ἐγεννήθησαν is a metaphor, and considered the ancient associations of these images, it remains to be seen whether this reading is 'able to fit in the context of the sentence'[55] and

---

54 Olyan, *Disability in the Hebrew Bible*, 50.
55 Ricoeur, 'Metaphor and the Main Problem', 307.

enable 'an audience to "see" something in a particular way and in a way that it might not have seen before'.[56]

6. Matthew 19:10–12

Jesus' eunuch logion occurs in response to the disciples' exasperation οὐ συμφέρει γαμῆσαι "It is better not to marry" (v.10). Jesus responds to the disciples' prejudice against singleness/ celibacy with two known examples of the unmarried and infertile from everyday life (e.g. Proverbs 25:3).[57] Chrysostom identifies the logic of the passage well when he writes:

> For since to speak of virginity seemed to be grievous [...] to show the possibility of it, he says, There are some eunuchs, who were so born from their mother's womb, there are some eunuchs which were made eunuchs of men, and there be eunuchs which have made themselves eunuchs for the kingdom of Heaven's sake.[58]

These two examples of the unmarried and the infertile (εὐνοῦχοι ... ἐγεννήθησαν and εὐνοῦχοι ... εὐνουχίσθησαν ὑπὸ τῶν ἀνθρώπων) force the disciples to reflect on those who live without the particular goods of marriage, sex and procreation. These particular bodies undermine the grounds for the disciples' objection. As Blomberg discerns, 'Jesus thus strikingly repudiates the typical Jewish prejudice against celibacy [...] even while he advocates a stricter faithfulness to one's spouse than Judaism officially promoted'.[59] By showing living examples of the unmarried and infertile, Jesus has offered justification for voluntarily forgoing married life and its blessings: εὐνοῦχοι οἵτινες εὐνούχισαν ἑαυτοὺς διὰ τὴν βασιλείαν τῶν οὐρανῶν. Such a sacrifice for the kingdom of heaven is in keeping with Jesus' teaching regarding the pearl of great value: When he found one of great value, he went away and sold everything he had and bought it (Matt 13:46).

---

56 Huber, 'Knowing is Seeing', 236.
57 Davies and Allison, *Saint Matthew*, 22.
58 John Chrysostom, Homily 62 on Matthew.
59 Blomberg, 'Marriage, Divorce, Remarriage, and Celibacy', 185.

Appreciating the *eunuch since the mother's womb*, we believe, strengthens the legitimacy of using the eunuch logion as a resource for Intersex/DSD. As a metaphor, εὐνοῦχοι ... ἐγεννήθησαν covers a wider range of bodily variations than simply castrated males. Consequently, the metaphor creates new avenues for describing the correspondence between this image and the conditions of Intersex/DSD. The situatedness of the metaphor εὐνοῦχοι ... ἐγεννήθησαν requires the interpreter to engage the imagery of the ancient world. This, we believe, avoids Marchal concern of an 'unreflective, ahistoricizing identification' of Intersex/DSD with the ancient eunuch.

Having observed the ancient world's familiarity with eunuchs, Megan DeFranza has suggested that 'people in the ancient world were more familiar with variations of sex development than many contemporary Christians are'.[60] Whatever the awareness of contemporary Christians may be on these issues, we take the same confidence as Lisa Isherwood and Elizabeth Stuart, who counsel 'the issues that theologians of the body face today—issues of gender, desire, change and decay, issues of difference and meaning—are all ones familiar to our ancestors in the faith'.[61] If the eunuch logion sheds theological and pastoral light on the Intersex/DSD body, what might the full radiance of the Gospel of Matthew reveal about our understanding of the body and embodiment?

---

60 DeFranza, *Sex Difference in Christian Theology*, 103.
61 Isherwood, 'Introducing Body Theology', 76–77.

Bibliography

Alexander, J. S.   'Self-Made Eunuchs as Model Disciples: Matthew 19:12 in Narrative and Historical Context', in W. M. Bailey and L. C. Barrett (eds.), *The Theologically Formed Heart: Essays in Honor of David J.* Gouwens (Eugene, OR: Wipf and Stock, 2014), 89–116.

Bauer, W.   'Matth. 19.12 und die alten Christen', in *Neutestamentliche Studien Georg Heinrici zu seinem 70. Geburtstag (14. März 1914) dargebracht.* (Chapter 7. Leipzig: J.C. Hinrich'sche Buchhandlung, 1914), 235–244.

Bauer, W. and F. W. Danker   *A Greek-English Lexicon of the New Testament and other Early Christian Literature.* (3rd Edition. Revised and Edited by Frederick William Danker. Chicago, IL: University of Chicago Press, 2000), 409.

Beardsley, C., and O'Brien, M. (eds.)   *This Is My Body: Hearing the Theology of Transgender Christians*, (London: Darton, Longman & Todd 2016).

Bird, P. A.   Missing *Persons and Mistaken Identities: Women and Gender in Ancient Israel* (Minneapolis, MN: Fortress Press, 1997).

Blinzler, J.   'Eisen Eunouchoi: Zur Auslegung von Mt 19:12', *ZNW* 48 (1957), 264–67.

Blomberg, C. L.   'Marriage, Divorce, Remarriage, and Celibacy: An Exegesis of Matthew 19:2–12', *Trinity Journal 11* n.s. (1990), 161–96.

Caner, D. F.   'The Practice and Prohibition of Self-Castration in Early Christianity', *Vigiliae Christ.* 51.4 (1997), 396–415.

Cornwall, S.   *Sex and Uncertainty: Intersex Conditions and Christian Theology.* (Gender, Theology and Spirituality. London: Equinox, 2010).

Cox, J. A.   *Intersex in Christ: Ambiguous Biology and the Gospel* (Eugene, OR: Wipf and Stock, 2018).

Davies, W. D., and D. C. Allison   *A Critical and Exegetical Commentary on the Gospel According to Saint* Matthew (International Critical Commentary on the Holy Scriptures of the Old and New Testaments. London: T & T Clark International, 2004).

DeFranza, M. K.   *Sex Difference in Christian Theology: Male, Female, and*

	Intersex in the Image of God (Grand Rapids, Michigan: Eerdmans, 2015).
DeFranza, M. K.	'Virtuous Eunuchs: Troubling Conservative and Queer Readings of Intersex and the Bible', in S. Cornwall (ed.) *Intersex, Theology, and the Bible: Troubling Bodies in Church, Text, and Society* (New York, NY: Palgrave Macmillan, 2015), 55–78.
Farla, P.	'"The Two Shall Become One Flesh": Gen.1.27 and 2.24 in the New Testament Marriage Texts', in S. Draisma, *Intertextuality in Biblical Writings : Essays in Honour of Bas van Iersel* (Kampen: Kok, 1989), 67–82.
Freire, A. V., M. G. Ropelato, and R. A. Rey	'Chapter 37 – Development and Function of the Ovaries and Testes in the Fetus and Neonate', in C. S. Kovacs and C. L. Deal (eds.), *Maternal-Fetal and Neonatal Endocrinology* (Cambridge, MA: Academic Press, 2020), 625–41. 2020
Garroway, K. H.	*Growing up in Ancient Israel : Children in Material Culture and Biblical Texts*, (Archaeology and Biblical Studies. Atlanta, GA: SBL Press, 2018).
Gross, S.	'Intersexuality and Scripture', *Theology and Sexuality* 11 (1999), 65–74.
Gundry, R. H.	*Matthew: A Commentary on His Literary and Theological Art* (Grand Rapids, MI: Eerdmans, 1982).
Harvey, A. E.	'Eunuchs for the Sake of the Kingdom' (The Ethel M. Wood Lecture. Univ. of London, 15th March, 1995).
Hays, R. B.	*The Moral Vision of the New Testament: A Contemporary Introduction to New Testament Ethics* (Edinburgh: T & T Clark, 1997).
Hester, J. D.	'Eunuchs and the Postgender Jesus: Matthew 19.12 and Transgressive Sexualities', *Journal for the Study of the New Testament,* 28.1 (2005), 13–40.
Hester, J. D.	'Intersexes and the End of Gender: Corporeal Ethics and Postgender Bodies', *Journal of Gender Studies* 13.3 (Nov 2004), 215–25.

Hester, J. D.   'Queers on Account of the Kingdom of Heaven: Rhetorical Constructions of the Eunuch Body', *Scriptura* 90 (2005), 809–23.

Hewitt, J. K., and G. L. Warne,   '46,XY DSD', in J. M. Hutson, G. L. Warne, and S. R. Grover (eds.), *Disorders of Sex Development: An Integrated Approach to Management*, (Berlin, Heidelberg: Springer, 2012).

Hippocrates   *Hippocratic Writings* (ed. G. Lloyd, trans. I. M. Lonie, J. Chadwick, and W. N. Mann; E. T. Withington; New edition. London: Penguin, 2005).

Huber, L. R.   'KNOWING IS SEEING: Theories of Metaphor Ancient, Medieval, and Modern', in V. K. Robbins, R. H. von Thaden Jr., and B. B. Bruehler (eds.), *Foundations for Sociorhetorical Exploration: A Rhetoric of Religious Antiquity Reader* (Atlanta, GA: SBL Press, 2016), 235–84.

Hutson, J. L.   'Abnormal Embryology in DSD', in J. M. Hutson, G. L. Warne, and S. R. Grover (eds.), *Disorders of Sex Development: An Integrated Approach to Management* (Berlin, Heidelberg: Springer, 2012), 41–52.

Instone-Brewer, D.   *Divorce and Remarriage in the Bible: The Social and Literary Context* (Grand Rapids, MI: Eerdmans, 2002).

Isherwood, L.   'Introducing Body Theology / Lisa Isherwood and Elizabeth Stuart', *Introductions in Feminist Theology 2* (Sheffield, UK: Sheffield Academic Press, 1998), 76–77.

Jung, P. B.   'Christianity and Human Sexual Polymorphism: Are they Compatible?', in S. E. Sytsma (ed.), *Ethics and Intersex* (Dordrecht: Springer, 2006), 293–309.

Kleist, J. A.   'Eunuchs in the New Testament', *CBQ* 7.4 (1945), 447–49.

Lebacqz, K.   'Difference or Defect? Intersexuality and the Politics of Difference', in *Annual of the Society of Christian Ethics* 17 (1997), 213–29.

Lev, S. L.   'They Treat Him As a Man and See Him As a Woman: The Tannaitic Understanding of the Congenital Eunuch', *Jew. Stud. Q.* 17.3 (2010), 213–43.

Lev, S. L.   'How the 'Aylonit Got Her Sex', *AJS Rev.* 31.2 (2007), 297–316.

Llewelyn, S. R., G. J. Wearne, and B. L. Sanderson   'Guarding Entry to the Kingdom: The Place of Eunuchs in Mt. 19.12', *JSHJ* 10.3 (2012), 228–46.

Looy, H.   'Male and Female God Created Them: The Challenge of Intersexuality', *Journal of Psychology and Christianity* 21.1 (2002), 10–20.

Luz, U.   *Matthew 8-20: A Commentary on the Gospel of Matthew.* (Translated by J. E. Crouch. Hermeneia. Minneapolis, MN: Fortress, 2001).

Marchal, J. A.   'Who Are You Calling a Eunuch?! Staging Conversations and Connections between Feminist and Queer Biblical Studies and Intersex Advocacy', in S. Cornwall (ed.), *Intersex, Theology, and the Bible: Troubling Bodies in Church, Text, and Society* (New York, NY: Palgrave Macmillan, 2015), 29–54.

Mazur, T., M. Gardner, A. M. Cook, and D. E. Sandberg   'Disorders of Sex Development (DSD): Definition, Syndromes, Gender Dysphoria, and Differentiation from Transsexualism', in R. Ettner, S. Monstrey, and E. Coleman (eds.), *Principles of Transgender Medicine and Surgery* (2nd edn. Milton Park, UK: Routledge 2016), 222–49.

Mollenkott, V. R.   *Omnigender: A Trans-Religious Approach* (Revised and expanded edn. Cleveland, OH: Pilgrim Press, 2007).

Moxnes, H.   'Body, Gender, and Social Space: Dilemmas in Constructing Early Christian Identities', in B. Holmberg and M. Winninge, *Identity Formation in the New Testament* (Wissenschaftliche Untersuchungen Zum Neuen Testament. Tübingen: Mohr Siebeck, 2008), 163–82.

O'Brien, M.   'Intersex, Medicine, Diversity, Identity and Spirituality', in C. Beardsley and M. O'Brien (eds.), *This Is My Body: Hearing the Theology of Transgender Christians* (London: Darton, Longman & Todd 2016), 45–55.

Olyan, S. M.   *Disability in the Hebrew Bible: Interpreting Mental and Physical Differences* (New York, NY: Cambridge University Press, 2008).

Quarles, C. L.   *Matthew* (Exegetical Guide to the Greek New Testament. Nashville, TN: B&H Publishing Group, 2017).

Ricoeur, P.	'Metaphor and the Main Problem of Hermeneutics', *New Lit. Hist.* 6.1 (1974), 95–110.
Skylar, J.	*Leviticus: An Introduction and Commentary* (Tyndale Old Testament Commentary 3. Downers Grove, IL: Inter-Varsity Press, 2014).
Sloane, A.	'"Male and Female He Created Them"?: Theological Reflections on Gender, Biology, and Identity', in E. Murphy and D. Starling (eds.), *The Gender Conversation: Evangelical Perspectives on Gender, Scripture and the Christian Life* (Macquarie Park: Morling Press, 2016), 347–58.
Spencer, F. S.	'The Ethiopian Eunuch and His Bible: A Social-Science Analysis', *Biblic. Theol. Bull. J. Bible Cult.* 22.4 (1992), 155–65.
Trautman, D. M.	*The Eunuch Logion of Matthew 19,12: Historical and Exegetical Dimensions as Related to Celibacy* (Rome: Catholic Book Agency, 1966).
Vanhoozer, K. J.	*The Drama of Doctrine: A Canonical-Linguistic Approach to Christian Theology* (Louisville, KY: Westminster John Knox Press, 2005).
Vanhoozer, K. J.	*Pictures at a Theological Exhibition: Scenes of the Church's Worship, Witness and Wisdom* (London: Inter-Varsity Press, 2016).
Wenham, G. J.	*Jesus and Divorce* (Biblical & Theological Classics Library, 9. Carlisle: Paternoster, 1997).
Wolff, H. W.	*Anthropology of the Old Testament* (Philadelphia, PA: Fortress Press, 1974).

CHAPTER 6

Jesus' Imperial Authority Over the Sea in Mark 6:45–52

Michael J. Kok

Abstract

The pericope about Jesus walking on the water in Mark 6:45–52 has been central to the debates over the Christology of Mark's Gospel and whether it describes Jesus as fully divine or as an idealised human agent. Nevertheless, in line with some recent scholarship that reads Mark's language of divine sonship in light of the Davidic messianic expectations within Second Temple Judaism on the one hand and the Roman imperial cult on the other, this essay will argue that the evangelist has been influenced by an older imperial ideology and that a Davidic Christology is the hermeneutical key to interpreting Mark 6:45–52. Specifically, the Markan Jesus was empowered to conquer and rule over the forces of chaos symbolised by the sea as the representative of the God of Israel and the royal heir of King David.

There have been two major trends in the current study of Mark's Christology. First, there is continued discussion over whether or not Mark identified Jesus as a *Davidic* messianic figure. Some exegetes argue that, by affirming that the 'Messiah' (Χριστός) was David's 'lord'

(κύριος), Mark rejected the common assumption that the Messiah had to be David's 'son' (υἱός) or royal heir in Mark 12:35–37.[1] Other exegetes find a two-stage Christology in this passage: Jesus was a descendant of David, but he inherited a higher station than his ancestor and his lordship was more cosmic in its orientation.[2] The debate has mainly focused on the exegesis of a handful of explicit references to David in Mark 10:47–48, 11:10, and 12:35–37, but a few recent studies have moved beyond this methodological impasse by showing how a Davidic Christology is supported by the scriptural resonances throughout Mark's narrative as a whole (e.g., Mark 1:11/Psalm 2:7; cf. 2 Sam. 7:14).[3] Secondly, there is an increasing emphasis on how Mark's audience would have comprehended the language of Jesus' divine sonship in the light of Roman political propaganda and the imperial cult as well.[4]

The aim of this essay will be to demonstrate how a royal, Davidic Christology can inform our understanding of the pericope in Mark 6:45–52 about Jesus walking on the water. Biblical scholars have combed through Jewish, Hellenistic, and Roman literature to uncover any parallels to Jesus' extraordinary feat.[5] Building on the research of J. R. Daniel Kirk, Stephen L. Young, and Debra Scroggins Ballentine,[6] I will argue that Mark 6:45–52 reproduced an older imperial ideology

---

1   For example, see Tyson, 'Blindness', 266, 266 n.17; Kelber, *The Kingdom*, 95–97; Achtemeier, '"And He Followed Him"', 127–30; Telford, *Theology*, 51–54; Horsley, *Hearing the Whole Story*, 251; Malbon, *Mark's Jesus*, 159–69; Crossley, 'Mark's Christology', 126–27. Botner, *Jesus Christ as the Son of David*, 4–9, traces this negative answer to the *Davidssohnfrage* back to William Wrede.

2   For example, see Hahn, *Titles*, 252–53; Burger, *Jesus als Davidssohn*, 64–70; Kingsbury, *The Christology*, 109–114; Juel, *Messianic Exegesis*, 143–44; Watts, *Isaiah's New Exodus*, 287–88; Ahearne-Kroll, *The Psalms of Lament*, 161–66; Collins and Collins, *King and Messiah*, 134 n.42; Whitenton, *Hearing Kyriotic Sonship*, 225–35.

3   See, for instance, Ahearne-Kroll, *The Psalms of Lament*, 59–226; Whitenton, *Hearing Kyriotic Sonship*, 15–320; Botner, *Jesus Christ as the Son of David*, 27–194.

4   For example, see Kim, 'The Anarthrous Υἱος Θεου', 151–57; Evans, 'Mark's Incipit', 67–81; Collins, 'Mark and His Readers', 88, 94–99; Peppard, *The Son of God in the Roman World*, 67–131; Samuel, *A Postcolonial Reading*, 89–96, 152; Winn, 'The Gospel of Mark: A Response', 92–94, 95–96; Leander, *Discourses*, 185–99, 285–93.

5   For a sample of studies, see Ritt, 'Der "Seewandel Jesu"', 71–84; Heil, *Jesus Walking on the Sea*; Collins, 'Rulers, Divine Men', 207–27; Madden, *Jesus' Walking on the Sea*; Combs, 'A Ghost', 345–58; Cotter, *The Christ of the Miracles Stories*, 233–52; Kirk and Young, 'I Will Set his Hand to the Sea', 333–40; Ballentine, *The Conflict Myth*; McPhee, 'Walk, Don't Run' 763–77.

6   Kirk and Young, 'I Will Set his Hand to the Sea', 333–40; Ballentine, *The Conflict Myth*, 111–23, 174–83; Kirk, *A Man Attested by God*, 247–50, 435–36, 440–42.

which portrayed a sovereign ruler subduing the forces of chaos that were symbolised by the tumultuous sea. In this way, Jesus exercised the regal authority that had been delegated to him by Israel's national deity.

YHWH or YHWH's Appointed Human Agent?

The story in Mark 6:45–52 is somewhat enigmatic. As Mark sets up the scene, Jesus ordered the disciples to sail out to Bethsaida before he ascended a mountain to spend time alone in prayer. Then, Jesus came out to the disciples when their boat was stuck in the middle of the sea and when they were straining against a strong wind. Matthew 14:24 adds that they were being battered by the waves. One could follow John P. Heil's categorisation of this episode as a 'sea rescue epiphany', though the disciples may not have been in real danger and Jesus did not alleviate their plight like he did previously when he calmed a storm (cf. Mark 4:35–41).[7] Hence, some scholars prefer to simply classify the account as an epiphany,[8] but the Markan disciples did not comprehend the revelation because their hearts were hardened (6:49, 52). Indeed, they initially mistook Jesus for a 'ghost' (φάντασμα), which even went against prevalent beliefs at the time that ghosts could be destroyed by water and that water served as a boundary marker preventing the buried dead from escaping their resting place.[9] On the contrary, after witnessing this event, the Matthean disciples confessed Jesus' divine sonship and 'prostrated' (προσεκύνησαν) before him in Matthew 14:33, but it is an open question as to whether their actions amounted to the obeisance granted to a social superior (cf. Matt. 2:11) or to the cultic worship offered to a divine being.[10]

The ancient Near East combat myth may be the key to deciphering the Markan pericope. In his ground-breaking study comparing the

---

7 Heil, *Jesus Walking on the Sea*, 17, 30.
8 See the critique of Heil's categorisation of Mark 6:45–52 in Meier, *A Marginal Jew*, 908.
9 Combs, 'Absurdity', 353–56, 358, argues that the absurd deduction that Jesus was a ghost supports the larger Markan theme about the disciples' ignorance of the 'messianic secret' in the pre-Easter period. For a fascinating reading about how the followers of Jesus were haunted by their traumatic memories of the historical Jesus' suffering and by the risen Jesus' seeming absence in their current plight, see Choi, *Postcolonial Discipleship*, 63–84.
10 Contrast Kirk, *A Man Attested by God*, 252 and Hurtado, *Lord Jesus Christ*, 338.

Babylonian *Enuma Elish* to the priestly creation narrative in Genesis, which noted the vestiges of a primordial conflict running through the Hebrew and Christian writings (e.g., Job 3:8; 7:12; 9:13; 26:12; 40:15–41:34; Ps. 74:13–15; 89:9–10; 104:25–26; Isa. 27:1; 30:6–7; 51:9–10; Rev. 12), Herman Gunkel brought the *Chaoskampf* theme to the forefront of scholarly attention.[11] He looked to Mesopotamian sources, but we now have Babylonian, Assyrian, and Ugaritic extant narratives as well as epitomes or summaries from Mari, Israel, and Judah about a warrior god (e.g., Ninurta, Marduk, Aššur, Ba'al) defeating a sea deity or monster (e.g., Anzu, Tiamat, Yamm) to become the supreme ruler.[12] Concerning the use of the conflict motif in Job and the Psalms, Ballentine lists the following common elements: the representation of Yahweh as an incomparable and majestic deity, as a victorious warrior battling superhuman opponents, and as a sovereign creator whose universal dominion extends over the waters.[13]

For this reason, many exegetes infer that Mark 6:45–52 deliberately imitated the imagery of a theophany in the Hebrew Bible. Jesus descended from the *axis mundi* on a mountain, displayed his glory at the 'fourth watch of the night' when the light was about to dawn, approached the boat 'walking on the sea' (περιπατῶν ἐπὶ τῆς θαλάσσης) in a verbal echo of Job 9:8 LXX, intended 'to pass by' (παρελθεῖν) the disciples (cf. Exod. 33:7–34:8; 1 Kgs 19:11–13), advised the disciples to not fear, and used the divine name 'I am' (ἐγώ εἰμι) as a self-designation (cf. Exod. 3:14; Isa. 41:4; 43:10–11).[14] Patrick J. Madden only stresses a few minor variations—the absence of the article before the word 'sea' and the inclusion of the clarification 'as if on dry ground' (ὡς ἐπ' ἐδάφους)

---

11 Gunkel, *Schöpfung und Chaos*.
12 For an up-to-date survey of the ancient data that is also informed by modern theories of myth, see Ballentine, *The Conflict Myth*, 1–126.
13 Ballentine, *The Conflict Myth*, 90.
14 See Ritt, 'Der "Seewandel Jesu"', 79; Heil, *Jesus Walking on the Sea*, 37–59, 79–80, 459; Blackburn, *Theos Aner*, 145–52; Gundry, *Mark*, 336–37; Collins, 'Walking on the Water', 212–13, 224; Meier, *Mentor, Message and Miracles*, 914–19; Frenschkowski, *Offenbarung und Epiphanie*, 179–80; Madden, *Jesus' Walking on the Sea*, 24–32, 100–102; Watts, *Isaiah's New Exodus*, 161–62; Boring, 'Markan Christology', 466–67; Marcus, *Mark 1–8*, 430–34; Hurtado, *Lord Jesus Christ*, 285–86; Gathercole, *The Pre-existent Son*, 63–64; Cotter, *Miracle Stories*, 247–50; Hays, *Reading Backwards*, 24–26; Geddert, 'Implied Yhwh Christology', 332–34; Ballentine, *The Conflict Myth*, 180; Whitenton, *Hearing Kyriotic Sonship*, 193–97.

in Job 9:8 LXX—to challenge Mark's direct literary dependence on the text of Job.[15] All of these observations lead Timothy J. Geddert to conclude that Mark depicts Jesus as 'the embodiment of Yhwh.'[16]

Adela Yarbro Collins and Wendy J. Cotter broaden the scope of their surveys to encompass the Greek and Roman parallels as well.[17] For instance, there were tales of Poseidon/Neptune riding his chariot on the surface of the sea (e.g., Homer, *Il.* 13.26–29; Virgil, *Aen.* 5.1081–85), a feat that the Persian emperor Xerxes allegedly mimicked when he rode his chariot on a pontoon bridge over the Hellespont (cf. Dio Chrysostom, *3 Regn*. 30–31), and Poseidon's offspring Euphemus and Orion could dash across the sea (Apollonius Rhodius, *Argon.* 1.182–184; Hyginus, *Fab.* 14.15; *Poet. astr.* 2.34; Pseudo-Eratosthenes, *Cat.* 32). The ability to travel over water was not restricted to Poseidon, whose domain was the sea, for the goddess Hera possessed the same ability (cf. Homer, *Il.* 14.225–30).[18] Yet Brian McPhee points out that the proverbial imagery of running at super-speeds on ears of grain without breaking their heads or on top of waves without sinking stands out from the Gospels inasmuch as 'Jesus's ambulatory pace indicates a type of levitation miracle'.[19] McPhee is adamant that there is no indisputable, pre-Christian example in Graeco-Roman mythology of a divinity or hero *walking* (i.e. περιπατέω) on water.[20] Likewise, Madden highlights the lexical differences between Mark and these other sources and underscores that Mark stands out from them in chronicling a one-time occurrence during Jesus' ministry rather than what a legendary hero or demi-god could theoretically do on a regular basis.[21] Therefore, the picture of Yhwh walking on the unruly waters may be a closer parallel.

Yet there are weaknesses to the theophanic interpretation of Mark

---

15 Madden, *Jesus' Walking on the Sea*, 65.
16 Geddert, 'Implied Yhwh Christology', 327.
17 Collins, 'Walking on the Water', 214–23; Cotter, *Miracle Stories*, 241–46.
18 McPhee, 'Walk, Don't Run', 767 n.11.
19 McPhee, 'Walk, Don't Run', 769; cf. 765–69.
20 McPhee, 'Walk, Don't Run', 770–75. For example, the verbs πορεύεσθαι, διαβαίνειν, and διαπορεύεσθαι are used for the actions of Orion and Euphemus (cf. Pseudo-Eratosthenes, Cat. 32; Pseudo-Apollodorus, Bib. 1.4.3; scholium ad Pindar, Pyth. 4.61), but, contrary to Collins ('Walking on the Water', 215–16), have a wider semantic range than strictly 'to walk' and denote traveling in general.
21 Madden, *Jesus' Walking on the Sea*, 54–57.

6:45–52. First, ἐγώ εἰμι could be translated as a simple form of self-identification (i.e. 'it is I') and Jesus may have planned 'to pass by' the disciples so that they would follow him on the way of discipleship. Secondly, in the parallel passage in Matthew 14:22–33, Jesus invited Peter to perform the same action that he did by stepping out of the boat onto the water in a piece of Matthean *Sondergut* in 14:28–31. Kirk recognises that 'Peter's participation, however brief, curtails sharply the possibility that Jesus is being depicted as ontologically distinct rather than vocationally or dispositionally superior'.[22] Thirdly, the theophanic interpretation may stand in tension with Mark's overarching agency Christology, which portrays Jesus as the 'son' commissioned by his heavenly father (cf. 1:11; 9:7) to whom he prays (1:35; 6:46; 14:32–40; 15:34) and to whose will he yields (10:40; 13:32; 14:36).[23] To account for the supposed tension within Mark's christological presentation, John P. Meier imagines that there was originally a 'grab bag' of heterogeneous christological images that the evangelist freely drew from without a care for internal consistency or systematisation.[24] Yet this may be a relic of the form critical view of the evangelists as 'scissor and paste' compilers of oral units rather than creative composers in their own right. Thus, Ballentine reckons that Mark only intended to communicate Jesus' incomparability among mortals as approximating Yhwh's incomparability among celestial beings.[25]

An alternative solution is that Mark depicts Jesus as an 'idealised human agent', defined by Kirk as 'non-angelic, non-pre-existent human beings, of the past, present, or anticipated future, who are depicted in textual or other artefacts as playing some unique role in representing God to the rest of the created realm, or in representing some aspect of the created realm before God'.[26] For Richard Horsley, the Markan Jesus followed the 'prophetic script' modeled by popular Israelite

---

22 Kirk, *A Man Attested by God*, 251.
23 This is not to devalue the importance of canonical or systematic theological approaches that consciously bring Mark's text into dialogue with other voices in the canon or with the ecumenical creeds. It is just to concede that, from a historical-critical standpoint, the earliest audiences of Mark's Gospel were not yet cognisant about how the text could be profitably read through a later Nicene lens.
24 Meier, *Mentor, Message and Miracles*, 919.
25 Ballentine, *The Conflict Myth*, 178–79.
26 Kirk, *A Man Attested by God*, 3.

prophets such as Moses and Elijah.[27] A comparison between Jesus and Moses may be instructive.[28] The combination of sea and feeding miracles (cf. Mark 4:35–41; 6:30–44, 45–52; 8:1–10) is reminiscent of the crossing of the sea (Exod. 14:1–31) and the provision of manna in the wilderness (Exod. 16:4–36; Num. 11:7–9). Likewise, Moses' successor, Joshua, led the people of Israel through the Jordan River (Josh. 3:1–4:24) and the prophet Elijah divided the Jordan River by striking the water with his mantle (2 Kgs 2:8). Philo lauded Moses as a god and king of the Israelite nation who had command over the elements (Philo, *Mos.* 1.55–58), while Josephus defended the miracle attributed to Moses on the grounds of the similar reports that Alexander the Great marched through the Pamphylian Sea (*Ant.* 2.347–48). The drowning of the 'legion' of demons in Mark 5:13 may also evoke the fate that befell Pharaoh's army (Exod. 14:26–28).[29]

The main objection against likening Jesus to Moses is that Jesus does not carve a path through the sea to pass through it on dry ground, but treads upon the water as in LXX Job 9:8.[30] Even so, this foundational epic of Israel's origins in the exodus adapts the imagery of the combat myth, celebrating Yhwh's supremacy over Egypt's gods after throwing the horse and its rider into the sea (cf. Exod. 15:21). There is a general principle that Yhwh could empower humans to compel the sea to bend to their wills. In fact, there may be a third approach where Yhwh extends his imperial authority over the sea to a human vicegerent.

The Power of Human Rulers over the Sea?

There is plenty of corroborating evidence for the indissoluble connection between the ancient Near East conflict myth and imperial ideology. There is an extant letter dating as far back as the eighteenth century B.C.E. from Nur-Sin of Aleppo to Zimri-Lim, the king of Mari, about

---

27 Horsley, *Hearing the Whole Story*, 236–43.
28 For the following points, see Achtemeier, 'Origin and Function', 202–3, 210–12; Mack, *A Myth of Innocence*, 216–22; Collins, 'Walking on the Water', 215; Horsley, *Hearing the Whole Story*, 104–5; Cotter, *Miracle Stories*, 247; Crossley, 'Mark's Christology', 136, 140–42.
29 Horsley, *Hearing the Whole Story*, 141.
30 Hays, *Figural Christology*, 24.

how the god Adad restored Zimri-Lim to his throne, anointed him with victory/luminosity oil, and gifted him with the weapons by which he crushed the Sea (Mari Letter A.1968).[31] In a proverb about royal power in a fifth-century B.C.E. Aramaic work found at Elephantine, the orders that proceed from the king's tongue 'breaks the ribs of a dragon' (*Ahiqar* col. 6, 1.89–90).[32] Ballentine illuminates how this myth functioned as a 'taxonomy in narrative form' that sanctioned the social order:

> Ancient West Asian stories of divine combat generate a narrative hierarchical relationship among their characters, and the taxonomy of those mythical characters was consciously projected onto historical persons and polities for ideological purposes. Those aligned with the victorious deity are validated and endorsed by association with that deity. Those aligned with the sea or dragons are, the authors hope, destined for defeat, invalidated, and delegitimized.[33]

As for Hellenistic and Roman sources, the Persian emperor Xerxes I (cf. Herodotus, *Hist.* 7.35–57; Lys. 2.29; Isocrates, *Pan.* 4.88–89; Dio Chrysostom, *Regn.* 3.30–31) and the Roman emperor Gaius 'Caligula' (cf. Dio Cassius, *Hist.* 59.17.1–11; Seutonius, *Cal.* 19; Josephus, *Ant.* 19.6) drove a chariot over the Hellespont and the Bay of Baiae respectively.[34] Xerxes bridged the Hellespont in 480 B.C.E. to launch the second Persian invasion of Greece. Herodotus painted Xerxes as a stereotypical despot when, after a storm wrecked the first bridge that he had constructed, he had the builders executed and the Hellespont scourged under the assumption that the natural elements were obliged to comply with his bidding (Herodotus, *Hist.* 7.56).[35] Explanations for Gaius' pageantry ranged from attempting to imitate Xerxes to inspiring terror in Germany and Britain over the Romans' technological advancement, but Suetonius amusingly speculates that Gaius wished to

---

31 Ballentine, *The Conflict Myth*, 112–16.
32 Ballentine, *The Conflict Myth*, 121.
33 Ballentine, *The Conflict Myth*, 1.
34 Collins, 'Walking on the Water', 218–219; Cotter, Miracle Stories, 218, 241, 244–45; Kirk, *A Man Attested by God*, 448–49.
35 For the argument that Herodotus misunderstood an ancient 'religious' custom as an act of hubris (ὕβρις), see Briquel, 'The Punishment of the Hellespont', 51–60.

rebuff the astrologer Thrasyllus' declaration that Gaius had no more a chance of becoming emperor that riding over the gulf of Baiae on horseback (*Cal.* 19). It is true that these accounts document technological marvels rather than miracles.[36] Nevertheless, Xerxes' accomplishment drew comparisons with Zeus (Herodotus, *Hist.* 7.56) or Poseidon (Dio Chrysostom, *3 Regn.* 30–31) and Josephus scorned Caligula's presumption about controlling the sea (Josephus, *Ant.* 19.6).

There were also Jewish traditions about a presumptuous, imperial ruler who presumed that he had power over the sea in 2 Maccabees 5:21.[37] The 'arrogance' (ὑπερηφανία) of Antiochus IV 'Epiphanes' in plundering the temple was related to his delusions that he could alter the laws of nature by making the land swimmable (τὴν... γῆν πλωτήν) and the sea walkable (τὸ πέλαγος πορευτόν). After recounting Antiochus's fatal illness, the final parting shot in 2 Maccabees 9:8 is that the tyrant supposed that he was able to command the waves of the sea and weigh the mountains on a scale (cf. Isa. 40:12).[38] Heil judges it to be doubtful that Mark was influenced by a proverbial expression in 2 Maccabees 5:21 lambasting Antiochus' pride.[39] Yet Ballentine detects the inversion of the legitimating function of the conflict motif here, for Antiochus' rule had no divine authorisation and he attempted to usurp divine prerogatives for himself.[40] Although Antiochus was not able to accomplish his incredible boasts, Collins comments that 'the figure of speech expresses proverbial impossibility and implies that human beings who claimed divinity, or to whom divinity was attributed, especially kings, were associated with such feats within the cultural context of this work'.[41] To corroborate this point, one could look at the interpretation of dreams about walking on the sea collected at various ports by Artemidorus of Daldis in the second century C.E. Such a dream may signify different things depending on the status of the dreamer, but, for statesmen or leaders, it may be a good omen of profit and fame as the

---

36 Madden, *Jesus' Walking on the Sea*, 57–59.
37 Collins, 'Walking on the Water', 220; Ballentine, *The Conflict Myth*, 180–83. I would also like to thank my colleague Carolyn Tan for her insights about the exegesis of this verse.
38 Ballentine, *The Conflict Myth*, 182.
39 Madden, *Jesus' Walking on the Water*, 63.
40 Ballentine, *The Conflict Myth*, 180–81.
41 Collins, 'Walking on the Water', 220.

dreamer has risen above the unstable crowd (*Onir*. 3.16).[42] For this reason, Dio Chrysostom deems the fantasies about walking on water to be the product of overactive imaginations and dreams (*Troj*. 129).[43]

In contrast to the stereotypical hubris of a tyrant like Antiochus, Kirk, Young, and Ballentine have uncovered biblical precedent in Psalm 89:25 (Ps. 88:26 LXX) that Yhwh's authority over the sea could be delegated to the legitimate Davidic king. The psalmist re-deployed the conflict motif recounted in Psalm 89:9–10 to endorse David's reign in 89:25 as inseparably linked to Yhwh's victory over mythic foes and control over the created order, ironically at a time when Yhwh's cosmic enemies appeared to be triumphant and the covenant about a perpetual Davidic dynasty seemed to have been broken (cf. 89:38–51).[44] While there is disagreement between the commentators about whether the idiom about setting David's hand on the sea and the rivers is an allusion to the combat myth or merely refers to the geographical extent of David's idealised empire, Marvin E. Tate urges commentators to avoid an either/or choice when deciding between mythical or socio-geographical readings of verse twenty-five. His balanced conclusion is that '[t]he powers overcome by Yahweh (Ps 89:10–13) have their counterpart in the Davidic ruler's domination of an earthly kingdom (vv.26). The cosmic taming power of Yahweh in vv.10–13 is demonstrated in the ruling power of the king'.[45] Moreover, Ballentine highlights how Psalm 78 similarly moves from the foundational miracle at the sea in the exodus narrative (78:13) to the election of David to shepherd the flock of Israel (78:70–72).[46]

We can trace the reception history of Psalm 89 in early Jewish and Christian writings. The *Testament of Judah* 24.2 foretold the reinstatement of kingship from the line of Judah and borrowed its 'eschatological Davidic language' from select verses in LXX Psalm 88:4–5, 29–30,

---

42 Collins, 'Walking of the Water', 222–23; Cotter, *Miracle Stories*, 245–46 n.25, 246.
43 McPhee, 'Walk, Don't Run', 774–75.
44 Kirk and Young, 'I Will Set his Hand to the Sea', 333–40; cf. Kirk, *A Man Attested by God*, 247–50, 435–36, 440–42; Ballentine, *The Conflict Myth*, 116–120, 144. See also Hossfeld and Zenger, *Psalms 2*, 410.
45 Tate, *Psalms 51–100*, 423.
46 Ballentine, *The Conflict Myth*, 120–21.

and 36–37.⁴⁷ Kirk and Young observe, '[t]he parallels between *T. Jud.* 22:4 and Ps. 88:4–5 are especially strong, with both stressing that God's swearing an oath (ὄμνυμι) to David involves ensuring the kingship for his offspring (τὸ σπέρμα) forever (ἕως τοῦ αἰῶνος)'.⁴⁸ Although far too late to have informed the evangelists, Kirk further points to the midrashic interpretation of Psalm 89:25 in the ninth-century C.E. *Pesiqta Rabbati* 36:1 on how the seas and rivers will stop flowing before Messiah Ephraim.⁴⁹ In the Amoraic era, *Genesis Rabbah* 2.4 on Genesis 1:2 credited R. Simeon b. Lakish with equating the spirit or wind hovering over the formless waters with the spirit of the Messiah.⁵⁰ Divine sovereignty over the forces of chaos typifies both the original primordial state and the coming messianic age.

Additionally, Donald Juel pinpoints several potential allusions to Psalm 89 in early Christian writings such as Luke 1:51 (cf. Ps. 89:11), 1:69 (cf. Ps. 89:24), John 12:34 (Ps. 89:36), Acts 2:30 (cf. Ps. 89:4), Colossians 1:15 (cf. Ps. 89:27), Hebrews 1:6 (cf. Ps. 89:27), 11:26 (cf. Ps. 89:50–51), 1 Peter 4:13–14 (Ps. 89:50–51), and Revelation 1:5 (cf. Ps. 89:27, 37), though not all of his proposed allusions are equally compelling.⁵¹ Although Psalm 89 connects David's ascent to power with his humiliation, it does not go into great detail about the nature of David's trials, which may be why the Markan passion narrative drew on other laments such as Psalm 22 to elucidate Jesus' suffering.⁵² The points of contact between Mark and Psalm 89 that Kirk and Young highlight are suggestive but not definitive: both address the deity in personal terms as 'my father' and anticipate that the anointed one will be delivered (Ps. 88:27; Mark 14:36), affirm the divine sonship of David and Jesus (Ps. 88:28; Mark 1:11; 9:7), designate David and Jesus as a δοῦλος or 'servant' (Ps. 88:21; Mark 10:44–45), and focus on the rejection and scorn that David and Jesus received from their enemies (Ps. 88:39–40,

---

47 Kirk and Young, 'I Will Set his Hand to the Sea', 338–40. For later Jewish midrashic interpretations of Psalm 89, see Juel, *Messianic Exegesis*, 105–6.
48 Kirk and Young, 'I Will Set his Hand to the Sea', 338.
49 Kirk, *A Man Attested by God*, 250, 436.
50 Crossley, 'Christ of Faith', 142.
51 Juel, *Messianic Exegesis*, 107–9; cf. Hossfeld and Zenger, *Psalms 2*, 414–15; Kirk and Young, 'I Will Set his Hand', 338.
52 Juel, *Messianic Exegesis*, 109.

42–46; Mark 15).[53] Even so, Kirk and Young do not require the psalm to have been the primary intertext shaping the Markan or pre-Markan tradition, for they have the modest aim of showing that Mark 'created a discursive world that trades on a set of descriptions of God's coming Messiah similar to those found in the psalm'.[54]

The question of whether a direct intertextual relationship between Mark 6:45–52 and Psalm 88:26 LXX can be proven may be beside the point, for the *raison d'être* of the combat myth was that civilisation was predicated on a deity keeping destabilising forces at bay and entrusting the governance of society to an appointed human acting as the deity's proxy. Horsley objects that Mark would not be influenced by an ancient imperial myth,[55] but Mark is more ambiguous than Horsley's treatment of the text as a straightforward discourse of anti-imperial resistance allows, and several postcolonial studies explore how Mark simultaneously deconstructs and reinscribes the logic of imperialism through the processes of colonial mimicry.[56] Mark 1:15 proclaims a vision of God's empire (βασιλεία) that counters *Roman* imperialism and overthrows other spiritual and political oppressors (cf. 3:23–27; 5:1–20).[57] The Markan Jesus was enthroned in heaven (12:36–37), will inherit this empire (12:6–11), and will triumphantly return to the earth in glory (13:26–27; 14:62). Ballentine spots one more point of distinction in Mark 6:45–52, insofar as 'David is never portrayed as actually wielding power over the sea, however, so the portrayal of Jesus actualizing this authority would be innovative'.[58] Just as the transfiguration in Mark 9:2–8 is a proleptic vision of Jesus' future glorious state when the kingdom of God fully arrives in power (9:1), so Mark 6:45–52 provides a glimpse of Jesus' future triumph over all rival powers.

---

53 Kirk and Young, 'I Will Set his Hand', 337–38. Whitenton, *Hearing Kyriotic Sonship*, 181–82, finds these parallels to be too weak when compared to the verbal echo of Job 9:8 LXX.
54 Kirk and Young, 'I Will Set his Hand', 338.
55 Horsley, *Hearing the Whole Story*, 105.
56 On ambivalence and colonial mimicry, see Liew, *Politics of Parousia*, 93–94; Moore, 'Representing Empire in Mark', 24–44; Samuel, *A Postcolonial Reading*, 26–32; Leander, *Discourses of Empire*, 44–48.
57 For a lengthy list of scholars who read the demoniac 'legion' in Mark 5:1–20 as negatively alluding to the Roman military occupation of the land, see Leander, *Discourses of Empire*, 201–202 n.1.
58 Ballentine, *The Conflict Myth*, 178.

To conclude, the portrayal of Jesus as the royal heir of King David, subjugating the hostile forces of chaos that threaten to undo civilisation as the representative of the God of Israel, was built upon an older imperial edifice and is consistent with Mark's christological presentation as a whole. Hopefully, this reading will provide a way forward between the scholarly debates over whether Mark 6:45–52 supports a divine or an idealised human agent Christology.

Bibliography

Achtemeier, P. J.   '"And He Followed Him": Miracles and Discipleship in Mark 10:46–52', *Semeia* 11 (1978), 115–45.

Achtemeier, P. J.   'The Origin and Function of the Pre-Markan Miracle Catenae', JBL 91.2 (1972), 198–221.

Ahearne-Kroll, S. P.   *The Psalms of Lament in Mark's Passion: Jesus' Davidic Suffering* (Cambridge: Cambridge University Press, 2007).

Ballentine, D. S.   *The Conflict Myth and the Biblical Tradition* (Oxford: Oxford University Press, 2015).

Blackburn, B.   *Theos Aner and the Markan Miracle Traditions: A Critique of the Theios Aner Concept as an Interpretive Background of the Miracle Traditions Used by Mark* (Tübingen: Mohr Siebeck, 1991).

Boring, M. E.   'Markan Christology: God-Language for Jesus?' NTS 45.4 (1999), 451–71.

Botner, M.   *Jesus Christ as the Son of David in the Gospel of Mark* (SNTSMS 174; Cambridge: Cambridge University Press, 2019).

Briquel, D.   'The Punishment of the Hellespont by Xerxes: Perception of Religious Behaviour of the Enemy in Conflict Situations', *Graeco-Latina Brunensia* 21.2 (2016), 51–60.

Burger, C.   *Jesus als Davidssohn: Eine traditionsgeschichtliche Untersuchung* (Göttingen: Vandenhoeck & Ruprecht, 1970).

Choi, J. Y.   *Postcolonial Discipleship of Embodiment: An Asian and Asian American Feminist Reading of the Gospel of Mark* (New York, NY: Palgrave Macmillan, 2015).

Collins, A.   'Mark and His Readers: The Son of God among Greeks and Romans', *HTR* 93.2 (2000), 85–100.

Collins, A. Y.   'Rulers, Divine Men, and Walking on the Water (Mark 6:45-52)', in L. Bormann, K. del Tredici, and A. Standhartinger (eds.) *Religious Propaganda and Missionary Competition in the New Testament World: Essays Honoring Dieter Georgi* (Leiden: Brill, 1994), 205–27.

Collins, A. Y., and J. J. Collins,   *King and Messiah as Son of God: Divine, Human, and Angelic Messianic Figures in Biblical and Related Literature* (Grand Rapids, MI: Eerdmans, 2008).

Combs, J. R.   'A Ghost on the Water? Understanding an Absurdity in Mark 6:49-50', *JBL* 127.2 (2008), 345–58.

Cotter, W. J.   *The Christ of the Miracles Stories: Portrait through Encounter* (Grand Rapids, MI: Baker Academic, 2010).

Crossley, J.   'Mark's Christology and the Scholarly Creation of a Non-Jewish Christ of Faith', in J. Crossley (ed.), *Judaism, Jewish Identities and the Gospel Tradition: Essays in Honour of Maurice Casey* (London: Equinox, 2010), 118–51.

Evans, C.   'Mark's Incipit and the Priene Calendar Inscription: From Jewish Gospel to Greco-Roman Gospel', *Journal of Greco-Roman Judaism and Christianity* 1 (2000), 67–81.

Frenschkowski, M.   *Offenbarung und Epiphanie: Die verborgene Epiphanie in Spätantike und frühem Christentum* (WUNT II. Reihe; Tübingen: Mohr Siebeck, 1997).

Gathercole, S. J.   *The Pre-existent Son: Recovering the Christologies of Matthew, Mark, and Luke* (Grand Rapids, MI: Eerdmans, 2006).

Geddert, T. J.   'The Implied Yhwh Christology of Mark's Gospel: Mark's Challenge to the Reader to "Connect the Dots"', *Bulletin for Biblical Research* 25.3 (2015), 325–40.

Gundry, R. H.   *Mark: A Commentary on His Apology for the Cross* (Grand Rapids, MI: Eerdmans, 1993).

Gunkel, H.   *Schöpfung und Chaos in Urzeit und Endzeit: Eine religionsgeschichtliche Untersuchung über Gen 1 und Ap Joh 12* (Göttingen: Vandenhoeck & Ruprecht, 1895).

Hahn, F.   *Titles of Jesus in Christology: Their History in Early Christianity* (trans. H. Knight and G. Ogg; London: Lutterworth, 1969).

Hays, R.   *Reading Backwards: Figural Christology and the Fourfold Gospel Witness* (London: SPCK, 2015).

Heil, J. P.   *Jesus Walking on the Sea: Meaning and Gospel Functions of Matt. 14:22– 23, Mark 6:45–52 and John 6:15b–21* (AnBib 87; Rome: Biblical Institute Press, 1981).

Horsley, R. A.   *Hearing the Whole Story: The Politics of Plot in Mark's Gospel* (Louisville, KY: Westminster John Knox, 2001).

Hossfeld F.-L., and E. Zenger   *Psalms 2: A Commentary on Psalms 51–100* (trans. L. M. Maloney; *Hermeneia*; Minneapolis, MN: Fortress, 2005).

Hurtado, L. W.   *Lord Jesus Christ: Devotion to Jesus in Earliest Christianity* (Grand Rapids, MI: Eerdmans, 2003).

Juel, D.   *Messianic Exegesis: Christological Interpretation of the Old Testament in Early Christianity* (Philadelphia, PA: Fortress, 1988).

Kelber, W.   *The Kingdom in Mark: A New Place and a New Time* (Philadelphia, PA: Fortress, 1974).

Kim, T. H.   'The Anarthrous Υιος Θεου in Mark 15,39 and the Roman Imperial Cult', *Biblica* 79.2 (1998), 221–41.

Kingsbury, J. D.   *The Christology of Mark's Gospel* (Minneapolis, MN: Fortress, 1983).

Kirk, J. R. D.   *A Man Attested by God: The Human Jesus of the Synoptic Gospels* (Grand Rapids, MI: Eerdmans, 2016).

Kirk, J. R. D., and S. L. Young,   'I Will Set his Hand to the Sea: Psalm 88:26 (LXX) and Christology in Mark', *JBL* 133.2 (2014), 333–40.

Leander, H.   *Discourses of Empire: The Gospel of Mark from a Postcolonial Perspective* (SBLSemS 71; Atlanta: SBL, 2013).

Liew, T. S. B.   *Politics of Parousia: Reading Mark Inter(con)textually* (Leiden: Brill, 1999).

Mack, B.   *A Myth of Innocence: Mark and Christian Origins* (Philadelphia, PA: Fortress, 1988).

Madden, P. J. *Jesus' Walking on the Sea: An Investigation of the Origin of a Narrative Account* (BZNW 81; Berlin: De Gruyter, 1997).

Malbon, E. S. *Mark's Jesus: Characterization as Narrative Christology* (Waco, TX: Baylor University Press, 2009).

Marcus, J. *Mark 1–8: A New Translation with Introduction and Commentary* (AB; New York, NY: Doubleday, 2000).

McPhee, B. D. 'Walk, Don't Run: Jesus's Water Walking is Unparalleled in Greco-Roman Mythology', *JBL* 135.4 (2016), 763–77.

Meier, J. P. *A Marginal Jew: Rethinking the Historical Jesus, vol. 2: Mentor, Message and Miracles* (New York, NY: Doubleday, 1994).

Peppard, M. *The Son of God in the Roman World: Divine Sonship in its Social and Political Context* (Oxford: Oxford University Press, 2011).

Ritt, H. 'Der "Seewandel Jesu" (Mk 6, 45–52 par): Literarische und theologische Aspekte', *BZ* 23 (1979), 71–84.

Samuel, S. *A Postcolonial Reading of Mark's Story of Jesus* (London: T&T Clark, 2007).

Tate, M. E. *Psalms 51–100* (Word; Dallas, TX: Word Books, 1990),

Telford, W. R. *The Theology of the Gospel of Mark* (Cambridge: Cambridge University Press, 1999).

Tyson, J. 'The Blindness of the Disciples in Mark', *JBL* 80 (1961), 261–68.

Watts, R. E. *Isaiah's New Exodus in Mark* (Tübingen: Mohr Siebeck, 1997).

Whitenton, M. R. *Hearing Kyriotic Sonship: A Cognitive and Rhetorical Approach to the Characterization of Mark's Jesus* (Leiden: Brill, 2016).

Winn, A. 'The Gospel of Mark: A Response to Imperial Roman Propaganda', in A. Winn (ed.), *An Introduction to Empire in the New Testament* (Atlanta: SBL, 2016), 91–106.

CHAPTER 7

'With a Noble and Good Heart'
ἐν καρδίᾳ καλῇ καὶ ἀγαθῇ
(Luke 8:15) in Graeco-Roman Cultural-communicative Context

Chris Spark

Abstract

The addition of *kale kai agathe* in Luke's rendition of the Parable of the Sower (8:15) has cultural-communicative significance for Graeco-Roman hearers in his audience. Luke's use of *agathos* across his narrative regularly carries ethical weight in characterisation, consistent with the use of this term in the Graeco-Roman benefaction system. The full term, *kalos kai agathos*, carried significant cultural weight in describing the ideal person, which is illustrated by a number of literary and inscriptional examples. This cultural weight is also reflected in the term's limited use in Jewish sources—a limited use which, in itself, also points to the predominantly Graeco-Roman currency of the term. The combined weight of this evidence suggests that Luke intentionally uses this addition to interpret Jesus' meaning for Graeco-Roman ears.

In Luke's rendering of the Parable of the Sower, we see a number of differences to Mark's version (Luke 8:5–15; Mark 4:3–20). Assuming Markan priority, a couple of these differences seem to be examples of Luke's interest in communicating Jesus' words in culturally significant ways to Graeco-Roman members of his audience.[1] This essay will focus on one of these differences, and the Graeco-Roman cultural significance of it.

Luke makes a unique addition to Jesus' interpretation of the final lot of seed in the parable of the sower. In Mark, Jesus says that this episode represents 'those who hear the word' (οἵτινες ἀκούουσιν τὸν λόγον; 4:20), to which Luke adds 'with a good and noble heart' (ἐν καρδίᾳ καλῇ καὶ ἀγαθῇ; 8:15).[2] There are two major elements to this addition: the noun καρδία, and the double adjective phrase καλὸς καὶ ἀγαθός. Of these, as we shall see, the latter is most significant in terms of Luke's concern for Jesus connecting with Graeco-Roman readers. Therefore, we will focus on this double term in this investigation, though we will also touch briefly on its combination with καρδία.

The particular construction καλὸς καὶ ἀγαθός was widely used as a double term in ancient Greek. This usage resulted in the creation of combined terms including καλοκἀγαθός and καλοκἀγαθία, however the combination was still written in divided forms (as here in Luke), especially by earlier writers.[3] Therefore, we will be considering the significance of this double term as a unit.

Bovon considers Luke's use of the term to be directed particularly at the Greek thought world: 'In order to make comprehensible the special character of Christian existence, Luke uses the Greek concept

---

[1] Luke's intended audience is very likely to have particularly included people of Gentile origin, and it is likely that such people were at the forefront of his mind as he wrote (Barnett, *Jesus and the Rise*, 378; Bock, *Luke*, 1:14–15; Bovon, *Luke 1*, 9; Bruce, *Book of Acts*, 11–13; Caird, *Gospel of Luke*, 44; Chen, *Luke*, 4–5; Fitzmyer, *Gospel According to Luke*, 1:57–59; Fleming, *Contextualization*, 250; Guthrie, *New Testament Introduction*, 109; Johnson, *Gospel of Luke*, 3). Harnack furnishes some examples of non-explicit indicators of Luke's Gentile readership which, though at points overstated, have considerable cumulative weight (*Luke the Physician*, 119 n.2; 126 n.1). Even commentators who are wary of emphasising a particular audience tend to see notable factors in Luke's work that fit with a high degree of Graeco-Roman or Gentile concern (for example, Carroll, *Luke*, 2–3; Green, 'Luke', 550; Parsons, *Luke*, 17; cf. Wright and Bird, *New Testament in its World*, 614–16).

[2] He also changes Mark's present verb to an aorist participle.

[3] LSJ καλοκἀγαθός; Grundmann, *TDNT* 3:538.

of ideal existence, καλοκἀγαθία ("noble goodness")'.[4] Marshall suggests that it is more likely that Luke has 'simply used a current form of words suggested by the description of the soil' without particular force.[5] Marshall's conclusion may seem justified due to the use of ἀγαθός and καλός to describe the good earth in 8:8 and 8:15 respectively. However, it misses two important factors: firstly, the use of ἀγαθός in verse 8 (and more widely) is itself intentional and fits with Luke's employment of καλὸς καὶ ἀγαθός in verse 15; and secondly, there was a freight of meaning contained in the term καλὸς καὶ ἀγαθός in the Graeco-Roman world, and consequent significance for Graeco-Roman ears. We will look at these factors in turn, seeking to evaluate the significance of Luke's change.

ἀγαθός in Luke 8:8 and the wider narrative

In Jesus' telling of the fourth lot of seed, Mark has him say that the seed fell 'into the good earth' (εἰς τὴν γῆν τὴν καλήν; Mark 4:8). Luke's only change is the adjective for 'good' (εἰς τὴν γῆν τὴν ἀγαθήν; Luke 8:8). This change may seem difficult to explain because Luke uses καλός at other times, including in verse 15 of this parable.[6] However, observing the *way* Luke uses both καλός and ἀγαθός gives reason to think that Luke's change to ἀγαθός in 8:8 may well be intentional and significant.

While Mark uses ἀγαθός only four times and καλός eleven times, Luke uses ἀγαθός more often than καλός in both the Gospel and Acts.[7] Particularly notable is his usage in Acts. Both uses of καλός are in stereotyped phrases: the name Fair Havens (27:8); and the phrase 'as you know very well' (ὡς καὶ σὺ κάλλιον ἐπιγινώσκεις; 25:10). On the other hand, while three uses of ἀγαθός are in the courtesy title 'most excellent' (23:26; 24:3; 26:25),[8] the other three all have ethical weight in descriptions of believers: firstly, Paul, before the Sanhedrin, describes

---

4 Bovon, *Luke 1*, 311.
5 Marshall, *Gospel of Luke*, 327; cf. Marshall 'Tradition and Theology', 72–73.
6 See Bock, *Luke*, 1:726 n.18.
7 He uses ἀγαθός sixteen times in Luke and six times in Acts; καλός nine times in Luke and twice in Acts.
8 See Barrett, *Acts of the Apostles*, 2:1082; Bruce, *Book of Acts*, 29 n.3.

his conscience as ἀγαθός (23:1); secondly, in the characterisation of an exemplary disciple, Tabitha's works are described as ἀγαθός (9:36); and most significantly Barnabas is described as ἀνὴρ ἀγαθός in relation to his good work in Antioch (11:24). This last description is also applied to Joseph of Arimathea (by Luke only), with the addition of 'righteous' (ἀνὴρ ἀγαθὸς καὶ δίκαιος; Luke 23:50).

The term ἀνὴρ ἀγαθός was associated with the benefaction system in the Graeco-Roman world, which was centred around generosity and reciprocity between benefactors and those they helped.[9] It was characterised by the term ἀρετή which spoke of 'distinction and excellence of the highest order', and ἀνὴρ ἀγαθός was a 'common synonym for a person marked by arete'.[10] Hence, in a fourth century B.C.E. inscription, Menelaos of Peiagonia is officially commended 'as a good man [ἀνὴρ ἀγαθός], who does whatever good he can for the people of Athens'.[11] A Hellenistic inscription from Smyrna describes Dionysius son of Dionysius as a benefactor of the people (εὐεργέτην τοῦ δήμου), honouring him as a 'virtuous man [ἄνδρα ἀγαθόν] with regard to the body of citizens'.[12] Another ἀνὴρ ἀγαθός, Opramoas (early-mid second century C.E.), is described as a model citizen.[13] Dio Chrysostom's description of the memorials given to his family by his city of Prusa provide a developed example of this phenomenon. In the course of this description, he speaks of the 'honours bestowed upon [his father] for being a good citizen (ἄνδρα ἀγαθόν) and for administering the city with uprightness as long as he lived' (*Orat.* 44.3–4).

In light of this, it is notable that Luke presents both Joseph and Barnabas as men of great character who do beneficent acts in connection with their description as ἀνὴρ ἀγαθός: Joseph had not consented to the Sanhedrin's action against Jesus, was waiting for the kingdom of God, and acted to give Jesus a proper burial (Luke 23:50–53); Barnabas encouraged the church at Antioch, was full of the Holy Spirit and faith, is associated with large numbers of people coming to

---

9 Danker, *Benefactor*, 318, 487.
10 Danker, *Benefactor*, 318–19.
11 Danker, *Benefactor*, 87; cf. p. 319.
12 *New Docs* 9, 6. This inscription can be viewed at: https://inscriptions.packhum.org/text/255053 (accessed 8 May 2020).
13 Danker, *Benefactor*, 115; cf. 319. Further examples are noted by Danker (*Benefactor*, 318–19).

the Lord, and brings Saul to Antioch to teach the church (Acts 11:23–26). The term is applied to these men in a way very much in keeping with Graeco-Roman benefaction language.

In Luke 8:8, the term ἀγαθός is applied to the earth and is associated with bearing fruit, and this in turn is representative of *people* who respond to the word of God rightly. When this is seen in light of his usage of ἀγαθός across his work, it would seem Luke's change here is quite intentional.[14] He seems to be tapping into Graeco-Roman understandings of moral characterisation. Hence, Luke's use of καλὸς καὶ ἀγαθός in 8:15 is unlikely to be an innocuous combination of terms simply suggested by the adjectives used to describe the fourth soil in the parable telling and its interpretation. The change to ἀγαθός in the telling of the parable was itself intentional and purposed, so we might expect any appropriation of this term in the interpretation to reflect that intentionality. These expectations are indeed confirmed when we consider the second factor mentioned above: the freight of meaning in the term καλὸς καὶ ἀγαθός for Graeco-Roman readers.

The significance of καλὸς καὶ ἀγαθός[15]

This term 'plays a most important role in Gk. life'.[16] It originated in the political sphere of the Greek world, and from there penetrated the social and ethical spheres of Graeco-Roman life more generally.[17] It seems often to have designated someone of noble birth, especially in an earlier period, but later to have more often described 'a perfect character',[18] 'exceptional citizens',[19] a person 'of lofty moral character and

---

14 In addition to those instances already discussed, see 6:45; 19:17 for further examples of ἀγαθός being significantly used of right action.
15 Weaver, 'Noble and Good Heart' is the most significant treatment of this term in its context in Luke 8. Weaver has an especially helpful investigation of the use of καλὸς καὶ ἀγαθός (and related terms) in the Greek moral philosophy tradition, even if at times the conclusions he draws from his analysis (including the perceived emphasis on the divine λόγος in his sources [e.g. pp. 164, 170–71]) do not seem sufficiently demonstrated by the evidence provided.
16 Grundmann, *TDNT* 3:538.
17 Grundmann, *TDNT* 3:538–9.
18 LSJ καλοκἀγαθός.
19 BDAG καλός 2.b.

civic-mindedness'.²⁰ Danker calls it 'one of the highest terms of praise in the Greek vocabulary', and, significantly, notes that it is a synonym for ἀνὴρ ἀγαθός.²¹ This was clearly a phrase of considerable weight in Graeco-Roman usage.

Some instances from Graeco-Roman literature will illustrate. According to Epictetus, the Stoic philosopher roughly contemporaneous with Luke,²² the καλὸς καὶ ἀγαθός is a person who deals with 'his impressions according to nature' (*Diss.* iii.3.1), and aligns his own life and will with God's will (iii.24.95–102). This is exactly the sort of person Epictetus is encouraging philosophy students to aspire to be (cf. iii.3; iii.24.103). Dio Chrysostom similarly, in a story he tells of Socrates' exhortations on what is necessary for good citizenship (and particularly for fulfilment of public office), says 'if a man strives earnestly to be good and honourable (καλὸς καὶ ἀγαθός), that is nothing but being a philosopher' (*Orat.* 13.27–28). Again, this is what he (and his Socrates) are seeking to encourage. An honorary decree from Delphi (79 C.E.) declares that Marcus Tourranius Hermonikos is awarded citizenship along with all the other 'honors that are accorded to exceptional men [καλοκἀγαθοί]'.²³ A decree of consolation states that the deceased youth in question 'strove to be a model of arete' and was a 'fine young man' (νεανίαν καλὸν καὶ ἀγαθόν; MAMA 412c *ll*. 4–6).²⁴

A search of inscriptions contained in the Packard Humanities Institute online database reveals scores of occurrences of καλὸς καὶ ἀγαθός in its various inflections.²⁵ The majority of these seem to be used as appellations of people for their virtuous acts and gifts. Further, a considerable majority occur in the stereotyped phrase ἀνὴρ καλὸς καὶ ἀγαθός (or its inflected equivalent), further reinforcing the impression

---

20 BDAG καλοκἀγαθία. The article at this point refers to the adjectival combination rather than the noun.
21 Danker, *Benefactor*, 319.
22 Scholer, 'Writing and Literature', 1287.
23 Danker, *Benefactor*, 71; cf. p. 319–20.
24 This inscription can be viewed at http://insaph.kcl.ac.uk/iaph2007/iAph120704.html#edition (accessed 8 May 2020). See Danker 1982, 67, 320.
25 https://inscriptions.packhum.org/. In the singular alone, there are 102 occurrences in the nominative, 14 in the genitive, 11 in the dative, and 147 in the accusative.

that this was a standard term that would be recognisable to Graeco-Roman hearers.²⁶ A couple of particular examples from amongst these inscriptions will illustrate. In an inscription from around the start of the third century B.C.E., the town of Arcesine on the Aegean island of Amorgos granted citizenship to a certain Epianaktides, who was from the nearby island Therai, due to his provision of grain for them. Epianaktides is designated an ἀνὴρ καλὸς καὶ ἀγαθός who did 'whatever good he was able' (ποιε[ῖ] ἀγαθὸν ὅτι ἂν δύνηται; IG XII 7.11 *ll*. 3–5).²⁷ In a funerary inscription from Aphrodisias, Hermias Glykon is honoured as 'a fine and good man' (ἄνδρα καλὸν καὶ ἀγαθόν), having served the city in various official capacities and with much financial generosity (PHI Aphrodisias 485 = *MAMA* 8.471 *ll*. 3–13). This ἀνὴρ καλὸς καὶ ἀγαθός is said to have lived with the display of 'every virtue' (πάσης ἀρετῆς) and to have been honoured with other decrees commemorating his outstanding citizenship (*ll*. 14–16).²⁸

There are also some instances of a feminine version of this term.²⁹ For example, a first-century inscription from Mantinea in Arcadia praises one Julia Eudia (IG V 2.269). She is introduced as a 'good and noble woman' (γυνὴ καλὴ καὶ ἀγ[α]θ[ή] [*ll*. 2–3]), and the inscription goes on to describe her 'magnanimity and goodness', calling her a 'benefactor' (εὐεργέτις; *ll*. 13–18).³⁰

It seems clear that the term καλὸς καὶ ἀγαθός denoted outstanding virtue and character in Graeco-Roman usage.

One reason Marshall gives for questioning Luke's intentional

---

26 83 of the 102 nominative singular occurrences of καλὸς καὶ ἀγαθός appear in this phrase (along with at least 4 others that have very similar phrases, only having ἀνήρ occurring in a slightly different word order [Priene 34; Priene 45; Iasos 29; Priene 48]), 7 of 11 in the dative singular, and 121 of the 147 in the accusative singular. The situation with genitive is slightly different, with only 2 of the 14 singular occurrences being with ἀνδρός. However, another stereotyped phrase dominates the genitive occurrences: the noble and good (i.e. honourable) *state* (δήμου καλοῦ καὶ ἀγαθοῦ), which constitutes 8 of the 14 genitive occurrences.
27 Translation mine. See Reger, 'Aspects of the Role', 179. Inscription can be viewed at https://inscriptions.packhum.org/text/78652 (accessed 8 May 2020).
28 Translation taken from http://insaph.kcl.ac.uk/iaph2007/iAph120306.html (accessed 8 May 2020), where the inscription can also be viewed.
29 Danker notes that, just as the combined term καλοκἀγαθός can describe a man, so καληκἀγαθή can describe a woman (*Benefactor*, 319).
30 Translation mine. Inscription can be viewed at https://inscriptions.packhum.org/text/32305 (accessed 8 May 2020).

Graeco-Roman allusion through this term is its use in Hellenistic Judaism with 'no trace of its characteristic Classical Greek meaning'.[31] However, a closer examination of such use shows that this term, though it had crossed to some extent into Hellenistic Judaism, did in fact retain the meaning which it had in the wider Graeco-Roman world. In 2 Maccabees 15:12 the former high priest Onias is spoken of as ἄνδρα καλὸν καὶ ἀγαθόν, followed by further acclamations of his character. Onias is described with the same terms in connection with his unimpeachable character in 4 Maccabees 4:1. Tobit uses καλὸς καὶ ἀγαθός in much the same way, applying it to both lineage and people of exemplary character (5:14 [LXX]; 7:6; 9:6 [G^II text]),[32] including that of Tobit himself, whose pious character and good deeds are a major theme of the book.[33] These uses of καλὸς καὶ ἀγαθός exhaust its occurrences in the LXX, and fit very comfortably into the 'excellence of character' semantic field which we saw in Graeco-Roman examples.[34]

Philo's usage of the term is similar. He sees Adam as the only man who has been truly good and noble (ὁ γὰρ ἀληθείᾳ καλὸς καὶ ἀγαθὸς οὗτος ὄντως ἦν; *Opif.* 136). He speaks approvingly of Phinehas' action against Moabite and Israelite collusion in the wilderness (cf. Num. 25:5–8) as bold but appropriate ἀνδρὶ καλῷ καὶ ἀγαθῷ (*Mos.* 301). He notes that 'in the land of the barbarians' there are companies of 'good and noble men' (καλῶν καὶ ἀγαθῶν [...] ἀνδρῶν), their finest examples of virtue (*Prob.* 74).[35] Again we clearly see in Philo's usage, in his strongly Hellenised way, the idea of excellence in character and

---

31 Marshall, 'Tradition and Theology', 73; cf. Marshall, *Gospel of Luke*, 327, where he notes Tobit and 2 Maccabees as examples.
32 Although Tobit is very likely originally written in a Semitic language (Di Lella, 'To the Reader', 457–58), the use of καλὸς καὶ ἀγαθός in the Greek translations still at least reflects the selection of this term to express excellent character and nobility.
33 Helyer, 'Tobit', 1238.
34 Additionally, the noun καλοκἀγαθία occurs in 4 Maccabees five times, in keeping with that book's wider Hellenistic-Jewish picture of virtue and character, again supporting our picture of the semantic field Luke 8:15 evokes (4 Macc 1:10; 3:18; 11:22; 13:25; 15:9). See further Weaver, 'Noble and Good', 163, who also notes a connection in 4 Maccabees between καλοκἀγαθία and ὑπομονή ('endurance'), as there is in Luke 8:15.
35 Philo's other usages of the term, confirming the picture we get from those examined, are in *Det.* 134; *Migr.* 88; *Mut.* 31; *Virt.* 198; *QG* 2.41. He additionally uses the noun καλοκἀγαθία over 80 times, largely in ways that reflect the general Graeco-Roman history of usage for exemplary noble character (cf. Weaver, 'Good and Noble', 155–60, 162, for discussion of some of this usage).

exemplary humanity.

From looking at the uses of καλὸς καὶ ἀγαθός in the LXX and Philo, two things seem clear. Firstly, while this term did not thoroughly penetrate Hellenistic Judaism, to the extent that it did it was strongly in line with Graeco-Roman usage, denoting exemplary character, ideal humanity, and occasionally noble birth. It was very often associated with good works reflecting the virtuous character of the person in question.

Secondly, though, the term *does not* seem to have penetrated Judaism deeply. There are no occurrences in the LXX translations of the canonical Old Testament books, and the only New Testament usage is our reference in Luke. The related noun is found only in the very Hellenised 4 Maccabees.[36] While the term was not unknown in Judaism, its employment by Luke is likely to be aimed at Graeco-Roman, rather than Jewish, ears.

Luke applies this term to the heart (καρδία) of the one who hears the word and produces a crop (8:15). While καλὸς καὶ ἀγαθός is usually simply applied to a person or group of people, the heart is 'the OT term for the seat of human reaction to God and his promptings',[37] and was not unknown in Greek literature as 'a seat of moral and intellectual life'.[38] So Luke's use of it here with καλὸς καὶ ἀγαθός, most likely under the influence of Isaiah 6,[39] would probably not be totally foreign to Graeco-Roman readers, and would be clarified through the introduction of the heart in the parable already in this connection (8:12), and by Luke's wider use of the term.

---

36 In Codex Sinaiticus, James 5:10 reads the noun καλοκἀγαθία in place of UBS⁴'s κακοπαθίας (suffering) (Danker, *Jesus and the New Age*, 177). This variant is lightly attested, but does seem to show that a (presumably Graeco-Roman) scribe thought it natural to say the prophets were 'examples of *good-nobleness* and patience'.
37 Fitzmyer, *Gospel According to Luke*, 1:714; cf. Meadors, 'Hardness of Heart', 360.
38 Behm, *TDNT* 3:611–13.
39 The prominence of καρδία in Isaiah 6:9–10, quoted in part by Luke a few verses earlier (8:10), and in full by Matthew (13:14–15), probably explains both evangelists adding it to Mark here (Nolland, *Gospel of Matthew*, 540; *pace* Wenham, 'Interpreting the Parable', 310). This Isaiah reference remains important for interpretation of the parable in Luke, as it is in Mark and Matthew (*pace* Weaver, 'Noble and Good', 165 n.54).

Conclusion

It would seem, then, that Luke's unique description of right response to the word ἐν καρδίᾳ καλῇ καὶ ἀγαθῇ was intentionally used in order to tap into the prominent semantic field of benefaction in the Graeco-Roman world, and especially to the καλὸς καὶ ἀγαθός as the ideal citizen, a person as one should be.[40] Luke's replacement of καλός with ἀγαθός in the parable telling (8:8) to describe the same people reinforces this, especially in light of Luke's wider application of ἀγαθός to exemplar figures—in two cases also using benefaction language (ἀνὴρ ἀγαθός). In employing καλὸς καὶ ἀγαθός in this way, Luke makes it clear that the response to the word of God seen in the fourth lot of seed is the right response. He is, in effect, using this Hellenistic ethical term to say 'surely this is the only honourable way to be hearers!'[41] For those who hear Jesus speak in Luke, this term acts to align them with the 'good earth'. They are moved to want to be like this fourth group. This is, of course, very similar to a major effect of the parable in Mark,[42] although it may be heightened in Luke. But, notably, Luke's addition taps into the picture of an ideal person *for Graeco-Roman hearers* in particular. Danker's conclusion about Luke more widely seems apt here: 'Luke found in the Graeco-Roman world's preoccupation with civic and private benefactors an opportunity to interpret for a wider audience the significance of Jesus as Israel's Messiah'.[43] To that end he modified Jesus' words at this point to interpret Jesus' meaning for his particular audience: the one who wishes to exhibit the characteristics of the καλὸς καὶ ἀγαθός will respond to Jesus' word of the kingdom by hearing it, retaining it, and persevering with it.

---

40 '[N]o subject dominates Graeco-Roman literary and non-literary texts as does the remembered benefactor' (Danker, *Benefactor*, 488). Whether or not the totality of this claim is accepted, the vital prominence of benefaction in the Graeco-Roman world is beyond question (cf. also Walker, 'Benefactor', 157).
41 Nolland, *Luke*, 1:387.
42 Lane, *Gospel of Mark*, 161–63.
43 Danker, *Jesus and the New Age*, xv.

Bibliography

Barnett, P. W. — *Jesus & the Rise of Early Christianity: A History of New Testament Times* (Downers Grove, IL: IVP Academic, 1999).

Barrett, C. K. — *A Critical and Exegetical Commentary on the Acts of the Apostles* (2 vols.; International Critical Commentary; Edinburgh: T&T Clark, 2004).

Bauer, W. — *A Greek-English Lexicon of the New Testament and Other Early Christian Literature* (F. W. Danker [ed.] 3rd edn.; Chicago, IL: University of Chicago Press, 2000. BibleWorks. v.10).

Behm, J. — 'καρδία, καρδιογνώστης, σκληροκαρδία', in G. Kittel and G. W. Bromiley (eds.), *Theological Dictionary of the New Testament, Volume 3, Θ–Κ* (Grand Rapids, MI: Eerdmans, 1965. [German: 1938]), 608–14.

Bock, D. L. — *Luke* (2 vols.; Baker Exegetical Commentary on the New Testament; Grand Rapids, MI: Baker Academic, 1994–1996).

Bovon, F. — *Luke 1: A Commentary on the Gospel of Luke 1:1–9:50* (edited by Helmut Koester; translated by C. M. Thomas; Hermeneia; Minneapolis, MN: Fortress, 2002 [German: 1989]).

Bruce, F. F. — *The Book of the Acts* (The New International Commentary on the New Testament; revised edn; Grand Rapids, MI: Eerdmans, 1988).

Caird, G. B. — *The Gospel of St Luke* (Pelican New Testament Commentaries; Middlesex: Penguin, 1963).

Carroll, J. T. — *Luke: A Commentary* (New Testament Library; Louisville, KY: Westminster John Knox, 2012).

Chen, D. G. — *Luke* (New Covenant Commentary Series; Eugene, OR: Cascade Books, 2017).

Danker, F. W. — *Benefactor: Epigraphic Study of a Graeco-Roman and New Testament Semantic Field* (St. Louis, MO: Clayton Pub. House, 1982).

Danker, F. W. — *Jesus and the New Age: A Commentary on St Luke's Gospel* (revised edn; Philadelphia, PA: Fortress, 1988).

Di Lella, A. A.	'To the Reader of Tobit', in *A New English Translation of the Septuagint* (New York, NY: Oxford University Press, 2007), 456–58.
Dio Chrysostom	*Dio Chrysostom II: Discourses 12–30* (translated by J. W. Cohoon; Loeb Classical Library 339; Cambridge, MA: Harvard University Press, 1939).
Dio Chrysostom	*Dio Chrysostom IV: Discourses 37–60* (translated by H. Lamar Crosby; Loeb Classical Library 376; Cambridge, MA: Harvard University Press, 1946).
Epictetus	*The Discourses as Reported by Arrian, The Manual, and Fragments* (translated by W. A. Oldfather; 2 vols; Loeb Classical Library; Cambridge, MA: Harvard University Press, 1925–1928).
Fitzmyer, J. A.	*The Gospel According to Luke: Introduction, Translation and Notes* (2 vols; Anchor Bible 28; New York, NY: Doubleday, 1981–1985).
Flemming, D.	*Contextualization in the New Testament: Patterns for Theology and Mission* (Downers Grove, IL: IVP, 2005).
Green, J. B.	'Luke, Gospel Of', in J. B. Green, J. K. Brown, and N. Perrin (eds.), *Dictionary of Jesus and the Gospels* (Downers Grove, IL.: IVP Academic, 2013 2nd edn. [1992]), 540–52.
Grundmann, W.	'καλός', in G. Kittel and G. W. Bromiley (eds.), *Theological Dictionary of the New Testament, Volume 3, Θ–K* (Grand Rapids, MI: Eerdmans, 1965 [German: 1938]), 536–50.
Guthrie, D.	*New Testament Introduction* (4th edn; Master Reference Collection; Downers Grove, IL.: InterVarsity Press, 1990).
Harnack, A.	*Luke, the Physician: The Author of the Third Gospel and the Acts of the Apostles* (translated by J. R. Wilkinson; London: Williams & Norgate, 1907 [German: 1906]).
Helyer, L. R.	'Tobit', in S. E. Porter and C. A. Evans (eds.), *Dictionary of New Testament Background: A Compendium of Contemporary Biblical Scholarship* (Downers Grove, IL: IVP, 2000), 1238–41.
Johnson, L. T.	*The Gospel of Luke* (Sacra Pagina, vol. 3; Collegeville, MN: Liturgical, 1992).

Lane, W. L. *The Gospel of Mark* (New International Commentary on the New Testament; Grand Rapids, MI: Eerdmans, 1974).

Liddell, H. G., and R. Scott *A Greek-English Lexicon* (9th edn; revised and augmented by H. S. Jones, with the assistance of R. McKenzie; supplement edited by P. G. W. Glare; Oxford: Clarendon, 1996).

Llewelyn, S. R. (ed.) *New Documents Illustrating Early Christianity Vol. 9* (Macquarie University Ancient History Documentary Research Centre; Grand Rapids, MI: Eerdmans, 2002).

Marshall, I. H. 'Tradition and Theology in Luke (Luke 8:5–15),' *Tyndale Bulletin* 20 (1969), 56–75.

Marshall, I. H. *The Gospel of Luke: A Commentary in the Greek Text* (New International Greek Testament Commentary; Exeter: Paternoster, 1978).

Meadors, E. P. 'Hardness of Heart', in J. B. Green, J. K. Brown, and N. Perrin (eds.), *Dictionary of Jesus and the Gospels* (Downers Grove, IL.: IVP Academic, 2013 2nd edn. [1992]), 350–62.

Nolland, J. *Luke* (3 vols; Word Biblical Commentary 35; Dallas: Word, 1989–1993).

Nolland, J. *The Gospel of Matthew: A Commentary in the Greek Text* (New International Greek Testament Commentary; Grand Rapids, MI: Eerdmans / Bletchley: Paternoster, 2005).

Parsons, M. C. *Luke* (Paideia Commentaries on the New Testament; Grand Rapids, MI: Baker Academic, 2015).

Reger, G. 'Aspects of the Role of Merchants in the Political Life of the Hellenistic World', in Carlo Zaccagnini (ed.), *Mercanti e politica nel mondo antico*. Roma: "L'Erma" di Bretschneider, 2003), 165–97.

Scholer, D. M. 'Writing and Literature: Greco-Roman', in S. E. Porter and C. A. Evans (eds.), *Dictionary of New Testament Background: A Compendium of Contemporary Biblical Scholarship* (Downers Grove, IL: IVP, 2000), 1282–89.

Walker, D. D. 'Benefactor', in S. E. Porter and C. A. Evans (eds.), *Dictionary of New Testament Background: A Compendium of Contemporary Biblical Scholarship* (Downers Grove, IL: IVP, 2000), 157–59.

Weaver, J. B.	'The Noble and Good Heart: Καλοκἀγαθία in Luke's Parable of the Sower', in P. Gray and G. R O'Day (eds.), *Scripture and Traditions: Essays on Early Judaism and Christianity in Honor of Carl R. Holladay* (Supplements to Novum Testamentum; Leiden: Brill, 2008), 151–71.
Wenham, D.	'Interpreting the Parable of the Sower,' *New Testament Studies* 20/3 (1974), 299–319.
Wright, N. T., and M. F. Bird	*The New Testament in its World: An Introduction to the History, Literature, and Theology of the First Christians* (London: SPCK; Grand Rapids, MI: Zondervan Academic, 2019).

CHAPTER 8

Breathing in Enoch to Breathe out Jesus. Two Examples of Luke's Apocalypticism

Peter G. Bolt

Abstract

Apocalyptic Judaism was simply the air breathed by Jesus and by the Jesus movement. Although not all of the literature associated with the name of Enoch has survived, its wide influence on apocalyptic perspectives is apparent. After noting previously identified Enochic influences within the Gospel of Luke, this chapter draws attention to the Enoch-influenced genealogy and the Lucan additions to the Parable of the Figtree, as two examples lying on the 'surface' of the narrative which indicate a deeper connection with the 'Enochic' world-view, especially in relation to time. These soundings add further weight to the suggestion that Luke's Gospel is, in fact, an apocalyptic narrative about Israel's Messiah/Son of Man at the End of Days.

1. Introduction

By 1953, when the father of Lukan redaction criticism published *Die Mitte der Zeit*—subsequently translated into English with the less dramatic title *The Theology of Luke*—nineteenth-century liberal scholars had already expressed their distaste for apocalyptic, and twentieth-century form critics had continued the trend by detaching the Gospel material from any concrete historical circumstances in favour of a generalized context of usage in which it developed across an unspecified but necessarily lengthy period of time. Writing from within this legacy of ideas, Conzelmann brought in a new era of scholarship by drawing conclusions about Luke's editorial work that would, in turn, become axiomatic for subsequent generations of Gospel scholars.[1]

Amongst those conclusions, Luke was definitely not apocalyptic, but, on the contrary, Luke's 'struggle is essentially an anti-apocalyptic one'.[2] After the initial fervor of the earliest days of the Christian movement, things had settled down into a more regular pattern of existence and this gave it the so-called 'Problem of the Delay of the Parousia'.[3] Where is the return of Jesus Christ that the first generation of believers had so fervently hoped for and proclaimed? This delay is 'the most important factor' to Luke,[4] and, to help the Christian movement embrace its mission to the nations for the lengthy period ahead, he continued the correction of apocalyptic that had already commenced with Mark's rendition of the traditions,[5] but with even more finesse.[6]

Some thirty years prior to the 1980s' burgeoning of literary studies

---

1   Conzelmann, *Theology of Luke*.
2   Conzelmann, *Theology of Luke*, 123.
3   For example, according to Conzelmann, *Theology of Luke*, in 9:27, the idea of the coming of the kingdom is replaced by a timeless conception of it (p.104); at 12:38ff. the delay is directly referred to in a pre-Lucan form (p.108); Luke's 'characteristic' ἀπὸ τοῦ νῦν (1:48; 5:10; 12:52; 22:18; 22:69) makes the saying not about the end, but about an epoch of conflict (p.109); 8:15 prepares the church for endurance (8:15), an 'adjustment to a long period of persecution' (p.104); and on Luke 21: 'The account is transferred from an eschatological background to that of the Church. Time after time we meet the same readjustment from an immediate eschatology to martyrdom as a present fact in which the eschatological prospect provides consolation' (p.129).
4   Conzelmann, *Theology of Luke*, 131.
5   E.g. on Luke 21: '[Mark's] aim already is to correct an apocalyptic tradition which is predominantly Jewish'; the postponement of the Parousia can be already traced in him, since Mark 13:10 envisages 'a fairly long period of missionary activity'; Conzelmann, *Theology of Luke*, 126, 127.
6   Conzelmann, *Theology of Luke*, 127, on Luke 21: 'the imminence of the end has ceased to play any vital part in Luke'; p.128: dropping Mark 13:10, as in Luke 17, the aim is now to endure, adding the exhortation to ὑπομονή, i.e. 'to adjustment to a long period of persecution, for such is the existence of the Church in the world'; p.129: signs (21:11; cf. 17:21) are not pointers to imminence, but 'to a long period which comes first'.

of the Gospels with their narrative-reader focus,[7] Conzelmann's interest was solely on Luke's work as an editor of the sources he had immediately received. Untouched by the Biblical Theology Movement, his discussion of the eschatology of the earliest days of the Christian movement shows little interest in the Old Testament, or in any other writings (potentially) available to the first-century Evangelist. Too early to take any real advantage of the Dead Sea Scrolls, his only reference (1QpHab VII, 7ff) was to show that the Qumran sect also had to face a similar delay of the End,[8] evidently unconcerned that this effectively relegates Luke to being yet another person facing the suffering and malevolence of this world and asking questions,[9] rather than someone (potentially) offering distinctively Christian answers.

However, in the light of the wealth of productive results from narrative-reader criticism, Biblical Theology, and also of recent discoveries enabling better understanding both of ancient Judaism and Jesus and earliest Christianity, such scholarly axioms—no matter how well-entrenched they might have become—need to be radically reconfigured.[10] In fact, apart from the early Christian movement being a missionary movement, there is practically nothing in Conzelmann's reconstruction that should be retained.[11] In particular, contrary to the prevailing tastes of nineteenth and much twentieth-century Gospels scholarship, in first-century Judaism apocalypticism was simply the air

---

7   For one account of many, see Green, 'Narrative Criticism', 74–81.
8   Conzelmann, *Theology of Luke*, 132 n.1. Cave 4, 'Qumran's library', containing eleven manuscripts of 1 Enoch, was only discovered in September 1952; Barker, *Lost Prophet*, 12–14; Milik, *Ten Years*, 13. Even in 1962, Rist, 'Enoch, Book of', 103, was able to note that Enoch had emerged at Qumran, but the evidence had not been thoroughly evaluated.
9   Alongside the Qumran *pesher*, see, for example, the book of Habakkuk itself, Rom 2:4, 2 Peter 3, or the discussion in Plutarch's, *Delay of divine vengeances*.
10 Cf. Charlesworth, 'Date and Provenance', 54: 'If the Parables of Enoch is not only Jewish, but represents the thought of some intellectually influential Jewish groups in Galilee, then we should revisit some allegedly closed debates among New Testament scholars. There seem to be reasons now to postulate that, since some Jews were developing the concept of "the Son of Man," Jesus could have used the expression to denote a heavenly figure. This hypothesis seems more likely than ten years ago, thanks to intensive work on the Books of Enoch within the Enoch Seminar and spectacular discoveries in Galilee that date from Jesus' time'; Barker, *Lost Prophet*, 14–15: 'a knowledge of 1 Enoch is now a necessary preliminary to any responsible study of the New Testament'.
11 Cf. Green, 'Reading Luke', 1: 'Arguably, the pillars of Conzelmann's perspective on Luke—for example, his emphasis on the delay of the Parousia, his apology for Rome, or his presentation of Jesus' ministry as a Satan-free period—have been felled, one by one, by subsequent scholarship'.

that everyone breathed.¹²

Despite such long-standing scholarly 'intense aversion' to apocalyptic elements,¹³ we now know that, although apocalypticism was a cultural phenomenon wider than Israel,¹⁴ it was also a general feature of mainstream Judaism, not simply a feature of the various sects.¹⁵ In 1983 and still more than a decade prior to the full publication of the Dead Sea Scrolls, Charlesworth edited a collection of nineteen apocalypses and related documents for the first volume of *Old Testament Pseudepigrapha*. He noted that although the OT and NT each have only one apocalyptic book (Daniel; Revelation), they also have apocalyptic sections (Ezek 40–48; Isa 24–27, 34–35, 56–66; Zech 9–14; Mark 13 and par.; 1 Thess 4; 1 Cor 15).¹⁶ He also noted that 'other pseudepigrapha [...] contain apocalyptic sections, especially the Testaments of the Twelve Patriarchs, the Testament of Abraham, the Testament of Moses, Jubilees, the Martyrdom and Ascension of Isaiah, and 4 Baruch', and so too do the Dead Sea Scrolls, 'many of which are apocalyptic writings, and the apocalypses and apocalyptically inspired writings in the New Testament Apocrypha and Pseudepigrapha'.¹⁷

The 'environmental criterion' must now factor in, that the period in which Jesus lived was such 'an age of apocalypticism' that 'there can no longer be any doubt that Jesus was profoundly influenced by apocalypticism'.¹⁸ Even if Jesus was 'clearly *not* an apocalypticist in the narrowest sense',¹⁹ all the elements are there, from an expectation of a Messiah and an imminent kingdom; an imminent end of the world, associated with the coming of the Son of Man; through a pessimism, or even

---

12 Cf. Barker, *Lost Prophet*, 112–113: '1 Enoch represents the written deposit of these ideas; many of them, perhaps most of them, were transmitted in a more diffuse way; the old ways were breathed in with the air. There was probably no conscious transmission of many of these beliefs about angels and their roles. The beliefs were just there. They penetrated every aspect of life. [...] And it is because they were just there, a part of the accepted view of the world, that these beliefs are not spelt out as a separate issue in the New Testament'.
13 Robinson, 'Apocalypticism', 122, cf. 123–124.
14 Boccaccini, 'Jewish Apocalyptic Tradition', 35, as cited by Robinson, 'Apocalypticism', 129.
15 Robinson, 'Apocalypticism', 131.
16 Charlesworth, 'Introduction, Apocalyptic Literature', 3.
17 Charlesworth, 'Introduction, Apocalyptic Literature', 3–4.
18 Robinson, 'Apocalypticism', 126–128, who discusses Josephus, Qumran, the Pseudepigrapha, and the New Testament.
19 Robinson, 'Apocalypticism', 127–128.

hostility, towards the present social order and those empowered by it; to a belief in the two ages, and the periodization of history as it moved relentlessly towards its conclusion whenever the evil powers would be overthrown and the Kingdom of God would break in.[20]

Luke also clearly shares this apocalyptic view, for it is the framework in which he sets Jesus' ministry, from the devil's initial testing (4:1–13), through Jesus' vision of his fall (10:18), to his re-entry in the drama by entering Judas (22:3, cf. 4:13), before the final testing of both disciple and master (22:31–32, 39–46; cf. 4:1–13). In Luke's account, Jesus' arrest signals the apparent victory of Israel's corrupt leadership, who are cast as instruments of Satan himself through apocalyptic imagery: 'this is your hour and the authority of darkness' (22:53). Yet the true victory occurs behind the scenes, allowing Jesus to be confident of the arrival of his kingdom, even while hanging on the cross (23:43).

Jesus, earliest Christianity, and even Luke's Gospel need to be understood not over against their surrounding apocalyptic context, but as an integral part of it, and their views on time must be set in the light of apocalyptic time-tables of the End. As a small contribution towards this necessary re-envisioning of Jesus, earliest Christianity, and Luke, this essay asks after the potential influences of Enoch on the Gospel of Luke. After some general comments about the significant presence of Enoch in the first-century Jewish apocalyptic atmosphere, it will look at the influence of Enoch on Luke's genealogy of Jesus, and at one example of an Enoch-referring detail in Luke's special material. Rather than being mere embellishments, both tap into the deep structures of Luke's narrative and contribute to its apocalyptic understanding of time.

2. Enoch as part of Luke's Framework of Thought

The influence of Enochic ideas on the New Testament seems clear,[21] even if it is disputed exactly where that influence is most evident. Although attempts to demonstrate a literary dependency must be done

---

20 Robinson, 'Apocalypticism', 123, 127–128.
21 Rist, 'Enoch, Book of', 105: 'The summation of its contents reveals the indebtedness of early Christianity to this book, or to writings and traditions of a similar character'.

cautiously, since there were more Enochic writings than have survived and Enoch writings and traditions were circulating amongst Jesus' contemporaries, their influence would have been more extensive than mere literary dependency.[22]

a) Enoch's Journey from Primeval to Contemporary Times

The enigmatic Genesis account reporting Enoch, son of Jared (Gen 5:18–19; 1 Chron 1:3; Luke 3:37),[23] being translated to God's presence rather than dying (Gen 5:24; cf. Josephus, *Ant* 1.84–85; 9:28; Philo, *Names* 1:34; *Abr* 17), gave rise to many stories, including those in *1 Enoch*, that 'when he was taken by God, [he] saw the secrets of the mysteries of the universe, the future of the world, and the predetermined course of human history'.[24] According to Nickelsburg's summary, the 'major subject matter [of *1 Enoch*] is twofold: the nature and implications of the created structure of the cosmos and the origin, nature, consequences, and final judgment of evil and sin'.[25]

1 Enoch was well-known to the Early Church,[26] but, after its rejection by Origen, it fell out of favour in the West after the fourth century. It nevertheless continued as part of the Ethiopian and Manichaen Scriptures, and maintained popular influence sufficient to warrant its listing as apocryphal well into the sixth century.[27] After renewed attention in the late eighteenth and nineteenth centuries, by the turn of the twentieth century the work of R.H. Charles in particular had put it

---

22 Writing on 1 Enoch 1–5, Hartman, *Asking for a Meaning*, 146–147, argues that it is 'the degree of similarity or of relationship of contents' that should matter, which may indicate 1 Enoch was 'part of the spiritual environment in which a New Testament text belongs', or that it drew upon 'a Jewish tradition' which then became, in a later form, 'the direct background of a New Testament text or motif', even if the question may be difficult to decide.
23 As opposed to the son of Cain (Gen 4:17–18).
24 Isaac, 'Introduction', 5.
25 Nickelsburg, 'Enoch, First Book of', 508.
26 Isaac, 'Introduction', 8. It was used, e.g., by Epistle of Barnabas, Apocalypse of Peter, Justin Martyr, Irenaues, Origen, Clement of Alexandria; Tertullian. By the 4th c. it fell out of favour, criticized by Augustine, Hilary, and Jerome, to circulate only in Ethiopia. For citations, see Lawlor, 'Early Citations'. See also McDonald, 'The *Parables*', 329.
27 McDonald, 'The *Parables*', 330.

back on the scholarly table.²⁸ But it was the publication of fragmentary Aramaic manuscripts discovered amongst the Dead Sea Scrolls,²⁹ that both demanded and facilitated the re-presentation and re-interpretation of the texts.³⁰ This, in turn, added weight to a re-appreciation of the apocalyptic nature of first-century Judaism, Jesus, and earliest Christianity. In order to reach its proper goal, this journey of Enoch's re-evaluation also demands a re-assessment of some of the legacies of previous scholarship, especially that of Conzelmann, proposing that Luke was non- or anti-apocalyptic.

b) 1 Enoch and its Influence

Although originally written in Aramaic or Hebrew, *1 Enoch* is also known as Ethiopic Enoch, because, although portions of the text survive in Aramaic, Greek and Latin, the whole document survives only in Ethiopic.³¹ This 'creative masterpiece of Second Temple Judaism'³² is

---

28 Summarising information from Isaac, 'Introduction', 8, Barker, *Lost Prophet*, 6, 8–12, Stuckenbruck and Boccaccini, '1 Enoch and the Synoptic Gospels', 2: 1 Enoch was well-known to Christian writers of the second century; condemned after the fifth; lost to the West; rediscovered in Ethiopia by J. Bruce in 1769 and brought to Europe in 1773; in 1800 Silvestre de Sacy published excerpts into Latin; translated into English by Laurence 1821, and German by Hoffmann in 1838; in 1853 Dillmann's translation aroused much interest; more manuscripts brought back to Europe in the 19th c.; the next big discovery was in 1886, when the Greek text of 1 Enoch 1–32 was found in an Egyptian grave, bound in a 5–6th c. codex with the Gospel of Peter and the Apocalypse of Peter. Previously the Greek version had only been known in fragments (chs. 6–11, 15–16, 89, and some quotations). A new English translation was needed, produced by R.H. Charles in 1893, then a 2nd edition in 1912. 1930: discovery of a 4th c. papyrus codex of Enoch, = the Epistle of Enoch (Greek).
29 Milik, with Black, *The Books of Enoch*. For an account of their discovery, see Barker, *Lost Prophet*, 12–14.
30 Nickelsburg, 'Enoch, Book of', 265; 'The discovery of fragmentary Aramaic MSS of Enoch amongst the Dead Sea Scrolls, as well as the renewed discussion of apocalyptic, make the re-evaluation and reinterpretation of these materials both necessary and possible'.
31 Rist, 'Enoch, Book of', 103; Isaac, 'Introduction', 6. For Aramaic: Milik and Black, *The Books of Enoch*; Greek: Codex Panopolitanus (*1 Enoch* 1:1–32:6 = Ga), Chronographia of Georgius Syncellus (6:1–10:14; 15:8–16:1 = Gs), Chester Beatty papyrus of Enoch (97:6–104; 106–107 = Gp; see Bonner, *The Last Chapters of Enoch in Greek*); Latin: a fragment in the British Museum (106:1–18; see James, *Apocrypha Anecdota*, 146–50); Ethiopic: see the translations of Charles, *Ethiopic Version*, Isaac, and Knibb. Nickelsburg, 'Enoch 97–104', examines both Greek and Ethiopic for that section. For commentary, see Nickelsburg, *1 Enoch 1* and Nickelsburg and VanderKam, *1 Enoch 2*.
32 Charlesworth, 'Did Jesus Know?', 217, who finds it impossible that Jesus wouldn't have interacted with the people of the Enoch circles and their ideas. Similarly, Walck, 'Parables', 266.

made up of five books, with an introduction and a conclusion.³³

1–5	Introduction
6–36	The Book of the Watchers
37–71	The Book of Parables [Similitudes]
72–82	The Book of Astronomy
83–90	The Book of Dream Visions
91–104	The Epistle of Enoch
105–107	Appendix/Conclusion

1 Enoch is a composite work with ancient roots, put together over a long period, with the latest section being the Parables [Similitudes] of Enoch (37–71). The similarities between the Parables and the Gospels are such that, after it was discovered that this section was not amongst the Enoch material at Qumran,³⁴ Milik argued that it was a Christian work influenced by the Gospels.³⁵ Even by 1977,³⁶ however, his theory was largely rejected and by 2013 the consensus had emerged that it was originally composed during the last days of Herod the Great or in

---

33 Rist, 'Enoch, Book of', 104; Milik, 'Problèmes'; *Books of Enoch*, whose five parts combine 1–36 and 91–107; Isaac, 'Introduction', 5, who (following Milik) combines 1–5 and 6–36 into 'the first part'.
34 As with the absence of Esther at Qumran (Greenfield and Stone, 'Enochic Pentateuch', 55), other explanations have been mounted for the absence of the Parables, apart from their non-existence. Cf. Nickelsburg, 'Enoch, First Book of', 267, noting that 1 Enoch 105 was regarded as a Christian interpretation until it turned up at Qumran, comments that even if the Similitudes are not there, 'the hypothesis of a Christian origin seems highly unlikely in view of a total lack of Christological reference in the Son of Man passages'.
35 Although older scholarship tended to regard the Similitudes as Jewish (Knibb, 'Date', 345), with the discovery that these chapters were not amongst the Enoch material at Qumran, Milik, 'Problèmes', argued for a pre-Christian version which included the Book of Giants instead of the Similitudes, which was a Christian work of the 3rd c. AD, and that the latter had replaced the former by about AD 400. However, even by 1977, his view had been strongly criticized (Greenfield and Stone, 'Enochic Pentateuch'; Charlesworth, 'Seminar Report'; Knibb, 'Date'; Mearns, 'Dating'; Isaac, 'Introduction'), and the consensus had re-affirmed the older view that the Similitudes were Jewish, suggesting that they dated from the 1st c. AD, and were included in the book by the end of that century. 'Erik Sjöberg has convincingly demonstrated that the *Similitudes* were a unity and that the supposed Christian element is nothing more than a figment of scholarly imagination', Greenfield and Stone, 'Enochic Pentateuch', 58, referring to Sjöberg, *Der Menschensohn*.
36 Charlesworth, 'Seminar Report'.

the early decades of the 1st century,[37] in Aramaic, probably in Galilee and, if so, likely at Magdala.[38] This dating and provenance means that Enochide perspectives, as represented in 1 Enoch were simply part of the air that Jesus and his followers breathed.[39]

The influence of the Enoch material on the Jews of the first-century was both widespread and deep.[40] It is best to speak of 'the Enoch material', because beyond the books explicitly bearing Enoch's name lies a sprawling array of literature some of which has survived, but more has

---

37 The different sections of 1 Enoch have been dated variously; see Rist, 'Enoch, Book of', 104; Isaac, 'Introduction', 7; Nickelsburg, 'Enoch, First Book of', 509. The Parables/Similitudes have been dated from 2nd c. BC (Frey) to AD 270 (Milik); Mearns, 'Dating', 360. However, a consensus was emerging in 1977 (Charlesworth, 'Seminar Report') and established by 2013, that it was composed in the last days of Herod the Great, or early in the 1st AD—given that 55:5–7 refers to the Parthian invasion of Palestine in 40 BC; and 67:8–9 to Herod attempting to cure himself in the waters of Callirhoe (Josephus, *Ant* 17.6.5 §§171–73; *JW* 1.33.5 §§657–58); see the essays by Charlesworth, Bock, Owen, Mearns, VanderKam and Boesenberg, Aviam, in Bock and Charlesworth (eds.), *The Parables of Enoch* and Nickelsburg, 'Enoch, First Book of', 513. Knibb, 'Date', 352, 358, prefers the latter portion of the window between 63 BC to AD 135.
38 Isaac, 'Introduction', 8, has Judea, but according to the later growing consensus, it was Galilee. See Charlesworth, 'Date and Provenance', 54; Charlesworth, 'Did Jesus Know?', 216; Aviam, 'Book of Enoch'.
39 Although Enochide ideas were clearly part of the oral culture in Jesus' time and their influence on the Gospel writers is readily acknowledged, many would be too cautious to go along with McDonald, 'The *Parables*', 330, that Jesus was 'familiar with the *Parables of Enoch*' (cf. pp.333, 336, 362). He notes that Matthew's Gospel has 'the closest citations of or allusions to the *Parables of Enoch*' (p.336).
40 See for example: Hartman, *Asking for a Meaning*, 146: 'There are signs that indicate that *1 Enoch* 1–36 has played a role in Judaism which by far transcends its relative portion of Jewish literature—witness the references to Enoch's writings in other intertestamental literature as well as in the New Testament'. Greenfield and Stone, 'Enochic Pentateuch', 55, point out its breadth of influence from Sir 44:6, to the Testaments of the Twelve, the Samaritan Hellenistic historian, Pseudo-Eupolemus, and perhaps also the *Mani Codex* (pp.62–63).

Rist, 'Enoch, Book of', 104: Enoch was 'well known to Jews and later to Christians', being used by the writers of the Testaments of the Twelve, the Assumption of Moses, the Apocalypse of Baruch, 4 Ezra, but by the 2nd c. AD rarely mentioned by Jews.

Focusing on the Parables of Enoch, McDonald, 'The *Parables*', 330–31, notes: Sir 44:16; 49:14; Jub 5:5 (1 Enoch 10:11; 7:5,4; 10:9); 7:22 (1 Enoch 7:2–5); 8:3 (1 Enoch 8:3); TLevi 2–7 (cf. 1 Enoch 14); TSim 5:4; TLevi 10:5; 14:1; 16:1; TDan 5:6; TNaph 4:1; TBenj 9:1; TJud 18:1; TZeb 3:4 ['Moses' is probably a slip for 'Enoch']. After discussing the verbal parallels, he concludes 'that the Enochic traditions, including the *Parables of Enoch*, informed the faith of the Jews and Christian in the first century ce' (pp.362–63).

only left its trace in other extant writings.[41] In the Testaments of the Twelve, for example, although Enoch is explicitly mentioned, the underlying portion cannot always be readily identified in extant copies.[42]

To identify the 'influence' of Enoch on Luke is therefore a much more difficult task than identifying his quotations from the Old Testament.

c) Enoch in Luke

In 1962, Rist decried R.H. Charles' claim that 'nearly all the writers of the New Testament books were acquainted with [Enoch], and influenced by it, and that with the earlier fathers and apologists it had all the weight of a canonical book' as an overstatement.[43] However, subsequent research suggests that it may be less of an exaggeration than Rist initially imagined, and further research may close the gap even more[44]—especially when the quest is broadened from seeking a direct literary dependence to identifying Enoch's potential pervasive influence.

It is now common to declare the conceptual influence of Enoch on various New Testament books, including the Gospels and Revelation

---

41 This sprawling array does not only include 1 Enoch (Ethiopic): 2nd BC—1st AD (E. Isaac, *OTP*, 5–89), 2 Enoch (Slavonic): Late 1st AD (F.I. Andersen, *OTP*, 91–221), and 3 Enoch (Hebrew): 5th to 6th AD (P. Alexander, *OTP*, 223–315), but here was more Enoch material than what has survived. E.g. the 'Book of Giants', and the Enochic-Noachic traditions are not represented in Ethiopian Enoch; the Enoch texts alluded to in the Testaments of the Twelve, or Jude.

42 Barker, *Lost Prophet*, 8: 'We cannot place any of these in known Enochic texts, and we can only assume that there must have been far more Enochic literature than we now know'.

43 Rist, 'Enoch, Book of', 104; with the assent of Isaac, 'Introduction', 10. Seeking after proof of literary dependency, Knibb, 'Date', 355–56, also finds Charles' list 'difficult to accept seriously' and 'difficult to believe'. Despite finding Theisohn, *Der auserwählte Richter*, 149–201, 'a much more sophisticated attempt' (p.357), he still finds the similarities too commonplace to prove influence. For a somewhat more appreciative reception of Charles' comment, see Stuckenbruck and Boccaccini, '1 Enoch and the Synoptic Gospels', 2–3, noting that 'Charles was more specifically describing the nature of this significance in terms of "influence"'. Walck, 'Parables', speaks of verbal influence or a similar 'theological dynamic', or 'theological background / influence /undergirding', or 'working off the patterns of relationship of "the Chosen One" and "the Son of Man", or 'conceptual similarity', etc. (pp.240, 243, 251, 252, 259, 260, 267, 268).

44 Cf. Walck, 'Parables', 233, calling for Charles' list of similarites to be revisited, in the light of more recent approaches to studying ancient documents.

'clear' and 'without doubt'.[45] Verbal and conceptual correspondences between Luke and 1 Enoch can certainly be identified, as can some major ovelapping interests, especially a common concern with the Son of Man, conceived in similar ways (see below).[46] Working with the Greek text of 1 Enoch 92–105, Aalen (1966) regarded Enoch as one of Luke's possible sources, identifying parallels between exact phrases and concepts in similar context as well as a comparable eschatological schema lying behind each work.[47] Although Nickelsburg (1979) found many of Aalen's similarities too commonplace to prove dependency, he was nevertheless content to find Enoch in Luke's background, especially in a common approach to wealth (and poverty).[48] Shellard (2002), also declared Aalen 'a little overstated', concluding that 'we cannot, upon the verbal evidence offered by Aalen, regard the dependence of Luke upon the Greek text of *1 En.* 92–105 as proven'.[49] She nevertheless endorsed 'significant points of contact' that should not be dismissed, including (with Nickelsburg): 'a strongly negative view of possessions and their relation to salvation' (esp. *1 En.* 97.8–20; Luke 12:15–34; cf. Sir 11:18–19).[50]

---

45 See Isaac, 'Introduction', 8: 'it is clear that Enochic concepts are found in various New Testament books, including the Gospels and Revelation' and 'few other apocryphal books so indelibly marked the religious history and thought of the time of Jesus'; p.10: There is little doubt that 1 Enoch was influential in molding New Testament doctrines concerning the nature of the Messiah, the Son of Man, the messianic kingdom, demonology, the future, resurrection, final judgment, the whole eschatologcal theater, and symbolism' and 'there is no doubt that the New Testament world was influenced by its language and thought', listing Matthew, Luke, John, Acts, Romans, 1 and 2 Corinthians, Ephesians, Colossians, 1 and 2 Thessalonians, 1 Timothy, Hebrews, 1 John, Jude, and Revelation. Others add more NT texts, such as Mark and 2 Peter; Nickelsburg, 'Enoch, First Book of'; Barker, *Lost Prophet*, 16–17; McDonald, 'The *Parables*', 331, notes: Luke 3:37; Heb 11:5; Jude 14–15 [1 Enoch 1:9]; 1 Peter 3:19–20 [1 Enoch 19:1; cf. 15:4,6,7; and 2 Peter 2:1–4]; Jude 6 [1 Enoch 10:4–6,12–14; 12:4; 14:5]; Rev 5:11 [1 Enoch 14:22], 15:3 [1 Enoch 9:4; 25:5; 27:3], 19:16 [1 Enoch 9:4]. Stuckenbruck and Boccaccini, '1 Enoch and the Synoptic Gospels, 3: 'hardly anyone would doubt that the authors of 1 Peter 2:18–22, 2 Peter 2:4–5, and Jude 6 and 14–15 knowingly drew on traditions from 1 Enoch' (1 Enoch 6–11; 1:9). For overlaps and common themes, see also the essays in Stuckenbruck and Boccaccini, *1 Enoch and the Synoptic Gospels*.
46 According to Nickelsburg, 'The remarkable correspondence between the Son of Man in 1 Enoch 37–71 and the Gospels is primarily that in both he is judge', as reported in Charlesworth, 'Seminar Report', 316, 321; cf. Acts 17:31–32. Cf. Charlesworth, 'Date and Provenance', 54.
47 Aalen, 'St Luke's Gospel and 1 Enoch'.
48 Nickelsburg, 'Riches'.
49 Shellard, 'Excursus', 189, 190.
50 Shellard, 'Excursus', 191, 194, 195.

But alongside these (potential) verbal and conceptual similarities, overlapping viewpoints, perspectives, and underlying mythological structures are no less present, even if more difficult to document. Just like the 'apocalyptic imagination' itself, the influence of Enoch informs the deep structures of Luke's thought and so it also profoundly shapes its message. As happens with other instances of intertextuality, the occasional verbal echoes lying on the surface of Luke tap into the deeper structures by which he narrative gains its communicative power.[51]

Although Enoch's influence on Luke can be identified in quite a large number of passages and in a number of his central themes,[52] this essay focuses on two passages, both related to Luke's view of time. The genealogy of Jesus (Luke 3:23–38) is a lengthy passage which is recognised to be of some significance to Luke's account, even if its full significance has not always been fully appreciated. On the other hand, the Lukan addition of 'all the trees' (Luke 21:29), appears on first glance to be a rather minor redactional detail, worthy of the neglect that it has actually suffered. Both passages, however, aided by an Enochic intertextuality, tap into deep structures of Luke's narrative and play a part in promoting its apocalyptic understanding of time.

3. The Genealogy of Jesus (Luke 3:23–38)

The legacy of form criticism inherited by Conzelmann included the 'destruction of the chronological and topographical framework of the life of Jesus' in order to focus only on the embedded traditions.[53] After Gospels scholarship has become reacquainted with the sophisticated narrative art of the Evangelists, Luke's careful articulation of time can no longer be set aside so casually, and, when examined, it is clear that it

---

51 For exploration of Enoch's potential intertextuality with the Synoptic Gospels, see the essays in Stuckenbruck and Boccaccini, *Enoch and the Synoptic Gospels*.
52 Some of the passages which could be discussed, for example, include: 1:1,32,35, 46–55,52–53,79; 4:1–13; 6:24–26,47; 8:8 [cf. 1 Enoch 10:18–19]; 9:28–36; 9:51; 10:1; 10:18–22; 10:29; 11:22,40; 12:5,19; 12:15–21; 13:3,5,32; 14:18; 16:9,15,19–31, 27–31; 17:20–37; 18:1–8,9; 20:20,35,38; 21; 23:43; 24:51; and themes such as Archangels and angels, Demons and their demise, Christology (esp. Son of Man; Elect One, Righeous One; Christ; Servant), use of Parables, salvation, wisdom, the rich, wealth and poverty.
53 Funk, 'Conzelmann on Luke', 299, referring to Conzelmann, *Theology*, 9,10.

is a time-frame set within the apocalyptic mode.

The importance of time and its manipulation for narrative effect is axiomatic for narrative-reader criticism, for through time-manipulation a narrative not only draws its readers into the narrative drama, but also encourages them to set its events in the light of the past, just as it impels them forward into a new future.[54] But, as in the other Gospels, in Luke, time is not only a vehicle for furthering the narrative drama, but it is actually an integral part of its message. The narrative is *about* time, for it concerns 'the things that have been fulfilled amongst us' (1:1).[55] As the promises of the Old Testament are fulfilled in the coming of Jesus of Nazareth, time itself has actually changed. This is something that those within the narrative had to grasp as they were confronted by Jesus and his gospel (12:54–56), and those reading the narrative have to grasp as they are confronted by the same gospel, written down. Conzelmann certainly understood Luke to be saying something about time, but by declaring him anti-apocalyptic, he denuded his message of the apocalyptic urgency that is essential for the hearer to reckon with. As will be argued below, this is not only on the surface of Luke's account, and his narrative structure, but it is also embedded in its deep structures, perhaps to even more powerful effect, as indicated by a proper appreciation of the genealogy of Jesus.

After Luke's orderly narrative arrives at the point where Jesus commences his ministry at 'about thirty' (3:23; cf. David entering his kingship, 2Sam 5:4), and as it is poised to commence recounting the events of his ministry, Luke anchors both Jesus and those events in a family tree that sweeps backwards from Jesus to Adam. Claiming that, 'the Lukan Genealogy of Jesus is a more important historical document

---

54 For a brief account, see Green, 'Narrative Criticism', 92–93, 95–96; and for a classic discussion, see Licht, *Storytelling*, 96–120.
55 In the hint that the many who had taken up the pen before Luke were not quite right, Tilley, 'Crisis?', 28 n.51, finds an echo of 1 Enoch 69:8–12, decrying human beings writing down 'matters sacred and apocalyptic' (Tilley). If so, then Luke would be more like Enoch, and, of course, Jesus, announcing what had been given by revelation. Cf. Charlesworth, 'Did Jesus Know?', 216: 'Sociological and archaeological analysis shifts the pendulum towards a confrontation between the Enoch group and Jesus, before [AD] 30 and within the creative Jewish world of a vibrantly reinvigorated Galilee. While Enoch was allegedly given secret knowledge, he was instructed to announce it to all on the earth' (cf. 1 Enoch 37:1–5).

than has been generally appreciated',[56] Richard Bauckham has demonstrated that Luke's genealogical scheme follows the pattern of Enoch's *Apocalypse of Weeks* (1 Enoch 93:3–10; 91:11–17). According to Isaac's summary, this *Apocalypse* from the final section of 1 Enoch, The Epistle to Enoch, 'summarizes the events that would unfold upon the earth during ten [...] consecutive world weeks'.[57]

Sourced from members of Jesus' own family, it not only incorporates the family's own tradition of its ancestry, but it is 'a sophisticated theological document, carefully designed to express the central messianic convictions of the brothers of Jesus and their circle. It deserves a significant place in any attempt to reconstruct the character of the Palestinian Jewish Christianity of the first few decades'.[58]

Two major keys unlock the understanding of the genealogy.

a) The Davidic Dimension

The first, its Davidic dimension, will be only touched upon in this essay, namely, that Jesus' ancestry is not traced through the kings of Judah, but through, Nathan, David's son by Bathsheba (2 Sam. 5:14; 1 Chron. 3:5; 14:4; cf. Zech. 12:12), and then through Zerubbabel, through whom the family gained the right of royal succession (Luke 3:31,27).[59] Within the prophetic tradition, a strand of expectation promised the restoration of the monarchy, but not through the royal line of the rejected kings. In Isaiah's picture of 'a shoot (*ḥōṭer*) from the stump of Jesse, and a branch (*neṣer*) from his roots' (11:1; cf. 4:2): 'The royal house of David will be cut down in judgement, and the ideal king of the future will be derived, not from the royal line of the kings of Judah, but from the origins of the dynasty, indicated by the reference to Jesse'.[60] Because the Branch indicates a fresh start, he must come through another descent line, not that of Solomon (cf. Mic. 5:2 [Heb. 5:1]; Jer. 23:5–6, 33:15–16; Zech.

---

56 Bauckham, *Jude and the Relatives of Jesus*, 315.
57 Isaac, 'Introduction', 5. He notes that the fourth part of the Ethiopic *Book of the Mysteries of Heaven and Earth* 'recapitulates the Apocalypse of Weeks, brings the last three weeks through to the Christian era, and ends with the Antichrist in the tenth' (p.10).
58 Bauckham, *Jude and the Relatives of Jesus*, 315.
59 Bauckham, *Jude and the Relatives of Jesus*, 331.
60 Bauckham, *Jude and the Relatives of Jesus*, 334.

3:8 [Zerubbabel]; 6:12 [Zerubbabel]; Hag. 2:23; cf. Jer. 22:24; Dan 11:7).[61] Language associated with this 'Branch Christology' can also be traced in 1 Enoch, especially associated with its presentation of the figure called the Son of Man, the Elect One, and the Messiah[62] (e.g. 10:16; 39:6-7; 46:3-4; 48;[63] 49:1-4; 62:2; 93:2,5,8,10) —just as elsewhere in apocalyptic Judaism the Branch is the eschatological Messiah (e.g. Qumran:[64] 4Q161; 4Q162; 4Q285; 11Q14), often combined with another persistent image of the Messiah,[65] the Star of Num 24:17 (e.g. T.Jud 24; cf. Rev 22:16; Justin, *1 Apol* 32:12-13; *Dial* 126:1; cf. *Dial* 106:4). These two messianic images also lie behind the names of two Galilean villages settled, most likely, by faithful Jewish exiles returning from Babylon giving concrete expression to their hopes for the future, Kokhaba ('the Star'), near Sepphoris, and Nazareth (cf. 'the Branch'), the town in which Jesus grew up and by which he became known.[66]

---

61 In the fourth century, Eusebius (perhaps drawing upon Julius Africanus) referred to a Jewish tradition that traced the descent of the Messiah through Nathan, rather than Solomon:

> For differing opinions concerning the Messiah prevail among the Jews, though all agree in leading [the pedigree] up to David. But yet some are persuaded that the Messiah will come from David and Solomon and the royal line while others eschew this opinion because serious accusation was levelled against the kings and because Jeconiah was denounced by the prophet Jeremiah and because it was said that no seed from him [Jeconiah] should arise to sit on the throne of David. For these reasons, therefore, they go another way, agreeing [with the descent] from David; not, however, through Solomon but rather through Nathan, who was a child of David (they say that Nathan also prophesied, according to what is said in the books of Kings). They are certain that the Messiah would come forth from the successors of Nathan and trace the ancestry of Joseph from that point. Therefore, Luke, necessarily taking account of their opinion—though it was not his own—added to his account the ὡς ἐνομίζετο ["as was supposed"]. In doing this he allowed Matthew to relate [the matter], not on the basis of supposition but as having the truth in the matters of the genealogy.

    Eusebius, *Quaestiones Evangelicae ad Stephanum* 3:2. Translation from Johnson, *The Purpose*, 244 (Greek text: *PG* 22:896, reprinted on pp. 243-244), which is reproduced in Bauckham, *Jude and the Relatives*, 348-349. The Jewish tradition that expected the Messiah to come through the house of Nathan referred to by Eusebius has survived, but only in one late Jewish source, the medieval *Apocalypse of Zerubbabel*; Bauckham, *Jude and the Relatives of Jesus*, 347-354.

62 VanderKam, 'Righteous One'.

63 The description of the Son of Man is not only reminiscent of Isaiah 11 (Barker, *Lost Prophet*, 98), but also of Isaiah's Servant of the Lord.

64 Evans, 'Dead Sea Scrolls', 148, 150.

65 Bauckham, *Jude and the Relatives of Jesus*, 65: for Num 24:17 see: CD 7:18-21; 4QTest 9-13; 1QM 11:6-7; TLevi 18:3; [and also Targumim]; for Isa 11:1 see 4QPBless; 4QFlor 1:11-12; 4QpIsa^a frag.A; cf. allusions to other parts of Isa 11:1-5 in 1QSb 5:24; PssSol 17:35-37; 1 Enoch 49:3; 62:2.

66 Bauckham, *Jude and the Relatives of Jesus*, 64-65.

But the fact that the genealogy begins to identify Jesus as this promised Davidic Messiah, also indicates something about time and its fulfilment.

b) The Enoch Dimension: Weeks of Generations

Luke's genealogy crosses eleven generations of seven, running backwards from Jesus to Adam. It therefore consists of 77 generations, a number which already suggests some kind of numerical scheme (cf. 1 Chron 6:1–15; Matt 1:1–17).[67]

	7	6	5	4	3	2	1
11	[23]Jesus,	Joseph,	Heli,	[24]Matthat,	Levi,	Melchi,	Jannai,
10	Joseph,	[25]Mattathias,	Amos,	Nahum,	Esli,	Naggai,	[26]Maath,
9	Mattathias,	Semein,	Josech,	Joda,	[27]Joanan,	Rhesa,	Zerubbabel,
8	Shealtiel,	Neri,	[28]Melchi,	Addi,	Cosam,	Elmadam,	Er,
7	[29]Joshua,	Eliezer,	Jorim,	Matthat,	Levi,	[30]Simeon,	Judah,
6	Joseph,	Jonam,	Eliakim,	[31]Melea,	Menna,	Mattatha,	Nathan,
5	**David**,	[32]Jesse,	Obed,	Boaz,	Sala,	Nahshon,	[33]Amminadab,
4	Admin,	Arni,	Hezron,	Perez,	Judah,	[34]Jacob,	Isaac,
3	Abraham,	Terah,	Nahor,	[35]Serug,	Reu,	Peleg,	Eber,
2	Shelah,	[36]Cainan,	Arphaxad,	Shem,	Noah,	Lamech,	[37]Methuselah,
1	Enoch,	Jared,	Mahalaleel,	Cainan,	[38]Enos,	Seth,	Adam,
0	God.						

Since Enoch's *Apocalypse of Weeks* (1 Enoch 93:3–10; 91:11–17) is 'the only extant apocalyptic scheme of world history (from Adam to the End) which makes use of generations as its unit of measurement' (NB it is clear from 93:3 that it is weeks of generations, not years), it is 'much the most suitable for comparison with a *genealogical* scheme such as the Lukan genealogy of Jesus'.[68]

Although Luke's genealogy doesn't conform to the details of that in Enoch, it follows the principle in the *Apocalypse of Weeks* that 'the important generations are those at the end of each week'.[69] In Luke's

---

67 Bauckham, *Jude and the Relatives of Jesus*, 318.
68 Bauckham, *Jude and the Relatives of Jesus*, 321.
69 Bauckham, *Jude and the Relatives of Jesus*, 324. For the evidence, see the chart on pp. 316–317.

genealogy, Enoch occupies the seventh place (cf. Jude 14, ἕβδομος ἀπὸ Ἀδὰμ Ἐνώχ; 1 Enoch 93:3; Life of Adam and Eve [*Vita*] App. 9), which was a well-known position marking significance. This raises the expectation of some kind of relationship between Enoch in the special seventh position, and Jesus in the ultimate 77th—reinforced by the additional feature that Jesus's name also appears in the 49th 'Jubilee' position, with his namesake 'Joshua' (3:29). 'The number seventy-seven designates Jesus as the furthest the generation of world history will go, both in number and in significance'.[70]

This is 'confirmed by the text on which this genealogy of Jesus must have been based', *1 Enoch* 10:12 (=4QEn^b 1:4:10), which refers to the binding of the Watchers for 70 generations until the day of Judgement (cf. Jude 6). Since the binding of the Watchers is dated to the generation after Enoch, then the entire history of the world from Adam to the Day of Judgement lasts for 77 generations (cf. Dan 9:24–27). 'For anyone familiar with *1 Enoch* 10:12 the Lukan genealogy of Jesus would clearly designate Jesus the last generation of history before the end'.[71] Bauckham therefore draws the conclusion that, 'the genealogy designates Jesus as the climax and end of world history'.[72]

For many reasons, the theological significance and narrative power of Luke's genealogy has been overlooked.[73] When read against its Enochic background, the genealogy does more than provide Jesus with a family tree—which, given the family and the expectations associated with the promised Davidic Messiah, is impressive enough. It also prepares the reader to understand 'the things fulfilled amongst us' as integral components of God's plan, shaped by the timetabled expectations

---

70 Bauckham, *Jude and the Relatives of Jesus*, 319.
71 Bauckham, *Jude and the Relatives of Jesus*, 320.
72 Bauckham, *Jude and the Relatives of Jesus*, 319.
73 Despite recognizing Luke's 'outline of the successive stages in redemptive history according to God's plan', Conzelmann, *Theology of Luke*, 135, read it as an alternative to 'the early expectation' of the end, missing the fact that they were actually two sides of the one coin. If the successive stages are rightly discerned, with the coming of Christ, the End is nigh. Elsewhere, declaring Paul's speech in Acts 17 to be negating Luke 3:1, he found that 'no conception of world history is developed, nor are the periods into which it is divided set out', and 'Jesus' place in it is not one that can be demonstrated as part of a system, but is a "chance" one, as and when it pleases God' (p.168). This is a monumental misreading both of Luke's eschatology, and also of his Christology upon which it is determined.

current within apocalyptic circles.[74] It is not surprising, therefore, that the sense that time itself is reaching its divinely planned goal is reflected elsewhere as Luke's narrative proceeds 'like flint' towards its, and his, and *the*, End (cf. 9:51; Isa 50:7).

Although the other Gospels also use the primeval expression 'this generation' (Gen 7:1; Matt 11:16; 12:41–42; 23:36; 24:34; Mark 8:12; 13:30), Luke uses it with particular emphasis, stressing the responsibility of Jesus' contemporaries as the generation amongst whom the Messiah has arrived, and as the evil generation that failed to believe and by which he was rejected, and upon which God's judgement is about to fall (7:31 [Q]; 9:41 [Triple]; 11:29–32 [Triple/Q]; 11:50–51 [L, but cf. Matt 23:35]; 16:8 [L]; 17:25 [L]; 21:32 [Triple]). This echoes the apocalyptic timetable, with the last generation(s) before the coming of the Messiah/ the End being apostate from the priests down.

That 'this generation' is the one amongst whom the things of God have reached fulfilment (1:1) is an integral assumption behind the writing of Luke's Gospel. Luke reinforces the point that human history had reached a turning point with the events that took place in this generation by stressing, for example, the role of John the Baptist (16:16), and by using the expression 'from now on' (ἀπὸ τοῦ νῦν, 1:48; 5:10; 12:52; 22:18; 22:69).[75] By the end of the Gospel, this perspective on time then fuels the urgency of the message that must be proclaimed to the nations (24:46–47).

Alongside the narrative's constant and deeply-embedded reference to the fulfilment of prophecy, its account of Jesus' ministry is explictly set upon a time-frame for the fulfilment of God's plan. This is clear in the frequent attention to the John-Jesus linkage, as the last Elijah-like prophet before the coming judgement (Isa 40:3; Mal 4:5–6) and the Mightier One following him, that a person must recognise in order to be saved (1–2; 3–4; 7:18–28,31–35; 7:29–30; 9:7–9,18–20; 11:1–4; 16:16; 20:1–8). It is there in Jesus' and Luke's perception that he has a

---

74 These include and are related to the expectation of the eschatological Jubilee (cf. Dan 9:24–27), which has already been identified as contributing to Luke's Gospel in a number of specific passages (e.g. 4:16–21) and in a deep structural manner. See Wacholder, 'Chronomessianism'; Sloan, *Favourable Year*; Bergsma, *The Jubilee*.
75 Contra Conzelmann, *Theology of Luke*, see above n.3.

destiny that must be, and is being, fulfilled (e.g. 2:49; 3:21–22; 4:21; 7:21–23,31–35; 9:31,51; 10:18–20,23–24; 11:20; 12:49–53; 13:31–35; 16:16; 18:8), especially as the Son of Man (Dan 7:13–14; Luke 5:24; 6:5,22; 7:34; 9:22,26,44,58; 11:30; 12:8,10,40; 17:22,24,26,30; 18:8,31; 19:10; 21:27,36; 22:22,48,69; 24:7). In case the readers may have missed the significance of the events narrated thus far, on the other side of Christ's death and resurrection Luke's final chapter reiterates that two of the three major events on the divine timetable have now been fulfilled, leaving only the proclamation of forgiveness to the nations to be completed (24:25–27,44–49)—opening the way for Luke's second volume to recount the commencement of this mission to the nations which still continues through Luke's readers.[76]

At several points in the narrative, Luke portrays Jesus as deliberately calling upon his hearers from 'this [final] generation' to understand their times (12:54–59), which become increasingly urgent the closer he gets to the final events in Jerusalem (9:27,31,51; 10:9,11; 9:41; 18:35; 19:11–27;[77] 19:37,41; [cf. 21:8]; 21:20):[78]

> **Luke 12:54** He also said to the crowds: "When you see a cloud rising in the west, right away you say, 'A storm is coming,' and so it does. ⁵⁵ And when the south wind is blowing, you say, 'It's going to be a scorcher!' and it is. ⁵⁶ Hypocrites! You know how to interpret the appearance of the earth and the sky, but why don't you know <u>how to interpret this time</u>?

> **Luke 13:32** He said to them, "Go tell that fox, 'Look! I'm driving out demons and performing healings <u>today and tomorrow, and on the third day</u> I will complete My work.' ³³ Yet I must travel <u>today, tomorrow, and the next day,</u> because it is not possible for a prophet to perish outside of Jerusalem!

---

76 Bolt, 'Mission and Witness'.
77 For an explanation of this parable, so often mistakenly interpreted as speaking of the Delay of the Parousia, see Bolt, 'Preparing Israel'.
78 Rather than Luke's 'removals' of the notion of the kingdom's nearness found in Mark (and Matthew) indicating he was downplaying the kingdom's imminence (so Conzelmann, see above), by retaining the nearness theme in the second half of his narrative, he more firmly associates the imminent kingdom's coming with the final events in Jerusalem.

Understanding the arrival of Jesus Christ against the Enochic scheme of history, Luke is narrating his story of Jesus from this apocalyptic view of time: that he and his generation are the last, and they therefore have a very special place and an onerous responsibility in the history of Israel, and, indeed, the world, seen from the perspective of God's eternal plan. From his first verse, Luke informs his readers that he has undertaken 'to draw up a narrative concerning the things that have come to their conclusion amongst us' (1:1, ... ἀνατάξασθαι διήγησιν περὶ τῶν πεπληροφορημένων ἐν ἡμῖν πραγμάτων).

4. 'All the trees' (Luke 21:29)

That this view of time and human history underlies Luke's narrative is further reinforced by noticing what at first glance appears to be a minor redactional addition of almost no significance. As part of the 'apocalyptic discourse', in all three Synoptics, Jesus tells 'the Parable of the Figtree'. When examined more closely, Luke's unique features point back to Enoch and, by doing so, tap into the deep structures of both narratives in order to profoundly reinforce Luke's apocalyptic view of time.

a) The Context: the coming of the Son of Man as eschatological judge

The parable comes at the end of Luke's version of Jesus' 'apocalyptic discourse' (21:5–36), surrounded by the expected 'coming of the Son of Man' (vv.27–28,37). The difference in the time-frame from that of Daniel is immediately apparent, for, after seeing his vision of the Son of Man coming to the Ancient of Days to receive authority over the kingdom of God (Dan 7:13–14), and narrating the connection of that event with the Judgement Day, the eschatological Jubilee (9:24–27), and the Day of Resurrection (12:1–3), Daniel is told that these things will be beyond his lifetime, for they concern the End of Days (12:5–13). In contrast, as Jesus told his disciples, 'Blessed are the eyes that see the things you see! For I tell you that many prophets and kings wanted to see the things you see but didn't see them; to hear the things you hear but didn't hear them' (Luke 10:23–24). This was the time of the End.

Although Luke's frequent references to 'the Son of Man' always refer to the figure of Daniel 7:13–14, it also comes to his Gospel filtered through the Enochic perspectives of apocalyptic Judaism.[79] It is quite clear that Luke depicts *his* Son of Man, Jesus of Nazareth, by drawing upon titles applied to the Son of Man found in 1 Enoch (46, 48, 60, 62, 63, 69, 70, 71), each of which, frequent or not, is also deeply embedded in Luke's narrative:[80] 'the Righteous One' (e.g. 1 Enoch 46:3; see Luke 23:47; Acts 3:14; 7:52; 22:14), 'the Elect One' (1 Enoch 45, 49, 51, 55, 61; see Luke 9:35; 23:35; and cf. 3:22; Ps 2:7; Isa 42:1; 44:1–2; 49:1–7), the Messiah (1 Enoch 52; cf. Luke 2:11,26; 3:15; 4:41; 9:20; 20:41; 22:67; 23:2,35,39; 24:26,46; and Acts). Their interrelation in Luke's narrative, occasionally explicitly (22:67–70; 23:35), shows that they mutually describe the same person, as they do in 1 Enoch.[81].

But the most significant feature shared between 1 Enoch (e.g. 38:1–3; cf. 92:2–5; 49:2–4; 55:4; 61:8; 62:1–3) and Luke (and the other Gospels), is that, despite the biblical tradition that only God is judge, the Son of Man will be the cosmic and eschatological judge,[82] enthroned to give eternal life to the elect (1 Enoch 37:4).[83] This is the immediate context of the Parable of the Figtree, for it comes after Jesus

---

79 Enoch's Son of Man clearly draws on Dan 7:13–14, yet with 'exegetical expansions'; Charlesworth, 'Did Jesus Know?', 193, 202.
80 See Powell, *Who Are the Righteous?*, 127, who shows that Luke's earlier usage of δίκαιος prepares for Jesus to be disclosed as the righteous one at the crucifixion: 'The narrative reveals that the one who, from an outsider's perspective, appeared to be a criminal, a friend of sinners, is in reality the righteous one' (p.127). Similarly, 'the elect one' appears at significant narrative moments; see Walck, 'Parables', 267.
81 See VanderKam, 'Righteous One'; Charlesworth, 'Did Jesus Know?', 192; Walck, 'Parables', 264. Charlesworth, 'Date and Provenance', 55, also notes the title 'the Elect One' in 4Q534 ar, suggesting Enoch's influence even though 'Son of Man' is not in the extant fragments. Enoch also describes the Son of Man in terms of Isaiah's Servant of the Lord, just as Luke portrays Jesus as the Servant; e.g. Walck, 'Parables', 264; Theisohn, *Der auserwählte Richter*, 119–21. The conflation of the Servant and the Son of Man explains the Gospels' insistence on the Son of Man suffering; so also Walck, 'Parables', 242; with Nickelsburg, 'Son of Man', 149. This Son of Man in the role of judgement also has similarities to Melchizedek in 11QMelchizedek; see Kobelski, '11QMelchizdek', 130–137.
82 This has been frequently observed, see Charlesworth, 'Date and Provenance', 54–55 (see also 4Q245); Charlesworth, 'Did Jesus Know?', 174 (as part of the developing consensus), 192, 202 ('a theological pinnacle'), 206, 207, 216; Walck, 'Parables', 267, whose article examines the Enoch dimension in each of Luke's 24 Son of Man passages; Theisohn, *Der auserwählte Richter*; Knibb, 'Date of Parables', 351; Mearns, 'Dating', 366. See also Nickelsburg, n.48 above.
83 Charlesworth, 'Did Jesus Know?', 209.

tells his hearers that when the Son of Man comes, they are to 'stand up and lift up your heads, because your redemption is drawing near' (21:28; cf. 1 Enoch 51:2: 'the day on which they will be saved is drawing near'), and before he urges them to be ready for 'that day', so that they 'may be able to stand before the Son of Man' (21:34–36), that is, survive his searching judgement.[84] This is structurally significant for Luke's narrative, for the redemption for which Israel were waiting (1:68; 2:25,38; 24:21), would now come through the coming of the Son of Man, the eschatological judge.[85]

For those who viewed human history from the perspective of the divine timetable of the End, the big question about the Son of Man was, when will his coming be? (cf. 21:7) How long have we got? Evidently concerned with timing, the parable's function is to reinforce the imminence of the Kingdom of God, and therefore the urgent need for Jesus' hearers to be prepared for its inauguration with the coming of the Son of Man.

---

84 Grabbe, 'Son of Man', 193, 'implied is that the Son of Man will be a figure, perhaps a judge, of the end time'; Walck, 'Parables', 266, with Marshall, *Luke*, 783, 'to stand' being a Hebraism meaning to secure a favourable verdict. Nolland, *Luke*, 1013, declares it to be 'an image of deliverance [from eschatological trials], not standing in a judicial dock', apparently followed by Bock, *Luke*, 1695, 'standing with approval in deliverance'— all noting 1 Enoch 62:8,13; 1QH 4:21–22.

85 Walck, 'Parables', 263, notes that 21:36 and 18:8b both conclude significant discourses, 18:8b the Day of the Son of Man discourse; and 21:36 the 'Synoptic Apocalypse'. 'Deliberately and significantly Luke has placed these sayings in these positions of importance to draw each discourse to a close under the powerful image of the end-time Judge, the authority and sovereign of all, the Son of Man. It seems likely he is doing so deliberately, conscious of the image of the Son of Man in the Parables of Enoch'.

b) The Parable of the Figtree ... and all the Trees (καὶ πάντα τὰ δένδρα, Luke 21:29)

Matt 24:32–35	Mark 13:28–31	Luke 21:29–33
³² Ἀπὸ δὲ τῆς συκῆς μάθετε τὴν παραβολήν·	²⁸ Ἀπὸ δὲ τῆς συκῆς μάθετε τὴν παραβολήν·	²⁹Καὶ εἶπεν παραβολὴν αὐτοῖς· <u>Ἴδετε</u> τὴν συκῆν <u>καὶ πάντα τὰ δένδρα</u·
ὅταν ἤδη ὁ κλάδος αὐτῆς γένηται ἁπαλὸς καὶ τὰ φύλλα ἐκφύῃ, γινώσκετε ὅτι ἐγγὺς τὸ θέρος·	ὅταν ἤδη ὁ κλάδος αὐτῆς ἁπαλὸς γένηται καὶ ἐκφύῃ τὰ φύλλα, γινώσκετε ὅτι ἐγγὺς τὸ θέρος ἐστίν·	³⁰ ὅταν <u>προβάλωσιν</u> ἤδη, <u>βλέποντες ἀφ᾽ ἑαυτῶν</u> γινώσκετε ὅτι ἤδη ἐγγὺς τὸ θέρος ἐστίν·
³³ οὕτως καὶ ὑμεῖς, ὅταν ἴδητε <u>πάντα</u> ταῦτα, γινώσκετε ὅτι ἐγγύς ἐστιν ἐπὶ θύραις.	²⁹ οὕτως καὶ ὑμεῖς, ὅταν ἴδητε [...] ταῦτα γινόμενα, γινώσκετε ὅτι ἐγγύς ἐστιν ἐπὶ θύραις.	³¹ οὕτως καὶ ὑμεῖς, ὅταν ἴδητε [...] ταῦτα γινόμενα, γινώσκετε ὅτι ἐγγύς ἐστιν <u>ἡ βασιλεία τοῦ θεοῦ</u>.
³⁴ ἀμὴν λέγω ὑμῖν ὅτι οὐ μὴ παρέλθῃ ἡ γενεὰ αὕτη ἕως ἂν πάντα ταῦτα γένηται.	³⁰ ἀμὴν λέγω ὑμῖν ὅτι οὐ μὴ παρέλθῃ ἡ γενεὰ αὕτη μέχρις οὗ ταῦτα πάντα γένηται.	³² ἀμὴν λέγω ὑμῖν ὅτι οὐ μὴ παρέλθῃ ἡ γενεὰ αὕτη ἕως ἂν πάντα [...] γένηται.
³⁵ ὁ οὐρανὸς καὶ ἡ γῆ παρελεύσεται, οἱ δὲ λόγοι μου οὐ μὴ παρέλθωσιν.	³¹ ὁ οὐρανὸς καὶ ἡ γῆ παρελεύσονται, οἱ δὲ λόγοι μου οὐ μὴ παρελεύσονται.	³³ ὁ οὐρανὸς καὶ ἡ γῆ παρελεύσονται, οἱ δὲ λόγοι μου οὐ μὴ παρελεύσονται.

Although this parable appears in the triple tradition, Luke differs from the other two at several points.

Unlike Matthew and Mark, Luke explicitly introduces this saying as a parable (v.29a). 1 Enoch is also introduced as a parable (1 Enoch 1:2,3 Greek: παραβολή; cf. 4QEnᵃ 1:1) and the third section, the Parables/Similitudes, deliberately recalls this opening, claiming to tell the vision Enoch saw a second time and the wisdom he had previously commenced propounding (37:1-2). Contrary to the (older and) simplistic definition of a parable being 'an earthly story with a heavenly meaning', Enoch's parables are exactly the reverse. They are more akin to visions-explained, for what he sees in the heavenly places he then makes known for its significance for those on earth. This is the same relationship between the vision and its application in Daniel 7 (Dan 7:1-14,15-28), and it is in accord with Luke's views on heavenly realities being revealed (e.g. 10:18-24), especially through Jesus' parables, for those with ears to hear and eyes to see (cf. Luke 4-18).

In keeping with this visionary view of parables, whereas the other Synoptists call upon the audience to 'learn from', in Luke, Jesus calls upon them to 'see' or 'contemplate' (ἴδετε) (21:29b; cf. 2:26,30; 10:18,23-24; cf. 8:18 βλέπετε), which is exactly the language used in the Greek text of 1 Enoch (2:3; 3:1; 5:3; 102:7)[86] to direct the hearer to consider an aspect of creation for its lessons about God's ways. Whereas in Matthew and Mark the lesson is contained in the solitary figtree, in Luke Jesus points to the figtree, but then he adds 'and all the trees' (v.29c). Rather than this Lukan addition being a (rather meaningless) generalization for the sake of his Gentile audience, as is sometimes proposed,[87] it conforms Jesus' parable exactly with 1 Enoch 3:1 (Greek: καταμάθετε καὶ ἴδετε πάντα τὰ δένδρα).

1 Enoch 1:1-3 opens with Enoch taking up his parable while his eyes were open and he saw and understood the vision, speaking not for 'this generation' but for the generation to come. The vision was the coming judgement (1:4-8) and the destruction of sinners (1:9-10). His 'parable' continues to speak of the coming judgement in 5:5-6, but in the intervening section (2:1-5:4), he justifies why the judgement must fall. He does so by calling upon his hearers to 'see' or 'contemplate' various features of heaven and earth, to notice that everything belongs to God and he has fashioned them, and how 'his work proceeds and progresses from year to year' according to his order (5:2), just as the seasons (5:3). As the only thing not abiding by the created

---

86 Enoch also has a counterpart to Matthew and Mark's μάθετε in καταμάθετε, 'contemplate' (3:1; see also μανθάνω at 25:1; 99:10; 104:13), a verb found in the NT only at Matt 6:28.

87 Plummer, *Luke*, s.v., 'those to whom fig trees are unknown'; Nolland, *Luke*, 1008, to enable a parallel between Israel and the Gentile nations; Bock, *Luke*, 1687, 'any tree could reveal this lesson'.

order, he then turns on the hard-hearted, 'But not you'. Instead of being properly ordered like the rest of God's creation, they have not perservered and kept his command, and they will not find peace. At this point, his parable then returns to the coming judgement.

As part of the intervening exhortation, the hearers are called to 'Observe the summer and winter (2:3 [Greek], ἴδετε τὴν θερείαν καὶ τὸν χειμῶνα), consider and observe all the trees (3:1a [Greek], καταμάθετε καὶ ἴδετε πάντα τὰ δένδρα), that is, their characteristics as they pass through winter and summer. 'All their leaves appear as if they wither and had fallen' (3:1b [Ethiopic]), and consider the summer, how the scorching heat dominates the earth (4:1 [Ethiopic]), and yet inevitably, '[See]how the trees are covered with green leaves and they bear fruit to [their] honour and glory' (5:1a [Greek], πῶς τὰ φύλλα χλωρὰ ἐν αὐτοῖς σκέποντα τὰ δένδρα, καὶ πᾶς ὁ καρπὸς αὐτῶν εἰς τιμὴν καὶ δόξαν)'. This contemplation is with the goal of understanding God's works and perceiving how he fashioned them (5:1b).

This introduction (1–5) prepares for the books to follow, and, as noted already, it explicitly prepares for the third Book (37–71; see 37:1–2), which comes after the account of the fall of the Watchers (6–36). With the reader prepared for the coming judgement by the first two sections, the Parables introduce the Son of Man as the agent of that judgement, before this 'contemplation of the cosmos' theme is picked up at length in the Book of Astronomy (72–82) in order to demonstrate the created order of the heavens and drive home the same lesson. This order in nature and in the heavenly places reminds of God's faithfulness to what he intends to do, and so the departure of the watchers from their proper realms and the fall of humanity into their sinful state will eventually meet with God's judgement process.[88]

Thus, the allusion to 'all the trees' taps into 1 Enoch's narrative sub-structure and understanding of time, thus importing the same into Luke's own perspective on the apocalyptic time-frame in which Jesus operated.

---

88 In the OT, the image of 'all the trees' (although in LXX: πάντα τὰ ξύλα) not only resonates with the trees of Eden (cf. Ezekiel 31; and later 4 Bar 9:16–17), but is already loaded with additional eschatological freight. Their withering is associated with God's judgement (Exod 9:25; Joel 1:12, 19), and their springing into new life and joy with God's salvation (Ps 96:12; Isa 44:23; 55:12).

With a the single word προβάλωσιν (v.30), referring to the 'putting forth' of leaves, Luke's version passes over the detail given in Matthew and Mark, but retains the adverb ἤδη, with the combined effect being that the emphasis falls, not upon the process of change, but upon the final state of the trees when 'already' fully in leaf. Resuming the thought that Jesus' hearers ought to be 'seeing' (v.29, Ἴδετε), Luke's unique addition of the adverbial participial clause βλέποντες ἀφ' ἑαυτῶν in support of the next imperative, ensures the focus falls not upon the objective facts of what can be observed, but upon the subjective experience of the observer. At the moment when the trees are fully in leaf, 'seeing from yourselves,[89] *you know*'.[90] Their own personal experience of this feature of the world at exactly at the moment of their observation, brings them knowledge.

The ὅτι clause then provides the content of this empirically-derived knowledge and it relates to the character of the times. Inserting an additional ἤδη, Luke's version further stresses that present moment of perception, reinforced, in turn, by the word order stressing (by primacy effect) the time issue: for from the trees in leaf the hearers simply know that '*already near*, is the summer (τὸ θέρος)'. By the time the leaves are observed, the summer is already upon them. With the sign comes the reality, or, perhaps better, as the reality arrives, that is in itself the signal that it is here.

Luke's version of Jesus' application of this analogy to his hearers' current issue(s) (v.31, οὕτως καὶ ὑμεῖς, 'so also you') parallels that of Matthew and Mark, except for a substitution in the climactic final position (v.31), which clarifies the subject of the impersonal verb they had left ambiguous. Like the presence of the leaves—'whenever you see *these things* coming about',[91] 'you will know, that'—like the co-incident arrival of the summer—'*near is the kingdom of God*'.[92] The kingdom of God was

---

89 This prepositional phrase conveys the sense of a person drawing upon their own personal experience; see also the other two instances in the NT (Luke 12:57; 2 Cor 3:5).
90 This is after the fashion of the exodus (Exod 3:12).
91 For Matthew's πάντα ταῦτα, Mark and Luke have only ταῦτα.
92 Matthew and Mark's 'at the door' also stresses imminence, but their extra metaphor introduces a slight distance between the two comparanda, because the observer is pictured as inside, and the things arriving as outside, the door. For Luke at the moment of observing the sign, the signified is already present

the substance of Jesus' preaching (4:43; 8:1; cf. 9:2,11,60; 16:16), and yet its arrival was still a future prospect (6:20; 7:28). If his hearers were to have its secrets revealed, then they had to hear in order to see (8:10). After the transfiguration, he began to announce the imminence of its arrival, again with the language of 'seeing' (9:27), and the message took on a new urgency (10:9,11), for through acting as the Servant of the Lord, the kingdom of God had 'come upon them' (11:20; 17:21), and as they got closer to Jerusalem, its imminence grew more urgent by metres (9:27,31,51; 13:32–33; 19:11[93]). Poised for the final events of his life, Jesus now used his 'apocalyptic discourse' to reveal in answer to the question about the timing of God's eschatological events (21:7; cf. v.8). Its arrival would be experienced as they see *these things* coming about'. In context, *these things* are the desolations promised by Daniel before the End (v.20), which would be the context at which time 'they will see the Son of Man coming in a cloud with power and great glory' (v.27). And, 'when these things begin to take place, stand up and lift up your heads, because your redemption is drawing near (ἐγγίζει ἡ ἀπολύτρωσις ὑμῶν)' (v.28). According to the parable, at the moment they see these things coming about, they will know in their own experience that the kingdom of God is near. The coming of the Son of Man was specifically associated with the arrival of the kingdom of God. According to Daniel, his coming to the Ancient of Days was in order to receive the kingdom of God (Dan 7:13–14). In Luke's narrative, this expected vindication of the Son of Man (cf. 1 Enoch 46:3; 69:29; 70:1) will come in Jesus' exaltation (9:51; Acts 1:2,9; 2:36; 7:56).

But Jesus had not yet finished answering the question about timing. It is one thing to say that the arrival of the kingdom of God will be perceived in co-incidence with seeing the coming of the Son of Man, but its imminence can be also be given concrete dimensions. With a solemn introductory formula (v.32), he emphasised that 'this generation will not slip away, before *all things* come about'. The generation of Israel amongst whom Jesus has come is not only the final generation in God's timetable (see above), but it will therefore be the one which will

---

93 See note 77.

personally witness the End (cf. 9:27).⁹⁴ Once again, Luke has a significant variation that reinforces his eschatological perspective. Whereas Matthew and Mark include ταῦτα, which has the effect of restricting the referent to the things mentioned in the discourse (Danielic desolations; coming of the Son of Man; arrival of the kingdom of God), by dropping the demonstrative, Luke's 'all things' takes on the grander dimensions of Daniel's 'end of days' (cf. v.9; Daniel 12).⁹⁵

Jesus' final words make two extraordinary claims (v.33), both of which are rendered exactly the same in the triple tradition. However, following on from the change in the previous verse, Luke's version has 'all things coming about' (v.32), now encompassing the ultimate destruction of the cosmos. Whereas there was a permanency to 'heaven and earth' (Gen 1:14–15; Ps 148:5–6), that guaranteed God's promises to his people (Deut 11:21; Ps 103:11; cf. Zech 12:1; Isa 44:24; Jer 31:37), now Jesus says that the cosmos 'will [future indicative] pass away', which is an indication that God's judgement will surely fall (2 Sam 22:8; Joel 2:10; 3:16; Hag 2:16,21; Isa 13:13; Jer 4:23,28; Ezek 32:8). But, beyond the cosmic disaster of the judgement, God will bring about the renovation of all things, a new heaven and a new earth (Isa 65:17; 66:22; 1 Enoch 45), the glorious kingdom of God.

Although English translations tend to make the two halves of Jesus' statement a contrast, because the connective is simply δέ (rather than ἀλλά), it is more likely that they are co-ordinate expressions. Heaven and earth passing away, that is, the coming judgement, is exactly what Jesus has been pleading for Israel to 'see' and to respond to with repentance, while they are in this period of grace (13:6–9). Like the Law of God itself (16:17), 'my words will by no means pass away', for the judgement is certain, the Son of Man is about to come to the Ancient of Days, and when his hearers within this final generation see that event happening, exactly as they do so, the kingdom of God will have also come near.

---

94 'This cannot well mean anything but the generation living when these words were spoken'; Plummer, *Luke*, s.v.; cf. 7:31; 11:29–32,50,51; He therefore takes it to refer to the destruction of Jerusalem, but the coming of the Son of Man in the resurrection/ascension/exaltation is a much better fit.

95 Similarly, Conzelmann, *Theology of Luke*, 131, 'the saying does not refer ot the matters that have just been mentioned, but to the whole of the Divine plan'.

So to summarise the relationship between 'all the trees' in Luke 21:29, and in Enoch: 1. It is a parable; 2. The exact phrase is found; 3. It is related to time reckoned in generations; 4. It is about the signs of the arrival of the end, and so indicates they are in the last times, or better, the last generation; 5. It therefore looks to the arrival of the messianic age/ Son of Man/ kingdom of God (NOT the destruction of the temple). As Jesus was speaking, Israel were in a time of grace (13:18–19). This is when they are in the season of the 'Green tree' (22:31, ἐν τῷ ὑγρῷ ξύλῳ; cf. Ezek 17:22–24). If they do not 'see' that the summer is here, what will happen when the judgement falls?

The reference to 'all the trees' is not simply pictorial detail in Enoch, it is structurally significant, for it falls in the introduction to the narrative. One of the two main aims of the book according to Nickelsburg's summary, is 'the nature and implications of the created structure of the cosmos', but this actually serves the second and major purpose, namely, after exploring the 'origin, nature, [and] consequences' of evil and sin, to lay out the course of history that remains until the final judgement.[96] For Luke, the coming of the Davidic Messiah, of the lineage of Nathan, signals the final stage of that expected course. As the Son of Man is exalted to the right hand of the Father, not only does the Messiah (Son of God; Servant; Righteous One; Elect One) complete his destiny (9:51; 24:26), but the plan of God is all but finished, apart from the preaching of forgiveness to the nations (24:45–49). This is the activity the exalted Lord is now overseeing, in these last days before the End (Acts).

5. Conclusion

The discoveries at the Dead Sea and their subsequent publication in the latter decades of the twentieth century have forced a reassessment of Judaism and of Jesus within it and the Jesus movement arising from it. This reassessment has resulted in a greater appreciation of the Enochic influence on the New Testament writers in general, and the Evangelists in particular. The apocalyptic perspective(s) on life—and especially on

---

96 Nickelsburg, 'Enoch, First Book of', 508.

time—was simply the air that they breathed.

This reassessment needs to progress into a reassessment of the legacy of previous Gospels scholarship, which was not enamoured with the apocalyptic viewpoint and honed methods and conclusions that missed the drama of the historical moment in which Jesus and his followers operated. Conzelmann's conclusions played a big part in setting the framework in which subsequent Lukan scholarship became almost straight-jacketted. But, far from being non-apocalyptic or anti-apocalyptic, Luke shows evidence of having drunk at Enoch's well and, like his contemporaries, when he wrote his orderly narrative of the events fulfilled amongst us, he knew that time itself had entered its final stage.

Despite Luke 'contain[ing] the largest collection of [Enoch] traditions', Nickelsburg nevertheless felt that 'few would argue that Luke's theology is apocalyptic'.[97] However, whereas many define apocalyptic as a genre of narrative with its own set of unique characteristics, others argue that '"apocalyptic" does not denote a specific genre but a religious bearing that is preoccupied by the approach of the end of all normal time and history'.[98] Insofar as it is constrained to recount the history of Jesus of Nazareth, perhaps on the surface the Gospel narrative does not seem to be *generically* 'apocalyptic'. But there are sufficient indicators on that same surface, that the apocalyptic world view such as found in 1 Enoch is very much a part of Luke's deeper structures, just as it was native to Jesus' himself. One of the main burdens of such an apocalyptic view of history is that the plan of God will unfold according to a timetable through to the final apostate generation, and then the Messianic Son of Man will come, bringing the judgment day, and with his coming to the Ancient of Days, the kingdom of God will finally arrive before lasting forever. In this regard, Luke's orderly account is thoroughly apocalyptic, for from the midst of first-century Israel, it announces to the wider world 'the things that have been fulfilled amongst us' (1:1).

Peter G. Bolt
Sydney College of Divinity

---

97 Nickelsburg, 'Riches', 343.
98 Charlesworth, 'Introduction, Apocalyptic Literature', 3.

Bibliography

Aalen, S. — 'St Luke's Gospel and 1 Enoch', *NTS* 13 (1966), 1–13.

Aviam, Mordechai — 'The Book of Enoch and the Galilean Archaeology and Landscape', in D.L. Bock & J.H. Charlesworth (eds.), *The Parables of Enoch. A Paradigm Shift* (LBS; London: Bloomsbury, T&T Clark, 2013), 158–169.

Barker, M. — *The Lost Prophet. The Book of Enoch and its influence on Christianity* (London: SPCK, 1988).

Bauckham, Richard — *Jude and the Relatives of Jesus* (London: T&T Clark, 1990, repr. 2004).

Bergsma, J.S. — *The Jubilee From Leviticus to Qumran: A History of Interpretation* (VTSupp 115; Leiden: Brill, 2007).

Boccaccini, G. — 'Jewish Apocalyptic Tradition: The Contribution of Italian Scholarship', in J.H. Charlesworth & J.J. Collins (eds.), *Mysteries and Revelations: Apocalyptic Studies Since the Uppsala Colloquium* (Sheffield: Sheffield Academic Press, 1991), 33–50.

Bock, D.L. — *Luke 9:51-24:53* (BECNT; Grand Rapids: Baker Academic, 1996).

Bock, D.L. & J.H. Charlesworth (eds.), *Parables of Enoch: A Paradigm Shift* (LBS; London: Bloomsbury, T&T Clark, 2013).

Bolt, Peter G. — 'Preparing Israel for the Arrival of the Son of Man. Jesus' Kingship Parable (Luke 19:11–28) in its Historical and Literary Context', *JGAR* 1 (2017), 23–41.

Bolt, Peter G. — 'Mission and Witness', in David G. Peterson and I. Howard Marshall (eds.), *Witness to the Gospel. The Theology of Acts* (Carlisle & Grand Rapids: Paternoster & Eerdmans, 1998), 191–214.

Bonner, Campbell — *The Last Chapters of Enoch in Greek* (Studies and Documents, 8; London: Chatto and Windus, 1937).

Charles, R.H. — 'The Book of Enoch', *Apocrypha and Pseudepigrapha of the Old Testament* (2 vols.; Oxford: Clarendon, 1913), 2.163–281. This is incorporated from his *The Book of Enoch* (Oxford: Clarendon, 1912; London: SPCK, 1917, repr. 1987).

Charles, R.H.   *The Ethiopic Version of the Book of Enoch, together with the fragmentary Greek and Latin versions* (Oxford: Clarendon, 1906).

Charles, R.H.   *The Book of Enoch* (Oxford: Clarendon, 1893).

Charlesworth, J.H.   'Introduction, Apocalyptic Literature and Related Works', in J.H. Charlesworth (ed.), *The Old Testament Pseucepigrapha*. Vol. 1: *Apocalyptic Literature & Testaments* (New York: Doubleday, 1983), 3–4.

Charlesworth, J.H.   'Seminar Report. The SNTS Pseudepigrapha Seminars at Tübingen and Paris', *NTS* 25 (1979), 315–23.

Charlesworth, J.H.   'The Date and Provenance of the *Parables of Enoch*', in D.L. Bock & J.H. Charlesworth (eds.), *The Parables of Enoch. A Paradigm Shift* (LBS; London: Bloomsbury, T&T Clark, 2013), 37–57.

Charlesworth, J.H.   'Did Jesus Know the Traditions in the *Parables of Enoch*?', in D.L. Bock & J.H. Charlesworth (eds.), *The Parables of Enoch. A Paradigm Shift* (LBS; London: Bloomsbury, T&T Clark, 2013), 173–217

Conzelmann, H.   *The Theology of Luke* (G. Buswell, transl.; London: Faber & Faber, 1960, ²1961 [German: *Die Mitte der Zeit*, 1953, ²1957]).

Evans, C.A.   'Dead Sea Scrolls', in Mark J. Boda and J. Gordon McConville (eds.), *Dictionary of the Old Testament: Prophets* (Downers Grove, Il.: IVP, 2012), 143–152.

Funk, R.   'Conzelmann on Luke', *JBR* 30.4 (1962), 299–301.

Grabbe, Lester L.   '"Son of Man" in Second Temple Judaism', in Loren T. Stuckenbruck and Gabriele Boccaccini (eds.), *Enoch and the Synoptic Gospels: Reminiscences, Allusions, Intertextuality* (Early Judaism and its literature, 44; Atlanta: SBL Press, 2016), 169–197.

Green, Joel B.   'Reading Luke', in Joel B. Green (ed.), *Methods for Luke* (Methods in Biblical Interpretation; Cambridge: Cambridge University Press, 2010), 1–8.

Green, Joel B.   'Narrative Criticism', in Joel B. Green (ed.), *Methods for Luke* (Methods in Biblical Interpretation; Cambridge: Cambridge University Press, 2010), 74–112.

Greenfield, J.C., and M.E. Stone   'The Enochic Pentateuch and the Date of the Similitudes', *HTR* 70.1-2 (1977), 51-65.

Hartman, L.   *Asking for a Meaning. A Study of 1 Enoch 1-5* (Coniectanea Biblica NT 12; Lund: CWK Gleerup, 1979).

Isaac, E.   '1 (Ethiopic Apocalypse of) Enoch', in J. H. Charlesworth (ed.), *The Old Testament Pseudepigrapha*. Vol. 1: *Apocalyptic Literature and Testaments* (New York: Doubleday, 1983), 1.5-89 [Introduction: 5-12; Translation: 13-89].

James, M.R.   *Apocrypha Anecdota. A Collection of Thirteen Apocryphal Books* (Texts and Studies 2.3; Cambridge: Cambridge University Press, 1893, repr. 1967).

Knibb, Michael A.   *The Ethiopic Book of Enoch. A New Edition in the Light of the Aramaic Dead Sea Fragments* (2 Vols.; Oxford: Oxford University Press, 1978). Also incorporated in H. D. F. Sparks (ed.), *The Apocryphal Old Testament* (Oxford: Oxford University Press, 1984), which is a revision of Charles, *Apocrypha and Pseudepigrapha*.

Knibb, Michael A.   'The Date of the Parables of Enoch: A Critical Review', *NTS* 25 (1979), 345-59.

Kobelski, P.J.   '11QMelchizedek and the Son of Man Question', in *Melchizedek and Melchiresaʻ* (CBQMS, 10; Wasnington: CBA, 1981), 130-137.

Lawlor, H.   'Early Citations from the Book of Enoch', in W. Wright, I. Bywater, & H. Jackson (eds.), *The Journal of Philology* (Cambridge: Cambridge University Press, 2012), 164-225. doi:10.1017/CBO9781139523783.015.

Licht, Jacob   *Storytelling in the Bible* (Jerusalem: Magnes, 1978).

McDonald, Lee M.   'The *Parables of Enoch* in Early Christianity', in D.L. Bock & J.H. Charlesworth (eds.), The Parables of Enoch. A Paradigm Shift (LBS; London: Bloomsbury, T&T Clark, 2013), 329-363.

Marshall, I. Howard   *The Gospel of Luke: A Commentary on the Greek Text* (NIGTC; Grand Rapids: Eerdmans, 1978).

Mearns, Christopher L.   'Dating the Similitudes of Enoch', *NTS* 25 (1979), 360-69.

Milik, J.T., with M. Black   *The Books of Enoch. Aramaic Fragments of Qumran Cave 4* (Oxford: Clarendon, 1976).

Milik, J.T.   'Problèmes de la littérature Hénochique à la lumière des fragments araméens de Qumrân', *HTR* 64.2–3 (1971), 333–78.

Milik, J. T.   *Ten Years of Discovery in the Wilderness of Judaea* (SBT 26; London: SCM, 1959; Eugene: Wipf and Stock, 2009 reprint).

Nickelsburg, George W.E., and James C. VanderKam   *1 Enoch 2. A Commentary on the Book of 1 Enoch, Chapters 37–82* (Hermeneia; K. Baltzer, ed.; Minneapolis: Augsburg Fortress, 2012).

Nickelsburg, George W.E.   *1 Enoch 1. A Commentary on the Book of 1 Enoch, Chapters 1–36; 81–108* (Hermeneia; K. Baltzer, ed.; Minneapolis: Augsburg Fortress, 2001).

Nickelsburg, George W.E. 'Enoch, First Book of', *The Anchor Bible Dictionary* (6 vols.; New York: Doubleday, 1992), 2.508–516.

Nickelsburg, George W.E.   'Son of Man', *The Anchor Bible Dictionary* (6 vols.; New York: Doubleday, 1992), 6.137–150.

Nickelsburg, George W.E.   'Riches, the Rich, and God's Judgment in 1 Enoch 92–105 and the Gospel of Luke', *NTS* 25.3 (1979), 324–344.

Nickelsburg, George W.E.   'Enoch 97–104, a Study of the Greek and Ethiopic Texts', in Michael E. Stone (ed.), *Armenian and Biblical Studies* (*Sion* Supp. 1; Jerusalem: St James Press, 1976), 90–156.

Nolland, John   *Luke 18:35–24:53* (WBC 35C; Grand Rapids: Zondervan, 1993).

Plummer, Alfred   *The Gospel According to St. Luke* (ICC; Edinburgh: T. & T. Clark, ^{5}1922 [1896]).

Powell, Denise   *Who are the Righteous? The Narrative Function of the* Dikaioi *in the Gospel of Luke* (Lantham: Lexington Books/ Fortress Academic, 2021).

Rist, M.   'Enoch, Book of', *Interpreters Dictionary of the Bible* (5 Vols.; Nashville: Abingdon, 1962), 2.103–105.

Robinson, S.E.   'Apocalypticism in the Time of Hillel and Jesus', in James H. Charlesworth & Loren L. Johns (eds.), *Hillel and*

	Jesus. Comparative Studies of Two Major Religious Leaders (Minneapolis: Fortress, 1997), 121–136.
Shellard, Barbara	'Excursus: An Examination of the Connections Between Luke–Acts, *1 Enoch* 92–105 and Revelation', *New Light on Luke. Its Purpose, Sources and Literary Context* (JSNTSup 215; London: T&T Clark, repr. 2004 [2002]), 189–99.
Sjöberg, E.	*Der Menschensohn im äthiopischen Henochbuch* (Lund: Gleerup, 1946).
Sloan, R. B.	*The Favourable Year of the Lord: A Study of the Jubilary Theology in the Gospel of Luke* (Ann Arbor, MI: Scholars, 1977).
Stuckenbruck, Loren T., and Gabriele Boccaccini,	'1 Enoch and the Synoptic Gospels: The Method and Benefits of a Conversation', in Loren T. Stuckenbruck and Gabriele Boccaccini (eds.), *Enoch and the Synoptic Gospels: Reminiscences, Allusions, Intertextuality* (Early Judaism and its literature, 44; Atlanta: SBL Press, 2016), 1–17.
Theisohn, J.	*Der auserwählte Richter. Untersuchungen zum traditionsgeschichtlichen Ort der Menschen- sohngestalt der Bilderreden des Äthiopischen Henoch* (Studien zum Umwelt des Neuen Testaments 12; Göttingen: Vandenhoeck & Ruprecht, 1975).
Tilley, Robert	'Crisis? What Crisis?' Gospel Criticism and the Ideological Use of an Illiterate Jesus Movement', *JGAR* 3 (2019), 15–40.
VanderKam, James C.	'Righteous One, Messiah, Chosen One, and Son of Man in 1 Enoch 37–71', in James H. Charlesworth (ed.), *The Messiah. Developments in Earliest Judaism and Christianity* (Minneapolis: Augsburg Fortress, 1992), 169–191. Republished in James C. VanderKam, *From Revelation to Canon: Studies in the Hebrew Bible and Second Temple Literature* (Leiden: Brill, 2002), 413–438.
Wacholder, Ben Z.	'Chronomessianism. The Timing of Messianic Movements and the Calendar of Sabbatical Cycles', *Hebrew Union College Annual* 46 (1975), 201–218. Reprinted in *Essays on Jewish Chronology and Chronography* (New York: Ktav, 1976), 240–257.

Walck, L.W.   'The *Parables of Enoch* and the Synoptic Gospels', in D.L. Bock & J.H. Charlesworth (eds.), *The Parables of Enoch. A Paradigm Shift* (LBS; London: Bloomsbury, T&T Clark, 2013), 231–268.

CHAPTER 9

Nathanael as a Remnant Figure in the Gospel of John: A Fresh Look at an Enigmatic Character

Stephen Rockwell

Abstract

Nathanael is an enigmatic figure in the Fourth Gospel. The narrative reveals so little about him and as readers we are left wanting so much more. However, what is disclosed about him is significant. Jesus, on seeing Nathanael for the first time, declares to the other disciples with him, ἴδε ἀληθῶς Ἰσραηλίτης ἐν ᾧ δόλος οὐκ ἔστιν (1:47).

There are three key lexemes (ἀληθῶς, Ἰσραηλίτης, δόλος) within this description, all of which require careful attention if we are to understand the meaning of Jesus' words accurately. These terms have been variously understood within scholarship, although there is a broad consensus that they should be read within the backdrop of the Jacob narrative in Genesis, and also Psalm 32.

Whilst acknowledging the contribution of such scholarship, this chapter presents an alternate reading of this crucial description of Nathanael. Rather than seeing Nathanael as a 'new Jacob', this paper will propose that Nathanael is introduced by Jesus and by the author of the gospel as being a remnant figure of faithful Israel.

This will be demonstrated by a careful consideration of the three key terms read within the backdrop, not of Genesis, but rather of the prophetic writings of the Old Testament and in particular the book of the twelve minor prophets.

Introduction

Nathanael is an enigmatic figure in the fourth Gospel. The narrative reveals so little about him and readers are left wanting so much more. However, what is disclosed about him is significant. He is mentioned in Chapter 1 and only again at the end of the Gospel. In Chapter 21 he is one of the disciples who goes out fishing with Peter, Thomas, the Sons of Zebedee, and two other unnamed disciples. There we are told that he comes from Cana in Galilee. Apart from that, and what we have recorded in John 1, very little is known about him. The fact that he is not listed amongst the disciples in any of the Synoptic Gospels has led to much speculation about his identity. There are those who suggest that he wasn't a real person, but just a literary figure employed by John. Others suggest perhaps that he wasn't one of the Twelve, although that is a difficult position to maintain in the light of John's account. Others try to place him in the lists found in the Synoptic accounts and Acts and equate him with either Bartholomew or James the son of Alphaeus. After all, John never gives a list of the twelve disciples and happily refers to unnamed disciples at various times.[1]

For the purpose of this paper, the discussions surrounding Nathanael's identity will be left aside in order to focus rather on Jesus' description of him in their first encounter—ἴδε ἀληθῶς Ἰσραηλίτης ἐν ᾧ δόλος οὐκ ἔστιν ('See truly an Israelite in whom there is no deceit', John 1:47).

---

1   For a good summary of the options see Bennema, *Encountering Jesus*. For a tentative presentation in favour of understanding Nathanael to be the same person as James son of Alphaeus, see Hill, 'Identity'.

Nathanael as a new Jacob?

These words have been almost universally read in light of the Jacob narrative in Genesis. Jacob was indeed a deceiver of great notoriety. He deceived his brother Esau out of his birthright by making him exchange it for soup (Gen. 25:29-34). Then, with the help of his mother Rebekah, Jacob deceived his blind father into giving him the family blessing rather than giving it to Esau (Gen. 27). Significantly at that point in the narrative, according to the LXX, Isaac says to his son Esau, 'your brother, coming with guile (δόλος) has taken your blessing' (Gen. 27:35). It is the same word for what Jesus says is not to be found in Nathanael.

Also, a few verses on, Jesus promises that some shall see 'heaven open and the angels of God ascending and descending on the Son of Man' (1:51)—which is undoubtedly an intertextual reference to Jacob's dream recorded in Gen 28:12. There Jacob is fleeing for his life after Esau was so angry at his deception that he wanted to kill him. Moreover, Jacob, on returning to his brother later in the narrative after spending time with his uncle Laban, deceiving him and being deceived by him, wrestles with God, and has his name changed by God from Jacob to Israel (Gen. 32:28).

Because all three of the above links are tied so closely together, the overwhelming majority of those who have studied Nathanael conclude that he is to be understood as a new Jacob, a new Israel, in whom there is not deceit. The manner in which Hill refers to this idea is indicative of the seeming universality of this reading within biblical scholarship. After making a statement that there are three direct allusions to the Jacob narrative in these verses, Hill provides a footnote that simply says, 'See the commentaries'.[2] And he is correct in his assessment, for almost all the commentaries read this pericope in light of the Jacob narrative. So Carson, whilst not definitive, is most certainly indicative of the scholarly consensus when he concludes that Nathanael 'was

---

2 Hill, 'Identity', 56 n. 39.

an Israelite without deceit, an "Israel" and not a "Jacob".[3] Trudinger rather quirkily paraphrases Jesus' statement as 'Look, Israel without a trace of Jacob left in him'.[4]

The Jacob I never knew

However, whilst this notion of reading Nathanael in light of Jacob is seemingly universal, there are some dissenters amongst the scholars. Schnackenberg is one example. Having stated that 'on account of the logion v.51 (Jacob's dream), many commentators have seen here an allusion to Jacob, the patriarch of Israel', he concludes rather that 'this is improbable'.[5] More recently Chennattu has also brought this assumption into question. She states a valid concern that the interpretation that sees Jacob as the paradigmatic deceiver 'does not seem to respect the Johannine presentation of Jacob elsewhere in the Gospel'.[6] We might want to add that neither does it suit the presentation of Jacob elsewhere in the New Testament.

This does appear to be a problem for the all too common approach to this text. If we are to read the text as we are told by many of the commentators, we must first assume that when anyone talks about δόλος in the context of Israel, then the original hearers' minds would go directly to Jacob, the greatest of tricksters.[7] However, this seems unlikely, and difficult to reconcile with the reverence in which Jacob is uniformly esteemed in the New Testament.

---

3   Carson, *John*, 161. See also Barrett, *John*, 185: 'In view of the use in v. 51 of Gen 28.12 it seems probable that there is here a reference to the cunning of Jacob (later called Israel) in robbing Esau of his blessing'; Köstenberger, *John*, 82: 'Nathanael differs from the original "Israel", who was deceitful. Nathanael was free from such duplicity of heart'; Michaels, *John*, 130: 'Nathanael is a true "Israel", forever free of the "deceit" (*dolos*) that marked the life of the old "Jacob"'; Lincoln, *John*, 120: Nathanael 'surpasses the original Israel by being without guile or deceit'; Bennema, *Encountering Jesus*, 66: 'Nathanael is *contrasted* to Jacob in that Nathanael represents the new Jacob or true Israel'; Moloney, *John*, 56: 'Nathanael is an Israelite without guile, unlike wily Jacob'; Westcott, *John*, 1.55: 'There is already here a reference to Jacob's victories of faith (v. 51) which is made even clearer by the second clause'; Keener, *John*, 1.485–486: 'By calling Nathanael an Israelite "in whom there is no deceit", Jesus deliberately contrasts this representative Israelite with his ancestor Jacob'.
4   Trudinger, 'Israelite', 117.
5   Schnackenburg, *John*, 1.316.
6   Chennattu, *Johannine Discipleship*, 37.
7   Patterson, 'Old Testament Use'.

Jacob, the son of Isaac, the grandson of Abraham, is referred to twenty-five times within the New Testament. Ten of those occurrences are merely biographical—like the inclusion of his name in a genealogy, or the narrative in Stephen's speech about his birth and descent down to Egypt where he died.[8] However, on seven occasions he is listed alongside Abraham and Isaac, giving the impression that he, with them, is one of the great patriarchs of the faith—for instance when God meets Moses in the burning bush and declares himself to be the God of Abraham, Isaac, and Jacob, which Jesus reflects on in his discussions with the Sadducees to show that he is the God of the living and not the dead.[9] That in itself is enough to make us question the automatic association of Jacob as the great deceiver. Moreover, Jacob is also listed with the great heroes of the faith in Hebrews 11,[10] and when the angel Gabriel visits the Virgin Mary, he declares to her that her child will reign over the House of Jacob forever.[11]

This high regard in which Jacob is esteemed in the New Testament is paralleled by the manner in which he is spoken about in the intertestamental Jewish apocryphal writings also. There Jacob is listed frequently alongside Abraham and Isaac as one of the great patriarchs of the faith, even being described as a 'faithful servant' (2 Macc 1:2), the 'sainted one' (3 Macc 6:3) and as 'our wise father' (4 Macc 2:19).

Overall the impression given in both the New Testament and the intertestamental Jewish writings is that for Jews and followers of Jesus alike, Jacob was revered as one of the forefathers of the people of God, one of the great Patriarchs.

More importantly, this impression of Jacob is confirmed within the Gospel of John itself, as Chennattu has already observed.[12]

In discussions with the woman at the well in John 4, in response to Jesus' offer of living water, the woman asks the question, 'Are you greater than our father Jacob?' (4:12). Importantly, the question begins with μή, indicating that, at least in the mind of the Samaritan woman

---

8   Matt 1:2 (x 2); Luke 3:34; John 4:5,6; Acts 7:8 (x 2), 12, 14, 15.
9   Matt 8:11; 22:32; Mark 12:26; Luke 13:28; 20:37; Acts 3:13; 7:32.
10 Heb 11:9, 20, 21.
11 Luke 1:33. Other passages which mention Jacob include Acts 7:46; Rom 9:13; 11:26.
12 Chennattu, *Johannine Discipleship*, 37.

at this stage in the conversation, she didn't believe that he was greater than Jacob (μὴ σὺ μείζων εἶ τοῦ πατρὸς ἡμῶν Ιακώβ). The readers of the Gospel, however, know better.

This is significant, since once again, this time within the Johannine narrative, we see Jacob being revered as the great forefather of the people of God, even amongst the Samaritans, and not as the paradigmatic trickster. Even more significant is the manner in which this question is repeated by Jesus' Jewish interlocutors in John 8, only changing the Patriarch to whom they compare Jesus. With the same grammar as 4:12, they ask: 'Are you greater than our father Abraham?' (8:53, μὴ σὺ μείζων εἶ τοῦ πατρὸς ἡμῶν Αβραάμ). The parallel between the two questions is difficult for the reader of John's Gospel to miss. John wants his readers to know that, despite the dubious questioning of those in Jesus' day, he is indeed greater than both Abraham and Jacob. Also we must observe here that in this context, within John's Gospel, Jacob is held, alongside Abraham, to be the great patriarch of the people of God.

To assume that the original hearers of Jesus' words (that Nathanael was an Israelite in whom there was no deceit) would have automatically understood him as making a comparison with the great deceiver Jacob is to fly in the face of every reference to Jacob in the New Testament. Thus, Trudinger's comments that 'the name Jacob [...] had become virtually a synonym for "deceit"', and that 'the character of Jacob was somewhat an embarrassment and a perplexity to many a devout Jew' seem to be both unsubstantiated and unsustainable in the light of the New Testament and other evidence to the contrary.[13] He is not the great deceiver, he is the great, revered Patriarch. That Jacob deceived his brother is not in question, but seeing him as the paradigmatic deceiver would be akin to remembering Moses, not as the great prophet and leader of the people of God but as the murderer, or to remembering David, not as the great King who followed after God's own heart, but as the adulterer. There is no evidence that Jacob was seen and remembered in such a light in Jesus' day.

---

13 Trudinger, 'Israelite', 117.

The dislocation of 1:51

Some will say that the undeniable link to Jacob's vision in 1:51 is the interpretive key that unlocks the true meaning of what Jesus was alluding to in these initial words concerning Nathanael in 1:47.[14] However, we must ask if this is as legitimate as some might argue.

First, are we to assume that the disciples who heard Jesus' declaration regarding Nathanael in 1:47 scratched their heads wondering what it was that he was saying about Nathanael until he finally mentioned his words in 1:51 when suddenly it all began to make sense to them? I think not. However, there is something even more significant in the grammar of 1:51 that dislocates this verse from the rest of the Nathanael narrative.

Two things are worth observing in regards to this verse. Firstly, this is the first time in the Gospel that Jesus employs the unique ἀμὴν ἀμήν formula. The double ἀμήν is not attested in the Synoptic Gospels, and yet it is a characteristic feature of John, occurring twenty-five times throughout the Gospel and never once singularly. This appears to be John's way of giving emphasis to a solemn pronouncement by Jesus, confirming the trustworthiness and importance of what is about to be said.[15] Nathanael can be told that he will see greater things than Jesus' prescient knowledge of him under the fig tree in verse 50, but what is said in verse 51 is of a different order, 'ἀμὴν ἀμήν, I say [...]'.

Secondly, note the importance of the change of number. The addressee changes from verse 50, the singular Nathanael, to the plural in verse 51. Jesus is clearly no longer just addressing Nathanael. This solemn promise of seeing heaven open is a promise made to a plural audience. ἀμὴν ἀμὴν λέγω ὑμῖν, 'truly, truly I say to you [*plural*]', ὄψεσθε 'that you (*plural*) will see' heaven open and so on and so forth. The change of number cannot be ignored here. This is now a solemn declaration, not just for Nathanael, but for all of those present, and arguably an invitation for all of John's readers to come and see heaven open for us in the person of Jesus.

---

14 See for example Barrett, *John*, 185: 'In view of the use of v.51 of Gen 28.12 it seems probable that there is here (in 1:47) a reference to the cunning of Jacob (later called Israel) in robbing Esau of his blessing'.
15 Barrett, *John*, 186. Carson, *John*, 162.

Thus 1:51 should not be read as the interpretive key to unlocking the meaning of the previous Nathanael pericope, but rather it should be understood as a summary declaration to all the disciples who have gathered around Jesus by the end of these eventful first days (at least Andrew, Peter, Philip, Nathanael, and an unnamed disciple—possibly the Beloved Disciple himself) and indeed an invitation to the reader of the Gospel.

Thus we conclude that the high regard in which Jacob was held as a Patriarch and the dislocation of 1:51 from the Nathanael narrative should lead us to question the veracity of understanding Jesus' declaration on seeing Nathanael in light of the Genesis accounts of Jacob and his trickery. Once free from the restraints of such an interpretation, we are now able to approach the text with some fresh eyes in order perhaps to understand it and its background anew.

To do that we must pay careful attention to the three key lexemes within Jesus statement: namely, ἀληθῶς, Ἰσραηλίτης, and δόλος.

Firstly, then ἀληθῶς.

ἀληθῶς— Adjective or Adverb?

Many commentators and translations understand ἀληθῶς in this verse adjectivally. In this reading then Jesus would be saying something along the lines of, 'Look here is a true Israelite'. The NIV '84 is a good example of that translation, and possibly even a motivating factor for some commentators to read it in this fashion. However, it must be observed that ἀληθῶς is not an adjective but an adverb. Despite this fact, many commentators still persist with the adjectival reading. Barrett, who of course predates the NIV '84, is none the less a good example of this tendency. Despite initially distinguishing Nathanael as one who 'truly is an Israelite' in one paragraph, in the very next he seemingly succumbs to the irrepressible gravitational force of the adjectival reading by stating that 'the true Israelite is further described' as being without δόλος.[16] Others have attempted more explicitly to justify the adjectival reading of the adverb here. Chennattu states unreservedly that 'the adverb ἀληθῶς

---

16 Barrett, *John*, 184–185.

here serves as the equivalent of the adjective ἀληθής or ἀληθινός.[17] Whilst BDF does outline that 'adverbs could be used as adjectives' and BDAG lists one of the uses of ἀληθῶς as being 'in attributive relation with substantives' it is not simply enough to note this possibly to assert this use here in John.[18] For although John is well aware of the adjectives ἀληθής and ἀληθινός and employs them frequently throughout his Gospel, he does not choose to do so here.[19] In fact, John chooses to utilise the adverb ἀληθῶς here in 1:47 and six other occasions within his Gospel over and above his other uses of the adjectives, and, contra to Chennattu, Carson insists correctly that ἀληθῶς is 'consistently deployed in the Fourth Gospel as an adverb'.[20]

This is important since the adverbial and adjectival readings change the way we understand Jesus' statement. If adjectival, then Jesus is making a statement about Nathanael being a true Israelite as opposed to others whose qualification for such a description might be in question. However, if, as argued above, the adverb should carry with it the sense it does in its Johannine usage elsewhere in the Gospel, then Jesus is stating something about the nature of truly being an Israelite. As Bauckham rightly observes, 'this use of the adverb [...] links this description of Nathanael with descriptions of Jesus himself elsewhere (in John): "truly the saviour of the world" (4:42), "truly the prophet that is to come into the world" (6:14), "truly the prophet" (7:40). It indicates that Nathanael really deserves the name "Israelite".[21] To understand more fully why Jesus might say that about Nathanael we need to look more closely at the two words that Jesus uses to describe Nathanael, i.e. an Israelite (Ἰσραηλίτης) in whom there is no guile (δόλος).

---

17 Chennattu, *Johannine Discipleship*, 37.
18 BDF §434. BDAG, s.v. ἀληθῶς.
19 ἀληθής on fourteen occasions (3:33; 4:18; 5:31,32; 6:55 [x2]; 7:18; 8:13,14,17,26; 10:41; 19:35; 21:24) and ἀληθινός on nine occasions (1:9; 4:23,37; 6:32; 7:28; 8:16; 15:1; 17:3; 19:35).
20 Carson, *John*, 160.
21 Bauckham, *Gospel of Glory*, 168.

'Israelites' and 'Jews'

To investigate more fully Jesus' description of Nathanael as an Israelite is to enter into the tempestuous waters of the discussions surrounding the nature of 'the Jews' in Johannine scholarship. An in-depth analysis of such discussions and their many and varied strata is beyond the scope of this essay. It is worth noting that here, in 1:47, we find the only use of the term 'Israelite' in the whole of John's Gospel, over and against the seventy-one uses of 'the Jews' and four occurrences of 'Israel'. On the surface of things, that should immediately raise the question whether there isn't something significant in the description of Nathanael being an Israelite. Bauckham, however, following both Tomson and Kuhn, cautions the careful reader of the Gospel about seeing anything significant in such a designation.[22] Tomson's excellent work in analysing the various usages of the terms in both biblical and extra-biblical sources leads to the following conclusions regarding the social context in which each various term was regularly employed: 'the dual usage typical of Judaism in the Graeco-Roman period involves semantic equivalence but social differentiation of the two names, "Israel" being the self-appellation Jews use in inner-Jewish situations, and "Jews" when including non-Jews among the intended hearers'.[23] This is a very helpful observation and saves the interpreter of the Gospel from possible unintended exegetical overstatements. Bauckham observes that the 'Gospel of John conforms almost entirely consistently to these facts of usage'.[24] So for instance, it is not surprising that Nicodemus is introduced as a ruler of the Jews (3:1) by the narrator of the fourth Gospel as it is assumed he is writing for a largely Gentile audience. It is similarly not surprising that in the midst of the recorded conversation, Jesus can refer to Nicodemus as a teacher of Israel (3:10), since now the conversation is within an inner-Jewish context. The same can be said regarding the title 'King of Israel' ascribed to Jesus by Nathanael (1:51) and the Jewish crowds upon Jesus' arrival into Jerusalem at the beginning of his passion week (12:31), and the title the 'King of the Jews' given by Pilate (18:33, 39; 19:19), and the

---

22 Bauckham, *Gospel of Glory*, 168. See also, Bauckham, *Testimony*, 230; Tomson, '"Jews"'; Kuhn, Ἰσραήλ, κτλ.
23 Tomson, '"Jews"', 339.
24 Bauckham, *Testimony*, 230.

soldiers (19:3), and the chief priests when speaking to Pilate (19:21). This, it is argued, is all in accordance with the usage rule which John was *obliged* to consistently follow within his Gospel[25] and so too with Jesus' description of Nathanael as an Israelite in 1:47. In accordance with the usage outlined by Tomson, this is exactly in accordance with what one would expect as part of an inner-Jewish conversation.

However, whilst this is extremely helpful, it is seemingly not as obligatory as one might first be led to believe. Whilst recognising the value of the contribution of Tomson and others, Thiel has questioned the veracity of the conclusion.[26] He observes several occasions where the supposed rule of dual-usage doesn't hold. Significantly he refers to the introductory salutation of 2 Maccabees (1:1–9), in which the Jews of Jerusalem are writing to their Jewish brothers in Egypt and encouraging them to remember and celebrate the Festival of Dedication or Hanukkah. In such a context, the letter opens, 'The Jewish brothers in Jerusalem and those in the land of Judea, to the Jewish brothers in Egypt, Greetings and true peace' (1 Macc 1:1).[27] As Thiel rightly observes, 'this is a letter written in Judea by Jews to Jews concerning a Jewish festival; it is inner-Jewish in any conceivable sense'.[28] Yet here the term 'Jew' is employed rather than 'Israelites' as one would expect if we were to be following Tomson's dual-usage hypothesis.

However, one does not need to venture much further than the Gospel of John itself to find such exceptions to the rule. Two such anomalies are acknowledged by Tomson himself. In 13:33 and 18:20 Jesus, speaking to a Jewish audience (the disciples in 13:33 and the High Priest in 18:20), refers not to his fellow Israelites as one would expect, but rather to 'the Jews'. So in 13:33 Jesus reminds his disciples that 'Just as I told the Jews, so I tell you now: Where I am going, you cannot come', and in 18:20 Jesus refers to the fact that he has spoken openly and publicly in the 'temple, where the Jews come together'. Whilst acknowledging their existence, Tomson does not allow these

---

25 Bauckham, *Testimony*, 231. Italics original.
26 Thiel, "'Israel'".
27 τοῖς ἀδελφοῖς τοῖς κατ' Αἴγυπτον Ἰουδαίοις χαίρειν οἱ ἀδελφοὶ οἱ ἐν Ἱεροσολύμοις Ἰουδαῖοι καὶ οἱ ἐν τῇ χώρᾳ τῆς Ἰουδαίας εἰρήνην ἀγαθήν.
28 Thiel, "'Israel'", 88.

anomalies to impact his general rule, preferring rather to state that 'this is a clear departure from the Jewish usage which we should expect here', and leaving it at that.[29] Bauckham also, whilst stating that the Gospel conforms 'almost entirely' to the above mentioned pattern, acknowledges, alongside the two passages already mentioned, a third in 11:8. However, he describes these passages as simply places in the Gospel where 'the rules are broken', with little justification or explanation as to why this might be so.[30] The passage in 11:8 is illuminating in this regard. There the disciples of Jesus remind him that returning to Jerusalem for Lazarus is a risky endeavour because 'a short while ago the Jews tried to stone you'.

So whilst we acknowledge the great contribution of Tomson's work in this regard, it is perhaps not quite as robust an hypothesis as it might first appear. As Thiel postulates: 'It is sometimes said that an exception proves the rule, but when exceptions mount it is natural to ask if the rule has lost its explanatory power'.[31] More than that, the aforementioned 'exceptions' might cause one to question if not the singular use of the phrase 'Israelite' in the Gospel could be seen as an exception also. After all, given that it is the sole use, it is already, by definition, an exception of some sort for John. Perhaps these exceptions might give us pause to reconsider Bauckham's forthright statement that there 'is no significance [...] in the fact that Jesus calls Nathanael an Israelite'.[32] Thiel speaks very differently when he suggests that 'for authors looking back to a golden age and looking forward to national restoration in the age to come, "Israel" expressed an idealized self-identity'.[33] It is this idea that will be explored in the remainder of this essay.

In this light, it is important to observe that Jesus does not simply call Nathanael 'an Israelite', but rather, 'an Israelite in whom there is no δόλος'. The two phrases cannot be separated—to understand properly the use of Israelite in this context, one needs to read it in light of this further qualification. In this vein we might be tempted to concede

---

29 Tomson, '"Jews"' 326.
30 Bauckham, *Testimony*, 230 n.96.
31 Thiel, '"Israel"', 98.
32 Bauckham, *Gospel of Glory*, 168.
33 Thiel, '"Israel"', 99.

Bauckham's previous assertion that there 'is no significance [...] in the fact that Jesus calls Nathanael an Israelite', but qualify it with the notion that there is great significance in the fact that Jesus calls Nathanael 'an Israelite in whom there is no deceit'. So we must now ask, how does the lack of δόλος contribute to our understanding of the designation 'Israelite' in this context in John's Gospel?

Another background to δόλος in the Old Testament

It has already been observed that δόλος is a term applied to the patriarch Jacob in the Genesis narrative. However, the Genesis account is not the only significant background to this noun and its cognate adjective in the Old Testament. In fact, it seems that we've been searching in the wrong place for the intertextual link that would help our understanding of this verse. The appropriate background is not in the Genesis account but rather the prophetic writings of the Old Testament and, in particular, the Book of the Twelve minor prophets, specifically Zephaniah.

The notion of a faithful and godly remnant makes an important contribution to the overall theology of the prophetic books of the Old Testament as a whole, and the Book of the Twelve in particular. Scholars agree that the Book of the Twelve minor prophets should be understood as a unity and within that unity, Zephaniah makes an important contribution to the overall theme of remnant.[34] Zephaniah 3:11–13 in particular 'depicts a situation in which YHWH will remove the arrogant ones (within Jerusalem) while leaving a pious remnant'.[35]

> [11] 'On that day you, Jerusalem, will not be put to shame
>   for all the wrongs you have done to me,
> because I will remove from you
>   your arrogant boasters.
> Never again will you be haughty
>   on my holy hill.

---

34 See House, *Unity*, 414–427.
35 Nogalski, *Book of the Twelve*, 41.

> ¹² But I will leave within you
>   the meek and humble.
> The remnant of Israel
>   will trust in the name of the LORD.
> ¹³ They will do no wrong;
>   they will tell no lies.
> A deceitful tongue
>   will not be found in their mouths.
> They will eat and lie down
>   and no one will make them afraid.'

Here many of the facets of remnant theology are contained in such a few short verses—in particular the notions of divine judgement that purges away the wicked and refines the righteous, and the nature and character of the remnant of Israel that remains.[36]

Zephaniah's prophecy describes the remnant of Israel in five different ways in these verses. They are first the meek and the humble whom God will leave after his judgement (3:12a); they are those who will trust in the name of the LORD (12b); they will do no wrong (13a); tell no lies (13b); and, importantly regarding our understanding of Jesus' words on meeting Nathanael, one will never find in their mouth a tongue of deceit (13d).

Significantly, the only place in the LXX where the term Israelite and the notion of deceit are paired together in a positive manner is in Zephaniah 3:13. Jesus is not making some pun on the name Jacob/Israel when he meets Nathanael, he is announcing that Nathanael is a representative of the righteous, remnant Israel.[37] He is not the sole representative, but is one of a growing number of disciples that have gathered around Jesus and are unified by their 'trust in the name of the LORD', as Zephaniah 3:12b describes them.

Nathanael is portrayed by both Jesus and John as a remnant figure in light of Zephaniah's prophecy of such a community. Jesus' words, that Nathanael is 'truly an Israelite in whom there is no deceit', not only make more sense when read in light of Zephaniah 3 than in light

---

36 King, 'Remnant', 415–417.
37 Bauckham, *Gospel of Glory*, 170.

of the Genesis account, but by understanding the reference as fulfilling some of the remnant theology of the Book of Twelve, the further conversation between Jesus and Nathanael is also clarified.

Why under a fig tree?

Much has been made about Jesus' statement that he saw Nathanael under the fig tree. Some see nothing in this statement except a display of omniscience which was enough to convince Nathanael that Jesus surely was the one Philip had suggested.[38] Others see the significance of being under the fig tree in light of later Rabbinic literature that suggests that such a place was common for a devout Jew to be studying Torah.[39] Some even go as far as to speculate exactly what it was that Nathanael was contemplating or reading under the fig tree.

Trudinger speculates the following: 'Nathanael, we suggest, is contemplating the fulfilment of Israel's history and thinking in particular about the patriarch Jacob who was privileged to be brought to the very gate of heaven'.[40] How he can be confident of such a suggestion is unknown.

However, all such Jacobian speculation is unnecessary when the pericope is seen in light of the remnant theology of the Book of the Twelve. Jesus has already identified Nathanael with the remnant figure of Zephaniah 3:13 by declaring him to be truly an Israelite in whom there is no deceit. By taking us back to this prophecy and context, we are assisted further in understanding the reference to the fig tree.

There is one more aspect, one more description of the remnant Israelite given in Zephaniah 3 that has thus far been unmentioned. In Zephaniah 3:13d, we are told that the remnant of Israel 'will eat and lie down and no one will make them afraid'. This is significant for our understanding of John 1, since, as Bauckham rightly points out, through the exegetical principle of *gezerah shavah* this passage and

---

38 See for instance Lincoln, *John*, 121: 'The main point of the reference [...] is the part it plays in demonstrating Jesus' unique knowledge'; Carson, *John*, 161: 'John's chief point here is Jesus' supernatural knowledge'.
39 Trudinger, 'Israelite', 118.
40 Trudinger, 'Israelite', 118.

Micah 4:4 are closely connected.[41]

Gezerah shavah refers to a rabbinic hermeneutical rule which compares and relates two separate passages on the basis of shared vocabulary or phrases. In this case it is the phrase 'no one will make them afraid'. This exact phrase occurs in Zephaniah 3:13 and also in Micah 4:4. But Micah 4:4 also brings into the discussion of remnant ideology the notion of the eschatological age when the nations stream into Jerusalem and when every man will sit under his own vine and under his own fig tree.

> Everyone will sit under their own vine and under their own
>   fig tree,
> and no one will make them afraid,
>   for the LORD Almighty has spoken.

Hence Bauckham can conclude, 'As the Israelite without guile, he (Nathanael) enjoys the peace and security of the people of God in the Messianic age. Of course, he does so only symbolically (his actual session under the fig tree was merely a transient feature of entirely ordinary life)'.[42]

Seeing both of these utterances of Jesus to Nathanael in light of the eschatological expectations established in the Book of the Twelve, particularly in Zephaniah 3:13 and Micah 4:4, appears to have far more warrant than the often cited Genesis background of Jacob, and gives a more consistent reading of the pericope.

Does John have a Remnant Theology?

However, it does not suffice to simply demonstrate some linguistic connections to these prophetic passages. One must ask the question, does this understanding of Jesus' interaction with Nathanael fit the aims and structure of the Gospel? What is the significance of this intertextual reference for the purposes of John's Gospel? Does John have a reason for portraying Nathanael as 'Israel without a trace of Jacob left in him', or does the idea of Nathanael as a remnant figure align more consistently within

---

41 Bauckham, *Gospel of Glory*, 167.
42 Bauckham, *Gospel of Glory*, 168.

the purposes of John's Gospel? Does John have a remnant theology?

The answer to that question appears to be: yes, he most certainly does, and Nathanael is a key representative remnant figure for John. Although space does not allow us to fully develop the remnant theology of John here in any detail, suffice to mention a few ideas that illustrate the certain presence of the theme within the Gospel.

First, and most importantly, the notion of remnant is clearly identifiable within the prologue. 1:11–12 tells us that the pre-existent divine Word 'came to that which was his own, but his own did not receive him. Yet to all who received him, to those who believed in his name, he gave the right to become children of God'.

This notion of 'his own' is picked up again throughout the Gospel at various significant points as this theme is developed. Particularly it plays an important role in the Good Shepherd discourse in chapter 10. The good shepherd calls his own sheep and he knows them by name (10:3). But the Jewish leaders themselves are not even Jesus' sheep (10:26). It is not all Israel who will be a part of this eschatological flock, just the remnant who hear his voice and follow him.

The culmination of this theme arrives in 13:1 where we are told that 'having loved his own who were in the world' Jesus now showed them the full extent of his love. This verse which introduces the second half of John's Gospel and the whole farewell discourse sets the scene for our understanding. 'His own' are now the disciples in the upper room. They constitute the nucleus of remnant Israel who will become the foundation of the new people of God under the new covenant following the crucified and resurrected Messiah. Köstenberger appropriately labels John 13–17 'The Messiah and the Believing Remnant'.[43]

There are other places where this remnant theology plays a significant role in John's theology, but these cannot be pursued here. However, even just this simple taste is enough to demonstrate that John does indeed have a remnant theology that runs throughout his Gospel and that Nathanael's introduction as a representative remnant figure in the early stages of Jesus' ministry accords seamlessly with John's overall intentions.

---

43 Köstenberger, *Theology*, 354.

Conclusion

Jesus' interaction with Nathanael has almost universally been read in light of the Genesis narratives of the patriarch Jacob. However, we have demonstrated that this is not as obvious as most commentators simply assume. In fact, there are some difficulties in maintaining this understanding, not least the negative portrayal of the great patriarch that must be present for such a reading to be comprehensible. Whilst the promised vision of the heavens opening and the angels ascending and descending on the Son of Man is indeed a reference to Jacob's dream recorded in Genesis, this does not imply that the whole pericope needs to be understood in light of the Jacob narrative. In fact, the plurality of the address and the solemn ἀμὴν ἀμήν that opens 1:51 demonstrates that this vision is a summary conclusion of the whole first chapter of John's Gospel, relevant for all the new followers of Jesus and indeed relevant for all future readers of the Gospel.

Bauckham is right to observe that 'the commentators have missed the significance' of Zephaniah 3:13 for the understanding of this passage. This essay has sought to highlight it.[44] Read in light of this prophetic utterance, John and Jesus paint Nathanael as a representative remnant figure within the Gospel narrative. This reading in light of the remnant theology of the Book of the Twelve also provides us with the most coherent and least speculative understanding of the mention of Nathanael under the fig tree.

John has a remnant theology of 'Jesus' own', and he expects his readers to see Nathanael as a representative figure in that vein in line with the prophetic fulfilment of the eschatological age that he, as the Messiah, is bringing into existence with the calling of the disciples.

See, truly an Israelite in whom there is no deceit.

Stephen Rockwell
George Whitefield College, Cape Town, Republic of South Africa

---

44 Bauckham, *Gospel of Glory*, 168.

Bibliography

Barrett, C. K. *The Gospel According to St John: An Introduction with Commentary and Notes on the Greek Text* (London: SPCK, 1962).

Bauckham, R. *Gospel of Glory: Major themes in Johannine Theology* (Grand Rapids, MI: Baker, 2015).

Bauckham, R. *The Testimony of the Beloved Disciple* (Grand Rapids, MI: Baker, 2007).

Bennema, C. *Encountering Jesus: Character Studies in the Gospel of John* (Carlisle: Paternoster, 2009).

Carson, D. A. *The Gospel According to John* (Pillar New Testament Commentary; Leicester: Apollos, 1991).

Chennattu, R. M. *Johannine Discipleship as a Covenant Relationship* (Peabody, MS: Hendrickson, 2006).

Hill, C. E. 'The identity of John's Nathanael', *JSNT* 67 (1997), 45–61.

House, P. A. *The Unity of the Twelve* (Sheffield: Almond, 1990).

Keener, C. S. *The Gospel of John. Vol 1* (Peabody, MS: Hendrickson, 2003).

King, G. A. 'The Remnant in Zephaniah', *Bibliotheca Sacra* 151 (1994), 414–427.

Köstenberger, A. J. *John* (BECNT; Grand Rapids, MI: Baker, 2004).

Köstenberger, A. J. *A Theology of John's Gospel and Letters* (Grand Rapids, MI: Zondervan, 2009).

Kuhn, K. G. "Ἰσραήλ, Ἰσραηλίτης, Ἰουδαῖος, Ἰουδαία, Ἰουδαϊκός, ἰουδαΐζω, Ἰουδαϊσμός, Ἑβραῖος, Ἑβραϊκός, ἑβραΐς, ἑβραϊστί: Β. "Ἰσραήλ, Ἰουδαῖος, Ἑβραῖος in Jewish Literature after the OT', *TDNT* 3.359–369.

Lincoln, A. T. *The Gospel According to St John* (Black's New Testament Commentaries; Peabody, MS: Hendrickson, 2005).

Michaels, J. R. *The Gospel of John* (NICNT; Grand Rapids, MI: Eerdmans, 2010).

Moloney, F. J. *John* (Sacra Pagina; Collegeville, MN: Liturgical Press, 1998).

Nogalski, J. D.   *The Book of the Twelve and Beyond* (Atlanta, GA: SBL Press, 2017).

Patterson, R. D.   'The Old Testament Use of an Archtype: The Trickster', *JETS* 42.3 (1999), 385–394.

Schnackenburg, R.   *The Gospel According to St John. Vol 1* (K. Smyth, trans.; London: Burns & Oates, 1968).

Thiel, N.   '"Israel" and "Jew" as Markers of Jewish Identity in Antiquity: The Problems of Insider/Outsider Classification', *Journal for the Study of Judaism* 45 (2014), 80–99.

Tomson, P. J.   '"Jews" in the Gospel of John as Compared with the Palestinian Talmud, the Synoptics and Some New Testament Apocrypha', in R. Bieringer, D. Pollefevt and F. Vandecasteele-Vanneuville (eds.), *Anti-Judaism and the Fourth Gospel* (Louisville, KY: Westminster John Knox, 2001), 301–340

Trudinger, L. P.   'An Israelite in Whom There is No Guile: An Interpretative Note on John 1:45–51', *EvQ* 54 (1982), 117–120.

Westcott, B. F.   *The Gospel According to St John. Vol 1* (Grand Rapids, MI: Eerdmans, 1954).

CHAPTER 10

Many Abidings (John 14:2)

John A. Davies

Abstract

Jesus' words of comfort to his disciples on the eve of his 'glorification' about the 'many abidings' in his 'Father's house' say nothing about what is to happen after their deaths. At this Passover time, Jesus employs the language of Jewish eschatological temple-building, the culmination of the exodus, to speak of the fulfilment of the divine dwelling with his people on earth. Observations of a Johannine bilingual play on words and the chiastic arrangement of John 14 strengthen the case for seeing a sustained theme of the coming of Jesus through the Spirit to empower the church for its continued mission.

A popular text at Christian funerals is John 14:2–3, with these familiar words of Jesus: 'In my Father's house there are many dwelling places. If it were not so, would I have told you that I go to prepare a place for you? And if I go and prepare a place for you, I will come again and will take you to myself, so that where I am, there you may be also.'[1] As generally understood, Jesus, in his farewell discourse, comforts his disciples by

---

1   Unless otherwise indicated, Bible quotations are from the NRSV.

promising to secure a place in heaven for them after their deaths.[2]

Alternative readings have been advocated.[3] Robert Gundry proposes a dual interpretation, an already and a not yet: the Father's house is in the first instance God's family and the dwelling places are 'spiritual positions in Christ', but there are also heavenly abodes awaiting the disciples as a secondary meaning.[4] Some scholars have explored in some depth the temple imagery of 14:2, while still understanding the referent to be heaven.[5] A few see the temple imagery being applied to the community of Jesus and the indwelling of its members by the Spirit with no reference to heaven.[6]

But such scholars are in the minority and their suggestions have gained little traction in the popular Christian understanding of the pericope. However, a closer look at the context and its background would suggest that a heavenly home for dead disciples might not be what Jesus is teaching. This article builds on the insights of scholars such as McCaffrey, Bryan, Kerr, and Coloe, strengthening the case for seeing the temple imagery fulfilled in the promised divine indwelling of the disciples, the new temple-community, as the culmination of the exodus.

Towards the end of the discourse Jesus says that he has been speaking in figures of speech (παροιμίαι, John 16:25; cf. 10:6; 16:29), so we should carefully enquire as to the extended meanings and associations of his words.[7] The Fourth Gospel is steeped in the language and thought of Jewish traditions, so we should be alert to any OT and Second Temple themes and language, particularly those associated with the festival which serves as the backdrop for the address (13:1). Several of the disciples seek explanations or express misunderstandings

---

2   Barrett, *John*, 380; Morris, *John*, 638; Brown, *John*, 625; Carson, *John*, 489. For a consideration of the farewell discourse in the context of Jewish testamentary literature, see Brown, *John*, 587–601; For the Hellenistic rhetorical background, see Parsenios, *Departure and Consolation*; Stube, *Graeco-Roman Rhetorical Reading*.
3   For a survey of interpretations, see Fischer, *Die himmlische Wohnungen*, 58–74.
4   Gundry, 'In my Father's House', 70; Keener seems open to a similar *double entendre*: Keener, *John*, vol. 2, 932, but opts for the coming and indwelling of Jesus through the Spirit as 'the only way to make sense of the text as it now stands' (938).
5   McCaffrey, *House*; Bryan, 'Eschatological Temple'.
6   Kerr, *Temple*, 276–313; Coloe, *Dwelling*, 145–66; Coloe, 'Temple Imagery'.
7   Stibbe defines παροιμία as 'a cryptic word-picture which requires considerable expertise to unravel': Stibbe, 'The Elusive Christ', 27.

regarding what Jesus is talking about (vv.5,8,22). This alerts us to the likelihood that Jesus' meaning may not be easy to grasp, and that the questions and responses might all be linked with what precedes by way of expansion and clarification, so we need to look to these explanations for any interpretive clues for the locational and journeying metaphors of the opening verses.

Commentators typically treat the opening verses of chapter 14 as parenthetical—a word of consolation from Jesus at the long-term prospect of his disciples' deaths, while the rest of the chapter reverts to the more immediate concern of the effect of Jesus' imminent departure. But is it the issue of what may lie beyond the grave that troubles the disciples (14:1)? Rather, their concern is the thought of Jesus leaving them to continue his work without him, and Jesus is aware that this will leave them feeling like orphans (14:18) and grief-stricken (16:6,20).

That they are to continue Jesus' mission is clear. Their first duty is self-sacrificial love (13:34–35; 15:12,17). The work the disciples are to do and the responses they are to anticipate are further spelled out through chapters 14–16. Jesus says that they 'will do the works that I do and, in fact, will do greater works than these, because I am going to the Father' (14:12); they are to observe Jesus' words (14:24); they are to 'bear fruit' (15:16). They are sent out to bear testimony to a hostile world, for which they are to expect pain and persecution (15:18–20,27; 16:20,33; 17:18). So when Jesus says in 14:1, 'Do not let your hearts be troubled', we should expect him to begin addressing the disciples' real anxiety. Jesus' words of reassurance form an *inclusio* with their repetition in v.27 where they are expanded by 'and do not let them be afraid'. These sentiments echo the summons to the exodus generation not to be afraid in the face of entry to unknown territory (Deut. 31:8). The exodus with its goal of God's dwelling securely with his people would be very much in mind in this Passover week. The (new) exodus theme is never far from the surface in the Fourth Gospel.[8]

The consolation of v.1 proceeds: 'Believe (πιστεύετε) in God,

---

8 For the exodus theme in John, see Glasson, *Moses*; Willoughby, 'Word'; Coxon, *Exploring*; Smith, 'Exodus Typology'.

believe (πιστεύετε) also in me'. However we understand the syntax (are the verbs indicatives or, as I would understand them both, imperatives in continuity with the preceding clause?), the point is much the same for our purposes: in the face of the severest threat to their emerging faith, the disciples are urged to maintain their loyalty to Jesus, his mission and message. They are not to be like the unbelieving generation of the exodus (Num. 14:11; Deut. 9:23; Ps. 78:22; Heb. 4:2). They should maintain their commitment to Jesus and reliance on what he is about to say, as like a previous Jesus / Joshua (LXX Ἰησοῦς), he leads the way to the place where God will dwell with his people. It is this confident trust in Jesus that is indispensible for all that follows, for Jesus will speak of things not perceivable without such trust (John 14:7,10,17,19; 16:8–11). It is this loyal trust, expressed in love, that differentiates the disciples from 'the world' (14:17,19,22).

My Father's House (14:2)

Jesus proceeds to assure his disciples: 'In my Father's house there are many abidings. If it were not so, would I have told you that I go to prepare a place for you?' (v.2, my translation). I leave aside the issue of whether the second part of the verse is a statement or (as NA28) a question. Clearly Jesus is being allusive in speaking of his Father's house, many abidings, and preparing a place.

First, what is meant by 'in my Father's house (ἐν τῇ οἰκίᾳ τοῦ πατρός μου)'? While it is generally assumed to refer to heaven, heaven is never in the OT denoted by the standard Hebrew word for house (*bayit*) nor elsewhere in the NT by either οἶκος or οἰκία. The LXX does occasionally use οἶκος (but never οἰκία) for God's heavenly abode (Isa. 63:15; Mic. 1:2). All of the OT references to the 'house of God / the Lord' are to a physical earthly sanctuary, the place of God's dwelling among his people (e.g. Exod. 23:19; Judg. 18:31; 1 Chr. 6:48; 2 Chr. 4:11; Ps. 42:4; 118:26). Similarly the few NT references to a 'house of God' relate to an OT sanctuary (Matt. 12:4; Mark 2:26; Luke 6:4).

Most pertinently, Jesus has spoken of 'my Father's house (τὸν οἶκον τοῦ πατρός μου)' in connection with his disruption within the courts of the Jerusalem temple (John 2:16). This was a prophetic demonstration at the outset of his ministry (as John places it) of the Jerusalem temple's obsolescence now that its fulfilment has come, and a claim by Jesus to possess authority over the real temple as the messianic Son (cf. 2 Sam. 7:14; 1 Chr. 17:13; Ps. 2:7; 89:26).[9] Following this action, Jesus makes a declaration, or perhaps to be more precise, issues a directive (imperative, v.19) concerning the destruction of the temple and prophesies its rebuilding, but the reader is informed that he means that from now on the temple is to be found elsewhere, in Jesus himself, in his body that would be destroyed and raised again after three days (2:19). Jesus is the reality to which the earthly sanctuary pointed, the true presence of God among his people, possible only through sacrifice. Horsley and Thatcher make the case that in playing with multiple meanings of 'house', John is already including the notion of house as people of God,[10] and Lieu notes the programmatic character of the event, an opportunity for Jesus to exhibit his passion for this house (John 2:17; cf. Ps. 69:9).[11] The writer has set up an expectation that the reader, on seeing 'my Father's house' again in John 14:2, albeit with a subtle variation in vocabulary (οἰκία for οἶκος), should call to mind that earlier episode.[12]

To understand how shocking were Jesus' actions and words to those who heard him speaking of the Herodian temple, we need to consider something of temple ideology and aspirations in Second Temple times.[13] An important theme of Israel's Scriptures is the dwelling of God with his people.[14] This is particularly so in connection with the exodus and the prospect of entry to the land. That presence of God with his people was symbolised initially in the wilderness tabernacle (Exod. 25:8). The construction and dedication of Solomon's temple, treated at length in 1 Kings 6–8, is presented as the climax of the exodus (1 Kgs 6:1). God comes to live in the midst of his people when his glory (*kabôd*, LXX δόξα) enters the temple (1 Kgs 8:10–11). God's dwelling (*ma'ôn*) is in the temple (2 Chr. 36:15). A psalmist could rhapsodise,

9   Coloe, *Dwelling*, 131–43; Moloney, 'Reading'; Kerr, *Temple*, 67–101.
10 Horsley and Thatcher, *John, Jesus*, 162.
11 Lieu, 'Temple and Synagogue'.
12 See, e.g. Klauck, 'Himmlische Haus', 23–25.
13 For a treatment of temple ideology in the Bible generally, see Beale, *Temple*. For a general overview of temple imagery in the Fourth Gospel, see Busse, 'Tempelmetaphorik'.
14 Terrien sees it as *the* central motif: Terrien, *Elusive Presence*.

'O LORD, I love the house in which you dwell (*meʿôn bêteka*), and the place where your glory abides (*miškan kebôdeka*)' (Ps. 26:8). Note that this verse uses two of the words found in conjunction in John 14:2. Of course the writers of the OT acknowledge God's transcendence and can express that in terms of him having his abode in the heavens or beyond them (Deut. 26:15; 1 Kgs 8:27; Ps. 78:69; Isa. 66:1), but the earthly temple was a replica and a gateway to this realm. The longing to be in fellowship with God could be expressed in terms of a desire to share that space with God in the temple (Ps. 23:6; 27:4).

The temple, from the outset the focal point for the people of God, in some circles takes on eschatological significance as the gathering place for a future restored Israel, and even the nations (Neh. 1:9; Isa. 2:2; 27:13; 66:18–22; Jer. 29:14; 31:8; Mic. 4:1; Hag. 2:6–9; Zech. 2:11; 14:16; Tob. 14:4–7; Jdt. 4:3; 1 Macc. 3:43; 2 Macc. 1:27–29; 2:17–18). Ezekiel envisages God taking his people into his land and establishing his temple in their midst (Ezek. 37:21,26) and then devotes a considerable proportion of his prophecy to a visionary depiction of an ideal temple and its cult (40–48), with God returning in glory to take up residence in it (43:4–5), something that is not said of the historic Second Temple.[15] The prophecy of Malachi declares: 'See, I am sending my messenger to prepare the way before me, and the Lord whom you seek will suddenly come to his temple' (Mal. 3:1). Apocalyptic literature can contemplate a sanctuary created in the beginning and kept in readiness for its end-time revelation (e.g. *2 Bar.* 4). The *Temple Scroll* from Qumran envisages a future building of the temple on a monumental scale, an idealised universe, with room to accommodate all the tribes of Israel (11Q19; cf. *4 Ezra* 13:36). Herod's temple, the one before which Jesus and 'the Judeans' stood in John 2:18–20, was a massive and as yet unfinished expansion and enhancement of the Second Temple, the power base of the priestly class.[16] In some minds at least, it also took on something of the char-

---

15 On the mixture of visionary and practical elements in Ezekiel's temple and the motif of the return of the Lord in glory, see Joyce, 'Temple and Worship'. For John's use of Ezekiel, particularly the vision of an ideal temple, see Peterson, *John's Use of Ezekiel*, 187–99; Fowler and Strickland, *Influence*, 67–89.
16 For John's term 'the Judeans' (traditionally 'the Jews'), which I take to be a geo-political rather than ethno-religious designation, see Horsley and Thatcher, *John, Jesus*, 106.

acteristics of an ideal end-time sanctuary.[17] All the more devastating then, from the perspective of John's readers, was this temple's destruction in 70 C.E., and over the ensuing decades Jews were forced to come to terms with this vacuum at what was for many the centre of their religious, political, social, and economic life. Köstenberger helpfully locates John's temple theme in the context of Jewish literature dealing with this loss.[18]

The OT writers could also move beyond the symbolism and speak of God being present with his people apart from the cult. Isaiah parallels the transcendent dwelling of God in heaven with his immanent dwelling with individuals: 'For thus says the high and lofty one who inhabits eternity, whose name is Holy: I dwell (*šoken*) in the high and holy place, and also with those who are contrite and humble in spirit' (Isa. 57:15). The Psalms also speak more abstractly of God himself as the dwelling place (*ma'ôn*) of his people: 'Lord, you have been our dwelling place in all generations' (Ps. 90:1; cf. Ps. 91:9) and Ezekiel has God declaring himself to be a sanctuary (*miqdaš*) for his people during the exile (Ezek. 11:16).

Besides the mention of 'my Father's house' in 2:16, we have been prepared for the identification of the temple with Jesus and his community, beginning with the prologue which identifies the 'Word' as God come to tabernacle (ἐσκήνωσεν) among us (1:1,14). Likewise at 4:21 Jesus informs the Samaritan woman that the time is approaching when any material temple will be redundant. So, with this temple background in mind, we are on the lookout for an extended meaning for 'my Father's house' in 14:2.[19] We may see this in Psalm 114:2 which speaks of Judah becoming God's sanctuary (*qodšô*, LXX ἁγίασμα) at the time of the exodus. Second Temple texts develop the theme of God's people as a sanctuary.[20] The Qumran *Florilegium* (4Q174 1:6) possibly envisages an eschatological temple consisting of humanity (*miqdaš 'adam*) who would offer thanksgiving (cf. Heb.

---

17 See, e.g. Josephus, *Jewish War* 5.222.
18 Köstenberger, 'Destruction'.
19 A number of scholars who treat the temple theme in John dismiss or fail to mention 14:2 as having any temple background in view: McKelvey, *New Temple*; Hoskins, *Jesus*, 10–18; Köstenberger, 'Destruction'.
20 See Gärtner, *Temple*; Davies, 'Missing Temple'.

13:15), though this interpretation is debated.[21] Somewhat clearer is the Qumran *Manual of Discipline,* which regards the community members as a 'holy house' (1QS 9.5–6; cf. CD 3.18–4.10; 1QpHab 12.3–4).[22] The Animal Apocalypse of *1 Enoch* represents the nation as the 'house' and the temple as a 'tower' (e.g. *1 Enoch* 89:50). But it is the emerging Christian church which particularly comes to own the idea of the faith community as a living temple. The writers of the NT, who see the physical temple as being rendered obsolete with the coming of Jesus, redefine God's house or temple as the Christian community where God now lives among his people (Eph. 2:21; 1 Tim. 3:15; Heb. 10:21; 1 Pet. 4:17). Paul can refer to believers as the temple of the Spirit (1 Cor. 3:16; 6:19).

John may already have provided the link between Jesus as the temple and believers as the temple. At the Feast of Tabernacles, when water-pouring was a prominent part of the celebration, having announced his departure, Jesus proclaimed in the temple courts: 'Let the one who believes in me drink. As the scripture has said, "Out of the believer's heart shall flow rivers of living water"' (John 7:38).[23] John then interprets this remark: 'Now he said this about the Spirit, which believers in him were to receive; for as yet there was no Spirit, because Jesus was not yet glorified' (7:39). The image seems to be drawn from the life-giving water flowing from the eschatological temple of Ezekiel 47, Joel 3:18, or Zechariah 14:8, a concept with deep roots in ancient temple ideology.[24] When Jesus is no longer visibly present, those who believe in him will perpetuate his life-giving ministry through the Spirit as the eschatological temple.

In John 14, then, as Jesus prepares to return to the Father, is he extending the meaning of 'my Father's house' to embrace the community, the 'body of Christ' to use Pauline language (1 Cor. 12:27)? Augustine held to such an interpretation: '[W]hat else can we suppose the house of God to mean but the temple of God? And what that

---

21 See Brooke, *Exegesis*, 178–93. Brooke canvasses interpretations of *miqdaš ʾadam* as a sanctuary made by men, or a sanctuary among men, but supports the understanding that it refers to the community.
22 For further examples, see Kerr, *Temple*, 296–98.
23 McKelvey, *New Temple*, 81.
24 See Greene, 'Integrating Interpretations'; Kerr, *Temple*, 226–50.

is, ask the apostle, and he will reply, "For the temple of God is holy, which temple you are"'.[25] This is the most natural understanding of the phrase 'my Father's house', which in the OT always refers to a household, a family (e.g. Gen. 20:13). The Nathan oracle (2 Sam. 7:5–17; 1 Chr. 17:4–15) plays with both meanings—house as temple and house as family or dynasty. The rarer word Jesus chooses, οἰκία, while capable of referring to a structure, is never used of the Jerusalem temple and lends itself better to this extended meaning (cf. 4:53).[26] Jesus would be saying that God will now come to reside with the new family Jesus entrusts to carry on his work, and with each individual within it. This is the outworking of the words of the Gospel's prologue, 'But to all who received him, who believed in his name, he gave power to become children of God' (1:12) and is reinforced with the new family relationship terms Jesus subsequently uses ('my brothers ... my Father and your Father', 20:17). God will now come to reside with the new family Jesus entrusts to carry on his work, and with each individual within it.

Many Abidings (14:2)

The notion that heaven consists of apartments within a grand palace and that Jesus' reassurance that heaven will not run short of such accommodation is, in view of the limitless scope of heaven (e.g. Jer. 31:37), rather absurd. While the meaning of μονή could extend to denoting a place to stay, its primary meaning is not concrete ('abode') but abstract, a verbal noun cognate with μένειν 'remain, abide', which BDAG glosses as 'state of remaining in an area, *staying, tarrying*'. Herodotus uses μονή in the sense of 'staying' in opposition to ἔξοδος 'leaving' (1.94.5). The only LXX usage has the sense of 'opportunity to live' in contrast with 'let them fall by the sword' (1 Macc. 7:38). Had John wanted in 14:2 to use the image of a room or apartment within a building, there was a more appropriate Greek word available: οἴκημα 'an individual room in a dwelling, *room, apartment*' (BDAG).

Why are there 'many abidings'? Is it many as opposed to few, or, as I

---

25 Augustine, *Tractates on the Gospel of John* 68.2.
26 Coloe, *Dwelling*, 145–48.

would suggest, many as contrasted with one—Jesus' physical presence (v.25)? Note that it is left unsaid in v.2 who experiences the μοναί. As it is a verbal noun, 'abidings', who is to *do* the abiding? Who or what is to be indwelt? We may have been too quick to assume that it is the disciples dwelling in heaven. As frequently noted, the only other occurrence of μονή in the NT is at v.23 of this chapter and its cognate verb μένειν is found thirty-three times in John, including three times in chapter 14 (vv.10,17,25), though insufficient weight is generally given to this observation. Verse 23, which comes pursuant to the disciples' requests for explanations, reads, 'Jesus answered him [Judas (not Iscariot)], "The one who loves me will keep my word, and my Father will love that one, and we will come to that one and make our abiding (μονή) with that one"' (my translation). It is Jesus and the Father who are doing the abiding. Likewise the three uses in this chapter of the cognate verb μένειν ('remain, abide') all have the Father or Jesus or the Spirit as their subject (14:10,17,25).

So the Father abides with the Son, while the Father, Jesus, and the Spirit are all said to abide with the disciples. An alternative expression is with (εἶναι) ἐν '(be) in': 'You know him, because he abides (μένει) with you, and he will be in (ἐν) you' (14:17; cf. vv.10,11,20). John will go on in chapter 15 to speak of the disciples abiding (μένειν) in him in the extended imagery of the vine and the branches (15:1–11).

Ought this not give us pause before interpreting the cryptic remark of v.2, the many μοναί, as rooms in heaven for the disciples to take up occupancy on their deaths? Ought we not at least to take seriously the indications that the two occurrences of the noun μονή and the three occurrences of the verb μένειν in this chapter all refer to the same thing, such that Jesus, in his compressed saying of v.2, is promising a continued mode of his own and his Father's abiding with each disciple after his present mode of abiding with them ceases; or better, a mutual indwelling of Father and Son and the disciples?[27] This mutual indwelling manifests itself in mutual love (14:15,21,23,24,28). The 'many' may also suggest an expansion beyond the immediate circle of disciples, and the borders of Israel, to include the 'other sheep', 'the Greeks', and those who would yet come to declare their loyalty to Jesus (10:16; 12:20; 17:20). Taken this way, the rest of the chapter unpacks the compressed remark of v.2.[28]

Further, I suggest a phonological parallel which has gone unnoticed. John's bilingual word-play in 1:14 has long been observed: 'The Word became flesh and lived (ἐσκήνωσεν) among us', where ἐσκήνωσεν (lit. 'tented') takes on some of the glory associations of Hebrew *shekinah* 'dwelling' whose consonants it shares. In chapter 14 John may similarly be reinforcing his point with another bilingual word-play, choosing the rare Greek word μονή (otherwise unattested in the NT), in part because of its resonance with Hebrew *ma 'ôn*, both also meaning 'dwelling', so that the passages which speak of God's dwelling with his people, or God himself as a dwelling, such as those cited above, come to mind.[29]

This connection is strengthened by the specific link with Psalm 68:5: 'Father of orphans and protector of widows is God in his holy habitation (*ma 'ôn*)'. This is likely the background for Jesus' reassurance, 'I will not leave you orphans; I am coming to you' (John 14:18). The disciples might feel they are about to be 'orphaned' but are being assured of Jesus' continued dwelling with them in fulfilment of the psalm and its exodus background.

Is Jesus, then, in John 14:2 announcing, in typically Johannine realised eschatological terms, the reality of which those OT references

---

[27] Lindars appears to move in this direction when he suggests the reference is to 'the mutual indwelling which will obtain in the post-Resurrection situation of the Church', while maintaining that the μοναί are rooms in heaven: Lindars, *John*, 470–71. Noting the explanatory role of v.23, Martyn observes that the comfort Jesus brings the anxious disciple is 'not by recalling that at the close of his own lifetime there will be a room for him in heaven, but rather by knowing that in the present time both the Father and the Son come and make their home with him': Martyn, *History*, 140.

[28] Schnackenburg, though he sees the ones dwelling as different in vv.2 and 23, suggests John 14:23 is 'to some extent an elaboration of the previous image of "dwelling" in John 14:2': Schnackenburg, *John*, vol. 3, 81.

[29] The consonants are again identical as the Hebrew consonant ʿ (ʿayin) is not represented in Greek.

of God's dwelling with his people were adumbrations as he enters his glory (i.e. goes to the cross), and concurrently takes up residence in his new temple, the believing community?[30] This glory and dwelling would seem to be the fulfilment of these conjoined themes from the exodus tradition, in words originally spoken of the wilderness tabernacle: 'I will meet with the Israelites there, and it shall be sanctified by my glory (*kabôd*, LXX δόξα); I will consecrate the tent of meeting and the altar; Aaron also and his sons I will consecrate, to serve me as priests. I will dwell (*šakan*) among the Israelites, and I will be their God' (Exod. 29:43–45).

Preparing a Place (14:2,3)

Where is the 'place' (τόπον) Jesus prepares (John 14:2,3)? The word τόπος can have the nuance of 'sanctuary' (e.g. LXX Gen. 12:6; Deut. 12:2; Josh. 9:27; Mic. 1:3; John 4:20; 11:48), continuing the temple theme.[31] A key passage is in the Nathan oracle, 2 Samuel 7:10: 'I will appoint a place (LXX τόπον) for my people Israel', which came to be interpreted in Second Temple times as a prophecy of an eschatological temple. Deuteronomy speaks of the 'place that the LORD your God will choose' (Deut. 12:5 and *passim*), so the temple functions as a symbol of the nation's unity, and in eschatological texts the gathering point for God's restored people.

Further, the word 'prepare' is given prominence by its repetition in connection with the 'place': 'If it were not so, would I have told you that I go to prepare (ἑτοιμάσαι) a place for you? And if I go and prepare (ἑτοιμάσω) a place for you . . .' (14:2–3). This echoes Exod. 15:17 'your prepared (ἕτοιμον) habitation, which you, O Lord, have accomplished; the sanctuary, O Lord, which your hands have prepared (ἡτοίμασαν)' (my translation of LXX), and the idea of a divinely prepared sanctuary,

---

30 In using the term 'realised eschatology', I am in no way denying that John also envisages a future beyond death. Käsemann notes the importance for John of a future hope: '[T]his futurist hope is simply taken for granted in John', though it is not, as Käsemann holds, 'the final unification of the community in heaven'. Rather, it is one of resurrection and judgement on the 'last day' (John 5:28; 6:39–40,44,54; 12:48): Käsemann, *Testament*, 72.

31 See maqôm, 3rd meaning in BDB; Köster, 'τόπος', 195–99.

perhaps with messianic agency, looms large in Jewish eschatological expectations (cf. LXX Isa. 2:2; Mic. 4:1; Zech. 6:12–13; Wis. 9:8; Rev. 12:6; *Sib. Or.* 5:414–33; *4 Ezra* 13:36; 4Q174; Targ. 1 Chr. 17:9).[32]

Jesus then appears to be using apocalyptic language with deep roots in Israel's temple ideology, telling his disciples that they are about to experience the long-anticipated eschatological temple, prepared by the messiah, where God can come to dwell with his people. But he is radically reinterpreting this tradition around himself and the new temple-community he is empowering to carry on his work on earth.

The Verbs 'Go', 'Come', 'Take' (14:2–4)

What then of the verbs of vv.2–3, 'go . . . come . . . take', and their traditionally understood directionality—'go (to heaven)' . . . 'come (back to earth)' . . . 'take (up to heaven)'?

Jesus informs his disciples, 'I go to prepare a place for you' (v.2). This is not the first time Jesus has spoken of his departure and it will not be the last. A variety of verbs with overlapping meanings is used to indicate Jesus' departure from this world: πορεύεσθαι, 'travel, journey' (14:2,3; 16:28); ὑπάγειν, 'go, depart' (7:33; 8:14,21,22; 13:3,33,36; 14:4,28; 16:5,10); ἀφιέναι, 'leave' (14:18; 16:28); μεταβαίνειν, 'depart, relocate' (13:1); ἀπέρχεσθαι, 'depart' (16:7); and finally ἀναβαίνειν, 'ascend' (20:17). The words πορεύεσθαι and ὑπάγειν at least can carry the sense of 'die', and certainly Jesus' going includes his death. 'The Judeans' take Jesus' remark about his intended departure to mean that he must be about to commit suicide (8:22), and Peter understands Jesus' going to involve his death or at least the risk of it (13:37). One word John does not use for Jesus' departure is ἔξοδος, which Luke uses (Luke 9:31). John casts Jesus' departure by way of the cross as a manifestation of his glory (δόξα / δοξάζειν, 7:39; 11:40; 12:16,23,41; 13:31,32; 17:1). In Jesus' departure, the goal and climax of the exodus has been reached as the Lord enters his temple in glory to abide

---

32 Bryan marshals further Second Temple and post-destruction evidence for the expectation of messiah's role in building the eschatological temple: Bryan, 'Eschatological Temple', 192–93. See also McKelvey, *New Temple*, 31; McCaffrey, *House*, 60–62; Davies, 'Ultimate Temple', 15–19.

with his people.³³ For John in chapter 14, however, the focus is not on the departure but on its antithesis, his continued presence (μονή). This is why Jesus' going should be a cause for rejoicing (14:28). He is departing this world to go back to the Father who sent him (7:33,34; 8:14,21; 13:1,3,33; 16:5,10,17,28; 20:9).³⁴ It is the glorified Jesus who is to return to the presence of the Father (2:19; 13:31–32; 17:1,5; 20:17). His going will bring understanding to the disciples (13:7), empowering them to do 'greater works' than Jesus himself (14:12).³⁵ And it is Jesus' going that enables the coming of the Spirit, that is to say, Jesus' own abiding presence (14:16-21; 16:7). If Jesus came 'from above', is 'not of this world' (8:23), and is ascending (20:17), we might assume his destination in 'going', conceived in spatial imagery, to be heaven, though the word is surprisingly absent from the farewell discourse.³⁶ The Fourth Gospel does place considerable emphasis on Jesus' connection with heaven, or the domain of the Father (1:32,51; 3:13,31; 6:32–58; 12:28; 16:28; 17:11–13). Jesus' going to heaven is not simply a Jewish way of saying he is going where all the righteous go on their deaths. Jesus, who was uniquely 'with God' (πρὸς τὸν θεόν, 1:1), is employing locational and journeying imagery, as expounded throughout chapter 14, to speak ultimately of relationships (cf. 1:18 for a similar locational image signifying relationship).

A key element of Jesus' reassurance to his disciples is that he will 'come again' (πάλιν ἔρχομαι, 14:3). In what sense will he come again? At his resurrection in three days? At the parousia or second advent, if this is different? Both of these views are advocated, and given John's use of multiple meanings, we perhaps should not rule out either of these as being encompassed at some level. But they are not the primary thrust. As already noted, Jesus refers several times later in this chapter to his coming to the disciples that will occur consequent upon his going, and is intimately connected with it (14:18,23,28). Judas

---

33 For the glory theme in John, see Koester, *Word of Life*, 120–23; Bauckham, *Gospel of Glory*, 43–62.
34 Stibbe develops the theme of Jesus' hiddenness in the Fourth Gospel: Stibbe, 'The Elusive Christ'.
35 See Köstenberger, 'Greater Works'.
36 Zimmermann deals with the conceptual metaphor of space 'above' and 'below' in John: Zimmermann, 'Imagery', 19–20. Humble, *A Divine Round Trip*, 113–20, treats the theme of Jesus' return to God / heaven.

apprehends that this coming, despite Jesus' use of ἐμφανίζειν (14:21), a word suggestive of public display, will be a secret manifestation, apparent only to the disciples (14:22). In one case, as we have seen, it is both the Father and Jesus who will come to make their abiding with those who love Jesus and keep his word (14:23), which does not readily fit with resurrection or parousia. These comings are juxtaposed with references to the giving (by the Father) or sending (by the Father or by Jesus) of the Spirit (14:16,17,26), who is also later said to 'come' (15:26; 16:13). Through the coming of the Spirit, the disciples will experience the presence of Jesus himself. He will be able to have an even closer relationship with each one than was possible in his bodily presence.

The close identification of the Spirit with Jesus is expressed in the congruence of their roles. Like the Spirit, Jesus has been a Paraclete (implied in his statement that he would send 'another Paraclete', 14:16). Just as Jesus has been 'with' his disciples (14:13), so the Spirit will be 'with' them (14:16). The abiding of the Spirit (14:17) is equivalent to the abiding of Jesus (14:23,25). The Spirit comes, says Jesus, 'in my name', that is, 'as my representative' (14:26), just as Jesus has come in his Father's name (5:43). The Spirit's teaching role will be in continuity with that of Jesus (14:26) and the Spirit will testify 'on behalf of' Jesus (15:26). The world's response to the Spirit will echo its response to Jesus (1:10; 14:17).

The successor to Jesus is ... Jesus, working through the Spirit-indwelt disciples.[37] Jesus goes and comes that his disciples, through the Spirit, might have a level of intimacy with him and the Father that was not possible before. The action might then find its point of contact with OT and Second Temple imagery in the coming of God to his temple or his people, often with salvation or aid in view (e.g. Ps. 22:19; 68:17; 96:13; 98:9; 141:1; 144:5; Isa. 31:4; 40:10; 59:19,20; 66:18; Hos. 6:3).

While 'take' in 14:3 is generally understood to mean 'take to heaven' at each believer's death, this is difficult if read in connection with Jesus' 'coming'. It would be an unparalleled notion that every time a believer dies, Jesus returns to earth to transport their soul to

---

37 See Woll, 'Departure'.

heaven. The word 'take' here is the compounded παραλαμβάνω which has warmer and more intimate associations than simply 'take' in the sense of 'convey, transport'. BDAG defines it as 'take into close association, *take (to oneself)*'. It is used, for example, of a husband taking a wife (Matt. 1:21,24). The only prior use of παραλαμβάνω in John refers to the lack of 'acceptance' of the Word by his own people (John 1:11). The notion of acceptance is reinforced in John 14:3 with the addition of 'to myself' (πρὸς ἐμαυτόν). In its exposition of v.2, v.23 informs us that the coming of Jesus is not to relocate his followers *post mortem*, but to be with them where they are in this life. Paradoxically it is the 'going' of Jesus that effects the new closeness of his intimate fellowship in coming and receiving and welcoming his disciples into a mutually indwelling relationship.

The purpose of the taking or accepting in John 14 is 'so that where I am, there you may be also' (14:3). A closely parallel text is found in Jesus' prayer: 'Father, I desire that those also, whom you have given me, may be with me where I am, to see my glory, which you have given me because you loved me before the foundation of the world' (17:24). McCaffrey draws attention to the present tense of 'where I am'.[38] Jesus is not referring to a future other-worldly location, but his present fellowship with the Father. This is clear when read in the light of its immediately preceding context which is about the indwelling of the Father and Jesus, and Jesus and the disciples, and the impact this has on the disciples in the sight of the world (v.23). The unity theme, prevalent in the discourse and following prayer (13:34,35; 15:12,17; 17:11,21,23), echoes the emphasis on the togetherness of the people in the eschatological temple texts. The 'glory' Jesus wishes his disciples to perceive, then, is something they could perceive in this world—the cross, and all that this accomplishes.

This, then, is the fulfilment of the hope and expectation of God's faithful people. At this time of exodus commemoration, Jesus appropriates the OT motif of Israel's departure to the goal—the manifestation of God's glory in the temple. He employs apocalyptic-type language, grounded in Israel's historical traditions, of expectations of an

---

38 McCaffrey, *House*, 44.

end-time ideal temple. God or his messiah prepares a temple in order to welcome his faithful people so that they might dwell together.

The idea of Jesus being 'with' the disciples is elsewhere closely linked with the master / servant relationship in John 12:26: 'Whoever serves me must follow me, and where I am, there will my servant be also', and in John 17:24 Jesus prays, 'Father, I desire that those also, whom you have given me, may be with me where I am, to see my glory, which you have given me because you loved me before the foundation of the world'. These references express the heart of discipleship in this life. The disciples will be with Jesus and he with them as they follow him in devoted service, a service henceforth characterised by friendship (15:15) and filial ties (20:17). They will perceive Jesus' glory not by dying and going to heaven, but by abiding in him, loving him, serving him, and coming to understand the true character of the cross.

The Way (14:4)

Finally Jesus extends the journeying metaphor as he rounds off his compressed assurance regarding his impending departure: 'And you know the way (ὁδόν) where I am going' (14:4; NET). English translations sometimes confuse the issue by adding the word 'place', as NRSV, NIV). Jesus has previously revealed that his path ahead will involve being 'lifted up', that is, on the cross, which is paradoxically his glorification, that God's purposes in salvation might be realised (2:19; 3:14; 12:23,32; 13:31,32).

The metaphor of a journey again evokes the theme of the exodus when God's people, under divine leading, were *en route* to dwell with him in his sanctuary land (Exod. 13:21; 23:20; Num. 14:25; Deut. 1:31; 8:2; Ps. 77:19). 'Way' is also an expression for the conduct of those who would associate themselves with the eschatological temple (Isa. 2:3; Mic. 4:2).

The Chiastic Structure of John 14

Evidence for the thematic unity of John 14 is to be seen when its chiastic structure is recognised. There are three interruptions to Jesus' discourse in chapter 14, a device John typically uses to clarify or bring out deeper meanings in Jesus' teaching:

Thomas's question: 14:5   Jesus' response: 14:6–7
Philip's question: 14:8   Jesus' response: 14:9–21
Judas's question: 14:22   Jesus' response: 14:23–31

While the responses of Jesus pick up on words the disciples have just used—'the way' (vv.5,6); 'show us the Father' (vv.8,9); 'the world' (14:22,27), they also serve to expound in chiastic order the compressed statements of vv.1–4. We may represent the chiastic structure as follows:

A. vv.1–2a No troubled heart; commitment to Jesus; many abidings.
μὴ ταρασσέσθω ὑμῶν ἡ καρδία ... πιστεύετε ... μοναὶ πολλαί.

   B. vv.2b–3 Jesus' going and coming; Jesus to be with the disciples.
   πορεύομαι ... ἔρχομαι ... ἵνα ὅπου εἰμὶ ἐγὼ καὶ ὑμεῖς ἦτε.

      C. v.4 You know the way. οἴδατε τὴν ὁδόν.
      C'. (to Thomas) vv.5–7 I am the way. ἐγώ εἰμι ἡ ὁδός.

   B'. (to Philip) vv.8–21 Jesus' going and coming; the Spirit to be with the disciples.
   πορεύομαι ... ἔρχομαι ... ἵνα μεθ' ὑμῶν εἰς τὸν αἰῶνα ᾖ.

A'. (to Judas) vv.22–31 The Father and Jesus to abide with each disciple; no troubled heart;
commitment to Jesus. μονὴν παρ' αὐτῷ ποιησόμεθα ... μὴ ταρασσέσθω ὑμῶν ἡ καρδία ... πιστεύσητε.

Central to the chiasm is the involvement of the disciples in the 'journey' (ἡ ὁδός, v.4), i.e. Jesus himself (v.6), the life-giving reality (ἡ ἀλήθεια καὶ ἡ ζωή) of which all else was an adumbration.[39] Their 'journey' is the way to a relationship with God which Jesus alone facilitates. Coming at the focal point of the chiasm, we should regard the journey metaphor, with its clarification, as determinative for the rest of the chapter. This

---

39 I take ἡ ἀλήθεια καὶ ἡ ζωή to be epexegetic of ἡ ὁδός as in the Wisdom literature (e.g. Prov. 2:19; 3:2); see Keener, *John*, 939–43.

chiastic structure serves to bind the chapter together, informing our understanding of the import of the figurative speech, the journey metaphor, expounded as the exodus-fulfilling presence of Jesus, and making it unlikely that we are to understand the opening verses as a parenthesis on the topic of life after death.

Conclusion

In John 14:1–4, at the time of the exodus commemoration, Jesus speaks of the fulfilment of the hope and expectation of God's faithful people, of God coming in glory to dwell with them. He uses language drawn from Israel's expectations of God's eschatological temple, but, as he so often does, Jesus redefines the terms around himself and his mission. The prepared place, where God is to dwell with his people, is being made a reality through Jesus' 'glorification', enabling the Father and the Son to indwell each disciple through the empowering presence of the Spirit. With the coming of Father, Son, and Spirit, heaven in effect comes to earth. Read this way, there is nothing directly stated here regarding what the disciples might expect after their deaths, but every encouragement to press on in love and service of their glorified and ever present Lord.

The opening few verses of John 14 are, then, a highly pregnant prologue to the rest of the chapter, indeed to the rest of the discourse. We might then paraphrase 14:1–4 (expanded in the light of the subsequent explanations) as follows.

> Don't be distressed at what I'm telling you about the fact that I must leave you to carry on the work. You need to keep trusting me, just as you must trust God. My Father's household, his real temple, is now, because you are mine, with each of you, and many more besides, through the indwelling of the Spirit. My going back to the Father now, through the glory that is the cross, as I have been telling you, is the way for each of you to be part of this new temple-community. For my going is also my coming to each of you, through the Spirit, to remain with you in close fellowship and empowerment to carry on my work.

Bibliography

Barrett, C. K.	*The Gospel according to St John: An Introduction with Commentary and Notes on the Greek Text* (London: SPCK, 1955).
Bauckham, R.	*Gospel of Glory: Major Themes in Johannine Theology* (Grand Rapids, MI: Baker Academic, 2015).
Beale, G. K.	*The Temple and the Church's Mission: A Biblical Theology of the Dwelling Place of God* (New Studies in Biblical Theology; Downers Grove, IL: InterVarsity Press, 2004).
Boyle, J.	'The Last Discourse (Jn 13,31–16,33) and Prayer (Jn 17): Some Observations of their Unity and Development', *Biblica* 56 (1975), 210–22.
Brooke, G.	*Exegesis at Qumran: 4QFlorilegium in Its Jewish Context* (Sheffield: JSOT Press, 1985).
Brown, R. E.	*The Gospel according to John: Introduction, Translation, and Notes*, vol. 2, xii–xxi (Garden City, NY: Doubleday, 1970).
Bryan, S. M.	'The Eschatological Temple in John 14', *Bulletin for Biblical Research* 15 (2005), 187–98.
Busse, U.	'Die Tempelmetaphorik als ein Beispiel von implizitern Rekurs auf die biblische Tradition im Johannesevangelium', in C. M. Tuckett (ed.), *The Scriptures in the Gospels* (BETL 131; Leuven: Leuven University Press, 1977), 395–428.
Carson, D. A.	*The Gospel according to John* (Leicester: Inter-Varsity Press, 1991).
Coloe, M. L.	*Dwelling in the Household of God: Johannine Ecclesiology and Spirituality* (Collegeville, MN: Liturgical Press, 2007).
Coloe, M. L.	'John 17:1–26: The Missionary Prayer of Jesus', *Australian Biblical Review* 66 (2018), 1–12.
Coloe, M. L.	'Temple Imagery in John', *Interpretation* 63 (2009), 368–81.
Coxon, P. S.	*Exploring the New Exodus in John: A Biblical Theological Investigation of John Chapters 5–10* (Eugene, OR: Resource Publications, 2015).
Culpepper, A.	*The Gospel and Letters of John* (Nashville, TN: Abingdon, 1998).

Davies, J. A. — 'The *Temple Scroll* and the Missing Temple of the New Covenant', *Reformed Theological Review* 57.2 (1998), 70–79.

Davies, J. A. — 'The *Temple Scroll* from Qumran and the Ultimate Temple', *Reformed Theological Review* 57.1 (1998), 1–21.

Dennis, J. A. — *Jesus' Death and the Gathering of True Israel* (WUNT 2:217; Tübingen: Mohr Siebeck, 2006).

Finkel, A. — 'The Theme of God's Presence and the Qumran Temple Scroll', in L. Frizzell (ed.), *God and his Temple: Reflections on Professor Samuel Terrien's* The Elusive Presence: Toward a New Biblical Theology (South Orange, NJ: Institute of Judaeo-Christian Studies, Seton Hall University, 1980), 39–47.

Fischer, G. — *Die himmlische Wohnungen: Untersuchungen zu Joh 14,2f* (Bern: Lang, 1975).

Fowler, W. G., and M. Strickland — *The Influence of Ezekiel in the Fourth Gospel: Intertextuality and Interpretation* (Leiden: Brill, 2018).

Gärtner, B. — *The Temple and the Community in Qumran and the New Testament: A Comparative Study in the Temple Symbolism of the Qumran Texts and in the New Testament* (Cambridge: Cambridge University Press, 1965).

Glasson, T. F. — *Moses in the Fourth Gospel* (Naperville, IL: Alec R. Allenson, 1963).

Greene, J. R. — 'Integrating Interpretations of John 7:37–39 into the Temple Theme: The Spirit as Efflux from the New Temple', *Neotestamentica* 47 (2013), 333–53.

Gundry, R. H. — '"In my Father's House Are Many Μοναί" (John 14 2)', *ZNTW* 58 (1967), 68–72.

Horsley, R. A. and T. Thatcher. — *John, Jesus, and the Renewal of Israel* (Grand Rapids, MI: Eerdmans, 2013).

Hoskins, P. M. — *Jesus as the Fulfillment of the Temple in the Gospel of John* (Waynesboro, GA: Paternoster, 2006).

Humble, S. E. — *A Divine Round Trip: The Literary and Christological Function of the Descent / Ascent Leitmotif in the Gospel of John* (Leuven: Peeters, 2016).

Joyce, P. M.	'Temple and Worship in Ezekiel 40–48', in J. Day (ed.), *Temple and Worship in Biblical Israel* (London: T&T Clark, 2007), 145–63.
Käsemann, E.	*The Testament of Jesus: A Study of the Gospel of John in the Light of Chapter 17* (NTL; London: SCM, 1968; tr. from German 1967).
Keener, C. S.	*The Gospel of John: A Commentary* (Peabody, MA: Hendrickson, 2003).
Kerr, A. R.	*The Temple of Jesus' Body: The Temple Theme in the Gospel of John* (London: Sheffield Academic, 2002).
Klauck, H.-J.	'Himmlische Haus und irdische Bleibe: Eschatologische Metaphorik in Antike und Christentum', *NTS* 50 (2004), 5–35.
Koester, C. R.	*The Word of Life: A Theology of John's Gospel* (Grand Rapids, MI: Eerdmans, 2008).
Köstenberger, A.	'The Destruction of the Second Temple and the Composition of the Fourth Gospel', in J. Lierman (ed.), *Challenging Perspectives on the Gospel of John* (Tübingen: Mohr Siebeck, 2006), 69–108.
Köstenberger, A.	'The "Greater Works" of the Believer according to John 14:12', Διδασκαλια (Spring 1995), 36–45.
Köster, H.	'τόπος', in *TDNT* 8, 187–208.
Lieu, J.	'Temple and Synagogue in John', *NTS* 45 (1999), 51–69.
Lindars, B.	*The Gospel of John* (Grand Rapids, MI: Eerdmans, 1972).
Martínez, F. G.	*The Dead Sea Scrolls Translated: The Qumran Texts in English* (rev. edn; Leiden: Brill, 1996; tr. from Spanish 1992).
Martyn, J. L.	*History and Theology in the Fourth Gospel* (3rd edn; Louisville, KY: Westminster John Knox, 2003).
McCaffrey, J.	*The House with Many Rooms: The Temple Theme of Jn. 14, 2-3* (AnBib 114; Rome: Pontifical Biblical Institute, 1988).
McKelvey, R. J.	*The New Temple: The Church in the New Testament* (Oxford: Oxford University Press, 1969).
Moloney, F. J.	'Reading John 2:13-22: The Purification of the Temple', *Revue biblique* 97 (1990), 432–52.

Morris, L.	*The Gospel according to John: The English Text with Introduction, Exposition and Notes* (Grand Rapids, MI: Eerdmans, 1971).
Parsenios, G. L.	*Departure and Consolation: The Johannine Farewell Discourses in Light of Greco-Roman Literature* (SNT 117; Leiden: Brill, 2005).
Peterson, B. N.	*John's Use of Ezekiel: Understanding the Unique Perspective of the Fourth Gospel* (Minneapolis, MN: Fortress, 2015).
Richardson, I.	*The Gospel according to Saint John: Introduction and Commentary* (London: SCM, 1959).
Schnackenburg, R.	*The Gospel according to St John* (New York, NY: Crossroad, 1982).
Smith, R. H.	'Exodus Typology in the Fourth Gospel', *JBL* 81 (1962), 329–42.
Stibbe, M. W. G.	'The Elusive Christ: A New Reading of the Fourth Gospel', *JSNT* 44 (1991), 19–38.
Stube, J. C.	*A Graeco-Roman Rhetorical Reading of the Farewell Discourse* (London: T&T Clark, 2006).
Terrien, S.	*The Elusive Presence: Toward a New Biblical Theology* (Eugene, OR: Wipf & Stock, 1978).
Walker, P. W. L.	*Jesus and the Holy City: New Testament Perspectives on Jerusalem* (Grand Rapids, MI: Eerdmans, 1996).
Willoughby, T. N.	'"The Word Became Flesh and Tabernacled among Us": A Primer for the Exodus in John's Gospel', in R. Michael Fox (ed.), *Reverberations of the Exodus in Scripture* (Eugene, OR: Pickwick, 2014), 121–38.
Wise, M. O.	'The Eschatological Vision of the Temple Scroll', *JNES* 49 (1990), 155–72.
Woll, D. B.	'The Departure of "The Way": The First Farewell Discourse in the Gospel of John', *JBL* 99 (1980), 225–39.

CHAPTER 11

The Meaning of πιστεύω in the Gospel of John

Christopher Seglenieks

Abstract

Recent trends in the study of *pistis* contribute to our understanding of belief in the Gospel of John. Beginning with one of the most recent studies on belief in John's Gospel from Nadine Ueberschaer, it is evident that Johannine belief has a propositional dimension focused on the identity of Jesus. Yet the contextual study by Teresa Morgan demonstrates that the use of *pistis* and *fides* in the Graeco-Roman world has a primarily relational focus, questioning the dominant emphasis on propositional belief. An alternative perspective on *pistis* in the New Testament comes from Matthew Bates, who argues that at times it ought to be translated 'allegiance' rather than 'faith'. While such a translation does not fit in the Johannine context, 'allegiance' is a useful term for discussing the broader concept of belief in John, which involves words and deeds, as well as trust and propositional belief.

1. Introduction

If you had to pick one word as the key word for John, it would be πιστεύω. The whole Gospel revolves around both the question of in whom to believe, but also what it means to believe. But answering either of those questions requires an important clarification. What does this word πιστεύω mean? There are two primary options when it comes to understanding πιστεύω. One, shaped by tradition and the central role of creeds and doctrines within Christianity, assumes πιστεύω is primarily about propositional belief.[1] Thus with John, many have asked the question, what does John say we need to believe? 'Believing' is understood as being closely connected to 'knowing', albeit with a greater volitional emphasis.[2] The alternative is to focus on πιστεύω as a relational term, conveying personal trust and commitment.[3] In this view, the primary goal of the Gospel of John is that the reader place their trust in Jesus. Some have, of course, suggested that both aspects are in view.[4] What follows is an exploration of these two interpretative options through the lens of recent work on πιστεύω, before turning to a third option that might prove useful in talking about πιστεύω in John.

2. Πιστεύω as Propositional Belief

The most common way to understand πιστεύω in studies focused on John is as primarily conveying propositional belief. A recent example is Nadine Ueberschaer's 2017 work, 'Das Johannesevangelium als

---

[1] Significant in the understanding of πιστεύω as propositional is the idea of a distinctly Christian use of the language of πίστις for 'acceptance of kerygma' as argued by Bultmann, 'πιστεύω κτλ.', *TDNT* 6.208. Others to understand πιστεύω as referring to propositional belief include: Tam, *Apprehension*, 1; Zumstein, *L'apprentisage de la foi*, 59–61; Moloney, 'From Cana to Cana'; Forestell, *Word of the Cross*, 103–13; J. Gaffney, 'Believing and Knowing'; Hawthorne, 'Concept of Faith'.

[2] Gaffney, 'Believing and Knowing', 240. While there may be some epistemological concerns connected with πιστεύω (as Gupta suggests), the primary emphasis in John is not on how one knows but on the acceptance of a message, whether that message is encountered through the signs, Scripture, the witness of Jesus, of the witness of others. See Gupta, *Paul*, 74–5.

[3] A focus on the relational dimension is evident in: Koester, *The Word of Life*, 62–4; O'Brien, 'Written', 291; Jensen, *John's Gospel*, 115; Thompson, 'Signs and Faith'.

[4] Dodd, *Interpretation*, 179–85; see also Gupta, *Paul*, 74; Bultmann, 'πιστεύω κτλ.', *TDNT* 6.205–7.

Medium der Glaubensvermittlung.'[5] Her argument first tackles the use of πιστεύειν with the dative. Rather than attempting to read the different constructions used with πιστεύω as indicating significantly different kinds of belief with one being inadequate and the other indicating genuine belief, Ueberschaer instead asks what the function of the construction might be.[6] By arguing that the use of the dative has a distinct function, Ueberschaer goes against Bultmann, who sees the dative and the use of εἰς as essentially synonymous.[7] Her argument is that πιστεύω with the dative focuses on belief in Jesus as messenger of God. It is this construction that connects most closely to the title of her work, as she sees it indicating the role of John's Gospel as 'a medium of faith-transmission.'[8] The use of the dative also indicates that both the words and works of Jesus are to lead to faith. Effectively, taking this approach assumes that there is some propositional content that is to be conveyed by the Gospel.

The second part of her work addresses the use of εἰς and ὅτι with πιστεύω, which both present a similar focus upon Jesus. From these, she argues that Jesus' death and resurrection are the key event to which faith refers. While the Gospel refers to faith in the transmitted words of Jesus, she argues the use of the singular λόγος (2:22) focuses on the message of death and resurrection.[9] While πιστεύω with the dative presents the function of the Gospel in terms of transmitting faith, εἰς and ὅτι primarily convey the object of faith. The propositional content of faith is centred upon Jesus in his relationship to God, a focus of the Gospel from the prologue. Thus, Ueberschaer argues that while faith is directed at Jesus in 1:12, Jesus has been connected to God already, so all instances of πιστεύω must be read in light of this connection. Alongside the connection to God, Jesus is also presented as the one in whom messianic hopes are fulfilled. Thus for Ueberschaer, faith entails acceptance of Jesus' identity and its related

---

5   Ueberschaer, 'Das Johannesevangelium', 451–71.
6   An argument for distinguishing quality of belief by the construction used is made by Hawthorne, 'Concept of Faith', 118–23; arguing against that view are Harris, *Prepositions*, 236; Painter, 'Eschatological Faith', 40.
7   Ueberschaer, 'Das Johannesevangelium', 458; Bultmann, πιστεύω κτλ., *TDNT* 6.222.
8   Ueberschaer, 'Das Johannesevangelium', 452–8.
9   Ueberschaer, 'Das Johannesevangelium', 454.

soteriological meaning, with both founded in the relationship of Jesus to the Father.¹⁰ Throughout this work, the focus is upon πιστεύω as propositional.¹¹

2.1 The Problem with πιστεύω as Propositional Belief

As an investigation of the propositional content of πιστεύω in John, Ueberschaer provides a good, comprehensive analysis. It stands in a line of similar approaches, in her case particularly influenced by Schnackenburg.¹² It reflects the concern of the Gospel for the identity of Jesus, and the call for people to acknowledge that identity. Yet there are flaws in this approach, and these flaws are less an indictment of Ueberschaer as they are a shortcoming of many works addressing πιστεύω in John.¹³ The two broader critiques are the absence of any definition of πιστεύω and the lack of consideration of the contextual use of the term.

In this chapter, Ueberschaer assumes both that πιστεύω is equivalent to *glaube*, and that it conveys propositional belief. There is no attempt to justify such a position, or to provide any explicit definition. This is a problem that plagues works on belief. The definitions both of 'belief' and of πιστεύω are assumed and the reader is left to figure out the definition the author is working with. There are at least two main positions in terms of the focus of πιστεύω, either on propositional belief or relational trust, and sometimes it is unclear whether an author is adopting one or the other, or the two together. The lack of any consideration of the meaning of πιστεύω in such studies as

---

10 Ueberschaer, 'Das Johannesevangelium', 467–70. The extent of the information that must be believed is debated, for while most see John as highlighting the identity of Jesus, the extent to which his mission or any soteriological dimension must be believed is more contentious. See Seglenieks, *Johannine Belief*, 106–110.
11 While Ueberschaer acknowledges a personal, relational element, this is limited to a brief reference. Ueberschaer, 'Das Johannesevangelium', 467.
12 Schnackenburg, *John*, 1:563–67.
13 One concern that is specific to Ueberschaer's work is the failure to interact outside the bounds of German scholarship. None of the English-language works referenced in this paper are mentioned, which means regrettably Ueberschaer does not interact with Morgan's work. Neither is there reference to important French works on the Gospel as a means of faith transmission, particularly the work of Jean Zumstein, including: 'L'évangile johannique'; 'Croire et comprendre'; and *L'apprentisage de la foi*. Ueberschaer's focus is more exegetical than Zumstein's narrative approach, yet the intersection of ideas makes the omission surprising.

Ueberschaer's is striking. The absence of a definition not only leaves the reader to make assumptions, but it also leaves open the possibility that the author is similarly making assumptions. While it may be presumptuous to begin a study with a firm definition, at the least a working definition would resolve some ambiguity, while still allowing for refining the definition as the evidence is presented.

The lack of definition leads to the second critique, since any serious consideration of the definition of πιστεύω would have to consider how the term is used not only in the Gospel, but in the wider context. An extensive survey of contextual use may not be possible in an article or chapter. Yet the absence of any reference to the meaning of the term in any literature outside the Gospel itself is a significant methodological flaw. As with the lack of definition, neglecting contextual use is a common flaw. For example, in Raymond Brown's excursus on πιστεύω in his commentary, he makes mention of the possible Hebrew background but says nothing of the use of the term in the Graeco-Roman world.[14] One of the few exceptions where, in the context of the Fourth Gospel, the Graeco-Roman use of πιστεύω is given attention is the work of C. H. Dodd. Dodd discusses both Greek and Jewish backgrounds of the term, concluding that the Greek use was more intellectual, and therefore was limited in the extent to which it could convey the personal connection entailed in the Hebrew background.[15] As will be seen, his conclusions may be flawed, but methodologically his work is an improvement over others. For when we consider the Graeco-Roman context, we find that not only is there extensive evidence for the use of πιστεύω, but the sense of propositional belief is at best an uncommon use.

---

14   Brown, *John*, 1:512–15; cf. Morris, *John*, 296–98; Gaffney, 'Believing and Knowing'.
15   However, this conclusion rests heavily on the use of πιστεύω in the Hermetic literature. Dodd, *Interpretation*, 179–82. A more balanced, although still at times problematic, assessment of the Graeco-Roman background is found in Bultmann's TDNT article. Bultmann, 'πιστεύω κτλ.', *TDNT* 6:222.

3. Πιστεύω as Trust

The need for definition, and the importance of context, leads to the second key work, Teresa Morgan's *Roman Faith and Christian Faith*.[16] Her work has two primary parts. The first surveys the use of πίστις and *fides*, the Latin equivalent, in the Graeco-Roman world, across all contexts, religious and otherwise. The second part then turns to the New Testament and studies the New Testament use of πίστις in light of the contextual use.

3.1 Πίστις in the Graeco-Roman world

Morgan makes the argument that the predominant sense of πίστις in the Graeco-Roman world is trust. This meaning is the core sense, although she notes that πίστις, the noun, can take reified meanings. That is, where trust might be taken primarily as a disposition, sometimes trust needs to be made more concrete, and thus πίστις can also refer to a pledge, assurance, or proof. Πίστις plays a role in the religious sphere, albeit not with anywhere near the prominence that it has in Christianity. It primarily conveys the gods as ultimately trustworthy (except Tyche/Fortuna) and thus people are to trust them. It rarely, Morgan argues, has a propositional sense, and where it does that is largely subordinate to the more relational idea of trust. Such relational trust is not abstract or merely internal, but expresses itself actively in the conduct of relationships of all kinds, whether in family, business, military, or political contexts.

Turning from the Graeco-Roman world to the biblical text, Morgan sees the New Testament as essentially fitting within its context. At a few points, she acknowledges that there may be some shifts or different nuances. These do not amount to radical differences, but rather the New Testament use opens the door for the much greater propositional focus that Morgan sees as developing in the early church. But she argues that even instances such as ἡ πίστις in Gal. 1:23–24, which is traditionally taken as a set of doctrines, can instead be read in a relational sense.[17]

---

16 Morgan, *Roman Faith*. The significance of Morgan's work can be seen in the responses it has provoked, including: Watson, Seifrid and Morgan, 'Quaestiones disputatae'; Konstan, 'Trusting'; Oakes, 'Pistis'; Alexander, 'A Map'; Lieu, 'Faith'; Driediger-Murphy, 'Do Not Examine'; Howard-Snyder, 'Pistis'.

17 Morgan, *Roman Faith*, 265–7.

3.2 Πιστεύω in John

When Morgan comes to John, unsurprisingly she sees the focus of John's use of πίστις as focused on the relational. Morgan aligns her conclusions with Bultmann, understanding πιστεύω in a way that minimises propositional content and focuses on relationship with Jesus. She points to two key themes around πιστεύω in John: the importance of trusting/ believing Jesus, and the evolution of that trust/belief.[18]

While Morgan focuses on the relational element, the propositional aspect is not ignored. Morgan notes the close connection of πιστεύω to Christology and focuses on the question of divine equality versus subordination.[19] πιστεύω is based upon evidence, notably the signs.[20] Yet the propositional elements are constantly framed as subordinated to the relational. Thus Morgan presents trust preceding testimony, reading the later trust in Scripture or the words of Jesus as a confirmation of earlier trust, rather than as a greater understanding of Jesus.[21] While the close connection of knowing and believing is acknowledged, Morgan reads most uses of γινώσκω as relational knowledge.[22] In addition, Morgan places belief within a framework of pre-election, which also prioritises the relational over the propositional.[23] The overall picture is that any propositional elements of belief are secondary and flow out of a prior relational connection—the content is only what is necessary to evoke trust.[24]

There are some aspects of Morgan's approach to πιστεύω in John that are useful. It is a corrective to approaches that simply assume πιστεύω is a matter of propositional belief. Reading πιστεύω as relational places the term more obviously in connection with other relational language in John: terms of love and friendship, receiving Jesus, being in Jesus, and abiding in him. A relational sense of πιστεύω also makes the best sense of the Johannine emphasis on εἰς. This is not to say, as Dodd argued, that John needed to use εἰς to convey a relational idea,

---

18 Morgan, *Roman Faith*, 433, 397.
19 Morgan, *Roman Faith*, 398–400.
20 Morgan, *Roman Faith*, 406–7.
21 Morgan, *Roman Faith*, 411–15; for the argument that these instances reflect greater understanding, see Seglenieks, 'Faith and Narrative'.
22 Morgan, *Roman Faith*, 411–12, 428.
23 Morgan, *Roman Faith*, 406–7, 427.
24 Morgan, *Roman Faith*, 428.

but as with 'being in' and 'abiding in', the use of the preposition intensifies the relational idea.[25] As de la Potterie suggests, it may even convey a dynamic sense of moving into relationship.[26] This synergy with the rest of the Gospel supports Morgan's argument that πιστεύω has a relational sense in John, and thus that the solely propositional view is untenable.

3.3 The Problem with πιστεύω as Trust

However, there are some shortcomings of Morgan's assessment of πιστεύω in John. The central problem is that she underplays the role of propositional belief, with the focus on the relational aspect leading the propositional elements to be subsumed under the relational.[27] Such downplaying of the propositional aspect begins in the Graeco-Roman material, for while the dominant emphasis of πίστις is trust, there are occasions when the Greeks talk about knowing and believing things about the gods. It may play a less significant role than it does in Christian texts, but it is present, and such propositional belief is expressed using more than just the language of πίστις.[28]

The downplaying of the propositional aspect of πίστις is more pronounced when it comes to John. There are reasons why many scholars have simply assumed a propositional reading of πιστεύω in John, and it is because they are picking up on a key element within the Johannine presentation. In a response to Morgan's work, Judith Lieu raises some concerns regarding Morgan's assessment, and some of her key critiques are around a lack of engagement with Johannine scholarship, along with a failure to interact with John as narrative.[29] Some of the problems Lieu highlights are different from those raised here, and her article is primarily raising questions more than giving counter arguments, but nevertheless those critiques intersect with the key problem regarding the propositional aspect of belief.

---

25   Malatesta, *Interiority*, 60.
26   Potterie, 'L'emploi dynamique', 376.
27   Concerns with Morgan underplaying the propositional aspect in the NT are raised by Francis Watson and Mark Seifrid, in 'Quaestiones disputatae'.
28   Examples where πίστις reflects a propositional aspect in a Graeco-Roman religious context are found particularly in Plutarch (*Pyth. orac.* 18; *Amatorius* 13; *Quaest. rom.* 11) and Lucian (*Pseudol.* 8; *Philop.* 13, 30; *Icar.* 10); see further Seglenieks, *Johannine Belief*, 131–7.
29   Lieu, 'Faith', 292–6.

As a way of highlighting the effect of the two problems—the lack of scholarly engagement and the failure to treat John as narrative—we can examine Morgan's comments regarding John 8. First, Morgan refers to the use of πιστεύω with ἐγώ εἰμι in 8:24, connecting it to a call to trust Jesus as one would God.[30] Yet this overlooks the role that ἐγώ εἰμι may have either within the original discourse or for the Gospel audience. Either of these would suggest a more propositional reading of πιστεύω than Morgan makes—in the original setting it is a call to believe in Jesus' heavenly origin, while for a later audience a claim to divinity is possible in light of both the prologue and other uses of ἐγώ εἰμι in the Gospel.

Secondly, Morgan sees 8:12–20 as a case where propositional language is used to convey knowing as relational.[31] She argues that it is seeking to shift both the Pharisees and Gospel audience away from the idea of verification by human standards, that it is not about competing truth claims. The idea that the Gospel seeks to move away from truth claims clashes with the prominence of the language of witness and the courtroom motif that plays a key role in the first half of the Gospel.[32] A reading of 8:12–20 that aligns with the Gospel narrative is that the scene shows that 'knowing relationally' and 'knowing about' are entwined and the one requires the other. It is easy to see how both of Morgan's readings make sense when doing detailed exegesis of a verse or paragraph, but they become problematic when the Gospel as a wider narrative is considered.

3.4 The Counterargument

Given Morgan's work, we cannot simply assume a propositional focus for belief in John, and so the case that belief is propositional must be argued.[33] One of the central reasons that the propositional aspect of πίστις must be taken seriously in John is the statement of purpose in 20:31, 'these things are written so that you might believe that Jesus is the Christ, the Son of God'. While Morgan asserts that ὅτι with πιστεύω

---

30 Morgan, *Roman Faith*, 400.
31 Morgan, *Roman Faith*, 429–31.
32 On the trial motif, see especially Lincoln, *Truth on Trial*.
33 I make this argument more extensively in Seglenieks, *Johannine Belief*, 106–10.

merely repeats the ideas expressed in more relational contexts, subordinating the propositional entails a failure to recognise the narrative function of expressions such as 20:31. If the purpose of the narrative can be expressed in such propositional terms, then we need substantial evidence within the text to argue that the propositional idea should be seen as subordinate to the relational. Yet at times the Gospel appears to show the relational in fact depends upon the propositional. In 16:27, the Father's love for the disciples is not based solely on their love for Jesus, but also their propositional belief that he came from God. Curiously, in Morgan's analysis she points to pieces of evidence that should lead towards acknowledging that propositional belief is significant in John. She states that πιστεύω is more often linked to titles than in the Synoptics, as well as observing Jesus' connection to key judicial and life-giving roles.[34] The awareness of such evidence makes it surprising that Morgan consistently decides to subordinate the propositional to the relational.

As noted already, Morgan sees the development of πιστεύω as one of the key features of the Johannine presentation. But she states that how πιστεύω develops is not explained, and that when characters such as the disciples have already been presented in terms of πιστεύω, subsequent instances of πιστεύω are merely confirmation of earlier trust.[35] Yet the disciples display greater understanding through the course of their time with Jesus (16:30), while the Gospel author also goes to significant lengths to show that the disciples also came to greater understanding after the resurrection (2:22; 12:16; 20:9).[36] One observation that may go further to understanding such a subordination is that Morgan reads πιστεύω in John through a framework of pre-election.[37] Morgan's framework of pre-election forces all these instances into an in/out paradigm which flattens out the development of propositional belief.[38] This overlooks the way that outside chapters six and twelve,

---

34 Morgan, *Roman Faith*, 400–2
35 Morgan, *Roman Faith*, 406–7, 413, 415.
36 On the development of the faith of the disciples see Seglenieks, 'Now You Believe', 97, 106; on their greater post-resurrection understanding see Seglenieks, 'Faith and Narrative', 29–34.
37 Morgan, *Roman Faith*, 427.
38 While John does speak at times in a binary fashion regarding acceptable and unacceptable responses, the characters within the narrative display greater complexity and are not always easily categorised as in or out.

rather than a context of divine election, πιστεύω often appears in contexts that present πιστεύω as a choice (e.g. 3:16–18, 32–36; 4:39–42; 5:40–47). In this way, the complexity of Johannine belief is overlooked, and therefore the extent to which believing involves learning and understanding is wrongly minimised.

Both the propositional and the relational are prominent strands within the Johannine use of πιστεύω, and neither should be minimised by an excessive focus on the other. These two senses are related, for in order to trust someone we must know something about them. As both Matthew Bates and Gerald Downing have argued, linguistics suggests that we should not expect precision in defining between possible connotations of πίστις-language.[39] In Johannine use, πιστεύω conveys both a relational sense of trust and propositional belief centred upon Jesus' identity, and both are presented by John as essential parts of the intended response to Jesus. At this point we need to ask, however, if these two aspects together comprise all we can or should say about the meaning of πιστεύω in John? In order to answer that question, I will bring into the discussion a third work.

4. Πιστεύω as Allegiance

The third work to consider is another that addresses the topic of πίστις, Matthew Bates' *Salvation by Allegiance Alone*.[40] Bates' focus is on Paul rather than John, and thus may not be an obvious conversation partner here. However, he proposes a novel thesis regarding the use of πίστις in the New Testament, which is that at least in some cases it should be understood as meaning allegiance. He is not the first to use the term 'allegiance' in connection with πίστις, but what is new is a sustained argument that πίστις should be understood and even translated this way.[41]

Bates' argument begins with an observation that in modern use, 'belief' can have an unhelpfully limited sense.[42] We have already seen

---

39 Bates, 'The External-Relational Shift', 188–92; Downing, 'Ambiguity', 139–62.
40 Bates, *Salvation*, see also *Gospel Allegiance*, 57–83.
41 Others to recently use the language of 'allegiance' in connection with faith include Gupta, *Paul*, 88; Wright, *Paul*, 90; Bennema, *Mimesis*, 27.
42 Bates, *Salvation*, 15–25.

that belief can be understood by some as limited to the idea of propositional belief or intellectual assent, a position rendered untenable in view of Morgan's work. Rather than focusing, as Morgan does, on relational ideas of trust, Bates highlights some contextual examples which he argues use πίστις in the sense of allegiance.[43] From there, he argues that the same meaning fits within some contexts in the New Testament. Bates also suggests that the idea of allegiance aligns with a broader understanding of the gospel and πίστις as a response to the reigning king Jesus.[44] Bates then goes a step further in his argument to say that not only is allegiance an appropriate translation of πίστις, but that allegiance is also an ideal term for representing a more comprehensive picture of the response that is required for salvation.[45]

4.1 Allegiance as a Translation for Πιστεύω

Bates' thesis has proved to be provocative, and in response Will Timmins argues that Bates' idea is untenable.[46] Timmins marshals a long list of critiques, and those relating to the exegesis of Pauline texts will be not be taken up here. Additionally, some of the objections are less than compelling. For example, Timmins points out that the contextual examples that Bates uses do not show πίστις used with prepositions, when in the NT ἐν, ἐπι and εἰς are commonly used. Morgan, and others previously, have shown that there is no significant difference in meaning between the use of the dative and the use of those prepositions with πίστις/πιστεύω.[47] However, several of Timmins objections are significant, including the assertion that Bates does not provide sufficient contextual evidence, and that he fails to recognise the distinction between a word study and a concept study.

Timmins argues that Bates fails to give sufficient contextual evidence for πίστις as allegiance. As a result, Timmins alleges there is the impression that Bates is trying to resolve problems rather than

---

43 Bates, *Salvation*, 5–6, 79–80.
44 Bates, *Salvation*, 78.
45 Bates, *Salvation*,
46 Timmins, 'A Faith'.
47 Morgan, *Roman Faith*, 425–6; Harris, *Prepositions*, 236; Painter, 'Eschatological Faith', 40; Bultmann, *TDNT* 6:222.

presenting an argument that is the best fit for the data. The section on contextual examples is relatively short, and limited primarily to instances from Maccabees (1 Macc. 10:25–27; 3 Macc. 3:2–4; 5:31) and Josephus (*Ant.* 12.47, 12.147, 12.396; *J.W.* 1.207, 2.341).[48] It raises questions around whether 'allegiance' was a standard use of πίστις in the wider Graeco-Roman context instead of merely within Jewish settings. However, while limited, the evidence does show that πίστις was used to indicate the sort of loyalty to a sovereign which could equally be termed allegiance. Bates also demonstrates this use in literature that is closely connected to the New Testament (in the case of the LXX) or coming out of the same socio-cultural context (Josephus). Morgan similarly provides examples where πίστις conveys loyalty to a superior, including military contexts of a soldier's loyalty to the commander.[49] While Timmins argues that allegiance, loyalty, and faithfulness are not synonymous, they have significant semantic overlap.[50] Thus, while faithfulness or loyalty may not imply a status differential in the way that allegiance does, there may be cases where those terms can function synonymously. Such is the case with the gospel context of Jesus as king, along with the imperial context into which the gospel was proclaimed.[51] Thus, while more evidence may be desirable, Bates raises the plausibility of πίστις being translated as allegiance in a first-century Jewish context.

One particular area where there is a lack of evidence adduced by Timmins is with regard to the use of the verb πιστεύω.[52] This is a critical problem when applying Bates' arguments to John, as John only uses the verb. As Morgan identifies, the verb has a more limited range of meaning than the noun. It is more focused on the core meanings of trust/believe, with the occasional use as 'entrust', in contrast to the noun which can also be used for deferred and reified meanings, such

---

48 Bates, *Salvation*, 79–80.
49 Morgan, *Roman Faith*,
50 Timmins, 'A Faith', 609.
51 Bates highlights both of these contexts. Bates, *Salvation*, 67–72, 87–9.
52 Bates refers to the presence of the verb in Josephus, *Ant.* 12.396. However, the use of the verb refers to entrusting one's self to someone in the context of physical protection, using the same construction as in John 2:24.

as assurance, persuasion, pledge, and proof.[53] Thus, in the absence of further evidence we cannot extend Bates' argument to suggest that πιστεύω in John might be translated as 'give allegiance'. While it is possible that there is contextual evidence that would open up 'give allegiance' as a possible translation of the verb, at this stage that the evidence has not been presented.

A second issue that Timmins raises is the blurring of the distinction between a word study and a concept study. This is a confusion that has long plagued biblical studies and can particularly be an issue in discussions of 'faith'.[54] Yet Timmins overstates the problem, for Bates differentiates between talking about translation and talking about a concept.[55] Word and concept are connected, as it is words which convey concepts, and thus it is to be expected that Bates would move from discussing individual instances of πίστις to their broader significance. A greater methodological clarity would be useful, but it is not a fatal flaw in the logic of his case. Nevertheless, the issue is important to consider here because of how we might appropriate his work in the context of John's Gospel. While the evidence that Bates provides is not sufficient to suggest that 'give allegiance' is an appropriate contextual sense for πιστεύω in John, nor is there an exegetical basis for such a translation in any specific instances within John, we can still consider whether allegiance conveys the concept of the response required for salvation, or in Johannine terms, to receive eternal life.

4.2 Allegiance and the Johannine Concept of Belief

While the question of translating πιστεύω as 'give allegiance' has been ruled out, there remains the possibility of allegiance playing a role as conceptual terminology. The shift from talking about a word to a concept is justified on account of the way πιστεύω is used in John. Far more than in the other Gospels, πιστεύω has a prominent conceptual role in John. That is, πιστεύω is used to summarise the intended response to

---

53 Morgan, *Roman Faith*, 6, 20–23, 395–96. Cf. Williams, 'Faith', 349.
54 The classic critique calling for distinguishing word and concept studies is Barr, *Semantics*, 206–62. Highlighting the issue in the context of faith is Campbell, *Quest*, 190. Both Timmins and Bates refer to the discussion in Campbell.
55 Bates, *Salvation*, 78.

Jesus which the Gospel seeks to evoke in the audience. The prologue sets up πιστεύω as the intended response to witness (1:7), initially in terms of the witness of John the Baptist, but also echoing with the role of the Gospel itself as witness (21:24). Πιστεύω is also presented as the ideal response to the incarnation (1:12–13), tied to other important ideas of receiving Jesus and birth from God. The statement of purpose in 20:30–31 summarises the goal of the Gospel to evoke πιστεύω which leads to life. Throughout the Gospel πιστεύω is used frequently, in significant passages, and in close connection to all the other important aspects of responding to Jesus which the Gospel encourages (ἀγαπάω, γινώσκω/οἶδα, μένω, ἔρχομαι, ἀκολουθέω).[56] Thus we can talk about a concept of belief in John, which centres on πιστεύω but is conveyed through a range of related terms.

The question then is, when talking about the Johannine concept of belief, whether allegiance might be an appropriate and even helpful term to use. To answer the question would require a definition of the concept of belief in John. I have recently argued elsewhere that Johannine belief entails a cognitive aspect, centred on Jesus identity, a relational aspect that involves a close personal connection of trust and love with Jesus, an ethical aspect, in terms of right conduct in adherence to Jesus' commands and example, a witness aspect, both confessing one's faith but presenting such faith in order that others might also believe, and an ongoing aspect, as all the above aspects are to be continuous.[57] If we take the idea of 'saving allegiance' as Bates defines it, there is some alignment with the concept in John. Bates' definition is '*mental affirmation* that the gospel is true, *professed fealty* to Jesus alone as the cosmic Lord, and *enacted loyalty* through obedience to Jesus as the king.'[58] It reflects the cognitive, ethical and witness aspects. As such, it could be a helpful term to convey something of the breadth of the concept in John. One shortcoming is that Bates' definition is not explicit about the relational aspect that might be conveyed by the idea

---

56 For a detailed analysis of these interconnected terms, see Seglenieks, *Johannine Belief*, 17, 31–105.
57 Seglenieks, *Johannine Belief*, 106–18.
58 Bates, *Salvation*, 92.

of trust.⁵⁹ In John 6:68–69, believing that Jesus has the words of life may indicate an affirmation of his message, but in the context it also conveys a trust in the person of Jesus despite incomplete understanding. The ongoing aspect of Johannine belief may be entailed in Bates' definition, but it is not made explicit. These problems do not require the rejection of the idea that allegiance may be a helpful term when it comes to discussing the concept of belief in John's Gospel.

One benefit of such terminology would be that 'allegiance' is less prone to a reductionistic understanding than 'belief'. Popular use of the term 'belief' is primarily cognitive, which as we have seen is too limited a sense in light of both the sense of πιστεύω in John and the broader Johannine concept of belief.⁶⁰ It can also have connotations of opinions that are counterfactual or unsupported by any form of evidence. As Morgan argues in her work, πιστεύω in John does have an evidential basis, as the signs and works of Jesus are presented as evidence that supports belief (John 10:38; 20:30–31).⁶¹ Using allegiance in talking of the Johannine concept of belief could avoid some of these limitations in the English term 'belief'. Additionally, in contemporary thought both propositional belief and trust are often conceived of as primarily internal and attitudinal. In contrast, the Johannine concept of belief incorporates active elements, which could be construed as acting in alignment with, or in imitation of, the king. Thus, allegiance is a helpful term to include in our vocabulary as it reduces the chance of assumptions that limit the idea of what is entailed by Johannine belief.

The use of 'allegiance' as a descriptor of Johannine belief will not resolve all the problems noted here. Popular understanding of allegiance still does not equate to the Johannine concept of belief, so it cannot be as simple as simply replacing one term with another. Most modern definitions of allegiance focus on ideas of loyalty and commitment. These are directed, in more traditional usage, towards the

---

59 While there is an acknowledgement that trust is involved, that is subsumed within allegiance, see Bates, *Salvation*, 90. Bates is clearer that πίστις is often trust in *Gospel Allegiance*, 64.
60 Bates observes the potential problems in the English terms 'faith' and 'believe', *Gospel Allegiance*, 59–60; see also Bates, 'External-Relational Shift', 176–7; Gupta, *Paul*, 2–5.
61 Morgan, *Roman Faith*, 403–18.

state or sovereign, and so it can entail some sense of obedience.[62] But it can be used more broadly to indicate loyalty and support for a group or cause. We can speak of allegiance to a political group, or a football team. It is always used in a sense of open commitment—someone who wears the team colours, goes to the game, the vocal supporter. Similar to Bates' definition, the common use of allegiance does not emphasise the relational aspect of belief. Therefore, rather than replacing other terms, speaking of allegiance alongside trust could go further towards conveying the breadth of the Johannine concept of belief, rather than merely relying on 'belief' or 'trust' alone.

5. Conclusion

We are now in a position to return to where we began and give an answer, in light of recent work on the subject, to the question of what πιστεύω means in John. In terms of the word itself, it has two senses that work together in John. It conveys a sense of relational trust, a trust that is directed towards the person of Jesus. This is a close, relational trust, with the use of εἰς emphasising the relational connection. Alongside the relational sense, there is a propositional sense. In particular with ὅτι, πιστεύω is used to convey information about Jesus which is presented as needing to be accepted. These two senses are both present throughout the Gospel, and neither is clearly subordinated to the other. Thus, we ought not speak only of knowledge that enables relationship, nor of relationship that is the means to knowledge. To believe in Jesus is to both know and accept his identity as the Christ, the Son of God, and to trust in him.

If we extend our focus to consider the concept of belief, which in John is centred upon but not limited to the term πιστεύω, we see both those aspects continue. The propositional aspect is reflected in use of 'know', as well as narrative features such as the prevalent confessions. The relational aspect is extended through language of love, friendship, and abiding. This concept, however, goes beyond these

---

62 Bates understands John as including obedience in the '*pistis* action' based on John 2:23–24; 3:36. *Gospel Allegiance*, 89.

two dimensions, including ethical actions and bearing witness to one's faith. Thus, while we do not have the evidence to make the case for 'allegiance' as a translation for πιστεύω, the idea of allegiance is helpful to convey the breadth of the Johannine concept of belief. It overcomes some of the limitations of popular conceptions of belief, and even of trust, and thus ensures that the richness of the Johannine concept is not obscured by modern English usage.

Christopher Seglenieks
Bible College of South Australia

Bibliography

Alexander, L.	'A Map of Understanding: The Riskiness of Trust in the World of the Early Christians', *JSNT* 40, no. 3 (2018), 276–88.
Barr, J.	*The Semantics of Biblical* Language (Oxford: Oxford University Press, 1961).
Bates, M. W.	*Gospel Allegiance* (Grand Rapids, MI: Brazos, 2019).
Bates, M. W.	*Salvation by Allegiance Alone: Rethinking Faith, Works, and the Gospel of Jesus the King* (Grand Rapids, MI: Baker Academic, 2017).
Bates, M. W.	'The External-Relational Shift in Faith (Pistis) in New Testament Research: Romans 1 as Gospel-Allegiance Test Case', *CBR* 18, no. 2 (2020), 176–202.
Bennema, C.	*Mimesis in the Johannine Literature* (LNTS; London: T&T Clark, 2017).
Brown, R. E.	The *Gospel According to John* (2 vols.; Garden City, NY: Doubleday, 1966–1970).
Campbell, D. A.	*The Quest for Paul's Gospel: A Suggested Strategy* (London: T&T Clark, 2005).
de la Potterie, I.	'L'emploi dynamique de εἰς dans Saint Jean et ses incidences théologiques', *Biblica* 43, no. 3 (1962), 366–87.
Dodd, C. H.	*The Interpretation of the Fourth Gospel* (Cambridge: University Press, 1968).

Downing, F. G.   'Ambiguity, Ancient Semantics, and Faith', *NTS* 56 (2009), 139–62.

Driediger-Murphy, L. G.   '"Do Not Examine, But Believe!" A Classicist's Perspective on Teresa Morgan's Roman Faith and Christian Faith', *RelS* 54, no. 4 (2018), 568–576.

Forestell, J. T.   *The Word of the Cross* (Rome: Biblical Institute, 1974).

Gaffney, J.   'Believing and Knowing in the Fourth Gospel', *TS* 26 (1965), 215–41.

Gupta, N. K.   *Paul and the Language of Faith* (Grand Rapids, MI: Eerdmans, 2020).

Harris, M. J.   *Prepositions and Theology in the Greek New Testament* (Grand Rapids, MI: Zondervan, 2012).

Hawthorne, G. F.   'The Concept of Faith in the Fourth Gospel', *BSac* 116, no. 462 (1959), 117–26.

Howard-Snyder, D.   'Pistis, Fides, and Propositional Belief', *RelS* 54, no. 4 (2018), 585–92.

Jensen, A. S.   *John's Gospel as Witness: The Development of the Early Christian Language of Faith* (Aldershot: Ashgate, 2004).

Koester, C. R.   *The Word of Life: A Theology of John's Gospel* (Grand Rapids, MI: Eerdmans, 2008).

Konstan, D.   'Trusting in Jesus', *JSNT* 40, no. 3 (2018), 247–54.

Lieu, J. M.   'Faith and the Fourth Gospel: A Conversation with Teresa Morgan', *JSNT* 40, no. 3 (2018), 289–98.

Lincoln, A. T.   *Truth on Trial: The Lawsuit Motif in the Fourth Gospel* (Peabody, MA: Hendrickson, 2000).

Malatesta, E.   *Interiority and Covenant* (Rome: Biblical Institute Press, 1978).

Moloney, F. J.   'From Cana to Cana (Jn 2.1–4.54) and the Fourth Evangelist's Concept of Correct (and Incorrect) Faith', in E. A. Livingstone (ed.), *Studia Biblica 1978 International Congress on Biblical Studies* (Sheffield: University of Sheffield, 1978), 185–213.

Morgan, T.   *Roman Faith and Christian Faith: Pistis and Fides in the Early Roman Empire and Early Churches* (Oxford: Oxford University Press, 2015).

Morris, L. L.	*The Gospel According to John* (NICNT; Grand Rapids, MI: Eerdmans, 1995).
Oakes, P.	'Pistis as Relational Way of Life in Galatians', *JSNT* 40, no. 3 (2018), 255–75.
O'Brien, K. S.	'Written that You May Believe: John 20 and Narrative Rhetoric', *CBQ* 67, no. 2 (2005), 284–302.
Painter, J.	'Eschatological Faith in the Gospel of John', in R. Banks (ed.), *Reconciliation and Hope: New Testament Essays on Atonement and Eschatology* (Grand Rapids, MI: Eerdmans, 1974), 36–52.
Schnackenburg, R.	*The Gospel According to St. John* (3 vols.; New York, NY: Herder & Herder, 1968–1982).
Seglenieks, C.	'Faith and Narrative: A Two-Level Reading of Belief in the Gospel of John', *TynBul* 70, no. 1 (2019), 23–40.
Seglenieks, C.	*Johannine Belief and Graeco-Roman Devotion: Reshaping Devotion for John's Graeco-Roman Audience* (Tübingen, Mohr Siebeck, 2020).
Seglenieks, C.	'"Now You Believe": The Faith of the Disciples in John 16:30–33', *Colloquium* 50, no. 2 (2018), 90–108.
Tam, J. C.	*Apprehension of Jesus in the Gospel of John* (Tübingen: Mohr Siebeck, 2015).
Thompson, M. M.	'Signs and Faith in the Fourth Gospel', *BBR* 1 (1991), 89–108.
Timmins, W. N.	'A Faith Unlike Abraham's: Matthew Bates on Salvation by Allegiance Alone', *JETS* 61, no. 3 (2018), 595–615.
Ueberschaer, N.	'Das Johannesevangelium als Medium der Glaubensvermittlung', in J. Frey et al. (eds.), *Glaube: Das Verständnis des Glaubens im frühen Christentum und in seiner jüdischen und hellenistisch-römischen Umwelt* (Tübingen: Mohr Siebeck, 2017), 451–471.
Watson, F., M. A. Seifrid, and T. Morgan	'Quaestiones disputatae: Roman Faith and Christian Faith', *NTS* 64 (2018), 243–61.
Williams, C. H.	'Faith, Eternal Life, and the Spirit in the Gospel of John', in J. M. Lieu et al. (eds.) *The Oxford Handbook of Johannine Studies* (Oxford: Oxford University Press, 2018), 347–62.

Wright, N. T.   *Paul: A Biography* (New York, NY: Harper Collins, 2018).

Zumstein, J.   'Croire et comprendre', in J. Zumstein (ed.), *Miettes exégétiques* (Geneva: Labor et Fides, 1991), 73–88.

Zumstein, J.   *L'apprentisage de la foi* (2nd ed.; Geneva: Labor et Fides, 2015).

Zumstein, J.   'L'évangile johannique: une stratégie du croire', in J. Zumstein (ed.), *Miettes exégétiques* (Geneva: Labor et Fides, 1991), 237–52.

CHAPTER 12

What did Paul's Companions Hear? How the Syntax of Ἀκούω Aids the Interpretation of Acts 9:7 and 22:9

Andrew Stewart

Abstract

Divergences between Luke's three accounts of Paul's conversion have long been at the centre of discussions about the historicity of Acts; and the question of what Paul's companions saw or did not see in Acts 9:7 and 22:9 is a significant crux. Various formulations of the syntax of ἀκούω have shaped this discussion. This essay examines the linguistic data in Luke-Acts and Paul in light of the basic functions of the accusative and genitive cases and suggests an alternative formulation which may aid the reader's understanding of the use of ἀκούω in the conversion narratives and other sections in Acts.

Hearing is an important activity in the book of Acts. It is the activity which complements proclamation, and proclamation of the apostolic testimony is the thread which binds the narrative together, from the commission of the risen Jesus in 1:8 to the climactic ministry of Paul in Rome in 28:30-32. The importance of hearing in Acts is demonstrated by the fact that the verb ἀκούω occurs eighty-eight times in Acts, and it is to be found in virtually every significant episode. This essay will argue that it is a word whose syntax will repay closer examination.[1]

As a contribution to that endeavour a series of passages will be examined where the significance of ἀκούω has been much debated, namely the passages which describe what Paul and his travelling companions heard on the road to Damascus. The three accounts of Paul's encounter with the risen Jesus give a clear and consistent account of what *Paul* heard. In all three accounts Paul heard a voice saying, 'Saul, Saul, why are you persecuting me?' (9:4; 22:7; 26:14).[2] However, the two reports of what *Paul's companions* heard in 9:7 and 22:9 leave the reader asking whether they heard anything at all.

Restricting our focus, for now, to the three passages relating Paul's conversion and call, we can note that:

- In 9:4 Paul 'heard the voice of one speaking to him'. Here the direct object of ἀκούω is the accusative φωνὴν λέγουσαν and refers to Jesus.
- In 9:7 Paul's companions stood, 'hearing the voice'. Here the participle takes a genitive direct object, ἀκούοντες μὲν τῆς φωνῆς.
- In 9:13 Luke recounts Ananias' response that he has heard from many (ἀπὸ πολλῶν) about the numerous evil things Paul has done against the saints in Jerusalem, ὅσα κακὰ τοῖς ἁγίοις σου ἐποίησεν ἐν Ἰερουσαλήμ. Here the direct object is in the accusative.
- In 22:1 Paul appeals for a hearing, with the imperative followed by a genitive direct object, ἀκούσατέ μου [...] ἀπολογίας.
- In 22:7, when Paul relates his first hearing the words of Jesus, the voice of one speaking takes the genitive, φωνῆς λεγούσης, rather than the accusative as in 9:4.

---

1   Green, *Conversion in Luke-Acts*, 116–17, 'Hearing well is thematic for Luke-Acts [...] Hearing well is realized in the formation of patterns of thinking, feeling, believing and behaving characteristic of one's community of reference. Hearing in this sense is metaphoric for conversion [...]'.
2   For the sake of consistency I will refer to Saul of Tarsus as Paul in this article, even though he is not referred to by his Roman cognomen until Acts 13:9. From his first mention in the narrative in Acts 7:58 until the first stage of his missionary travels in Cyprus (Acts 13:7, 9a) Paul is referred to by his Jewish name Saul. That, too, is how he is addressed by the risen Jesus on the road, see Acts 9:4; 22:7; and 26:14.

- In 22:9, when Paul retells the experience of his companions, he hears the voice which they do not hear and ἀκούω takes the accusative, τὴν δὲ φωνὴν οὐκ ἤκουσαν τοῦ λαλοῦντός μοι, and not the accusative as in 9:7.
- In 26:14, when Paul again relates how he heard the voice of Jesus, his description of the voice he heard reverts to the accusative as in 9:4, ἤκουσα φωνὴν λέγουσαν πρός με.

The most obvious question arising from this list concerns the apparent discrepancy between 9:7 and 22:9 in their descriptions of what Paul's companions heard as Jesus spoke to Paul. In 9:7 Luke tells us that 'they *heard* the voice but saw no-one', while in 22:9 Paul tells an angry crowd in Jerusalem that, 'they did *not hear* the voice of the one who spoke to me'. The tension between the two verses is obvious, and several ways of addressing it have been suggested.

i. One of the earliest was the claim that 9:7 and 22:9 refer to *two different voices*. Thus, in 9:7 the companions heard the voice of Paul, while in 22:9 they did not hear the voice of Jesus. This interpretation was advocated by Chrysostom[3] and more recently by F. F. Bruce.[4] It does not, however, enjoy widespread acceptance.

ii. Another interpretation accepts that the voice in both verses is that of Jesus, but ἀκούω is to be *understood differently*. In 9:7 it describes the faculty of hearing, while in 22:9 it describes the faculty of understanding. This is reflected in several translations.[5] Interpreters arrive at this conclusion by different routes. Some base their conclusion on the syntax of ἀκούω.[6] Others attribute a particular sense to ἀκούω because of the context in which it stands.[7]

---

3 Chrysostom, *Homilies on Acts*, Part II, Homily XLVII, 628: 'It is not at variance, no there were two voices, that of Paul and the Lord's voice [in that place, the writer] means Paul's voice; as in fact (Paul) here adds, "The voice of Him that spoke unto me"'.
4 Bruce, *Acts*, 199. However, writing in 1988, Bruce, *Book of Acts*, 185, acknowledges the problems with this explanation.
5 NASV, NIV, ESV, and NLT. The Message distinguishes what the companions heard in a different way, 'They could hear the sound (9:7) [...] but they didn't hear the conversation' (22:9).
6 Rackham, *Acts*, 131.
7 Brachter, 'Ἀκούω', 244.

iii. Yet another approach is to *abandon the quest for a reconciliation* between the two accounts and explain the apparent contradiction in terms of the author's compositional or rhetorical technique, or an apparent indifference to such insignificant points of detail among ancient writers.[8] This approach is facilitated by the now commonly accepted view that in Koine Greek ἀκούω takes accusative and genitive direct objects interchangeably, with little or no reference to the sense in which ἀκούω is to be understood.

With a view to gaining a better understanding of how ἀκούω is to be construed, not only in 9:7 and 22:9, but in other passages in Acts as well, my aim is to review the conclusion that ἀκούω takes accusative and genitive direct objects interchangeably. First of all, I will survey the application of the so called 'classical rule' of syntax, before considering the arguments in favour of interchangeability of case, before presenting the results of a fresh study of the NT data regarding the case of direct objects of ἀκούω. Finally, these conclusions will lead to several suggestions as to how to understand the occurrences of ἀκούω in Acts, with specific reference to Acts 9:7 and 22.9.

The Influence of the 'Classical Rule'

Underlying the question of whether case governs the meaning of direct objects of ἀκούω in the NT is a rule supposedly drawn from the grammar of classical Greek. Simply put, the accusative is used when referring to the *thing* heard, while the genitive is used when referring to the *person* heard. Herbert W. Smyth explained the use of the genitive case as a partitive genitive used with verbs of hearing and perception. Thus, '[t]he person or thing whose words, sound etc. are perceived by the senses, stands in the genitive; the words, sound etc. generally stand in the accusative'.[9]

This rule, or a version of it, has been applied by NT commentators

---

8 Craig S. Keener cites the differences between accounts of the same events as recounted by Josephus in his Jewish War and Antiquities. Keener, *Acts*, 1.1638.
9 Smyth, *Greek Grammar*, 232.

to Acts 9:7 and 22:9.¹⁰ James H. Moulton, for example, drew upon the rule in classical Greek to defend the consistency and reliability of Luke's two accounts of what Paul's companions heard or did not hear: 'The fact that the maintenance of an old and well-known distinction between the accusative and genitive with ἀκούω saves the author of Acts ix 7 and xxii 9 from a patent contradiction, should by itself be enough to make us recognise it for Luke, and for other writers until it is proved wrong'.¹¹ The Princeton exegete, Joseph A. Alexander, argued that the distinction was maintained in the NT even where the force of the rule had been qualified.¹²

According to Blass, Debrunner, and Funk the classical rule is generally applicable to the NT. 'The classical rule for ἀκούειν is: the person whose words are heard stands in the genitive, the thing about which (or whom) one hears in the accusative'.¹³ Maximillian Zerwick also drew upon the classical rule to explain NT usage:

> After ἀκούειν in classical usage the genitive is used of the person speaking and the accusative of the *thing (or person) of which one hears* [...] the accusative represents what is *directly grasped by the hearing* (sound, news, what is said) and the genitive the *source of what is heard*, whether the person speaking or a voice conceived not as a sound but as speaking, or the object making the noise which is heard. The attention to the source of what is said leads to the use of ἀκούειν not simply of the perception of sound, but with notions 'listen, attend, obey'.¹⁴

A. T. Robertson took a different approach to explaining the difference between Acts 9:7 and 22:9. He formulated the classical rule as follows: 'The accusative case (case of extent) accents the *intellectual apprehension*

---

10 Rackham, *Acts*, 131, who distinguishes between 'hearing the sound' and 'not hearing the articulate words'.
11 Moulton, *Grammar*, 1.66.
12 Alexander, *Acts*, 297–98, 'Another [possible but less natural explanation of the difference between 9:7 and 22:9] makes a difference between the accusative and genitive constructions of the verb to hear, the one denoting mere sensation, the other intellectual apprehension'.
13 BDF, §173. Allowance is made for the fact that the NT wavers between genitive and accusative in phrases meaning 'to hear a sound' and the fact that the NT displays a greater preference for the accusative over the genitive than is evident in classical Greek.
14 Zerwick, *Biblical Greek*, 24. Emphasis added.

of the sound, while the genitive (specifying case) calls attention to the *sound of the voice without accenting the sense*.[15]

This distinction, however, does not appear to hold good in other places where ἀκούω is used in the NT. Instances can be cited where ἀκούω with an accusative direct object expressly does not involve understanding (see, for example Matthew 13:19; Acts 5:24). In 9:4 Luke uses ἀκούω with an accusative direct object to describe how Paul heard the speaking voice, even though he did not know who was speaking and needed a further explanation (9:6). Moreover, in Paul's account of the same incident in 22:7 ἀκούω takes the genitive. Thus, C. F. D. Moule has called the boundary between the accusative and genitive in the NT 'disputed territory'. He claims that 'the NT usage varies in a way which defies classification, e.g., it seems to me to be impossible to find a satisfactory distinction in meaning between the genitive and accusative in Acts 9:7 and 22:9'.[16]

The apparent lack of a clear distinction in meaning between accusative and genitive direct objects of ἀκούω is often explained as a consequence of the abandonment of the precise distinctions observed by classical Greek, as the Koine form of the language came to be used around the Mediterranean and absorbed the influences of other languages. Despite the statement in his *Prolegomena* in support of the distinction between accusative and genitive in Koine Greek, Moulton observed the use of the genitive in 11:7 and 22:7, alongside the accusatives in very similar phrases in 9:4 and 26:14, and concluded: 'If this pointless variation can occur in a writer like Luke, the classical distinction between accusative and genitive has broken down'.[17]

Alternatively, it has been argued that the classical distinction remained active, but the writers of Koine Greek developed a preference for the accusative which displaced the genitive where it would have been preferred by classical writers. This is the suggestion of Gerhard Kittel in his article on ἀκούω: 'The classical rule of the genitive (or prepositions παρά, πρός, ἐκ) for the persons whom we hear, and the accusative for the persons or things about whom or which we

---

15 Robertson, *Grammar*, 506. Emphasis added.
16 Moule, *Idiom Book*, 36.
17 Moulton, *Grammar*, 3.161.

hear, is applied even more systematically in the NT, where the accusative tends to replace the more common classical genitive even in the case of hearing a sound, though the latter still occurs'.[18]

Nigel Turner acknowledges the difficulty of applying the 'classical rule' to the NT and suggests that 'it is worth examining in greater detail the view that the accusative involves an *understanding* of the object while the genitive merely records the physical *hearing* of it'.[19] Yet even this 'rule' admits exceptions, noting that 'several accusatives occur when there must be no idea of *understanding*, merely physical perception' (Matthew 26:65/Mark 14:65; Luke 1:41). However, when he examines these 'exceptions' Turner suggests that 'the accusatives, which appear at first to involve no more than physical perception, each bear a more subtle interpretation'. In other words, there is a measure of understanding which goes beyond merely hearing a sound.

With greater confidence Turner argues that when the direct object of ἀκούω is a participle 'there is some real difference between the accusative and genitive'. More specifically: 'It would appear that the accusative transforms the participle into a subordinate clause of indirect speech [...] while the genitive influences the participle to indicate the sound that was directly heard'. Thus, Paul's account of 'a voice speaking directly to him' in 22:9 is appropriately indicated by the genitive case. However, it is 'somewhat perplexing' to find accusatives in 9:4 and 26:14.[20] When he seeks to apply the 'classical rule' to the apparent discrepancy of 9:7 and 22:9 Turner falls back on the nature of the accusative as the case indicating extent: 'In the accusative, one does not so much hear *a* sound as hear the gist of it'.[21] I will argue that this is a point worthy of further examination, even when the direct object of ἀκούω is not a participle.

Two articles published in 1959 raised the question of which grammatical rules, if any, governed Luke's use of ἀκούω. Robert G. Brachter surveyed the use of ἀκούω in Luke-Acts and found that the accusative direct objects always refer to the thing heard. He also noted that this on its own would not resolve the contradiction between 9:7 and 22:9

---

18   Kittel, 'Ακούω', 216. Abbreviations not retained.
19   Turner, *Grammatical Insights*, 89.
20   Turner, *Grammatical Insights*, 87.
21   Turner, *Grammatical Insights*, 88.

unless a further assumption was made that to hear a thing implied understanding of what was heard. When it came to the rule that genitive direct objects refer to the person Brachter noted a significant number of exceptions.[22] Commenting on the difference between 9:7 and 22:9 he concluded that '[i]t can hardly be maintained, therefore, that Lucan usage supports the contention that Acts 9:7 ἀκούσαντες μὲν τῆς φωνῆς may be taken to mean "they heard (but did not understand) the voice" while τὴν δὲ φωνὴν οὐκ ἤκουσαν in 22:9 may mean that "they did not understand (although they heard) the voice"'.[23] He claimed that grammar alone does not explain the meaning of the text. 'The particular shade of meaning the verb acquires in a given sentence does not depend upon the case of the object [...] but on the whole context of the narrative in which the verb is used'.[24]

A fuller survey of the linguistic data was attempted by Horst R. Moehring.[25] Based on his survey of the usage of ἀκούω in classical literature, the LXX, the NT, and the works of Epictetus, Moehring concluded that neither the simple rule as stated by Blass (accusative for the thing and genitive for the person) nor the more complex rule as stated by Robertson (accusative for hearing with understanding and genitive for hearing without necessarily understanding) was followed in the NT. On this basis he argued: 'It is the thesis of this paper that the author of Acts used the verb ἀκούω with both the accusative and genitive *without a differentiation of meaning*'.[26]

His conclusion has been widely accepted both by grammarians[27] and commentators,[28] though not without protest. In 1989 Gert

---

22 Of the 42 instances where ἀκούω took a genitive direct object, 34 referred to a person while eight referred to a thing. See Brachter, 'Ἀκούω', 244.
23 Brachter, 'Ἀκούω', 245.
24 Brachter, 'Ἀκούω', 244.
25 Moehring, 'AKOYEIN', 80–99.
26 Moehring, 'AKOYEIN', 81. Emphasis added.
27 Wallace, *Greek Grammar*, 133. 'It is doubtful that this [Robertson's formulation of the rule] is where the difference lay between the two cases used with ἀκούω in Hellenistic Greek: the NT (including the more literary writers) is filled with examples of ἀκούω + genitive indicating understanding... as well as instances of ἀκούω + accusative where little or no comprehension takes place'.
28 Conzelmann, *Acts*, 71; Fitzmyer, *Acts*, 426; Keener, *Acts* 1.1639; and Barrett, *Acts*, 2.1039 cite Moehring and Brachter as to support the view that case was assigned interchangeably. Kistemaker, *Acts*, 336, notes the views of Moehring and Brachter, but cites Robertson as an adocate that case distinctions are significant, before concluding, 'The evidence, however, is inconclusive'.

Steuernagel questioned the consensus which had gathered around the thesis of undifferentiated meaning as set out by Moehring. Steuernagel argued that the genitive case of the voice (τῆς φωνῆς) which Paul's companions heard in 9:7 is exegetically significant.²⁹ Thus, the genitive with the article of 9:7 (τῆς φωνῆς) indicates a subtle distinction from the accusative without the article of 9:4 (φωνήν). He concluded that

> [t]he genitive [...] leaves something in suspense. What is captured here is the fact that there must have been a voice as Saul answers the question. His companions hear that Saul must have heard. But what is also captured is the fact that they possibly heard later as he told how he heard [...] Hence the suggested rendering: 'They heard that the voice of the Lord must have been present. But they indeed saw no-one'.³⁰

Even if one does not accept Steuernagel's conclusion as to the import of ἀκούσαντες μὲν τῆς φωνῆς in 9:7, the route he takes to arrive at his conclusion is worthy of note because of his critique of the thesis that accusative and genitive cases are used interchangeably with ἀκούω, as espoused by Moehring and others. His argument might be summarised as follows.

- First of all, there are only a very few instances where accusative and genitive direct objects of ἀκούω are found in close proximity in the same passage.
- Secondly, the passages where case is said to be used interchangeably have not been subject to the kind of thorough exegetical scrutiny which would justify the conclusion of interchangeability. He argues that examples have been listed rather than analysed. He criticises one grammarian for failing to consider '*why* a genitive or accusative was or could have been used'.³¹
- Thirdly, he suggests that the consensus which has formed around the thesis of interchangeability has discouraged a thorough

---

29   Steuernagel, 'ΑΚΟΥΟΝΤΕΣ ΜΕΝ ΤΗΣ ΦΩΝΗΣ'.
30   Steuernagel, 'ΑΚΟΥΟΝΤΕΣ ΜΕΝ ΤΗΣ ΦΩΝΗΣ', 624.
31   Steuernagel, 'ΑΚΟΥΟΝΤΕΣ ΜΕΝ ΤΗΣ ΦΩΝΗΣ', 620. Emphasis as in Steuernagel's article, '*warum* jeweils ein Genitiv oder Akkusativ gebraucht worden ist oder sein könnte'.

enquiry into the syntax of ἀκούω in both the LXX and the NT.³²

In view of the reliance placed upon Moehring's work by subsequent scholars, as well as Steuernagel's critique of Moehring, it is important to examine his methodology as well as his conclusion. Two aspects of Moehring's methodology deserve further scrutiny. The first is the *scope* of the linguistic data upon which he based his conclusions. Introducing his survey of the LXX data, he states: 'in view of the great mass of material a complete study of every single instance is very difficult and hardly necessary'.³³ When he comes to the NT data Moehring concentrates on the expression 'to hear a voice'. Selectivity is understandable as the scope for studying the syntax of ἀκούω is so large.³⁴ However, his method of selection has resulted in an imbalanced conclusion as it focused attention on a significant body of material which seems to defy grammatical classification, but in so doing it overlooks an even larger body of material where the direct objects of ἀκούω appear to conform to a pattern of sorts. His bold conclusion that the author of Acts—and other Koine authors—used case indiscriminately with ἀκούω surely needs to be based on a fuller survey of the available data.

The second aspect of Moehring's methodology that is problematic is his *polemical* approach towards the formulations of 'school-grammarians' such as Moulton and Robertson.³⁵ He is suspicious of their apologetic tendencies. However, he seems to believe that merely by showing exceptions to the rules which they postulated, he has thereby demonstrated that there is no pattern to which Koine authors adhered. This by no means follows. Further study, of the kind advocated by Steuernagel, may shed light upon patterns of syntax which, while falling short of the certainty of a grammatical rule, do indicate when a given speaker or writer is more likely to use either the accusative or the genitive as a direct object of ἀκούω.

---

32 Steuernagel, 'ΑΚΟΥΟΝΤΕΣ ΜΕΝ ΤΗΣ ΦΩΝΗΣ', 620, 'The concepts of interchangeability and fluctuation prevent him [Rehkopf, the editor of Blass and Debrunner's German language Grammar of New Testament Greek] from pursuing a more thorough enquiry'.
33 Moehring, 'AKOYEIN', 92–93.
34 The Thesaurus Linguae Graecae lists 17,327 occurrences of ἀκούω in the whole corpus of ancient Greek literature.
35 Moehring, 'AKOYEIN', 82.

Thus, it has been my goal to survey all the occurrences of ἀκούω in the NT with the aim of identifying predictable patterns of case use, which might then be compared with patterns of use in other Koine literature. But first it will be important to set out my proposed method of study.

The Use of Ἀκούω in the New Testament

The NT offers a sufficiently large number of occurrences of ἀκούω to allow us to observe patterns at work as it occurs 428 times. When direct objects of ἀκούω are identified as specific words or word forms they almost always display a marked preference for either the accusative or genitive case.

Several word forms show a marked preference for the accusative case. The most common direct object of ἀκούω is λόγος, and it overwhelmingly takes the accusative (as can be seen in the chart below). Naturally, it refers to verbal communication which is heard. The same preference can be observed when relative, indefinite, correlative, and demonstrative pronouns serve as direct objects of ἀκούω. Almost always they refer to the substance or content of what is heard. Where they occur in the genitive, it is clear that they do not refer to the content of what is heard, but the person speaking.[36]

	Accusative direct object	Genitive direct object
λόγος	32	3
Relative pronoun—ὅς	19	4
Indefinite pronoun—τίς	13	0
Correlative pronoun—ὅσος	4	0
Demonstrative pronoun—οὗτος	18	2

36 See, for example John 9:31, τούτου ἀκούει ('God hears him').

Several word forms demonstrate a corresponding preference for the genitive case. These are overwhelmingly personal. In their various forms (first, second, and third person, plural and singular) personal pronouns occur forty-five times as direct objects of ἀκούω. On only one occasion does the personal pronoun occur as an accusative direct object. This is the phrase εἴ γε αὐτὸν ἠκούσατε in Ephesians 4:21, where αὐτόν refers not to the person of Jesus, but the teaching of Jesus. Thus, the accusative direct object refers to the substance or content of what is heard.

A similar preference for the genitive case can be observed when the direct object of ἀκούω is a proper noun, a title, or another explicitly personal designation. Eleven such genitive direct objects can be cited, but none in the accusative.

- Matthew 2:9—the king
- Luke 16:31—Moses and the prophets
- John 9:31—sinners
- Acts 3:21—the prophet
- Acts 14:9—Paul speaking
- Acts 15:12—Barnabas and Saul
- Acts 25:22—the man
- Revelation 6:1—one of the four living creatures
- Revelation 6:3—the second living creature
- Revelation 6:5—the third living creature
- Revelation 16:5—an angel

There are, however, a number of direct objects which do not fit easily into the categories listed above. Yet when these accusative direct objects, which are neither pronouns nor the accusative forms of λόγος or φωνή (about which more will be said below) are listed, a theme can be seen to emerge, in that they refer to verbal communication. I have been able to list thirty-four such accusative direct objects in the NT.[37]

---

[37] Matthew 11:2; 12:42; 13:18; 14:1; 21:33, 45; 24:6; 26:65; Mark 13:7; Luke 1:41; 9:7; 11:31; 21:9; John 8:47; Acts 7:12; 10:22, 33; 17:32; 23:16; 28:15; 1 Corinthians 11:18; 2 Corinthians 12:4; Galatians 1:13; 4:21; Ephesians 1:15; 3:2; Philippians 1:27; Colossians 1:4; Philemon 5; James 5:11; 3 John 4; Revelation 5:13; 7:4; 9:16.

Examples include:
- Matthew 12:42—the wisdom of Solomon
- Matthew 13:9—the parable of the sower
- Luke 1:41—the greeting of Mary
- 1 Corinthians 11:18—reports of divisions among the Corinthians
- Galatians 1:13—Paul's former way of life
- Colossians 1:4—the faith of the Colossians
- Philemon 5—Philemon's love
- 3 John 4—that my children are walking in the faith

A similar observation can be made about the wide range of genitive direct objects which do not fit easily into the categories listed above. Most involve some reference to words spoken, but they refer to more than the mere content of those words. Sometimes they refer to groups of people making a noise, such as 'those disputing with him' in Mark 12:28. Or they may be a metonym for a person, such as 'my words' in John 12:47, which is another way of saying 'me'. The common factor is that these genitive direct objects tell us something of the character of what is heard. They may tell us about the identity of the speaker, or the source of the sound, or the quality of the sound.

As indicated above, the word φωνή demands special consideration. It is the second most common direct object of ἀκούω, occurring thirty-two times in the NT. At first sight it appears to take both cases indiscriminately. On fifteen occasions it takes the accusative case and on seventeen occasions it takes the genitive case, sometimes with the accusative (φωνήν) and genitive (φωνῆς) in close proximity.[38] For this reason, it provided the bedrock upon which Moehring's theory of interchangeability was based.

Yet here too, it is important to begin with several recurring features of the ἀκούω + φωνή combination. The voice heard in John 5:25, 28; 10:3, 16, 27; 18:37; Hebrews 3:7, 15; 4:7; and Revelation 3:20 is the voice of a person speaking. For example, to hear the voice of the Son of God in John 5:25, 28 is to hear the Son of God himself. In

---

38 For example, Acts 9:4, 7.

Revelation 11:12; 14:13; 16:1 and 21:3 the voice is 'a loud voice'. Thus, the emphasis is placed on the source and/or character of what is heard. So it comes as no surprise that in a majority of ἀκούω + φωνή combinations φωνή takes the genitive. That is its default setting.[39]

There is, however, a significant number of occasions when ἀκούω + φωνή bucks that trend by taking the accusative.[40] These accusative direct objects require particular attention. Sentences which contain φωνή as an accusative direct object of ἀκούω contain two further features.

  i. They contain some other indicator of the source or character of the voice, so that the function of the genitive is served by some other means. See, for example Revelation 1:10, 'as a trumpet'.
  ii. Emphasis is placed on the words spoken by the voice. For example, in John 5:37 Jesus states that the Father has borne witness about him, before telling his opponents that 'His voice (φωνὴν αὐτοῦ) you have never heard'. Likewise, in Revelation 6:1ff. John hears the living creatures speak as the seven seals are broken and God's judgements are released. When the living creatures are heard they are presented as genitive direct objects (see 6:1, 3, 5), but when John turns the reader's attention to their increasingly dark predictions in 6:6, 7 φωνή takes the accusative. 'And I heard what seemed to be a voice (ἤκουσα ὡς φωνὴν) in the midst of the four living creatures, saying, "A quart of wheat for a denarius"'.

Thus, it may fairly be argued that the shifts between accusative and genitive direct objects are not arbitrary but indicate significant, though subtle, changes of emphasis.

---

39 The three ἀκούω + φωνῆς combinations in Acts 9:7; 11:7; and 22:7 will be considered below.
40 On fifteen occasions in the NT: John 5:37; Acts 9:4; 22:14; 26:14; 2 Peter 1:18; Revelation 1:10; 6:6, 7; 9:13; 10:4; 12:10; 14:2; 18:4; 19:1, 6.

A Pattern Observed—or a Rule To Be Followed?

In view of the data gleaned from the NT the following observations can be made:

1. Accusative direct objects of ἀκούω direct the hearer's attention to the *information* communicated by words or sounds. This may be articulated verbal information, such as a report or proclamation, or it may refer to less clearly articulated, but nonetheless important, information—such as the presence of wars, or turbulence, or distinct musical notation.
2. Genitive direct objects of ἀκούω direct the hearer's attention to the *quality* of what the hearer hears. One aspect of that quality may be the source—the speaker, the musical instrument etc. Another may be its quality as speech or music. Still another may be the urgency underlying what is heard or the consequences which result from hearing it.

In an attempt to describe the ways in which case is used with direct objects of ἀκούω it may be helpful to bear in mind the distinction drawn by the linguist John Lyons between *transcendent rules* imposed from above, and rules which are *immanent or 'self-governed'*, expressed in the actual usage of the author or translator.[41] The former is more likely to have been formally defined and deliberately applied. The latter is unlikely to have been formally defined and it is, perhaps, misleading to call it a 'rule'. Although it has been applied sub-consciously, it is instinctively understood, and predictable patterns can be observed. This study has sought to describe the patterns of language use which can be observed in Koine Greek, on the basis of which the use of certain grammatical forms may be predicted. It is acknowledged that a fuller understanding of the data which I have presented may well emerge from a multi-disciplinary study drawing on the insights of linguistics, psychology, and literary studies. However, it is submitted that the pattern of use which I have described is best understood as one immanent in the usage of Luke and other Koine Greek authors.

---

41 Lyons, *Language and Linguistics*, 48.

The Use of Ἀκούω in Acts

An examination of the direct objects of ἀκούω in Acts shows that they follow the pattern observed in the NT as a whole. That is, accusative direct objects refer to the substance or content of what is heard, while genitive direct objects focus on the quality of what is heard. Thus, when λόγος occurs as a direct object of ἀκούω it always takes the accusative (9x). When the demonstrative pronoun refers to reported speech, it always takes the accusative (4x). There are seven other instances where the accusative direct object of ἀκούω is reported speech:

- 7:12—rumours that there was grain in Egypt;
- 10:22—words from Peter;
- 10:33—all that Peter had been commanded by the Lord;
- 17:32—Paul's preaching about the resurrection;
- 23:16—plans to ambush Paul;
- 28:15—reports about the arrival of Paul in Italy;
- 28:22—an account of what Paul believed.

As in the NT as a whole, personal pronouns (whether alone or in combination with a participle) prefer the genitive. In fact, in all seventeen instances of personal pronouns functioning as the direct object of ἀκούω they take the genitive case. In the two instances where a proper noun functions as a direct object of ἀκούω, it takes the genitive (14:9 and 15:12). In two further instances in Acts personal descriptors also take the genitive (3:23 and 25:22). These might simply be characterised as instances of the genitive referring to the person heard. The problem is that this 'classical rule' does not explain the ἀκούω + φωνῆς combinations in Acts.

One of the juxtapositions that has posed problems for the claim that Acts follows 'the classical rule' is found in 11:7, 18. There Peter told a group of sceptical believers in Jerusalem that he ate unclean food only when he heard 'a voice speaking to him' (11:7). That voice was the voice of God (10:15, 28). The fact that it occurs in the genitive case in 11:7 indicates not just that Peter heard a person speaking to him, but that this voice possessed an unusual quality—heavenly authority. When the narrator of Acts tells the reader that when Peter's hearers heard 'these things' they were silent, he switches to the accusative ταῦτα (11:18).

This switch is neither puzzling nor meaningless when we remember that the focus is thereby shifted to the content of Peter's report.

The most puzzling juxtapositions of accusative and genitive direct objects of ἀκούω in Acts are those found in the three accounts of what Paul and his companions heard on the road to Damascus. It is not only the apparent contradiction between the accounts of what Paul's companions heard in 9:7 and 22:9 which raises problems of interpretation, but the question of what Paul himself heard in 9:4; 22:7 and 26:14. If the author of Acts was following the patterns I have described, the following interpretations of ἀκούω may be offered.

First of all, the voice of the risen Jesus, which Paul heard on the road to Damascus, is introduced in 9:4 as an accusative direct object. This places the focus on the words of Jesus heard by Paul. The same can be said of Ananias' explanation of the event in 22:14; as well as Paul's retelling in 26:14. The accusative φωνήν is the default setting for a report of spoken words.

However, when Paul retold the same event in 22:7 before a crowd of hostile Jews in Jerusalem the 'speaking voice' of Jesus takes the genitive case. Here Luke depicts Paul as striving to communicate not only what he heard, but also the source of what he heard. In the following verse the Lord's answer expands to include the description of Jesus as 'the Nazarean' (22:8). Paul wanted his hearers to understand that his mission to the Gentiles was initiated by a voice from heaven, uttered by the risen Jesus himself.

Then secondly, we return to the question of what Paul's travelling companions heard in 9:7, and whether they heard anything at all in 22:9. In 9:7 they heard τῆς φωνῆς, a genitive which focuses attention on the character of the voice. This voice from heaven clearly amazed them, for they 'stood speechless [...] seeing no one'. The heavenly quality of what they heard was what amazed them. Yet they heard none of the words that Paul heard from Jesus. That point is clarified in 22:9 when Paul describes their experience. They 'saw the light but did not hear the voice (φωνήν) of the one who spoke to me'. There is no need to understand ἀκούω in the verse as 'hearing with understanding' for the narrative to make sense. The accusative tells us that they did not hear the words of Jesus as Paul did.

Conclusion

The conclusion I draw from the data surveyed in the NT as a whole, and Acts in particular, is that there are patterns of use which appear to govern the choice of case for the direct objects of ἀκούω. These patterns appear to explain a wide range of recurring phenomena, as well as some exegetical difficulties in Acts. Whether these patterns of use are firm enough to be called a 'rule' of grammar or the idiolect of a particular author remains a matter for debate. There is, however, a *prima facie* case for pursuing further research into other bodies of Koine literature, to discover whether the existence of a pattern can be confirmed or defined more precisely.

Bibliography

Alexander, J. A. *A Commentary on the Acts of the Apostles.* (London: The Banner of Truth Trust, 1963).

Barrett, C. K. *A Critical and Exegetical Commentary on The Acts of the Apostles* (Edited by J. A. Emerton, C. E. B. Cranfield, and G. N. Stanton; 2 vols. International Critical Commentary; Edinburgh: T & T Clark, 1994–98).

Brachter, R. G. 'Ἀκούω in Acts ix.7 and xxii.9', *ET* 71 (195–60), 243–245.

Bruce, F. F. *Acts* (Leicester: IVP, 1951).

Bruce, F. F. *The Book of The Acts* (Revised edn; NICNT; Grand Rapids, MI: Eerdmans, 1988).

Chrysostom, J. *The Homilies of St. John Chrysostom on the Acts of the Apostles* (Edited by E. B. Pusey, J. Keble, and C. Marriott; Library of Fathers of the Holy Catholic Church; London: Rivington, 1870).

Conzelmann, H. *Acts of the Apostles* (Translated by J. Limburg, A. T. Kraabel, and D. H. Juel; Hermeneia; Philadelphia, PA: Fortress Press, 1987).

Fitzmyer, J. A. *The Acts of the Apostles* (The Anchor Bible; New York, NY: Doubleday & Co., 1998).

Green, J. B.	*Conversion in Luke-Acts: Divine Action, Human Cognition, and the People of God* (Grand Rapids, MI: Baker Academic, 2015).
Keener, C. S.	*Acts: An Exegetical Commentary* (4 vols. Grand Rapids, MI: Baker Academic, 2012–15).
Kistemaker, S. J.	*Exposition of the Acts of the Apostles* (Grand Rapids, MI: Baker Academic, 1990).
Kittel, G.	'Ἀκούω', in G. Kittel (ed.), TDNT vol. 1 (10 vols. Grand Rapids, MI: Eerdmans, 1964), 216–20.
Lyons, J.	*Language and Linguistics: An Introduction* (Cambridge: CUP, 1981).
Moehring, H. R.	'The Verb ΑΚΟΥΕΙΝ in Acts IX 7 and XXII 9', *NovT* 1–2 (1959), 80–99.
Moule, C. F. D.,	*An Idiom Book of New Testament Greek* (Cambridge: CUP, 1971).
Moulton, J. H.,	*A Grammar of New Testament Greek* (3 vols. Edinburgh: T & T Clark, 1906).
Rackham, R. B.	*The Acts of the Apostles: An Exposition* (London: Methuen, 1901).
Robertson, A. T.	*A Grammar of the Greek New Testament in the Light of Historical Research* (Nashville, TN: Broadman Press, 1914).
Smyth, H. W.	*Greek Grammar* (Reprint edn. Oxford: Benediction Classics, 1915).
Steuernagel, G.	'ΑΚΟΥΟΝΤΕΣ ΜΕΝ ΤΗΣ ΦΩΝΗΣ (APG 9.7): Ein Genitiv in der Apostelgeschichte', *NTS* 35 (1989), 619–24.
Turner, N.	*Grammatical Insights into the New Testament* (Edinburgh: T & T Clark, 1965).
Wallace, D. B.	*Greek Grammar beyond the Basics* (Grand Rapids, MI: Zondervan, 1996).
Zerwick, M.	*Biblical Greek Illustrated by Examples* (Rome: Pontifical Biblical Institute, 1963).